"Nearly four centuries have passed since St. Teresa began to write, and, both in her own country and abroad, her fame is still widespread and still growing. Her purely human qualities and gifts, the saintliness of her life by which they were illumined and overshadowed, the naturalness and candour of her manner and style—these are some of the reasons why her name is not only graven upon the enduring marble of history but taken on the lips of generation after generation with reverence and love.

"She is a mystic—and more than a mystic. Her works, it is true, are well known in the cloister and have served as nourishment to many who are far advanced on the Way of Perfection, and who, without her aid, would still be beginners in the life of prayer. Yet they have also entered the homes of millions living in the world and have brought consolation, assurance, hope and strength to souls who, in the technical sense, know nothing of the life of contemplation. Devoting herself, as she did, with the most wonderful persistence and tenacity, to the sublimest task given to man—the attempt to guide others toward perfection—she succeeded so well in that task that she is respected everywhere as an incredibly gifted teacher, who has revealed, more perhaps than any who came before her, the nature and extent of those gifts which the Lord has laid up in this life for those who love Him. In past ages, of course, there had been many writers kindled with Divine love to whom He had manifested His ineffable secrets, but for the most part these secrets had gone down with them to the grave. To St. Teresa it was given to speak to the world, in her diaphanous, colloquial language and her simple, unaffected style, of the work of the Holy Spirit in the enamoured soul, of the interior strife and the continual purgation through which such a soul must pass in its ascent of Mount Carmel and of the wonders which await it on the mountain's summit."

—E. ALLISON PEERS

THE LIFE
OF TERESA OF JESUS

THE AUTOBIOGRAPHY
OF ST. TERESA OF AVILA
Translated and Edited by
E. ALLISON PEERS
from the Critical Edition of
P. SILVERIO DE SANTA TERESA, C.D.

IMAGE BOOKS

A Division of Doubleday & Company, Inc.
Garden City, New York

Image Books Edition 1960
by special arrangement with Sheed & Ward

Image Books edition published February, 1960

Nihil Obstat: Reginaldus Phillips, s.t.l.
                    Censor Deputatus
Imprimatur: E. Morrogh Bernard, *Vicarius Generalis*
Westmonasterii, die 16ᴀ Junii, 1944

COVER BY URSULA SEUSS

PRINTED IN THE UNITED STATES OF AMERICA

To the Gracious Memory of
P. EDMUND GURDON
Sometime Prior of the Carthusian Monastery of Miraflores

A MAN OF GOD

CONTENTS

TRANSLATOR'S PREFACE

I

For some time after completing my translation of the Complete Works of St. John of the Cross, in the year 1935, I had no thought of preparing a similar edition of the works of that other great Carmelite, to whom he owed so much, St. Teresa. Even when the welcome given to the works of *el Santo* in their new dress showed what an unexpectedly and encouragingly large public there now was for this type of literature, it seemed to me that *la Santa* was on the whole sufficiently well served by the translations already in existence. But many readers of St. John of the Cross were not of this opinion: not all St. Teresa's works, they said, had been satisfactorily translated; not all of them, even, were based on an up-to-date Spanish text; and, in any case, there was ample room for a fresh, modern version of the Complete Works, made by a single hand, with footnotes of an elucidatory rather than a piously discursive type—an edition, furthermore, which would facilitate individual study by providing comprehensive indices.

As time went on, this point of view was increasingly pressed upon me, and by a great variety of people. In Spain, a well-known Academician asked me when a complete St. Teresa was to appear in English; in the American Southwest, a remote community of Carmelite nuns whom I visited put the same question; in England, the remark became almost a commonplace. At last I began to reconsider the position. The only easily accessible versions of the *Life* and the *Foundations* were still, though they had been several times revised, essentially the versions made by David Lewis in 1870-1: as regards both language and interpretation they could certainly be greatly bettered. The Stanbrook Benedictines' translation of the *Interior Castle*, the *Way of perfection* and the Minor Works (in prose and verse) dated from the beginning of this century and were much superior to Lewis; yet since these volumes had first appeared P. Silverio de Santa Teresa had published his comprehensive and critical Spanish edition of the Complete Works, which would make it possible to add a good deal, especially in the *Way of perfection*, to what was already available. The most recently published translation was that made by the Benedictines of Stanbrook of the *Letters* (4 vols., 1919–24). This excellent piece of work was unfortunately completed before P. Silverio's three-volume edition of the *Letters* appeared, and, though in 1927 its editors brought out an appendix to their final volume consisting of twenty-two letters and some fragments to which they had not previously had access, there is a good deal in P. Silverio's three volumes which it would be worth while to pass on to the English reader. None the less, the *Letters* presented the least urgent part of the problem.

After full consideration, I decided to undertake an edition of the Complete Works, publishing them all, in one series, as soon as might be, with the exception of the *Letters*, a new edition of which it seemed better to postpone for the present, since it would be strange if the recent years of upheaval in Spain did not lead to fresh discoveries. Accordingly, the work was begun in the summer of 1939, continued throughout the whole period of the War and is only now completed.

II

It might be thought that St. Teresa—so often colloquial and matter-of-fact in her language—would be a great deal easier to translate than St. John of the Cross, but the truth is very nearly the exact opposite. There are certainly passages and phrases in St. John of the Cross which present the greatest difficulty, but they are relatively few: for all the sublimity of his teaching, his expression is, as a rule, crystal-clear, and at every turn the translator is assisted by his logical and orderly mind and by his great objectivity. Much of St. Teresa's work, on the other hand, is autobiographical narrative, and, even in that part of it which is not, every page bears the indelible impress of her forceful and vivid personality. In addition to the difficulty of interpreting that personality by means of a translation there are stylistic difficulties of a kind presented by few, if any, other Spanish writers of the first rank. As an appreciation of these two points will help us to a fuller understanding of the qualities of the work of St. Teresa, it will be worth our while to consider them in greater detail.

1. To Spaniards there is no writer whose personality communicates itself with greater immediacy and intensity than does that of St. Teresa—and this both because of her almost complete disregard of the literary conventions and because in nothing that she wrote could her strong individuality ever be concealed. No translator could hope to convey that impression as fully and forcibly as do the original words, but he is not therefore exempted from the obligation to convey as much of it as possible. In an attempt to do this, I have denied to her vigorous and pugnacious phrases the superfluous words in which another age might have clothed them. In such passages as these we can hear the authentic and virile note of a saint unlike any to be found in a stained-glass window:

"Rest, indeed!" I would say. "I need no rest; what I need is crosses."[1]

We can make use only of a single cell—what do we gain by its being very large and well built? What, indeed? We have not to spend all our time looking at the walls.[2]

"Oh, the devil, the devil!" we say, when we might be saying "God! God!" and making the devil tremble. Of course we might, for we know he cannot move a finger unless the Lord permits it. Whatever are we thinking of? I am quite sure I am more afraid of people who are themselves terrified of the devil than I am of the devil himself.[3]

If Thou wilt (prove me) by means of trials, give me strength and let them come.[4]

In rendering these and similar phrases I have had always in my mind the Teresa whom I have come to know through

Special Note: The references for the works of St. Teresa (except for *Life*) used in the footnotes throughout this work refer to *Complete Works of St. Teresa*, translated and edited by E. Allison Peers, 3 vols., Sheed & Ward, New York, 1957.

[1] *Life*, Chap. XIII (p. 140).
[2] *Foundations*, Chap. XIV (Vol. III, p. 66).
[3] *Life*, Chap. XXV (p. 243).
[4] *Way of perfection*, Chap. XXXII (Vol. II, p. 138).

close contact with her over many years. A woman who made her decisions and then stuck to them regardless of the consequences:

> I was well aware that there was ample trouble in store for me, but, as the thing was now done, I cared very little about that.[5]

Who, if she ever thought she was afraid of the Inquisition, would "go and pay it a visit of (her) own accord."[6] And who counselled her nuns to be like herself:

> Strive like strong men until you die in the attempt, for you are here for nothing else than to strive.[7]

Again, St. Teresa has continual outbursts of sanctified commonsense, humour and irony. "I just laughed to myself" is a type of phrase which we continually meet in her work and she has left us an excellent specimen of her sustained laughter in the "Judgment . . . upon various writings".[8] She particularly disliked pretentiousness, even in what was good, and castigated it with those most effective weapons. Even into that sublime commentary on the *Song of Songs* entitled the *Conceptions of the Love of God*, creeps a delightfully shrewd description of the lady whose self-importance was so intimately mingled with her devoutness. She, and others like her,

> were saints in their own opinion, but, when I got to know them, they frightened me more than all the sinners I have ever met.[9]

Some of her stories are shot through and through with an allusive humour which it needs all one's ingenuity to render—such are the accounts of her visit to Duruelo, with Fray Antonio sweeping out the porch and the depression caused in the business men who came with her from Medina by all those crosses and skulls[10]; her efforts to address a great lady

---

[5] *Life*, Chap. XXXVI (pp. 344–5).
[6] *Life*, Chap. XXXIII (p. 312).
[7] *Way of perfection*, Chap. XX (Vol. II, p. 86).
[8] Vol. III, pp. 229–31.
[9] *Conceptions of the Love of God*, Chap. II (Vol. II, p. 375).
[10] *Foundations*, Chap. XIV (Vol. III, p. 66).

as befitted her rank and how she "got it wrong";[11] poor María del Sacramento and her attack of nerves on All Souls' eve in the sparsely furnished convent at Salamanca[12]; the group of devout ladies at Villanueva, only one of whom could read with any ease, who tried to recite their Office using different versions of the Breviary: "God will have accepted their intention and labour, but they can have said very little that was correct."[13] No less apt to evade one are innumerable little natural touches which, in the English, if carelessly rendered, might easily pass unnoticed:

> I was . . . ashamed to go to my confessor . . . for fear he might laugh at me and say: "What a Saint Paul she is, with her heavenly visions! Quite a Saint Jerome!"[14]

> Blessed be Thou, Lord, Who hast made me so incompetent and unprofitable![15]

> I only wish I could write with both hands, so as not to forget one thing while I am saying another.[16]

> From foolish devotions may God deliver us.[17]

And in her less frequent ironical passages, such as the description in the *Way of perfection* of how the devil invents "laws by which we (nuns) go up and down in rank, as people do in the world",[18] or the animadversions in the *Life* upon the niceties of worldly etiquette:

> —the title "Illustrious" has to be given to a man who formerly was not even described as "Magnificent".[19]

The style here is so sedate that one has to pause for quite a long time before pressing the button lest the photograph should fail to catch the twinkle in the eye.

Then there are the thousand touches which reveal the temperamentally great writer who never became, or wanted to

[11] *Way of perfection*, Chap. XXII (Vol. II, p. 94).
[12] *Foundations*, Chap. XIX (Vol. III, p. 94).
[13] *Foundations*, Chap. XXVIII (Vol. III, p. 164).
[14] *Life*, Chap. XXXVIII (p. 361).
[15] *Life*, Chap. XIII (p. 147).
[16] *Way of perfection*, Chap. XX (Vol. II, p. 88).
[17] *Life*, Chap. XIII (p. 145).
[18] *Ibid.*, Chap. XXXVI (Vol. II, p. 156).
[19] *Life*, Chap. XXXVII (p. 360).

become, a professional one—the genius born, not made. This trait in herself St. Teresa never allows us to forget—which is just as well for the translator who might otherwise conventionalize her. She is "stupid", "incompetent" and always busy with really "important" things like her spinning-wheel. She has "no learning", suffers from "noises" in the head, a bad memory, and a "rough" and "heavy" style. It is useless for her to write anything on mystical theology, for—"I am unable to use the proper terms". She cannot prevent herself from digressing if she feels like it: otherwise, her writing "worries" her.[20] "How I do let myself wander!" begins Chapter XXIII of the *Way of perfection*.[21] As for the dates she quotes—"you must always understand (them) to be approximate—they are of no great importance."[22] And she scribbles at breakneck speed and with tremendous intensity, never revising her work —nor even rereading it to see what she has said last.[23] All the time the translator has to remember that he is dealing with this unique kind of woman—it would be nothing short of a tragedy if he turned her into a writer of text-books.

2. The second type of difficulty which should be referred to will perhaps be of greater interest to the student than to the general reader. In her "rough style", she says comfortingly at the end of Chapter XVI of the *Way of perfection*, her argument will be better understood "than in other books which put it more elegantly."[24] That no doubt was true, and may still be true, so far as the general trend of the argument is concerned—and one has constantly to be on one's guard, when there is some "elegant" word that exactly expresses her meaning, against using it—but it certainly does not apply to the exact sense of particular passages. Even Spaniards familiar with her books are continually baffled when asked the precise meaning of phrases which at first sight may seem perfectly simple. Vivid, disjointed, elliptical, paradoxical and gaily ungrammatical, the nun of Ávila continually confounds the successors of those "learned men" to whom in her life she turned so often for enlightenment. One often has frankly to guess at

[20] Such references as these are to be found everywhere. See, for example, p. 151, Vol. II, pp. 68, 234, 291, Vol. III, pp. xxii, xxiii.

[21] In the Escorial manuscript. See Vol. II, p. 97, n. 6.

[22] *Foundations*, Chap. XXV (Vol. III, p. 132).

[23] *Way of perfection*, Chap. XIX (Vol. II, p. 76).

[24] Vol. II, p. 68.

her exact meaning, and half a dozen people may make half a dozen different guesses, none of which anybody can pick out as definitely correct.

To illustrate these characteristics of her style, I have, for the sake of brevity, selected examples in which her meaning is fairly evident. When to the difficulty of rendering her words without paraphrasing them is added that of deciding between several possible meanings it can be imagined how much the task is magnified.

In the course of a discussion on melancholy in nuns, in the seventh chapter of the *Foundations*, St. Teresa observes that lack of discipline is often more to blame than temperament:

> Digo en algunas, porque he visto, que cuando hay a quien temer, se van a la mano y pueden.
>
> (*Lit.*: I mean in some, for I have seen that, when there is whom to fear, they become docile and can.)

This, in English, has to be expanded somewhat as follows:

> I know it is so in some; for, when they have been brought before a person they are afraid of, I have seen them become docile, so I know that they can.[25]

Again, in the *Interior Castle* (VI, viii), she has been considering how a person can be sure whether some vision is of Christ or of a saint:

> Aun ya el Señor, cuando habla, más fácil parece; mas el santo que no habla, sino que parece le pone el Señor allí por ayuda de aquel alma y por compañía, es más de maravilla.
>
> (*Lit.*: Even now the Lord, when He speaks, [it] seems easier; but the saint who speaks not, but seems to have been placed there by the Lord for aid to that soul and for company, is more remarkable.)

Which means:

> When it is the Lord, and He speaks, it is natural that He should be easily recognized; but even when it is a saint, and no words are spoken, the soul is able to feel that the Lord is sending him to be a help and a companion to it; and this is (still) more remarkable.[26]

[25] Vol. III, p. 39.
[26] Vol. II, p. 312.

Then there are shorter phrases, couched in a staccato, almost telegraphic style, hard enough to translate without a weakening of their generally considerable force—

> Con esto, mal dormir, todo trabajo, todo cruz!
> (*Lit.*: With this, bad sleep, all trial, all cross!)

And then, the scant sleep they get: nothing but trials, nothing but crosses![27]—

but quite devastating when the clipt phraseology makes one doubtful of the meaning. And there are words which St. Teresa uses in a sense entirely her own, and conjunctions which do not in the least mean what they say—e.g., "and" for "but" and *vice versa*, not to mention the conjunction *que*, which can stand for almost any other.

One has also to watch for, and preserve, the Saint's colloquialisms. Even in talking with God, she tells us, she has a "silly way"

> in which I often speak to Him without meaning what I am saying; for it is love that speaks, and my soul is so far transported that I take no notice of the distance that separates it from God.[28]

How much more unconventional, then, is she likely to be with her readers! Not only in her modes of address, but in the introduction of everyday, semi-proverbial phrases, some of which are no longer in use in Spain and might be unintelligible did she not thoughtfully accompany them with an "as one might put it" or "as they say". It would not be hard to turn into current English slang such phrases as:

> They see that these things are considered, as one might say, "all right".[29]

> (I am) so peevish and ill-tempered that I seem to want to snap everyone up.[30]

> We had not so much as a scrap of brushwood to broil a sardine on.[31]

---

27 *Life*, Chap. XIII (p. 147).
28 *Life*, Chap. XXXIV (p. 324).
29 *Life*, Chap. VII (p. 98).
30 *Life*, Chap. XXX (p. 282).
31 *Foundations*, Chap. XV (Vol. III, p. 74).

So with her homely and vivid metaphors: the Christian making progress "at a hen's pace" or even "like hens with their feet tied"; his adversary the devil "clapping his hands to his head" in despair of ever vanquishing him; love finding an outlet and not being "allowed to boil right over like a pot to which fuel has been applied indiscriminately";[32] worldly aids to devotion being of no more use to lean upon than "dry rosemary twigs" which break at the slightest pressure.[33] All these —and there are hundreds of them enlivening her narratives and illumining her expositions—can be so easily spoiled in translation.

Another stumbling block is repetition, a practice to which St. Teresa was greatly addicted. Some of her repetitions of words are merely careless and clumsy—as in her constant use of the word "great"[34]—and these I have been content to indicate rather than reproduce every time they occur. When she repeats phrases it is generally for emphasis—

> Oh, what terrible harm, what terrible harm is wrought . . . when the religious life is not properly observed![35]

and, except occasionally where our language necessitates another formula for the conveying of the effect, her phraseology can as a rule be reproduced as it stands. But often the same word is repeated in a different sense, sometimes so pointedly that it produces an obvious play upon the word's two or more meanings. Some of these usages cannot be conveyed in English; others are best translated freely with the point explained more fully in a footnote. But whenever possible I have rendered this characteristic Teresian trait quite literally: if it gives the reader a slight shock, that is probably what she often intended:

> How much more will anyone fear this to whom He has thus revealed Himself, and given such a consciousness of His presence as will produce unconsciousness![36]

[32] *Life*, Chaps. XIII, XXXVII, XXVI, XXIX (p. 140, 380, 244, 273).

[33] *Relations*, III (Vol. I, p. 316).

[34] See, for a typical example, *Life*, Chap. XXXVIII (p. 362).

[35] *Life*, Chap. VII (p. 98).

[36] *Interior Castle*, VI, ix (Vol. II, p. 316).

If I . . . used my unhappiness in order to serve God, it would serve me as a kind of purgatory.[37]

But . . . though my will is not yet free from self-interest, I give it to Thee freely. For I have proved, by long experience, how much I gain by leaving it freely in Thy hands.[38]

Alas that one cannot do more to give the English reader the unforgettable effect of intimacy with this woman of the sixteenth century still living and breathing in the twentieth as she writes in her own language! The fine shades of meaning which she creates with her untranslatable idioms, her love for inventing all kinds of diminutives, her characteristic metatheses and other forms of popular misspelling, her curious semiphonetic transliterations of Latin texts, her long, shambling, breathless sentences, as common as her short sprightly ones, which for reasons of clarity one cannot avoid splitting up—these make one feel that, when one has done everything possible, one has still done nothing. All I can say is that I have done my best.

Those acquainted with the Spanish text may care to have a few notes on the renderings normally adopted for characteristic words and phrases. One of the Saint's most frequent exclamations, *¡Válgame Dios!*, which can express any emotion from playful exasperation to profound distress, is as a rule translated literally, as "God help me!" Occasionally where the context will not suffice to indicate the shade of meaning, it becomes "Oh, God!", "Dear God!" or even "Dear me!" The polite form of address *Vuestra Merced* is translated "Your Honour" (or sometimes merely "you") when applied to a layman and "Your Reverence" when used to a priest. The word *letrados* is rendered literally "learned men", though the type of learning to which it refers is invariably theological. The characteristic and rather subtle uses of the word *honra* ("honour", "reputation", "good name") are dealt with, as they occur, in footnotes. Of terms used in specifically mystical passages, *arrobamiento* is normally translated "rapture"; *arrebatamiento*, "transport"; *amortecimiento*, "swoon"; *elevamiento* and *levantamiento*, "elevation"; *embebecimiento*, "absorption"; and *hablas*, "locutions" (or, rarely, "voices"). Three words which St. Teresa by no means always distin-

---

[37] *Life*, Chap. XXXVI (p. 343).
[38] *Way of perfection*, Chap. XXXII (Vol. II, p. 135).

guishes from one another are *gustos, contentos* and *regalos*, generally translated, respectively, "consolations", "sweetness" (in devotion) and "favours", *gustos* being more substantial than the evanescent *contentos* and often contrasted with them. The verb *regalar* may run through the gamut "caress", "pamper", "indulge", "delight", "gladden" and "cheer"; and the singular substantive *regalo* varies in the same way. *Descanso* can mean not only "rest" but something very much like "happiness", as also can *consuelo* ("comfort"). *Espíritu* can refer to a person's particular spiritual condition or to his or her spirituality. *Remedio* is more often "help" than "remedy". For convenience's sake, St. Teresa's usage here being very elastic, I have called all religious houses for men "monasteries" or "friaries" and those for women "convents". To the word "soul" the neuter pronoun is applied unless it seems to be equivalent to "person". Where the Spanish gender is ambiguous, "she" is used only if St. Teresa appears to have a woman definitely in mind.

III

Some idea of the principles which have guided me in the planning of this edition will be implicit in what has already been said. I have aimed at extreme literalness, and have seldom sacrificed this to smoothness and elegance of diction. In an attempt to present the text in the best and fullest form I have utilized all the manuscripts reproduced by P. Silverio; and particular care, as will be seen, has been devoted to the *Way of perfection*. The notes, greatly abridged from those of P. Silverio, whose discursiveness is not limited to his introductions, have been kept down to a minimum.[39] One need not remind avowed Teresians, but it may be worth while pointing out to the general reader, that the best possible commentary on many of St. Teresa's ascetic and mystical passages can be found by using a subject-index to the works of St. John of the Cross.[40] So much autobiographical material is found in the

[39] [All the footnotes to the text are P. Silverio's except where they are enclosed in square brackets, or where the contrary is stated. I have followed P. Silverio in not numbering the paragraphs of the text, as both he and I thought it advisable to do in the *Complete Works of St. John of the Cross*.]

[40] Such a subject-index will be found in Vol. III, pp. 445–54 of my edition of the Complete Works.

Life and the *Foundations*—and indeed in practically all the works—that no biographical introduction has seemed necessary; a brief outline of the main events in St. Teresa's career, however, supplemented by references to the works, has been thought worth including.

The style and tone adopted in the translation of the different works varies considerably, just as in the works of St. John of the Cross—even more so, indeed, than there, for the *Exclamations* are much farther in this respect from the *Foundations* than is the *Ascent of Mount Carmel* from the *Spiritual Canticle*. But, except in the *Exclamations* and in parts of the *Interior Castle* and *Conceptions*, St. Teresa's style is more pedestrian and colloquial than that of St. John of the Cross, and this I have indicated by the use of more "modern" language, without, I hope, entirely destroying the flavour of a past age. The same remark, *mutatis mutandis*, applies to the *Poems*.

St. Teresa's quotations from the Bible are often inexact: my rule has been to give her own words, approximating them as nearly as possible to the text of the Douai Version[41] but never allowing her to say in English anything that she does not say in Spanish. Her mind was so completely immersed in Biblical phraseology[42] that it is sometimes hard to tell if she is consciously quoting at all. Where a Scriptural reference is given in a footnote it is to be understood that I think her to be making a definite quotation.

It would have been attractive to have included a very large proportion of the numerous documents printed by P. Silverio in his nine volumes, which throw so many sidelights on St. Teresa's life and times. But if this translation, like its predecessor, was to be compressed into three volumes there was only a very little space to spare, even when the introductions to the individual works were cut down, as they have been, to a minimum. I have therefore confined myself to translating a few outstanding documents, making them as representative as possible. In order that the pages at my disposal for this purpose should be used to the best advantage, I have occasionally

---

[41] All footnote references are to this version. Where the numbering of chapters or verses in the Authorized Version differs from this, as in the Psalms, the variation has been shown in square brackets.

[42] Cf. her reference to the Bible in *Life*, Chap. XXV (p. 239).

omitted irrelevant passages or condensed their verboseness of expression, without, however (I hope), impairing their spirit.

IV

Chief among my acknowledgments are those to P. Silverio de Santa Teresa, the excellence of whose work I have had occasion to test again and again, and to the Benedictines of Stanbrook, who, holding exclusive copyright for the English translation of his edition, have most generously permitted me to make full use of it. For over twenty years I have been in constant correspondence with the Stanbrook nuns over Teresian matters and have thus been able to appreciate the knowledge as well as the devotion which they put into their labours. I trust that this edition will help to increase the public for their many translations in the field of Spanish mysticism, which includes not only St. Teresa and St. John of the Cross but the less known Francisco de Osuna and Luis de León.

My friend P. Edmund Gurdon, who, when Prior of the Cartuja de Miraflores, near Burgos, helped me so much in the interpretation of difficult passages in St. John of the Cross, died in October 1940, only a year or so after I had begun work on St. Teresa. This edition will be the poorer for the almost entire loss of his collaboration, particularly as he had lived for so many years in St. Teresa's own Castile, and either he or one of his Spanish monks could often suggest a possible meaning for many an obscure elliptical phrase which it was impossible to translate as it stood. Though the World War has made it hard for me to get as much help of this kind from Spain as I should have liked, I have often been able to consult Spanish friends about occasional difficulties—chief among them my colleague at Liverpool, Don José Castillejo, Don Luis Meana, of the University of Manchester, and Don Pedro Penzol, of the University of Leeds. To these, to my colleague Miss Audrey Lumsden, to the Carmelite Fathers of Kensington, and to the Benedictines of Ampleforth, I tender my most cordial thanks.

University of Liverpool   E. A. P.
    August 15, 1943

PRINCIPAL ABBREVIATIONS

A.V.—Authorized Version of the Bible (1611).

D.V.—Douai Version of the Bible (1609).

Letters.—Letters of St. Teresa. Unless otherwise stated, the numbering of the Letters follows Vols. VII–IX of P. Silverio. *Letters* (St.) indicates the translation of the Benedictines of Stanbrook (London, 1919–24. 4 vols.).

Lewis.—*The Life of St. Teresa of Jesus*, etc. Translated by David Lewis. 5th ed., with notes and introductions by the Very Rev. Benedict Zimmerman, O.C.D., London, 1916.

P. Silverio.—*Obras de Santa Teresa de Jesús.* Editadas y anotadas por el P. Silverio de Santa Teresa, C.D., Burgos, 1915–24. 9 vols.

Ribera.—Francisco de Ribera: *Vida de Santa Teresa de Jesús.* Nueva ed. aumentada, con introducción, etc., por el P. Jaime Pons. Barcelona, 1908.

S.S.M.—E. Allison Peers: *Studies of the Spanish Mystics.* London, 1927–30. 2 vols.

St. John of the Cross—*The Complete Works of Saint John of the Cross, Doctor of the Church.* Translated from the critical edition of P. Silverio de Santa Teresa, C.D., and edited by E. Allison Peers. London, 1934–5. 3 vols.

Yepes.—Diego de Yepes: *Vida de Santa Teresa.* Madrid, 1615.

AN OUTLINE OF THE LIFE
OF ST. TERESA

(Abbreviations: F = *Foundations*; I.C. = *Interior Castle*; L = *Life*; LL = *Letters*; R = *Relations*. Roman numerals after F, I.C., L, R refer to chapters; Arabic numerals after LL, to the numbers of the Letters. The numerals in brackets after the names of the foundations record their chronological sequence.)

1515 (March 28). Birth of Teresa de (Cepeda y) Ahumada at Ávila.

1528. Teresa loses her mother.

c. 1531. Enters Augustinian Convent of St. Mary of Grace, Ávila, as a boarder. Stays there for eighteen months (L III).

1536 (November 2). Enters Carmelite Convent of the Incarnation, Ávila, as a novice (cf. p. 77, n. 2. "It is forty years since this nun took the habit," wrote St. Teresa in 1576: R IV, p. 319).

1537 (November 3). Professed at Convent of the Incarnation.

1538 (Autumn: "before two years had passed": L V). Health gives way. Goes ("when the winter began") to stay with her half-sister, Doña María de Cepeda de Barrientos, at the village of Castellanos de la Cañada. On the way there, stays at Hortigosa with her uncle, Don Pedro de Cepeda, who gives her a copy of Osuna's *Third Spiritual Alphabet*.

1539 (April–July). Undergoes treatment at Becedas.

1539 (August 15). Attack of catalepsy, which leaves her helpless "for more than eight months" (L VI).

1540 (about Easter). Returns to Incarnation. An invalid till late in 1541: "This (illness) I suffered for three years"

(L V). The effects of the paralysis remain till the summer of 1542 (L VI) and recur intermittently (L VII) till about 1554.

1543 (December 24). Death of her father, Don Alonso Sánchez de Cepeda.

c. 1555–6. Begins to think she is "sometimes being addressed by interior voices and to see certain visions and experience revelations" (R IV).

c. 1556–7. Final "conversion" (after "nearly twenty years on that stormy sea": L VIII: p. 108). Cf. pp. 78, 117, n. 3. First contact with the Society of Jesus ("after almost twenty years' experience of prayer": L XXIII).

(1557. Visit of St. Francis Borgia to Ávila [L XXIV].)

1558. Experiences her first rapture (L XXIV) and perhaps (L XXVIII) an imaginary vision of Christ (usually dated January 25 or June 29–30, 1558. But a likelier date is 1560: see pp. 235, 260, 268, 271).
Discussions begin about the foundation in Ávila of a convent for Discalced nuns (R IV).

1559. P. Álvarez becomes her confessor. Transverberation of her heart (L XXIX).

1560. Makes a vow of greater perfection.

1561. P. Gaspar de Salazar comes to Ávila (April).
House for the first convent of the Reform bought in Ávila (August).

1562–7. At St. Joseph's, Ávila ("The most restful years of my life": F I).

1562

January–July. Stays with Doña Luisa de la Cerda at Toledo.

June. Finishes the first draft of the *Life*.

July. Brief (dated February) authorizing the foundation of St. Joseph's received from Rome on the night of her return to Ávila. The Bishop is persuaded by St. Peter of Alcántara to sanction the foundation.

August 24. Foundation of Convent of St. Joseph, Ávila (1).

August (to February 1563). "Commotion" in Ávila (L XXXVI).

(After August). Is commanded to write an amplified account of her life.

1563

(About March). Goes to live at St. Joseph's, Ávila.

July 3. Takes some further step (its exact nature not known) towards herself embracing the Reform.

August 22. Is granted a patent to transfer, with three companions, from the Incarnation to St. Joseph's.

1564

August 21. The Nuncio confirms the above-mentioned patent.

1565

(? December). Greater part of the second and final version of the *Life* written.
Completes the *Life* and sends it, at the end of the year, to P. García de Toledo (LL 3).
At about this time, begins the *Way of perfection*.

1566

(About August). Is visited by Fray Alonso Maldonado.

1567

February[1]. Visit to Castile of the Carmelite General, P. Rubeo (Rossi).

April. The General arrives (April 11) at Ávila and (April 27) visits St. Teresa, authorizing her to found further convents of the Reform, and later (August 14, from Barcelona) two monasteries.

August 15. Foundation of Convent at Medina del Campo (2).

[1] I.e., about six months after Maldonado's visit: cf. final words of F I (Vol. III, p. 4).

September–November. Remains at Medina till early November. During her stay there (? early in September) discusses with Antonio de Jesús and St. John of the Cross the foundation of the first monastery of the Reform (F III).

In November, goes to Madrid and stays for a fortnight with Doña Leonor de Mascareñas. Thence goes to Alcalá de Henares, consults P. Báñez and stays till February 1568.

1568

February. Visits Doña Luisa de la Cerda at Toledo.

March (late in). Leaves for Malagón.

April 11. Foundation of Convent at Malagón (3).

May 19. Leaves Malagón for Ávila. On the way, stays at Toledo in Doña Luisa de la Cerda's house, during her absence: (LL 6). Visits the Marchioness of Villena at Escalona (LL 6).

June 2–30. At St. Joseph's, Avila. Rafael Mejía offers her a house at Duruelo for use as a monastery. She leaves for Medina and Valladolid, calling at Duruelo on the way.

August 10. Arrives at Valladolid. St. John of the Cross has accompanied her from Medina to Valladolid and stays there till September 30 (F XIII; LL 10).

August 15. Foundation of Convent at Valladolid (4).

October. The Valladolid nuns fall ill and go to stay with Doña María de Mendoza, who takes over their house and gives them a new one.

(November 28. First Mass said at the Discalced monastery, Duruelo.)

1569

February 3. The Valladolid nuns enter their new house.

February 21. Leaves Valladolid for Medina, Ávila, Madrid and Toledo, revisiting Duruelo on the way (F XIV; cf. LL 13–15).

March 24. Arrives at Toledo (LL 19). (The King sends for her, believing her to be still in Madrid, after she has left for Toledo.)

May 14. Foundation of Convent at Toledo (5).

May 28. Receives a letter from the Princess of Éboli about a foundation at Pastrana.

May 30. Leaves Toledo. In Madrid, stays for a week at a Franciscan convent with Doña Leonor de Mascareñas. Refuses to found a convent in Madrid (LL 294).

July 9. Foundation of Convent at Pastrana (6). (A monastery founded there on July 13.)

July 21. Leaves for Toledo again. Stays there till August 1570.

NOTE.—The date of the *Exclamations of the Soul to God* is probably 1569. Cf. Vol. II, p. 401.

1570

(? July). Visits Pastrana and (August–October) Ávila. On October 31 arrives at Salamanca.

November 1. Foundation of Convent at Salamanca (7).

1571

January 25. Foundation of Convent at Alba de Tormes (8).

Mid-February. Leaves Alba. Goes to stay for some days with the Count and Countess of Monterrey. On March 29, is at Salamanca (LL 25); in May, by order of the Provincial of the Observance, P. Alonso González, at St. Joseph's; in June, at Medina del Campo; in mid-July, at Ávila.

August–October. Prioress at Medina (LL 27).

October 6. Goes from Medina to Ávila.

October 15 (to October 1574). Prioress of Convent of the Incarnation, Ávila (LL 29 ff.).

1572

(Between May and September). St. John of the Cross becomes confessor to Convent of the Incarnation, Ávila.

1573

June 11. Earliest extant letter (LL 45) written by St. Teresa to Philip II.

August. Visits the Salamanca Convent for the transference of the community there in September.

August 24. Begins to write the *Foundations* (at Salamanca: F VII). Writes about nine chapters: then stops on account of "numerous occupations".

1574

January. Leaves Salamanca. Spends some time at Alba de Tormes, staying for two days in the house of the Duke and Duchess of Alba. (I.C. VI, iv: Vol. II, p. 289.) Goes on to Medina and Ávila.

March. Travels to Segovia.

March 19. Foundation of Convent at Segovia (9).

Holy Week: April. Transfers Pastrana nuns to Segovia (F XVII). Remains there till September 30 (F XXI; LL 62).

October 6 (about). Returns to St. Joseph's, Ávila, as Prioress.

December (to January 1575). Visits Vallodolid (LL 66–70).

1575

February. Travels from Ávila, via Toledo, Malagón and Almodóvar, to Beas.

February 24. Foundation of Convent at Beas (10).

March 10. Agreement for the Caravaca convent signed (F XXVII).

Before May 11 (LL 71). First meeting with Gracián (F XXIV, R XXXIX). Makes vow of obedience to Gracián (R XL, XLI).

May 18–26. Journey to Seville (Leaves, May 18; at Ecija, May 23: R XL; arrives at Seville, May 26: F XXIV).

May 29. Foundation of Convent at Seville (11).

June 9. New licence for the Caravaca convent granted by Philip II (F XXVII).

(May–June. Chapter-General of the Order, held at Piacenza, adopts harsh measures towards the Discalced Reform.)

July 19. Writes from Seville to Philip II (LL 77) on behalf of the plan for dividing the Order and asking that P. Gracián be made Provincial of the Discalced.

August. Arrival of her brothers Lorenzo and Pedro from Spanish America (F XXV, R XLVI, LL 87, P. Silverio, IX, 246).

(Shortly before Christmas). Receives a written order from the General to leave Andalusia and to go to reside in a Castilian convent. P. Gracián authorizes her to stay at Seville till the summer (LL 87, 91).

1576

(From June 1576 to June 1580 St. Teresa is mainly at Toledo and Ávila. Strife within the Order holds up the foundations.)

January 1. Foundation of Convent at Caravaca (12) during her stay in Seville (LL 92).

(March. P. Jerónimo Tostado arrives in Spain armed with powers from P. Rubeo to suppress certain Discalced foundations and to take other measures against the Reform.)

April 5. Agreement for the new house at Seville signed.

(May 12. Provincial Chapter of the Observance, held at La Moraleja, takes stern measures against the Reform.)

May 28. Ceremony of the inauguration of the new house at Seville.

June 4. Leaves Seville for Toledo, via Almodóvar del Campo and Malagón. Arrives at Malagón on June 11 (LL 95) and stays for at least a week (LL 96). Is in Toledo before June 30 (LL 97).

(August 8. P. Gracián meets the Superiors of the Reform at Almodóvar: they refuse to accept the decisions of the Moraleja Chapter.)

June–November. Continues *Foundations*.

November 14. Completes Chapter XXVII of *Foundations* (See penultimate paragraph of that chapter).

1577

June 2. Begins *Interior Castle*.

(June 18. Death of the Nuncio Ormaneto.)

July. Goes from Toledo to Ávila to arrange for the transference of St. Joseph's from the jurisdiction of the Ordinary to that of the Carmelite Order. Interruption of her work on *Interior Castle* (I.C. V, iv).

(August 30. Arrival in Spain of the new Nuncio, Sega.)

September 18. Writes to Philip II on behalf of P. Gracián and of the Reform (LL 195).

October. Violent scenes at the election of a Prioress at the Incarnation, Ávila. Nuns voting for St. Teresa are excommunicated. Ana de Toledo chosen (LL 197–8, cf. 205–7).

(November 5. Royal Council opposes the policy of Tostado, who leaves for Rome.)

November 29. Finishes *Interior Castle*.

December 3. St. John of the Cross and a companion are carried off and imprisoned, at Toledo and La Moraleja respectively, by the friars of the Observance (LL 204, 219, 246–7).

December 4.[2] St. Teresa complains of this act to Philip II (LL 204).

December 24. Falls and breaks her left arm.

[2] Some authorities believe that, between December 11 and 17 of this year, St. Teresa had an interview with Philip II at El Escorial (cf. P. Silverio, IX, 266).

1578

(Persecution of the Reform continues throughout this year: LL 237 ff. St. Teresa is in Avila.)

(September 4. Death of P. Rubeo at Rome: LL 253.)

(October 9. Chapter-General of the Discalced held at Almodóvar.)

(October 16. Sega puts the Discalced under the jurisdiction of the Observance.)

1579

(April 1. Discalced removed from jurisdiction of the Observance: P. Ángel de Salazar becomes their Superior.)

(May. PP. Juan de Jesús [Roca] and Diego de la Trinidad leave for Rome, to attempt to effect the division of the Order: LL 273, 275.) P. Salazar authorizes St. Teresa to resume the visitation of her convents.

June 25. Leaves Ávila, with B. Ana de San Bartolomé, for Medina (stays 3–4 days), Valladolid (July 3–30), Salamanca (about 2½ months) and Alba (a week).

July. Sends the *Way of perfection* to the Archbishop of Évora (LL 285).

November (early). Returns to Ávila.

November. Goes to Toledo (mid-November: LL 291) and Malagón; arrives at Malagón, November 25; is there when (December 8) the community moves into its new house (LL 295). Stays till February 1580.

1580

February 13. Leaves Malagón for Villanueva de la Jara (LL 307–8, 313), arriving there February 21, after making stops at Toledo and La Roda.

February 21. Foundation of Convent at Villanueva de la Jara (13).

March 20. Leaves Villaneuva de la Jara.

March 26. Arrives at Toledo. On March 31 (LL 314) has a paralytic stroke. Asks the Archbishop of Toledo for a licence to make a foundation in Madrid: the request is not granted (LL 323).

June 7. Though still unwell, leaves for Madrid and Segovia. Reaches Segovia on June 15. While there, learns of the death (June 26) of her brother Lorenzo (LL 325-6, 342). Goes (July 6) from Segovia to Ávila, to settle his business affairs (LL 328). At Segovia, revises the *Interior Castle* in collaboration with P. Gracián and P. Yanguas. (Vol. II, p. 194.)

(June 22. The Discalced Reform is recognized as a separate province by a Bull of Gregory XIII.)

August (early). Goes on from Ávila to Medina del Campo and (August 8) Valladolid where she is to see the Bishop about the projected foundation in his diocese. At Valladolid has a recurrence of the Toledo complaint and becomes dangerously ill (LL 336).

December 28. Leaves Valladolid for Palencia (LL 344).

December 29. Foundation of Convent at Palencia (14) (LL 344).

1581

(March 3. Separation of Calced and Discalced Carmelites becomes operative at Chapter of Alcalá de Henares: cf. LL 350-4. P. Gracián appointed Provincial of the Discalced.)

June 2. Arrives at Soria, after spending the night of May 31 at Burgo de Osma (F XXX).

(June 1. The Palencia community moves to its new house.)

June 14. Foundation of Convent at Soria (15). (Cf. F XXX, Vol. III, p. 180, n. 3.)

August 16. Leaves for St. Joseph's, Ávila, via Burgo de Osma, Segovia (August 23-30: LL 376), Villacastín (September 4: LL 377).

September 5. Arrives at Ávila (LL 378).

September 10. Elected Prioress of St. Joseph's, Ávila.

1582

January 2. Leaves for Burgos, via Medina del Campo (January 4–9), Valladolid (staying four days through illness: LL 404) and Palencia (arrives January 16), arriving at Burgos on January 26.

January 20. Foundation of Convent at Granada (16) in St. Teresa's absence.

April 19. Foundation of Convent at Burgos (17).

(July) Completes *Foundations* (F XXXI was being written at "the end of June": Vol. III, p. 191, n. 2).

July 26. Leaves Burgos for Ávila, with B. Ana de San Bartolomé and her niece Teresita. Visits Palencia (in August), Vallodolid (again ill: leaves on September 15), Medina del Campo (September 16) and villages near Peñaranda. Though ill, goes to Alba de Tormes at the command of the Provincial, Fray Antonio de Jesús, to visit the Duchess of Alba.

September 20. Arrives at Alba de Tormes.

October 4. Dies at Alba de Tormes.

1614: April 24. Beatified by Paul V.

1617. Spanish Cortes votes her patroness of Spain. The vote not confirmed.

1622: March 12. Canonized by Gregory XV with SS. Isidro, Ignatius of Loyola and Francis Xavier.

1726. Benedict XIII institutes the Feast of the Transverberation of her Heart.

GENERAL INTRODUCTION
TO THE WORKS OF ST. TERESA

Nearly four centuries have passed since St. Teresa began to write, and, both in her own country and abroad, her fame is still widespread and still growing. Her purely human qualities and gifts, the saintliness of her life by which they were illumined and overshadowed, the naturalness and candour of her manner and style—these are some of the reasons why her name is not only graven upon the enduring marble of history but taken on the lips of generation after generation with reverence and love.

She is a mystic—and more than a mystic. Her works, it is true, are well known in the cloister and have served as nourishment to many who are far advanced on the Way of Perfection, and who, without her aid, would still be beginners in the life of prayer. Yet they have also entered the homes of millions living in the world and have brought consolation, assurance, hope and strength to souls who, in the technical sense, know nothing of the life of contemplation. Devoting herself, as she did, with the most wonderful persistence and tenacity, to the sublimest task given to man—the attempt to guide others toward perfection—she succeeded so well in that task that she is respected everywhere as an incredibly gifted teacher, who has revealed, more perhaps than any who came before her, the nature and extent of those gifts which the Lord has laid up in this life for those who love Him. In past ages, of course, there had been many writers kindled with Divine love to whom He had manifested His ineffable secrets, but for the most part these secrets had gone down with them to the grave. To St. Teresa it was given to speak to the world, in her diaphanous, colloquial language and her simple, unaffected style, of the work of the Holy Spirit in the enamoured soul, of the interior strife and the continual purgation through which such a soul must pass in its ascent of Mount Carmel and of the wonders which await it on the mountain's summit.

So she leads the soul from the most rudimentary stages of

the Purgative Way to the very heights of Union, bringing it into the innermost mansion of the Interior Castle, where, undisturbed by the foes that rage without, it can have fruition of union with the Lord of that Castle and experience a foretaste of the Beatific Vision of the life to come. But, despite the loftiness and sublimity of these themes, she is able to develop them without ever losing the most attractive of her qualities as a writer—simplicity. Continually she finds ready to hand apt and graphic comparisons, intelligible even to the unlearned. No mystical writer before her day, from the pseudo-Dionysius to Ruysbroeck, nor any who has written since, has described such high matters in a way so apt, so natural and to such a large extent within the reach of all. The publication of her treatises inaugurated for the mystics an epoch of what may almost be termed popularity. Those who love the pages of the Gospels, and whose aim in life is to attain the Gospel ideal of Christian perfection, have found in her works other pages in which, without any great effort of the intellect, they may learn much concerning the way. Her practical insistence upon the virtuous life, her faithfulness to the Evangelical counsels and the soundness of her doctrine even in the most obscure and recondite details—all these will commend her to them. Many, indeed, are the fervent lovers of Our Lord who have gone to the school of love kept by the Foundress of Ávila.

As a result, her works are read and re-read by Spaniards to this day and translated again and again into foreign languages. Probably no other book by a Spanish author is as widely known in Spain as the *Life* or the *Interior Castle* of St. Teresa, with the single exception of Cervantes' immortal *Don Quixote*. It is surely amazing that a woman who lived in the sixteenth century, who never studied in the Schools or pored over tomes of profound learning, still less aspired to any kind or degree of renown, should have won such a reputation, both among scholars and among the people. We cannot expect to find the reason for this in the purely scientific or literary merits of her writings: we must look for it by going deeper.

Essentially, her popularity has been due to Divine grace, which first inspired her to lay aside every aim but the quest for God and then enabled her to attain a degree of purity in her love for Him which sustained and impelled her. Before everything else it is the intense fervour of this love which speaks to lovers everywhere, just as it is the determination and courage of her virile soul which inspires those who long to be more determined and courageous than they are. But next to this, it is the purely human quality of her writings which makes so wide an appeal. Her methods of exposition are not rigidly logical—but neither are the workings of the human heart. Her books have a *gracioso desorden* [Herrick's "sweet disorder"] which the ordinary reader finds attractive, even illuminating. Her disconnected observations, her revealing parentheses, her transpositions, ellipses and sudden suspensions of thought make her, in one sense, easier to read, even if, in another, they sometimes make her more difficult to interpret. Even setting aside her lack of technical training as a writer, her robust and highly individual temperament would have led her into rebellion against academic mechanism of conventionality and style in language, had any attempt ever been made to force these upon her. Where she uses or imitates the phraseology of Holy Scripture she does so unconsciously. Often she never even re-read what she wrote; who that is not a professional writer, but just a man in the street, or a woman in the kitchen, can help loving her?

Her books were written at the command of her confessors —that is to say, under obedience. It seemed ridiculous to her that a person so imperfect and devoid of talent as herself— and a woman into the bargain!—could possibly write anything that would edify others. She was much better émployed, she herself thought, at the spinning-wheel, and it irked her to leave such a profitable occupation as spinning to take up her pen. "For the love of God," she once exclaimed, when importuned to write, "let me work at my spinning-wheel and go to choir and perform the duties of the religious life, like the other sisters. I am not meant to write: I have neither the health nor the intelligence for it."[1] The following passage gives as vivid an idea as any of the spirit in which she wrote:

The authority of persons so learned and serious as my confessors suffices for the approval of any good thing that I may say, if the Lord gives me grace to say it, in which case

[1] Jerónimo Gracián: *Lucidario del verdadero espíritu*, Chap. V. She did, however, eventually write the book she was asked for: it was the *Interior Castle*.

it will not be mine but His; for I have no learning, nor have I led a good life, nor do I get my information from a learned man or from any other person whatsoever. Only those who have commanded me to write this know that I am doing so, and at the moment they are not here. I am almost stealing the time for writing, and that with great difficulty, for it hinders me from spinning and I am living in a poor house and have numerous things to do.[2]

But, even had she left no such personal testimony, her writings would have shown how little she trusted for inspiration to her reading and how completely devoid she was of any constructional instinct or sense of literary proportion. Her ideas and sentiments spring spontaneously to her mind and spirit. Her pen runs freely—sometimes too freely for her mind to keep pace with it. Her memory, as she frequently confesses, is poor and her few quotations are seldom entirely accurate. But she is, without the slightest doubt, a born writer; and, when a person belonging to that rare and fortunate class knows nothing of artifice, casts aside convention, and writes as the spirit dictates, the result can never be disappointing.

Mysticism, furthermore, is in part an experimental science; and he who has the profoundest and most continuous experiences of Divine grace is the best qualified to speak of them. St. Teresa is remarkable both for the intensity and for the continuity of her mystical experiences, and she had a quickness of mind, a readiness of expression and a wealth of imagination which particularly well fitted her for describing them. Her descriptions are incomparably more vivid and intelligible than those of many professed students of mystical theology who have grown grey in the study of it. This superiority much more than compensates for any of her stylistic idiosyncrasies which may scandalize the literary preceptist. Had she not boldly snapped asunder the bonds of logic and literary rule, she would have been powerless to take wing and give us those finest of passages which describe the summit of Mount Carmel. We should have gained one more methodical writer aspiring to a "golden mediocrity"—but we should have lost work of a sublime beauty bearing the ineffaceable hallmark of genius.

[2] *Life*, Chap. X (p. 123).

But in any case she could never have written impeccable manuals or methodically ordered "guides" to the ascetic or the mystical life: her genius resembles the rushing torrent, not the scientifically constructed canal. She cannot even be said to separate asceticism from mysticism: the *Way of perfection* is an ascetic treatise which mystical ideas are constantly invading; while the *Interior Castle*, though fundamentally mystical, does not hesitate to lay down and develop ascetic principles. Here, again, she conforms, not so much to what is logical as to what is natural and human. Any divisions which she makes and adheres to are those made by nature and observable in life. By any and every test, she is a writer to be read by the many, by the people.

If obedience was St. Teresa's primary motive for writing, a secondary motive was to give an accurate and detailed account of her spiritual progress, as in the *Life*, or, as in most of her other books, to guide her spiritual daughters.

The seventeenth-century Carmelite, Fray Jerónimo de San José, a historian of the Discalced Reform and author of one of the earliest biographies of St. John of the Cross, makes the following enumeration of her writings:

> Our Mother St. Teresa wrote five books and seven opuscules. The books are: *The Book of her Life, The Way of perfection, The Mansions,*[3] *The Foundations* and *Meditations on the Songs*. The opuscules are: *Method for the visitation of her convents, Exclamations, Spiritual Maxims, Relations of her spirit, Favours granted her by the Lord, Devout verses which she composed, Letters to different persons*. So that, between books, opuscules and treatises, the number of books written by the Saint amounts in all to twelve.[4]

In addition to these works, several more have been credited to St. Teresa, though hardly on sufficient evidence. From a reference in the *Foundations* to "a tiny little book" in which she "believed she said something about" melancholy,[5] it has

[3] [This is the title nearly always given in Spanish to the *Interior Castle*.]

[4] *Historia del Carmen Descalzo*, Bk. V, Chap. XIII.

[5] *Foundations*, Chap. VII (Vol. III, p. 36, n. 2).

been inferred that a book of hers on this subject has been lost: the reference, however, might well be to the *Way of perfection*, which says a good deal about this, and, though the *Way of perfection* might hardly be thought "tiny", she refers to it elsewhere as "little" by contrast with her considerably larger *Life*.

Another book, which certainly exists, was thought to be the work of St. Teresa as long ago as 1630, when it was included by Baltasar Moreto in an edition of her works published in that year at Antwerp. The only reason for its inclusion appears to have been that it was found among some papers which had belonged to her, and afterwards became the property of Doña Isabel de Avellaneda, wife of Don Iñigo de Cárdenas, President of the Council of Castile. Its title is *Seven Meditations on the Paternoster*. It is a pious commentary on the Lord's Prayer, the seven petitions of which are treated as meditations, each intended to be read on a different day of the week, under the headings: Father, King, Spouse, Shepherd, Redeemer, Physician, Judge. The author was both a learned and a spiritually-minded person, well versed in Holy Scripture and with a decided literary bent. The most superficial examination reveals it to be clearly non-Teresian. Its style is quite unlike that of the Saint and it bears the marks of a careful revision entirely foreign to her habits and character. Her earliest biographers make no mention of it and her Order has never believed it to be hers. "I consider it quite certain that the treatise is not by our Holy Mother," says P. Jerónimo de San José, and gives the fullest reasons for his opinion.[6] "All who read it carefully," he adds, "and even those who read it without great care, will think likewise."

P. Ribera, St. Teresa's first biographer, and a particularly conscientious one, tells us that, when very young, in collaboration with her brother Rodrigo, she wrote a book on chivalry. "She had so excellent a wit, and had so well absorbed the language and style of chivalry, that in the space of a few months she and her brother Rodrigo composed a book of adventures and fictions on that subject, which was such that it attracted a great deal of comment."[7] This story is confirmed

[6] Quoted in full by P. Silverio, I, lxix.
[7] Ribera, Bk. I, Chap. V.

by Gracián in his notes to Ribera's book and has been frequently repeated and taken as accurate by later writers. There would be nothing intrinsically improbable in the idea that a writer with the initiative and imagination of St. Teresa, who, we know (for she tells us herself in great detail),[8] was attracted in her youth by romances of the *Amadis* type, should try to produce something of the sort herself by way of recreation, and we may be sure that, if she did so, the book in question would be well worth reading. P. Andrés de la Encarnación, an eighteenth-century editor and critic of St. John of the Cross,[9] took the suggestion very seriously, and debated where the book was to be found, and whether or no, supposing it were found, it ought to be published.[10] For ourselves, we suspect that, if it was ever written at all, it was soon destroyed by its own authors, either because of the nature of its contents or for fear that it would fall into the hands of their father, the austere Don Alonso, who for such an indiscretion would no doubt have meted out anything but a reward.

By great good fortune, the originals of nearly all St. Teresa's principal works have come down to us, together with those of a fair number of her letters and some account books bearing her signature. This fortune we owe to the great esteem shown for St. Teresa and her Reform by King Philip II, who, when collecting books and manuscripts for the library which he proposed to establish in his newly built palace-monastery at El Escorial, asked P. Doria (Fray Nicolás de Jesús María),[11] at that time Vicar-General of the Discalced Carmelites, if he could obtain for him any of St. Teresa's autographs. As a result, four of these are now to be found in the Escorial Library: namely, the *Life*, the *Way of perfection*, the *Foundations* and the *Method for the visitation of her convents*. The autograph of the *Interior Castle* is preserved in the Discalced Carmelite convent at Seville, and a second autograph of the *Way of perfection*, to be referred to later, has long been in the possession of the convent of the Discalced nuns at Valladolid. As a considerable number of facsimile reproductions of these manuscripts have been published, the careful study of

8 *Life*, Chap. II (p. 68).
9 [*St. John of the Cross*, I, liv ff., *et passim*.]
10 B.Nac. MS. 3180, Adiciones E., Nos. 13, 14.
11 [Cf. *S.S.M.*, II, 155–6.]

the Teresian writings in their original state has been brought
within the reach of all who are qualified to undertake it.

Needless to say, a great many copies of the Saint's writings
were made very soon after her death, and, needless to say,
too, these copies contained numerous errors. To put an end
to this circulation of defective versions of their Mother
Foundress' works, the Discalced Carmelites took steps towards the preparation of a complete edition. A beginning had
been made with their publication even in her own lifetime. A
great friend of hers, Don Teutonio de Braganza, Archbishop
of Évora, undertook to bring out an edition of the *Maxims*
and *Way of perfection*, based upon a corrected manuscript
(still extant) which she herself sent him, in 1579: this was
approved by the ecclesiastical censor in 1580 and published
at Évora in 1583. At Salamanca, in 1585, P. Gracián (Fray
Jerónimo de la Madre de Dios)[12] at that time Provincial of
the Reform, re-published the *Way of perfection*, which no
doubt was given precedence over the other works on account
of its practical utility in the training of religious. An impetus
must have been given to these activities by St. John of the
Cross, who, just about this time, wrote as follows in the commentary to his *Spiritual Canticle:*

> But since my intent is but to expound these stanzas
> briefly, as I promised in the prologue, these other things
> must remain for such as can treat them better than I. And
> I pass over the subject likewise because the Blessed Teresa
> of Jesus, our mother, left notes admirably written upon
> these things of the spirit, the which notes I hope in God
> will speedily be printed and brought to light.[13]

St. John of the Cross was in fact present at the meeting of the
General Chapter in 1586 which decided to publish the
Saint's complete works. The editorship was entrusted, not to
a Carmelite, but to an Augustinian—one of the leading men
of letters in Spain, the Salamancan professor Fray Luis de
León. The volume, of over a thousand octavo pages, was published at Salamanca in 1588, and includes the following
works, printed in the order here given: *Book of her life*; some
of the *Relations*; *Way of perfection*; *Maxims*; *Interior Castle*;

12 [S.S.M., II, 151–89.]
13 [*St. John of the Cross*, II, 72.]

Exclamations. The principal omission, it will be observed, is the *Foundations:* so many of the people mentioned in it were still living that its publication was thought to be premature.

On the whole, as one would expect of an editor who, besides being himself an author, had had a lifetime of academic experience, Fray Luis de León acquitted himself remarkably well. The edition has some omissions and variant readings of such length or importance that they can hardly have been due to accident, besides a considerable number of *errata*, notably in punctuation—and, owing to St. Teresa's often compressed and elliptical style, a misplaced comma is sometimes enough to alter the sense of an entire passage. None the less, judged by the standards of its day, the edition is a distinctly good one.

It was reprinted, at the same press, in the following year, after which date further editions came quickly. The works, in a more or less complete state, were published at Saragossa in 1592; at Madrid, in 1597 and 1615; at Naples, in 1604; at Brussels, in 1604; at Brussels, in 1610; at Valencia, in 1613 and 1623. The Brussels edition was the first to include the *Foundations.* The *editio princeps* was reprinted at Madrid in 1622 and 1627 and at Saragossa in 1623. In 1630, at Antwerp, Baltasar Moreto published an edition already referred to as including the apocryphal *Seven Meditations.* A single-volume edition, in 1635, and a two-volume edition, in 1636, came out in Madrid.

This rapidly increasing circulation of St. Teresa's works, however, was not altogether welcomed by her Order, for the printers' errors in each edition were handed down to the next, often with considerable additions, while undue liberties were sometimes taken with the text by editors less conscientious than Fray Luis de León. It was in about 1645 that P. Francisco de Santa María, the historian of the Discalced Reform, obtained permission from his superiors for a new collation of the printed works and the autographs, with a view to the preparation of a more reliable edition than any yet published. The collation was entrusted to a number of friars and the new edition—the second which may be described as "official" —was eventually published in Madrid in 1661.

We need not follow through the centuries the long tale of editions of the Saint's works—still less enumerate the editions of individual works which will be referred to later in the in-

troductions to each. It must suffice, in this brief survey, to remark on the continuity with which St. Teresa was read even
during the eighteenth and early nineteenth centuries, when
mysticism was little in favour, and to mention a few of the
editions which may be considered of outstanding interest.

In the mid-eighteenth century, the Order determined upon
still another "official" edition and entrusted the work of preparing one to that excellent critic already referred to, P. Andrés de la Encarnación, who enlisted the aid of a competent
palaeographer, a companion worthy of himself, P. Manuel
de Santa María. The results of their researches, both on
St. Teresa and on St. John of the Cross, remained in manuscript; and the three volumes of *Memorias historiales*, in the
National Library of Spain, at Madrid, are a major source for
critical work on the Reformers of Carmel. As many of the
archives which the two Fathers used are no longer in existence, their work has preserved much that would otherwise
have been irretrievably lost, including part of the magnificent
collection which we have of Teresian letters. In their work
upon the texts, they detected more than seven hundred errors in the *Life* of 1627 and twelve hundred in Moreto's edition of the *Foundations*. It is a pity that the Order found the
task of publishing a new edition too much for it and was content to reprint, in 1778, an edition of 1752, adding to it a
volume containing eighty-two previously unpublished letters.
In 1793 appeared another edition, which included a further
volume of letters and eighty-seven fragments, and was the
last to be published by the Order for a hundred and twenty
years. Not until 1851, when the religious persecutions of the
early years of the nineteenth century were over, was this edition reprinted, and ten years later came the edition of Don
Vicente de la Fuente, which forms part of the monumental
series of Spanish classics known as the "Biblioteca de Autores
Españoles."

The strides made in Spain, during the last half-century, by
Teresian criticism, and indeed by Spanish criticism in general, make it possible for Spaniards to look back from a great
distance at the work of La Fuente, both here and in his later
six-volume edition of 1881, and find in it faults of many
kinds: innumerable textual errors, frequent inaccuracies of
fact, exaggerations in judgment and an undue dogmatism of
tone. This Aragonese editor, though learned and devout in a

high degree, had the temperamental bluntness and stubbornness traditionally associated with Aragon, and from this his work frequently suffered. None the less, his edition remained unsuperseded for over half a century—until, in fact, in the year of the quatercentenary of St. Teresa's birth, appeared the first volume of the definitive Carmelite edition [which we owe to the indefatigable P. Silverio de Santa Teresa.]

[This edition, consisting of nine volumes (1915–24) of which the last three comprise the largest collection yet made of the Saint's letters—four hundred and fifty in all—concentrated upon the preparation of as correct as possible a text, using the autographs, or photostats of them, where previous editors had relied on copies. The notes to the text, which are not the strongest point of the edition, are brief and in the main factual, though occasionally they sin through the discursiveness which P. Silverio seldom for long avoids. A welcome feature was the inclusion of many newly discovered letters—for, while the sacking of religious houses during the nineteenth century had led to much destruction, it had also brought to light a good deal that had previously been unknown. P. Silverio's appendices contain numerous hitherto unpublished documents, many of them of capital importance for an intimate knowledge of St. Teresa's life.]

[The foregoing notes bear witness of the most practical kind to the continuous popularity which St. Teresa has enjoyed in her own country since the time of her death. In our own country it was her *Life* which at first chiefly attracted translators: the Antwerp translations of the Jesuit William Malone appeared as early as 1611; twelve years later, Sir Tobias Mathew's version, known as *The Flaming Hart*, was published in London, a second edition appearing at Antwerp in 1642; while the *Life* and *Foundations* were published by Abraham Woodhead in 1669–71, and a third volume, containing nearly all the remaining works, came out in 1675. After this nearly two centuries elapsed before the Saint began to be widely read once more, but since Dalton, with his new translation of the *Life* (1851), led the revival, interest in her has never ceased. Dalton's *Way of perfection* and *Interior Castle* (1852), *Foundations* (1853) and small selection of *Letters* (1853) were followed by the *Life* (1870) and *Foundations* (1871) in the translation of David Lewis: the *Life*, still leading the other works in popularity, went into four editions. The mantle of Lewis fell upon the shoulders of a Benedictine nun of Stanbrook Abbey, and the editions of the Benedictines of Stanbrook, already referred to, and notably their versions of the *Way of perfection* and the *Interior Castle* and their four-volume edition of the *Letters* (1919–24), have perhaps done more than any others to give St. Teresa a place in our spiritual life comparable to that which she holds in Spain. Finally we must not forget the valuable contributions made to our knowledge of the Saint and her times by the learned Carmelite, Father Zimmerman, whose revisions of, and introductions to, the Lewis and Stanbrook translations have so much enhanced their value. England, it will be seen, is not now behindhand in her appreciation of a Saint on whom one of her seventeenth-century poets wrote what is perhaps the finest panegyric in verse upon her in existence.

O thou undanted daughter of desires!
By all thy dowr of Lights and Fires;
By all the eagle in thee, all the dove;
By all thy lives and deaths of love;
By thy larg draughts of intellectuall day,
And by thy thirsts of love more large then they;
By all thy brim-fill'd Bowles of feirce desire;
By thy last Morning's draught of liquid fire;
By the full kingdome of that finall kisse
That seiz'd thy parting Soul, and seal'd thee his;
By all the heavn's thou hast in him
(Fair sister of the Seraphim!);
By all of Him we have in Thee;
Leave nothing of my Self in me.
Let me so read thy life, that I
Unto all life of mine may dy.[14]]

The translator, who, in the main, has followed P. Silverio in the order in which he has arranged St. Teresa's works, begs leave to append a note, adapted from P. Silverio, upon the principles underlying this arrangement.

He begins with the Saint's earliest and fundamental work, her *Life* (1562–5), which is followed by a shorter work closely connected with it in spirit, and hence forming a natural com-

[14] ["The Flaming Hart" ("Upon the book and picture of the seraphicall St. Teresa").]

plement to it—the *Relations*. It might be thought that the *Life* should rather have been followed by the autobiographical *Foundations*, but it must be remembered that the *Life* is an autobiography primarily in the spiritual sense—a history of the manifestations of Divine grace in the writer's soul— whereas the *Foundations* is mainly a record of practical achievements and is related as closely with the history of the Order as with the life of the Saint.

After the *Life* and the *Relations* comes the *Way of perfection* (c. 1565), written under obedience, as we have seen, for the edification of the nuns of the Saint's first foundation—St. Joseph's, Ávila—and based upon her own meditations on the Lord's Prayer. Since the *Life* contained so much intimate detail it was thought unsuitable for publication until after its author's death, and the *Way of perfection* was written, in one sense, to supply its place. Next comes the *Interior Castle* (1577), more mature and more intensely mystical than its two predecessors. These three works, taken together, may be thought of as a complete exposition of the ascetic and mystical system of St. Teresa. As closely connected with the *Interior Castle* in its nature and spirit as are the *Relations* with the *Life* are the *Conceptions of the Love of God*, and the *Exclamations of the Soul to God*, the two loveliest of St. Teresa's opuscules, both of them from beginning to end aglow with mystical love.

Following these, as standing outside their sphere and (despite some fine and noble passages) on a lower plane, comes the *Foundations* (1573 ff.), the last of the four major works, and, following these, we give the minor works, with the poems appropriately coming last, as it is in verse that St. Teresa is least noteworthy.

THE LIFE
OF TERESA OF JESUS

THE LIFE OF THE HOLY
MOTHER TERESA OF JESUS

INTRODUCTION

Like all servants of God to whom He has granted special
graces, St. Teresa, when led by unfamiliar paths, had continual misgivings lest she should be suffering from demoni-
acal delusions. These misgivings she frequently revealed to
her spiritual directors, keeping nothing back from them but
opening her soul with exemplary simplicity and humility, especially when what she had to tell was to her own disadvantage. Some of her confessors, so as the better to form judgments on matters of such extreme difficulty, ordered her to
write an account of the graces that she was receiving from
God, more particularly of the graces given her in prayer, and
to record anything further which might facilitate the understanding of them.

Such was the origin of this admirable autobiography,
which, for the naturalness with which it is written, for the
profundity and detail of its psychological analysis and for the
sublimity of the spiritual mysteries which it unfolds, is
worthy of a place beside the *Confessions* of St. Augustine.

The first part of the book (Chaps. I–X) is autobiographical in the ordinary sense of the word: it describes the author's
parentage, early life and education, the interior conflicts
which she had to endure before embracing religion, the alter-
nating lukewarmness and fervour of her life at the Convent
of the Incarnation, in Ávila, and finally the crisis which ended
in her resolve to seek perfection and walk in the way of
prayer. There then follows a parenthetical section (Chaps.
XI–XXVII)[1] which describes the contemplative life under
the figure of the Four Waters, each of which corresponds to

[1] [More properly this section may be considered as ending with
Chap. XXII. "I will now return to the place where I left off the
description of my life," says St. Teresa at the beginning of Chap.
XXIII; but she interpolates a further generalization on locutions, so
the narrative is not quite continuous.]

one stage of spiritual progress. Only at the end of these seventeen chapters does St. Teresa return to her own life, in order to describe (Chaps. XXVIII–XL) the surpassing favours which the Lord granted her and the spiritual trials in which she was so greatly helped by the Franciscan St. Peter of Alcántara.[2] Into this part of the book is introduced her account of the foundation of the first convent of the Reform, St. Joseph's, Avila. The *Life* closes with a moving enumeration of the new favours which she is receiving from God and of the effects produced by them in her soul. Into the whole of this narrative are intercalated discreet counsels for confessors, tender colloquies with God, shrewd maxims for souls desirous of attaining perfection and ardent apostrophes to all Christian people.

This is St. Teresa's most important treatise. Without it neither the *Way of perfection* nor the *Interior Castle* could be properly understood: she herself refers to it on several occasions as her "big book" (*libro grande*). Only the superficial student, however, is content for long to think of these three works as separate. So closely united are they, so essentially complementary to each other, that it is easier to regard them as three parts of one great whole.

Exactly when the *Life* was written it is by no means easy to determine. P. Domingo Báñez, in a deposition made at Salamanca, asserts that "she had written this book when I first came into contact with her and she wrote it with the leave of her previous confessors. . . . Afterwards she added to it and recast it".[3] This first draft, of which no copy is known, though most of it, no doubt, was incorporated in the definitive version, was apparently concluded while she was staying with Doña Luisa de la Cerda at Toledo[4] [where she would, of course, have had much more leisure for writing than in the ordinary way]. At any rate, the note appended to the letter at the end of the book describes it as having been finished in June 1562,[5] and we know that she went to Toledo in January 1562 and stayed there for six months.[6]

At the end of 1562 [or possibly early in 1563, when the

[2] [S.S.M., II, 99–120.]
[3] Cit. La Fuente: *Escritos de Santa Teresa*, Madrid, 1861, II, 377.
[4] Cf. p. 232.
[5] Cf. p. 300.
[6] Cf. p. 241.

foundation of St. Joseph's had been completed, the resulting "commotion" had ceased and her mind was once more at rest], the Saint began to rewrite the book, and, just as she had been ordered to write the first draft by P. Ibáñez, so, it appears, we owe the new version to the insistence of his fellow-Dominican P. García de Toledo. The evidence for this [so far as it can be taken as referring to the *Life* as a whole] comes from St. Teresa herself, for in the preface to her *Foundations* she writes as follows:

> In the year 1562, when I was in the Convent of Saint Joseph, at Ávila, which had been founded in that very year, I was commanded by the Dominican Father Fray García de Toledo who at that time was my confessor, to write an account of the foundation of that convent, and also of many other things, as anyone who reads the book, if it is ever published, will see.[7]

Further encouragement, according to Gracián,[8] came from the Inquisitor Francisco Soto, whom she met at Ávila, from "other confessors who had given her the same command" and from "the requests of many of her friends". For greater clarity, the new version was divided into forty chapters.

The work must have proceeded very slowly, for there are a number of indications that it was not finished until the very end of 1565. The following, in the approximate order in which they occur, are the most reliable of these[9]:

1. "The twenty-eight years which have gone by since I began prayer" (Chap. VIII: p. 109).

2. "The twenty-eight years and more that have gone by since I became (a nun)" (Chap. XXXVI: p. 343).

3. "The twenty-seven years during which I have been practising prayer" (Chap. X: p. 124).

4. "It is now, I believe, some five, or perhaps six, years since the Lord granted me this prayer [the Third Water] in abundance" (Chap. XVI: p. 163).

5. Her first contact with the Society of Jesus took place

[7] [Vol. III, p. xxi. The command was given her in 1562 but the actual writing may not have been begun till later.]

[8] *Lucidario*, etc., Part I, Chap. III.

[9] [Only Nos. 7 and 8 are given by P. Silverio and the discussion of them all is the translator's.]

"after almost twenty years' experience of prayer" (Chap. XXIII: p. 224–5).

6. "I am not yet fifty" (Chap. XXXVII: p. 359).

7. Mention of the death of P. Ibáñez (Chap. XXXVIII: p. 365. Cf. Chap. XXXIV: p. 326).

8. Mention of the receipt of a Brief from Rome which was dated July 17, 1565 (Chap. XXXIX: p. 380).

The first five of these references enable us to postulate and confirm an approximate date; the last three confirm this further and help us to fix it more exactly.

1–5. What St. Teresa means by "beginning prayer" is evident from No. 5. Despite the unflattering account which she gives of the state of her soul during her first years as a nun, she clearly takes the date of her profession as roughly the beginning of her life of prayer. Since we know that her relations with the Society of Jesus began about 1557, this puts the earlier date at 1537, and Nos. 1, 3 then prove that Chapters VII and X were being written in 1564–5. The fact that the date of Chapter X is apparently a year earlier than that of Chapter VIII may mean that the earlier chapter was revised a second time after the later one had been written, or more likely, as the Saint revised her work but little, it may merely be a reminder to us that her figures cannot be implicitly relied upon.

No. 2 supplies a check on these calculations. If by "becoming a nun" she means "making her profession", Chapter XXXVI was also being written in 1565;[10] if she means entering the convent, the date is 1564. In any case, the foregoing calculations seem definitely to put out of court the critics who attempt to date her profession 1535, or even earlier, as also does the reference in Chapter VIII to the "nearly twenty years on that stormy sea" which she spent before the intensification of her spiritual life, which we can date with fair accuracy at 1556–7.

The evidence so far considered suggests that whatever delays occurred during the writing of the definitive *Life* took place during the years 1562–4, and that from the end of 1564 onwards the pace of composition was greatly accelerated.

No. 6 proves that, if the Saint knew her own age (cf. p.

[10] But perhaps late in that year: note the "and more", which does not occur in the earlier passage.

360, below), Chapter XXXVII was being written before March 28, 1565, the day on which she was fifty. This is a little earlier than we should have expected and it is interesting that the evidence as to Chapter XXXVI may also point to a date slightly in advance of that suggested by other testimony. Can these two chapters be earlier than some which precede them?

No. 7 means that Chapter XXXVIII was written after February 2, 1565. If very soon after, this and the preceding chapter may well have been written consecutively.

No. 8 not only proves that Chapter XXXIX could not have been written before the late summer of 1565 (and there is nothing in the text to suggest that it was written immediately on receipt of the Brief) but indicates that, if this Brief took five months in getting from Rome to Ávila as its predecessor did (p. 339, n. 1, below), it was probably written as late as December, or even early in the next year.[11]

Our general conclusions, then, will be that, though St. Teresa was commanded to write the *Life* in the latter part of 1562, she did comparatively little of it for some two years, and then worked more rapidly and intensively, writing most of it during 1565 and finishing it only at the very end of that year or early in 1566.

Having written the book, she endeavoured to submit it, as Soto had recommended her to do, to the scrutiny of the famous preacher and confessor Juan de Ávila,[12] but was not immediately successful. A letter appended to the autograph manuscript of the *Life* tells us that the book had no sooner been completed ("I had not finished reading through what I had written") than the recipient of the letter[13] asked for it;

11 [Two references in Chap. XXIX, briefly discussed in footnotes to pp. 268, 270, seem to support the theory of a later rather than an earlier date within the limits we have laid down. If we assume the first imaginary vision to have occurred in 1560 (p. 28) they indicate that Chap. XXIX was written either in the late summer, or at the very end, of 1565. Of the references given in the text above, No. 6 provides the only strong evidence against the supposition that the latter part of the book was not written till later in 1565 and not finished until early in 1566.]

12 [S.S.M., II, 123–48.]

13 Yepes asserts that this was P. García de Toledo, a statement confirmed by documents preserved in the Dominican College at Ávila. P. Andrés de la Encarnación (*Memorias historiales*, N, No. 27)

whereupon the author begged him to make any emendations
in it which he thought well and before sending it to P. Ávila
to have it copied. As at this time P. Báñez, one of the Saint's
two confessors, was professor of theology at the Dominican
College of St. Thomas in Ávila, it is not improbable that the
two Fathers examined the manuscript together, which would
no doubt mean a delay in sending it on as its author had
asked.

Her wish was apparently in part prompted by the fame of
the great Apostle of Andalusia as a discerner of spirits and in
part due to the recommendation of the Inquisitor Francisco
Soto. That before sending him the book she had written to
him asking him to give her his opinion on it we deduce from
one of his own letters dated April 2 (probably 1568), which
is still extant, and in which he says:

> I want you to set your mind at rest with regard to the
> examination of that matter (*negocio*), for, if such persons
> as these have seen it, you have done everything that is in-
> cumbent upon you. I really do not believe that I could
> point out anything which these Fathers have not pointed
> out already.[14]

But neither this assurance nor the approval given to the
book by the two Dominican theologians could entirely satisfy
its author; she therefore had recourse to her good friend Doña
Luisa de la Cerda, whom Juan de Ávila also knew and esteemed highly. In May 1568 Doña Luisa apparently had the
manuscript in her possession, for St. Teresa writes begging
her to send it to him: "I cannot understand," she says, "why
Your Ladyship did not send it at once."[15] Nine days later,
she is desperate:

> I believe it is the devil who is preventing Master Ávila
> from seeing this thing (*negocio*) of mine. I should be
> sorry if he were to die first: that would be a great calamity.

---

shares the view. P. Gracián, however (*Lucidario*, Part I, Chap. III),
believes that the recipient was Francisco de Salcedo; M. Daza has
also been suggested.

[14] [My translation. Another version will be found in *Letters* (St.),
I, 41. (The heading there is incorrect, for Juan de Ávila had not
seen the manuscript when he wrote).]

[15] *Letters*, 5. Cf. *Letters* (St.), I, 18.

I beseech Your Ladyship, as you are so near, to send it him, sealed, by one of your own messengers.[16]

By June 23 it would appear that P. Ávila has it, or is about to have it, as she asks Doña Luisa to see that it is sent back to her as quickly as possible, together with his written opinion on it. It was actually returned to her, with "a long letter"[17] containing only minor criticisms, in September. Still she was not satisfied, and the next to read it were PP. Martín Gutiérrez and Jerónimo Ripalda, two priests of the Society of Jesus, the latter of whom urged her to write the history of her later foundations.[18] It was then read by Fray Bartolomé de Medina, a Dominican who at one time had been highly critical of the Saint but was converted into one of her strongest supporters.

And these were only the beginnings of the book's travels. Not merely religious, but secular clergy and lay-folk, wanted to see it or to show it to others; and soon a number of copies were in circulation, much to the disquiet both of the author and of P. Báñez, who feared that not all its readers might be as prudent as these first. Báñez, at one point, reproached St. Teresa for sending the book about too freely—"although", he adds in his own account of the affair, "I realize that the fault was not hers."[19]

Some trouble did in fact occur with that imperious and self-willed lady, Doña Ana de Mendoza, Princess of Éboli, whose character will be revealed more clearly in the Saint's narrative of her own foundations.[20] Hearing of the book, about the summer of 1569, the Princess insisted upon its being lent her, and its author, though at first demurring to her importunity, had eventually to yield. The Princess promised her that the manuscript should be read only by herself and her husband, but, whether by accident or by design, it got into the hands of the entire household, and soon its contents began to be widely known and its most intimate revelations to be scoffed at or denounced as fraud or delusion.

About the chronology of what happened next there is some

---

16 *Letters*, 6. Cf. *Letters* (St.), I, 23–4.
17 *Letters*, 11. Cf. *Letters* (St.), I, 39.
18 Cf. Vol. III, p. xxii.
19 Cit. P. Silverio, I, cxxiii.
20 *Foundations*, Chap. XVII (Vol. III, pp. 79–85).

disagreement, but the sequence of the facts is fairly clear. After the Princess's husband died, she herself took the Discalced habit and caused a great commotion, as a result of which the Pastrana foundation, of which she had been the patroness, was moved to Segovia.[21] It is believed that St. Teresa's opposition to her conduct led the Princess to denounce the *Life* to the Inquisition: in any case, it was so denounced, and P. Báñez, fearful for the result, made a few small emendations in the manuscript and then himself laid it before the Inquisitors. These events probably all took place in the years 1574–5. Another Dominican was charged with its official examination and his judgment was wholly in its favour, but the Inquisitors retained the manuscript and Gracián advised Teresa to allow them to do so. When eventually application was made to them for it, they at once returned it and allowed it to be copied further and circulated among the communities of the Reform.

As we have said, the autograph of the *Life* is now in the Library of El Escorial. On the second folio is the inscription (not by the author): "Life of the Mother Teresa of Jesus, written by her own hand." The manuscript has no punctuation and few divisions into paragraphs but the writing is vigorous, clear and legible and there are hardly more than a dozen erasures. Some of these are the author's; some are by P. Báñez; and some by a third person—perhaps P. Ávila [though P. Silverio is inclined to think not]. At the end of the manuscript is an autograph *aprobación* by P. Báñez, dated July 7, 1575.

P. Gracián had a number of copies made of the *Life*, but nearly all these have been lost. One of the oldest copies known, which is kept at El Escorial, was made by the Saint's niece Teresa, daughter of her brother Lorenzo, from the manuscript already referred to as having been held by the Inquisition. Another, preserved in the Discalced Carmelite convent at Salamanca, is dated June 26, 1585 and was apparently made by a nun of the Reform: were the autograph not still in existence, it would be of the first importance. In the same convent there was formerly a copy of the *editio principis* of St. Teresa's works, in which the pages containing the

[21] Cf. Vol. III, p. 85.

Life have some marginal notes in the handwriting of P. Gracián, referring principally to the identity of persons mentioned in the text. Since in some places he could have gained his information only from St. Teresa's own lips, these notes are of great value. The whereabouts of this book is now unknown, but, as the marginal notes were copied by P. Andrés de la Encarnación, this is of little moment. Some of these sources will be referred to in footnotes in the pages which follow.

THE LIFE OF THE HOLY
MOTHER TERESA OF JESUS

AND SOME OF THE FAVOURS GRANTED TO HER BY GOD,
DESCRIBED BY HERSELF AT THE COMMAND OF HER
CONFESSOR, TO WHOM SHE SUBMITS AND ADDRESSES IT
AS FOLLOWS.[1]

As I have been commanded and given full liberty to write
about my way of prayer and the favours which the Lord has
granted me, I wish I had also been allowed to describe clearly
and in full detail my grave sins and wicked life. To do this
would be a great comfort to me; but it has been willed otherwise—in fact, I have been subjected to severe restrictions in
the matter. So, for the love of the Lord, I beg anyone who
reads this account of my life to bear in mind how wicked it
has been—so much so that, among all the saints who have
been converted to God, I can find none whose life affords me
any comfort. For I realize that, once the Lord had called
them, they never offended Him again. I, however, became
worse; and not only so, but I seem to have studied how to
resist the favours which His Majesty granted me. I knew that
I had the obligation to serve Him better, but realized that, of
myself, I could not pay the least part of what I owed Him.
May He Who waited so long for me be blessed for ever. I
beseech Him with my whole heart to give me grace to write
this account of my life, according to my confessors' command,
with complete clarity and truthfulness. The Lord Himself, I
know, has long wished it to be written but I have not presumed to write it. May it be to His glory and praise; and may
it lead my confessors to know me better, so that they may
help my weakness and I may be enabled to render the Lord
some part of the service which I owe Him. May He be praised
by all things for ever. Amen.

[1] This title is from the *editio princeps*.

CHAPTER I

*Describes how the Lord began to awaken her soul in child-
hood to a love of virtue and what a help it is in this
respect to have good parents.*

If I had not been so wicked it would have been a help to me
that I had parents who were virtuous and feared God, and
also that the Lord granted me His favour to make me good.
My father[1] was fond of reading good books and had some in
Spanish so that his children might read them too. These
books, together with the care which my mother took to make
us say our prayers and to lead us to be devoted to Our Lady
and to certain saints, began to awaken good desires in me
when I was, I suppose, about six or seven years old. It was a
help to me that I never saw my parents inclined to anything
but virtue. They themselves had many virtues. My father was
a man of great charity towards the poor, who was good to the
sick and also to his servants—so much so that he could never
be brought to keep slaves, because of his compassion for
them. On one occasion, when he had a slave of a brother of
his in the house,[2] he was as good to her as to his own children. He used to say that it caused him intolerable distress
that she was not free. He was strictly truthful: nobody ever
heard him swear or speak evil. He was a man of the most
rigid chastity.

My mother, too, was a very virtuous woman, who endured
a life of great infirmity: she was also particularly chaste.
Though extremely beautiful, she was never known to give any

[1] St. Teresa's father, Don Alonso Sánchez de Cepeda, was twice
married. By his first wife he had three children; by his second, Doña
Beatriz Dávila y Ahumada, nine. Of these nine, Rodrigo and Teresa
were respectively the second and the third, while Lorenzo, father of
the Teresa who copied the *Life* (p. 62) was the fourth. Both parents
were well descended and the family was in comfortable circumstances, though not wealthy.

[2] At this time well-to-do families in Spain often kept as slaves
Moors whose families had remained in the country after the Re-
conquest.

reason for supposing that she made the slightest account of her beauty; and, though she died at thirty-three, her dress was already that of a person advanced in years. She was a very tranquil woman, of great intelligence. Throughout her life she endured great trials and her death was most Christian.[3]

We were three sisters and nine brothers: all of them, by the goodness of God, resembled their parents in virtue, except myself, though I was my father's favourite. And, before I began to offend God, I think there was some reason for this, for it grieves me whenever I remember what good inclinations the Lord had given me and how little I profited by them. My brothers and sisters never hindered me from serving God in any way.

I had one brother almost of my own age.[4] It was he whom I most loved, though I had a great affection for them all, as had they for me. We used to read the lives of saints together; and, when I read of the martyrdoms suffered by saintly women for God's sake, I used to think they had purchased the fruition of God very cheaply; and I had a keen desire to die as they had done, not out of any love for God of which I was conscious, but in order to attain as quickly as possible to the fruition of the great blessings which, as I read, were laid up in Heaven. I used to discuss with this brother of mine how we could become martyrs. We agreed to go off to the country of the Moors, begging our bread for the love of God, so that they might behead us there; and, even at so tender an age, I believe the Lord had given us sufficient courage for this, if we could have found a way to do it; but our greatest hindrance seemed to be that we had a father and a mother.[5] It used to cause us great astonishment when we were told that both

[3] Doña Beatriz had married at fourteen, having been born in 1495, and died in 1528.

[4] The reference is almost certainly to Rodrigo, who was four years her senior. He emigrated to America in 1535 and died two years later fighting the Indians on the banks of the Río de la Plata. On the incident in the text, see Yepes, Bk. I, Chap. II.

[5] Ribera (Bk. I, Chap. IV) describes the attempt as having actually been made. The children left Ávila and "went on over the bridge, until they were met by an uncle who took them back home to their mother, greatly to her relief, for she had been having them searched for everywhere with great anxiety".

pain and glory would last for ever. We would spend long periods talking about this and we liked to repeat again and again, "For ever—ever—ever!" Through our frequent repetition of these words, it pleased the Lord that in my earliest years I should receive a lasting impression of the way of truth.

When I saw that it was impossible for me to go to any place where they would put me to death for God's sake, we decided to become hermits, and we used to build hermitages, as well as we could, in an orchard which we had at home. We would make heaps of small stones, but they at once fell down again, so we found no way of accomplishing our desires. But even now it gives me a feeling of devotion to remember how early God granted me what I lost by my own fault.

I gave alms as I could, which was but little. I tried to be alone when I said my prayers, and there were many such, in particular the rosary, to which my mother had a great devotion, and this made us devoted to them too. Whenever I played with other little girls, I used to love building convents and pretending that we were nuns; and I think I wanted to be a nun, though not so much as the other things I have described.

I remember that, when my mother died, I was twelve years of age or a little less.[6] When I began to realize what I had lost, I went in my distress to an image of Our Lady[7] and with many tears besought her to be a mother to me. Though I did this in my simplicity, I believe it was of some avail to me; for whenever I have commended myself to this Sovereign Virgin I have been conscious of her aid; and eventually she has brought me back to herself. It grieves me now when I observe and reflect how I did not keep sincerely to the good desires which I had begun.

O my Lord, since it seems Thou art determined on my salvation—and may it please Thy Majesty to save me!—and on granting me all the graces Thou hast bestowed on me already, why has it not seemed well to Thee, not for my advantage

[6] Actually, as we have seen, she was thirteen. Doña Beatriz made her will, shortly before her death, on November 24, 1528.

[7] Tradition has it that the image was one which is now in Ávila Cathedral, and that Teresa and Rodrigo also commended themselves to this Virgin before setting out to be martyred. Yearly, on October 15, a ceremony commemorating the event described in the text takes place in Ávila.

but for Thy honour, that this habitation wherein Thou hast had continually to dwell should not have become so greatly defiled? It grieves me, Lord, even to say this, since I know that the fault has been mine alone, for I believe there is nothing more Thou couldst have done, even from this early age, to make me wholly Thine. Nor, if I should feel inclined to complain of my parents, could I do so, for I saw nothing in them but every kind of good and anxiety for my welfare. But as I ceased to be a child and began to become aware of the natural graces which the Lord had given me, and which were said to be many, instead of giving Him thanks for them, as I should, I started to make use of them to offend Him. This I shall now explain.

CHAPTER II

Describes how these virtues were gradually lost and how important it is in childhood to associate with people of virtue.

What I shall now describe was, I think something which began to do me great harm. I sometimes reflect how wrong it is of parents not to contrive that their children shall always, and in every way, see things which are good. My mother, as I have said, was very good herself, but, when I came to the age of reason, I copied her goodness very little, in fact hardly at all, and evil things did me a great deal of harm. She was fond of books of chivalry; and this pastime had not the ill effects on her that is had on me, because she never allowed them to interfere with her work. But we were always trying to make time to read them; and she permitted this, perhaps in order to stop herself from thinking of the great trials she suffered, and to keep her children occupied so that in other respects they should not go astray. This annoyed my father so much that we had to be careful lest he should see us reading these books. For myself, I began to make a habit of it, and this little fault which I saw in my mother began to cool my good desires and lead me to other kinds of wrongdoing. I thought there was nothing wrong in my wasting many hours, by day and by night, in this useless occupation, even though I had to hide it from my father. So excessively was I absorbed in it that I believe, unless I had a new book, I was never happy.

I began to deck myself out and to try to attract others by my appearance, taking great trouble with my hands and hair, using perfumes and all the vanities I could get—and there were a good many of them, for I was very fastidious. There was nothing wrong with my intentions, for I should never have wanted anyone to offend God because of me. This great and excessive fastidiousness about personal appearance, together with other practices which I thought were in no way sinful, lasted for many years: I see now how wrong they must have been. I had some cousins, who were the only people allowed to enter my father's house:[1] he was very careful about this and I wish to God that he had been careful about my cousins too. For I now see the danger of intercourse, at an age when the virtues should be beginning to grow, with persons who, though ignorant of worldly vanity, arouse a desire for the world in others. These cousins were almost exactly of my own age or a little older than I. We always went about together; they were very fond of me; and I would keep our conversation on things that amused them and listen to the stories they told about their childish escapades and crazes, which were anything but edifying. What was worse, my soul began to incline to the thing that was the cause of all its trouble.

If I had to advise parents, I should tell them to take great care about the people with whom their children associate at such an age. Much harm may result from bad company and we are inclined by nature to follow what is worse rather than what is better. This was the case with me: I had a sister much older than myself,[2] from whom, though she was very good and chaste, I learned nothing, whereas from a relative whom we often had in the house I learned every kind of evil. This person was so frivolous in her conversation that my mother had tried very hard to prevent her from coming to the house,

[1] Don Alonso's brother, Don Francisco, had a house near his own, in the Plazuela de Santo Domingo, where the seventeenth-century Discalced Carmelite monastery now stands. The cousins referred to were no doubt Don Francisco's children: he had at least four sons, as well as several daughters.

[2] This was her half-sister, Doña María, her father's only daughter by his first wife.

realizing what harm she might do me, but there were so many reasons for her coming that she was powerless. I became very fond of meeting this woman. I talked and gossiped with her frequently; she joined me in all my favourite pastimes; and she also introduced me to other pastimes and talked to me about all her conversations and vanities. Until I knew her (this was when I was about fourteen or perhaps more: by knowing her I mean becoming friendly with her and receiving her confidences) I do not think I had ever forsaken God by committing any mortal sin, or lost my fear of God, though I was much more concerned about my honour.[3] This last fear was strong enough to prevent me from forfeiting my honour altogether, and I cannot think that I would have acted differently about this for anything in the world; nor was there anyone in the world whom I loved enough to forfeit my honour for. So I might have had the strength not to sin against the honour of God, as my natural inclination led me not to go astray in anything which I thought concerned worldly honour, and I did not realize that I was forfeiting my honour in many other ways.

I went to great extremes in my vain anxiety about this, though I took not the slightest trouble about what I must do to live a truly honourable life. All that I was seriously concerned about was that I should not be lost altogether. My father and sister were very sorry about this friendship of mine and often reproved me for it. But, as they could not prevent my friend from coming to the house, their efforts were of no avail, for when it came to doing anything wrong I was very clever. I am sometimes astonished at the harm which can be caused by bad company; if I had not experienced it I could not believe it. This is especially so when one is young, for it is then that the evil done is greatest. I wish parents would be warned by me and consider this very carefully. The result of my intercourse with this woman was to change me so much that I lost nearly all my soul's natural inclination to virtue,

[3] [The word *honra*, which St. Teresa uses in various senses—good, bad and neutral—I often render "reputation" or "good name", but in this context—i.e., of a girl of St. Teresa's age, living in the Spain of her day—the translation "honour" does not seem too strong: indeed, the contrast which she makes between the two kinds of *honra* almost necessitates it.]

and was greatly influenced by her, and by another person who indulged in the same kinds of pastime.

From this I have learned what great advantage comes from good companionship; and I am sure that if at that age I had been friendly with good people I should have remained sound in virtue. For, if at that time I had had anyone to teach me to fear God, my soul would have grown strong enough not to fall. Later, when the fear of God had entirely left me, I retained only this concern about my honour, which was a torture to me in everything that I did. When I thought that nobody would ever know, I was rash enough to do many things which were an offence both to my honour and to God.

At first, I believe, these things did me harm. The fault, I think, was not my friend's but my own. For subsequently my own wickedness sufficed to lead me into sin, together with the servants we had, whom I found quite ready to encourage me in all kinds of wrongdoing. Perhaps, if any of them had given me good advice, I might have profited by it; but they were as much blinded by their own interests as I was by desire. And yet I never felt the inclination to do much that was wrong, for I had a natural detestation of everything immodest and preferred passing the time in good company. But, if an occasion of sin presented itself, the danger would be at hand and I should be exposing my father and brothers to it. From all this God delivered me, in such a way that, even against my own will, He seems to have contrived that I should not be lost, though this was not to come about so secretly as to prevent me from gravely damaging my reputation and arousing suspicions in my father. I could hardly have been following these vanities for three months when I was taken to a convent in the place where I lived,⁴ in which children like myself, though less depraved in their habits than I, were being educated. The reason for this was so carefully concealed that only one or two of my relatives and myself were aware of it. They had waited for an occasion to arise naturally; and now, as my sister had married, and I had no mother, I should have been alone in the house if I had not gone there, which would not have been fitting.

⁴ This was the Augustinian convent of Our Lady of Grace, a foundation some twenty years old situated outside the city walls, which took girls from good families as boarders.

So excessive was my father's love for me, and so complete was the deception which I practised on him, that he could never believe all the ill of me that I deserved and thus I never fell into disgrace with him. It had not been going on for long; and, although they had some idea of what I had been doing, nothing could have been said about it with any certainty. As *I had such concern for my good name,[5] I had made the greatest efforts to keep it all secret, and I had not considered that it could not be kept secret from Him Who sees all things. O my God, what harm is done in the world by forgetfulness of this and by the belief that anything can be kept secret which is done against Thee! I am sure that much wrongdoing would be avoided if we realized that our business is to be on our guard, not against men, but against displeasing Thee.

For the first week I suffered a great deal, though not so much from being in a convent as from the suspicion that everyone knew about my vanity. For I had already become tired of the life I had been leading; and even when I offended God I never ceased to be sorely afraid of Him and I tried to make my confessions as soon as possible after falling into sin. At first I was very restless; but within a week, perhaps even earlier, I was much happier than I had been in my father's house. All the nuns were pleased with me; for the Lord had given me grace, wherever I was, to please people, and so I became a great favourite. Although at that time I had the greatest possible aversion from being a nun, I was very pleased to see nuns who were so good; for in that house they were all very good—completely blameless in their lives, devoted to their Rule and prudent in their behaviour. Yet in spite of this the devil did not cease tempting me and my friends outside tried to unsettle me by sending me messages. As that was not allowed, it soon came to an end, and my soul then began to return to the good habits of my earlier childhood and I realized what a great favour God does to those whom He places in the company of good people. It seems as if His Majesty was trying and trying again to find a way of bringing me back to Himself. Blessed be Thou, Lord, Who for so long hast suffered me! Amen.

If my faults had not been so numerous, there is one thing which I think might have served as an excuse for them: that

[5] [Honra.]

my intimacy with this person was of such a kind that I thought it might end satisfactorily on her marriage;[6] and both my confessor and other persons told me that in many respects I was not offending God. There was a nun who slept with those of us who were seculars and it was through her that the Lord seems to have been pleased to begin to give me light, as I shall now explain.

CHAPTER III

Describes how good companionship helped to awaken desires in her and the way in which the Lord began to give her light concerning the delusion under which she had been suffering.

As I began to enjoy the good and holy conversation of this nun, I grew to delight in listening to her, for she spoke well about God and was very discreet and holy. There was never a time, I think, when I did not delight in listening to her words. She began to tell me how she had come to be a nun through merely reading those words in the Gospel: Many are called but few chosen.[1] She used to describe to me the reward which the Lord gives to those who leave everything for His sake. This good companionship began to eradicate the habits which bad companionship had formed in me, to bring

---

[6] [St. Teresa's reference to this intimacy is so delicately vague that it is difficult for the translator not to express more than she actually says. The interpretation here given to her words I have decided upon after some hesitation. Dissenting readers may choose between P. Grégoire's "Il s'agissait de relations qui semblaient pouvoir aboutir à une alliance honorable pour moi", and Lewis's "The conversation I shared in was with one who, I thought, would do well in the estate of matrimony", the editor's footnote inferring that St. Teresa had "listened only to the story of her cousin's intended marriage". In default of other information I take the meaning to be that, as this woman was of marriageable (i.e., mature) age, the writer assumed that she would soon marry and their intimacy would come to an end: all would then be well that ended well. This seems a much more natural interpretation than one which represents St. Teresa as predicting her own marriage.]

[1] St. Matthew xx, 16.

back my thoughts to desires for eternal things, and to remove some of the great dislike which I had for being a nun, and which had become deeply engrained in me. If I saw anyone weeping as she prayed, or giving evidence of any other virtues, I now greatly envied her; for my heart was so hard in this respect that, even if I read the entire narrative of the Passion, I could not shed a tear; and this distressed me.

I remained in this convent for a year and a half, and was much the better for it. I began to say a great many vocal prayers and to get all the nuns to commend me to God and pray that He would bring me to the state in which I was to serve Him. But I was still anxious not to be a nun, for God had not as yet been pleased to give me this desire, although I was also afraid of marriage. By the end of my time there, I was much more reconciled to being a nun—though not in that house, because of the very virtuous practices which I had come to hear that they observed and which seemed to me altogether excessive. There were a few of the younger ones who encouraged me in this feeling; if all the nuns had been of one opinion, it would have been much better for me. I also had a close friend in another convent,[2] and this gave me the idea that, if I was to be a nun, I would go only to the house where she was. I thought more about pleasures of sense and vanity than of my soul's profit. These good thoughts about being a nun came to me from time to time but they soon left me and I could not persuade myself to become one.

At this time, though I was not careless about my own improvement, the Lord became more desirous of preparing me for the state of life which was best for me. He sent me a serious illness, which forced me to return to my father's house. When I got better, they took me to see my sister, who was living in a village.[3] She was so fond of me that, if she had had her way, I should never have left her. Her husband was also very fond of me—at least, he showed me every kindness. This, too, I owe chiefly to the Lord, for I have always been well treated everywhere, and yet the only service I have rendered Him is to be what I am.

On the road leading to my sister's lived one of my father's

[2] Doña Juana Suárez, a nun in the Convent of the Incarnation at Ávila, where St. Teresa afterwards professed.

[3] Doña María, living at Castellanos de la Cañada. Cf. p. 79, n. 3.

brothers,[4] a widower, who was a very shrewd man and full of virtues. Him, too, the Lord was preparing for Himself: in his old age he gave up all that he had and became a friar, and he ended his life in such a way that I believe he is now rejoicing in God. He wanted me to stay with him for some days. It was his practice to read good books in Spanish and his conversation was ordinarily about God and the vanity of the world. He made me read to him; and, although I did not much care for his books, I acted as though I did; for in the matter of pleasing others, even when I disliked doing it, I have been so excessively complacent, that in others it would have been a virtue, though in me it was a great fault because I was often very indiscreet. O God, in how many ways did His Majesty gradually prepare me for the state in which He was to be pleased to use me! In how many ways, against my own will, did He constrain me to exercise restraint upon myself![5] May He be blessed for ever. Amen.

Though I stayed here for only a few days, such was the impression made on my heart by the words of God, both as read and as heard, and the excellence of my uncle's company, that I began to understand the truth, which I had learned as a child, that all things are nothing, and that the world is vanity and will soon pass away. I began to fear that, if I had died of my illness, I should have gone to hell; and though, even then, I could not incline my will to being a nun, I saw that this was the best and safest state, and so, little by little, I determined to force myself to embrace it.

This conflict lasted for three months. I used to try to convince myself by using the following argument. The trials and distresses of being a nun could not be greater than those of purgatory and I had fully deserved to be in hell. It would not be a great matter to spend my life as though I were in purgatory if afterwards I were to go straight to Heaven, which was what I desired. This decision, then, to enter the religious life seems to have been inspired by servile fear more than by love. The devil suggested to me that I could not endure the trials of the religious life as I had been so delicately brought up. This suggestion I met by telling him about the trials suf-

[4] Cf. p. 80, n. 4.
[5] [Lit.: "did He force me to exercise force upon myself." The play upon words cannot be fully brought out by any satisfactory translation.]

fered by Christ and saying that it would not be too much for
me to suffer a few for His sake. I must have thought that He
would help me to bear them but that I cannot remember. I
had many temptations in those days.

I had now begun to suffer from serious fainting fits, together with fever; my health has always been poor. The fact
that I had now become fond of good books gave me new life. I
would read the epistles of Saint Jerome;[6] and these inspired
me with such courage that I determined to tell my father of
my decision, which was going almost as far as taking the
habit; for my word of honour meant so much to me that I
doubt if any reason would have sufficed to turn me back from
a thing when I had once said I would do it. He was so fond
of me that I was never able to get his consent, nor did the
requests of persons whom I asked to speak with him about
it succeed in doing so. The most I could obtain from him
was permission to do as I liked after his death. As I distrusted
myself and thought I might turn back out of weakness, this
course seemed an unsuitable one. So I achieved my aim in
another way, as I shall now explain.

CHAPTER IV

*Describes how the Lord helped her to force herself to take
the habit and tells of the numerous infirmities which
His Majesty began to send her.*

During this time, when I was considering these resolutions,
I had persuaded one of my brothers, by talking to him about
the vanity of the world, to become a friar,[1] and we agreed to
set out together, very early one morning, for the convent
where that friend of mine lived of whom I was so fond. In
making my final decision, I had already resolved that I would
go to any other convent in which I thought I could serve God
better or which my father might wish me to enter, for by now

[6] A Spanish translation of these, by Juan de Molina, had been
published at Valencia, in 1520.
[1] Her younger brother Antonio, who became a Dominican, and
later a Hieronymite. Then ill health compelled him to return to the
world and he died in the Indies, in 1546.

I was concerned chiefly with the good of my soul and cared nothing for my comfort. I remember—and I really believe this is true—that when I left my father's house my distress was so great that I do not think it will be greater when I die. It seemed to me as if every bone in my body were being wrenched asunder; for, as I had no love of God to subdue my love for my father and kinsfolk, everything was such a strain to me that, if the Lord had not helped me, no reflections of my own would have sufficed to keep me true to my purpose. But the Lord gave me courage to fight against myself and so I carried out my intention.

When I took the habit,[2] the Lord at once showed me how great are His favours to those who use force with themselves in His service. No one realized that I had gone through all this; they all thought I had acted out of sheer desire. At the time my entrance into this new life gave me a joy so great that it has never failed me even to this day, and God converted the aridity of my soul into the deepest tenderness. Everything connected with the religious life caused me delight; and it is a fact that sometimes, when I was spending time in sweeping floors which I had previously spent on my own indulgence and adornment, and realized that I was now free from all those things, there came to me a new joy, which amazed me, for I could not understand whence it arose. Whenever I recall this, there is nothing, however hard, which I would hesitate to undertake if it were proposed to me. For I know now, by experience of many kinds, that if I strengthen my purpose by resolving to do a thing for God's sake alone, it is His will that, from the very beginning, my soul shall be

[2] The Convent of the Incarnation, Ávila, is situated on the north side of the city, outside the walls. It had been founded in 1479, as a residence for ladies who were members of the Third Order of Carmel but later it was converted into a convent with the title of Our Lady of the Incarnation. As to the date of her entry into the Convent, there has been a great deal of doubt, but documents [published by P. Silverio in his appendices] appear to have established that she took the habit on November 2, 1536, and made her solemn profession on November 3, 1537, at the ages of twenty-one and twenty-two respectively. [Previously Ribera's dates of 1535 and 1536 had been generally accepted, though there was also evidence in favour of 1533 and 1534.] Cf. Relation IV (p. 319): "It is forty years since this nun took the habit." This was written in 1576.

afraid, so that my merit may be the greater; and if I achieve my resolve, the greater my fear has been, the greater will be my reward, and the greater, too, will be my retrospective pleasure. Even in this life His Majesty rewards such an act in ways that can be understood only by one who has enjoyed them. This I know by experience, as I have said, in many very serious matters; and so, if I were a person who had to advise others, I would never recommend anyone, when a good inspiration comes to him again and again, to hesitate to put it into practice because of fear; for, if one lives a life of detachment for God's sake alone, there is no reason to be afraid that things will turn out amiss, since He is all-powerful. May He be blessed for ever. Amen.

O Supreme Good! O my Rest! The favours which Thou hadst given me until now should have sufficed me, since by Thy compassion and greatness I had been brought, along so many devious ways, to a state so secure and to a house in which there were so many servants of God from whom I might take example and thus learn to grow in Thy service. When I remember the way I made my profession and the great determination and satisfaction with which I made it and the betrothal that I contracted with Thee, I do not know how to proceed any farther with my story. I cannot speak of this without tears, and they ought to be tears of blood, and my heart ought to break, and even that would be showing no great sorrow for the offences which I afterwards committed against Thee. It seems to me now that I was right not to wish for so great an honour, since I was to make such bad use of it. But Thou, my Lord, wert prepared to be offended by me for almost twenty years, during which time I made ill use of Thy favour, so that in the end I might become better. It would seem, my God, as if I had promised to break all the promises I had made Thee, although at the time that was not my intention. When I look back on these actions of mine, I do not know what my intention could have been. All this, my Spouse, reveals still more clearly the difference between Thy nature and mine. Certainly distress for my great sins is often tempered by the joy which comes to me at being the means of making known the multitude of Thy mercies.

In whom, Lord, can they shine forth as in me, who with my evil deeds have thus obscured the great favours which Thou hadst begun to show me? Alas, my Creator! If I would make an excuse, I have none, and none is to blame but I. For, had I repaid Thee any part of the love which Thou hadst begun to show me, I could have bestowed it on none but Thyself; and had I but done this, everything would have been set right. But as I have not deserved this, nor had such good fortune, may Thy mercy, Lord, be availing for me.

The change in my life, and in my diet, affected my health; and, though my happiness was great, it was not sufficient to cure me. My fainting-fits began to increase in number and I suffered so much from heart trouble that everyone who saw me was alarmed. I also had many other ailments. I spent my first year, therefore, in a very poor state of health, though I do not think I offended God very much during that time. My condition became so serious—for I hardly ever seemed to be fully conscious, and sometimes I lost consciousness altogether—that my father made great efforts to find me a cure. As our own doctors could suggest none, he arranged for me to be taken to a place where they had a great reputation for curing other kinds of illness and said they could also cure mine. This friend whom I have spoken of as being in the house, and who was one of the seniors among the sisters, went with me. In the house where I was a nun, we did not have to make a vow of enclosure. I was there for nearly a year, and during three months of that time I suffered the greatest tortures from the drastic remedies which they applied to me. I do not know how I managed to endure them; and in fact, though I did endure them, my constitution was unable to stand them, as I shall explain. My treatment was to commence at the beginning of the summer and I had left the convent when the winter began. All the intervening time I spent in the house of the sister whom I referred to above as living in a village, waiting for the month of April, which was near at hand, so that I should not have to go and come back again.[3]

[3] [This last phrase has puzzled the commentators. I take the meaning to be that St. Teresa went to stay with her sister, Doña María, who had married a certain Don Martín de Guzmán y Barrientos, in the late autumn ("when the winter began"—but it begins early on the Castilian plateau), was under the supervision of the *curandera*, who lived near the sister, during the winter, and went to live with her, to take the intensive and painful course of treatment referred to in the text, in the following April, staying till July. It was presumably on a first visit to the *curandera*, made for the purpose of a

On the way there, I stopped at the house of this uncle of mine, which, as I have said, was on the road, and he gave me a book called *Third Alphabet*, which treats of the Prayer of Recollection.[4] During this first year I had been reading good books (I no longer wanted to read any others, for I now realized what harm they had done me) but I did not know how to practise prayer, or how to recollect myself, and so I was delighted with the book and determined to follow that way of prayer with all my might. As by now the Lord had granted me the gift of tears, and I liked reading, I began to spend periods in solitude, to go frequently to confession and to start upon the way of prayer with this book for my guide. For I found no other guide (no confessor, I mean) who understood me, though I sought one for fully twenty years subsequently to the time I am speaking of. This did me great harm, as I had frequent relapses, and might have been completely lost; a guide would at least have helped me to escape when I found myself running the risk of offending God.

In these early days His Majesty began to grant me so many favours that at the end of this entire period of solitude, which lasted for almost nine months, although I was not so free from offending God as the book said one should be, I passed over that, for such great care seemed to me almost impossible. I was particular about not committing mortal sin—and would to God I had always been so! But about venial sins I troubled very little and it was this which brought about my fall. Still, the Lord began to be so gracious to me on this way of prayer that He granted me the favour of leading me to the Prayer of Quiet, and occasionally even to Union, though I did not understand what either of these was, or how highly they were to be valued. Had I understood this I think it would have been a great blessing. It is true that my experience of Union

consultation, that St. Teresa was accompanied by the older nun. But Becedas, where the *curandera* lived, was over forty miles from Ávila, whereas Doña María's village of Castellanos de la Cañada was quite near Becedas, so that by going to stay with her sister she saved herself long journeys during the winter. This interpretation seems to me the only one which fits all the facts.]

[4] The uncle, Don Pedro, lived at Hortigosa, a village on the road to Castellanos. The Discalced Carmelite community of St. Joseph, at Ávila, still preserves the copy of Francisco de Osuna's *Third Spiritual Alphabet* [cf. S.S.M., I, 79–131] here referred to.

lasted only a short time; I am not sure that it can have been for as long as an *Ave Maria*; but the results of it were so considerable, and lasted for so long that, although at this time I was not twenty years old,[5] I seemed to have trampled the world beneath my feet, and I remember that I used to pity those who still clung to it, even in things that were lawful. I used to try to think of Jesus Christ, our Good and our Lord, as present within me, and it was in this way that I prayed. If I thought about any incident in His life, I would imagine it inwardly, though I liked principally to read good books, and this constituted the whole of my recreation. For God had not given me talents for reasoning with the understanding or for making good use of the imagination: my imagination is so poor that, even when I thought about the Lord's Humanity, or tried to imagine it to myself, as I was in the habit of doing, I never succeeded. And although, if they persevere, people may attain more quickly to contemplation by following this method of not labouring with the understanding, it is a very troublesome and painful process. For if the will has nothing to employ it and love has no present object with which to busy itself, the soul finds itself without either support or occupation, its solitude and aridity cause it great distress and its thoughts involve it in the severest conflict.

People in this condition need greater purity of conscience than those who can labour with the understanding. For anyone meditating on the nature of the world, on his duties to God, on God's great sufferings and on what he himself is giving to Him Who loves him, will find in his meditations instructions for defending himself against his thoughts and against perils and occasions of sin. Anyone unable to make use of this method is in much greater danger and should occupy himself frequently in reading, since he cannot find instruction in any other way. And inability to do this is so very painful that, if the master who is directing him forbids him to read and thus find help for recollection, reading is none the less necessary for him, however little it may be, as a substitute for the mental prayer which he is unable to practise. I mean that if he is compelled to spend a great deal of time in prayer without this aid it will be impossible for him to persist in it

[5] [St. Teresa must have been mistaken. She cannot possibly have been less than twenty-three and was probably a little older.]

for long, and if he does so it will endanger his health, since it is a very painful process.

I believe now that it was through the Lord's good providence that I found no one to teach me; for, had I done so, it would have been impossible, I think, for me to persevere during the eighteen years for which I had to bear this trial and these great aridities, due, as I say, to my being unable to meditate. During all these years, except after communicating, I never dared begin to pray without a book; my soul was as much afraid to engage in prayer without one as if it were having to go and fight against a host of enemies. With this help, which was a companionship to me and a shield with which I could parry the blows of my many thoughts, I felt comforted. For it was not usual with me to suffer from aridity: this only came when I had no book, whereupon my soul would at once become disturbed and my thoughts would begin to wander. As soon as I started to read they began to collect themselves and the book acted like a bait to my soul. Often the mere fact that I had it by me was sufficient. Sometimes I read a little, sometimes a great deal, according to the favour which the Lord showed me. It seemed to me, in these early stages of which I am speaking, that, provided I had books and could be alone, there was no risk of my being deprived of that great blessing; and I believe that, by the help of God, this would have been the case if at the beginning I had had a master or some other person to advise me how to flee from occasions of sin, and, if I fell before them, to get me quickly free from them. If at that time the devil had attacked me openly, I believe I should never in any way have begun to sin grievously again. But he was so subtle, and I was so weak, that all my resolutions were of little profit to me, though, in the days when I served God, they became very profitable indeed, in that they enabled me to bear the terrible infirmities which came to me with the great patience given me by His Majesty.

I have often reflected with amazement upon God's great goodness and my soul has delighted in the thought of His great magnificence and mercy. May He be blessed for all this, for it has become clear to me that, even in this life, He has not failed to reward me for any of my good desires. However wretched and imperfect my good works have been, this Lord of mine has been improving them, perfecting them and mak-

ing them of greater worth, and yet hiding my evil deeds and
my sins as soon as they have been committed. He has even
allowed the eyes of those who have seen them to be blind to
them and He blots them from their memory. He gilds my
faults and makes some virtue of mine to shine forth in splendour; yet it was He Himself Who gave it me and almost
forced me to possess it.

I will now return and do what I have been commanded.
I repeat that, if I had to describe in detail the way in which
the Lord dealt with me in these early days, I should need
much more intelligence than I have so as to be able to appreciate what I owe to Him, together with my own ingratitude
and wickedness, all of which I have forgotten. May He be for
ever blessed, Who has endured me for so long. Amen.

CHAPTER V

*Continues to tell of the grievous infirmities which she suffered
and of the patience given her by the Lord, and of how
He brings good out of evil, as will be seen from an incident which happened to her in the place where she went
for treatment.*

I forgot to tell how, in the year of my novitiate, I suffered
long periods of unrest about things which in themselves were
of little importance. I was very often blamed when the fault
was not mine. This I bore very imperfectly, and with great
distress of mind, although I was able to endure it all because
of my great satisfaction at being a nun. When they saw me
endeavouring to be alone and sometimes weeping for my
sins, they thought that I was discontented and said so. I was
fond of everything to do with the religious life but I could
not bear anything which seemed to make me ridiculous. I
delighted in being thought well of; I was particular about
everything I did; and all this I thought was a virtue, though
that cannot serve me as an excuse, because I knew how to get
pleasure for myself out of everything and so my wrongdoing cannot be excused by ignorance. Some excuse may be
found in the imperfect organization of the convent. But I, in

my wickedness, followed what I knew to be wrong and neglected what was good.

At that time there was a nun who was afflicted by a most serious and painful illness: she was suffering from open sores in the stomach, which had been caused by obstructions, and these forced her to reject all her food. Of this illness she soon died. I saw that all the nuns were afraid of it but for my own part I had only great envy of her patience. I begged God that He would send me any illness He pleased if only He would make me as patient as she. I do not think I was in the least afraid of being ill, for I was so anxious to win eternal blessings that I was resolved to win them by any means whatsoever. And I am surprised at this; for, although I had not then, I think, such love for God as I have had since I began to pray, I had light enough to realize how trivial is the value of all things that pass away and how great is the worth of blessings which can be gained by despising them, for these are eternal. Well, His Majesty heard my prayer; for, before two years had passed, I myself had an illness which, though not of the same kind, was, I think, no less painful and troublesome. And this I suffered for three years, as I shall now relate.

When the time had come which I was awaiting in the place where, as I said, I was staying with my sister before undergoing my treatment, I was taken away, with the greatest solicitude for my comfort, by my father and sister and that nun who was my friend and had accompanied me when I had first left the convent because she loved me so dearly. It was now that the devil began to unsettle my soul, although God turned this into a great blessing. There was a priest[1] who lived in the place where I had gone for the treatment: he was a man of really good family and great intelligence, and also of some learning, though not a great deal. I began to make my confessions to him, for I have always been attracted by learning, though confessors with only a little of it have done my soul great harm, and I have not always found men who had as much of it as I should have liked. I have discovered by experience that if they are virtuous and lead holy lives it is better they should have none at all than only a little; for then they do not trust themselves (nor would I myself trust them) un-

[1] [Lit.: "a person of the Church", but the context makes the meaning clear.]

less they have first consulted those who are really learned; but a truly learned man has never led me astray. Not that these others can have meant to lead me astray: it is simply that they have known no better. I had supposed that they did and that my only obligation was to believe them, as they spoke to me in a very broad-minded way and gave me a great deal of freedom: if they had been strict, I am so wicked that I should have looked for others. What in reality was venial sin, they would tell me was no sin at all; and the most grievous of mortal sins was to them only venial. This did me such harm that it is not surprising if I speak of it here to warn others against so great an evil, for I see clearly that in God's sight I have no excuse; the fact that the things I did were themselves not good should have been sufficient to keep me from doing them. I believe God permitted these confessors to be mistaken and lead me astray because of my own sins. I myself led many others astray by repeating to them what had been told me. I continued in this state of blindness, I believe, for more than seventeen years, until a Dominican Father,[2] who was a very learned man, undeceived me about certain things, and the Fathers of the Company of Jesus[3] made me very much afraid about my whole position by representing to me the gravity of these unsound principles, as I shall explain later.

After I had begun to make my confessions to this priest of whom I am speaking, he took an extreme liking to me, for at that time I had little to confess by comparison with what I had later—I had not really had much ever since I became a nun. There was nothing wrong in his affection for me, but it ceased to be good because there was too much of it. He realized that nothing whatever would induce me to commit any grave offence against God and he assured me that it was the same with him, and so we talked together a good deal. But at that time, full of love for God as I was, my greatest delight in conversation was to speak about Him; and, as I was such a child, this caused him confusion, and, out of the great affection that he had for me, he began to tell me about his unhappy condition. It was no small matter: for nearly seven years

[2] P. Vicente Barrón, a theologian of repute, who was also her father's confessor.

[3] [Spanish writers always describe the Society of Jesus as the "Company" and that word is kept throughout this translation.]

he had been in a most perilous state because of his affection for a woman in that very place, with whom he had had a good deal to do. Nevertheless, he continued saying Mass. The fact that he had lost his honour and his good name was quite well known, yet no one dared to reprove him for it. I was sorry for him because I liked him very much: at that time I was so frivolous and blind that I thought it a virtue to be grateful and loyal to anyone who liked me. Cursed be such loyalty when it goes so far that it militates against loyalty to God! This is a bewildering folly common in the world and it certainly bewilders me. For we owe to God all the good that men show us, yet we consider it a virtue not to break off friendships with men even if they cause us to act contrarily to His will. O blindness of the world! May it please Thee, Lord, that I may be completely lacking in gratitude to the whole world provided that in no respect I lack gratitude to Thee. But exactly the reverse has been true of me, because of my sins.

I got to know more about this priest by making enquiries of members of his household. I then realized what great trouble the poor man had got himself into and found that it was not altogether his own fault. For the unhappy woman had cast a spell over him, giving him a little copper figure and begging him, for love of her, to wear it round his neck, and no one had been able to persuade him to take it off. Now, with regard to this particular incident of the spell, I do not believe there is the least truth in it. But I will relate what I saw, in order to warn men to be on their guard against women who try to do such things to them. Let them be sure that, if women (who are more bound to lead chaste lives even than men) lose all shame in the sight of God, there is nothing whatever in which they can be trusted. In order to obtain the pleasure of following their own will and an affection inspired in them by the devil, they will stop at nothing. Wicked as I have been, I have never fallen into any sin of this kind, nor have I ever tried to do wrong in this way; and, even if I could have done so, I should never have wanted to force anyone's affection in my favour, for the Lord has kept me from this. If He had forsaken me, however, I should have done wrong in this respect, as I have done in others, for I am in no way to be trusted.

When I heard about this spell I began to show the priest

greater affection. My intentions here were good, but my action was wrong, for one must never do the smallest thing that is wrong in order to do good, however great. As a rule, I used to speak to him about God. This must have done something to help him, although I believe his liking for me did more; for, in order to please me, he gave me the little figure, which I at once got someone to throw into a river. When he had done this, he became like a man awakening from a deep sleep and he began to recall everything that he had been doing during those years. He was amazed at himself and grieved at his lost condition and he began to hate the woman who had led him to it. Our Lady must have been a great help to him, for he was most devoted to her Conception and he used to keep the day commemorating it as a great festival. In the end, he gave up seeing the woman, and never wearied of giving thanks to God for having granted him light. Exactly a year from the day when I first saw him he died. He had been active in God's service and I never thought there was anything wrong in the great affection that he had for me, although it might have been purer. There were also occasions when, if he had not had recourse to the presence of God, he might have committed the gravest offences. As I have said, I would not at that time have done anything which I believed to be a mortal sin. And I think his realization that that was so increased his affection for me; for I believe all men must have greater affection for women when they see them inclined to virtue. Even in order to obtain their earthly desires, women can get more from men in this way, as I shall explain later. I am convinced that that priest is in the way of salvation. He died very devoutly and completely delivered from that occasion of sin. It seems that the Lord's will was that he should be saved by these means.

I remained in that place for three months, suffering the greatest trials, for the treatment was more drastic than my constitution could stand. At the end of two months, the severity of the remedies had almost ended my life, and the pain in my heart, which I had gone there to get treated, was much worse; sometimes I felt as if sharp teeth had hold of me, and so severe was the pain they caused that it was feared I was going mad. My strength suffered a grave decline, for I could take nothing but liquid, had a great distaste for food, was in a continual fever, and became so wasted away that, after they had given me purgatives daily for almost a month, I was, as it were, so shrivelled up that my nerves began to shrink. These symptoms were accompanied by intolerable pain which gave me no rest by night or by day. Altogether I was in a state of great misery.

Seeing that I had gained nothing here, my father took me away and once again called in the doctors. They all gave me up, saying that, quite apart from everything else, I was consumptive. This troubled me very little: it was the pains that distressed me, for they racked me from head to foot and never ceased. Nervous pains, as the doctors said, are intolerable, and, as all my nerves had shrunk, this would indeed have been terrible torture if it had not all been due to my own fault. I could not have been in this serious state for more than three months: it seemed impossible that so many ills could all be endured at the same time. I am astonished at myself now and consider the patience which His Majesty gave me to have been a great favour from the Lord, for, as could clearly be seen, it was from Him that it came. It was a great help to my patience that I had read the story of Job in the *Morals* of St. Gregory,[4] for the Lord seems to have used this for preparing me to suffer. It was also a help that I had begun the practice of prayer, so that I could bear everything with great resignation. All my conversation was with God. I had continually in mind these words of Job, which I used to repeat: Since we have received good things at the hand of the Lord, why shall we not suffer evil things?[5] This seemed to give me strength.

And now the August festival of Our Lady came round: I had been in torment ever since April, though the last three months were the worst. I hastened to go to confession, for I was always very fond of frequent confession. They thought that this was due to fear of death, and, in order that I should not be distressed, my father forbade me to go. Oh, what an excess of human love! Though my father was so good a Cath-

---

[4] The Discalced nuns of St. Joseph's, Ávila, have an edition of St. Gregory's *Morals*, in two volumes, which, according to an inscription in the second volume, were read and marked by St. Teresa. Both in these volumes, however, and in the *Alphabet*, it can be stated with confidence that the majority of the marks were not made by the Saint.

[5] Job ii, 10.

olic and so wise—for he was extremely wise and so was not acting through ignorance—he might have done me great harm. That night I had a fit, which left me unconscious for nearly four days.[6] During that time they gave me the Sacrament of Unction, and from hour to hour, from moment to moment, thought I was dying; they did nothing but repeat the Creed to me, as though I could have understood any of it. There must have been times when they were sure I was dead, for afterwards I actually found some wax on my eyelids.

My father was in great distress because he had not allowed me to go to confession. Many cries and prayers were made for me to God. Blessed be He Who was pleased to hear them! For a day and a half there was an open grave in my convent, where they were awaiting my body, and in one of the monasteries of our Order, some way from here, they had performed the rites for the dead. But it pleased the Lord that I should return to consciousness. I wished at once to go to confession. I communicated with many tears; but they were not, I think, tears of sorrow and distress due only to my having offended God, which might have sufficed to save me, if there had not been sufficient excuse for me in the way I was misled by those who had told me that certain things were not mortal sins which I have since seen clearly were so. My sufferings were so intolerable that I hardly had the power to think, though I believe my confession was complete as to all the ways in which I was conscious of having offended God. There is one grace, among others, which His Majesty has granted me: never since I began to communicate have I failed to confess anything which I thought to be a sin, even if only a venial one. But I think that without doubt, if I had died then, my salvation would have been very uncertain, because my confessors, on the one hand, were so unlearned, and because I, on the other, was so wicked, and for many other reasons.

The fact is, when I come to this point, and realize how the Lord seems to have raised me from the dead, I am so amazed that inwardly I am almost trembling. It would be well, O my soul, if thou wouldst look at the danger from which the Lord

[6] According to Ribera (Bk. I, Chap. VII), she was believed to be dead, a grave was dug for her at the Incarnation and nuns came from that convent to keep vigil by her body. Her father, however, was convinced that there was still life in her and refused to consent to the burial.

has delivered thee, so that if thou didst not cease to offend Him through love, thou shouldst do so through fear. He might have slain thee on any of a thousand other occasions and in a more perilous state still. I do not believe I am straying far from the truth when I say "a thousand", though I may be reproved by him who has commanded me to be temperate in recounting my sins, which I have presented in a light only too favourable. I beg him, for the love of God, to excuse none of my faults, for they only reveal the magnificence of God and His longsuffering to the soul. May He be blessed for ever. And may it please His Majesty that I be utterly consumed rather than cease to love Him.

CHAPTER VI

Describes all that she owed to the Lord for granting her resignation in such great trials; and how she took the glorious Saint Joseph for her mediator and advocate; and the great profit that this brought her.

After this fit, which lasted for four days, I was in such a state that only the Lord can know what intolerable sufferings I experienced. My tongue was bitten to pieces; nothing had passed my lips; and because of this and of my great weakness my throat was choking me so that I could not even take water. All my bones seemed to be out of joint and there was a terrible confusion in my head. As a result of the torments I had suffered during these days, I was all doubled up, like a ball, and no more able to move arm, foot, hand or head than if I had been dead, unless others moved them for me. I could move, I think, only one finger of my right hand. It was impossible to let anyone come to see me, for I was in such a state of distress that I could not endure it. They used to move me in a sheet, one taking one end and another the other. This lasted until Easter Sunday.[1] My only alleviation was that, if no one came near me, my pains often ceased; and when I had rested a little I used to think I was getting well. For I was afraid my patience would fail me; so I was very glad when I

---

[1] [*Pascua florida*. Lewis (p. 33) erroneously translates "Palm Sunday".]

found myself without such sharp and constant pains, although I could hardly endure the terrible cold fits of quartan ague, from which I still suffered and which were very severe. I still had a dreadful distaste for food.

I was now so eager to return to the convent that they had me taken there. So, instead of the dead body they had expected, the nuns received a living soul; though the body was worse than dead and distressing to behold. My extreme weakness cannot be described, for by this time I was nothing but bones. As I have said, I remained in this condition for more than eight months, and my paralysis, though it kept improving, continued for nearly three years. When I began to get about on my hands and knees, I praised God. All this I bore with great resignation, and, except at the beginning, with great joy; for none of it could compare with the pains and torments which I had suffered at first. I was quite resigned to the will of God, even if He had left me in this condition for ever. My great yearning, I think, was to get well so that I might be alone when I prayed, as I had been taught to be— there was no possibility of this in the infirmary. I made my confession very frequently, and talked a great deal about God, in such a way that all were edified and astonished at the patience which the Lord gave me; for if it had not come from His Majesty's hand it would have seemed impossible to be able to endure such great sufferings with such great joy.

It was a wonderful thing for me to have received the grace which God had granted me through prayer, for this made me realize what it was to love Him. After a short time I found these virtues were renewed within me, although not in great strength, for they were not sufficient to uphold me in righteousness. I never spoke ill of anyone in the slightest degree, for my usual practice was to avoid all evil-speaking. I used to remind myself that I must not wish or say anything about anyone which I should not like to be said of me. I was extremely particular about observing this rule on all possible occasions, although I was not so perfect as not to fail now and then when faced with difficult situations. Still, that was my usual habit; and those who were with me and had to do with me were so much struck by it that they made it a habit too. It came to be realized that in my presence people could turn their backs to me and yet be quite safe; and so, too, they were with my friends and kinsfolk and those who learned from me. But in other respects I shall have to give a strict account to God for the bad example which I set them. May it please His Majesty to forgive me, for I have been the cause of much wrongdoing, though my intentions were not so harmful as were the actions which resulted from them.

My desire for solitude continued and I was fond of speaking and conversing about God; if I found anyone with whom I could do so, it gave me more joy and recreation than indulgence in any of the refinements (which are really coarsenesses) of the conversation of the world. I communicated and confessed very much more frequently—and this by my own wish; I loved reading good books; I was most sincerely penitent at having offended God; and I remember that often I dared not pray because I was afraid of the very deep distress which I should feel at having offended Him, and which was like a severe punishment. This continued to grow upon me and became such a torment that I do not know with what I can compare it. And its being greater or less had nothing to do with any fear of mine, for it would come when I thought of the favours which the Lord was giving me in prayer, and of all that I owed Him, and when I saw how ill I was requiting Him. I could not bear it; and I would grow very angry with myself at shedding so many tears for my faults, when I saw how little I improved and how neither my resolutions nor the trouble I took were sufficient to keep me from falling again when an occasion presented itself. My tears seemed to me deceptive and my faults the greater because I was conscious of the great favour which the Lord bestowed upon me in granting me these tears and this great repentance. I used to try to make my confession as soon as possible after I had fallen; and, I think, did all I could to return to grace. The whole trouble lay in my not cutting off the occasions of sin at the root, and in the scant help given me by my confessors. For, if they had told me how dangerous was the path I was taking and how incumbent upon me it was not to indulge in these conversations, I feel quite sure I could never have endured remaining in mortal sin for even a day with the knowledge that I was doing so. All these tokens of the fear of God came to me in prayer. The chief of them was that my fear was always swallowed up[2] in love, for I never thought about punishment. All the time I was so ill, I kept a strict

---

2 [*Envuelto*. *Lit.*: "wrapped up", "swathed".]

watch over my conscience with respect to mortal sin. O God, how I longed for health that I might serve Thee better! And that was the cause of all my wrongdoing.

For when I found that, while still so young, I was so seriously paralysed, and that earthly doctors had been unable to cure me, I resolved to seek a cure from heavenly doctors, for, though I bore my sickness with great joy, I none the less desired to be well again. I often reflected that, if I were to grow well and then to incur damnation, it would be better for me to remain as I was; but still I believed that I should serve God much better if I recovered my health. That is the mistake we make: we do not leave ourselves entirely in the Lord's hands; yet He knows best what is good for us.

I began by having Masses said for me, and prayers which had been fully approved; for I was never fond of other kinds of devotion which some people practise—especially women—together with ceremonies which I could never endure, but for which they have a great affection. Since then it has been explained to me that such things are unseemly and superstitious. I took for my advocate and lord the glorious Saint Joseph and commended myself earnestly to him; and I found that this my father and lord delivered me both from this trouble and also from other and greater troubles concerning my honour[3] and the loss of my soul, and that he gave me greater blessings than I could ask of him. I do not remember even now that I have ever asked anything of him which he has failed to grant. I am astonished at the great favours which God has bestowed on me through this blessed saint, and at the perils from which He has freed me, both in body and in soul. To other saints the Lord seems to have given grace to succour us in some of our necessities but of this glorious saint my experience is that he succours us in them all and that the Lord wishes to teach us that as He was Himself subject to him on earth (for, being His guardian and being called His father, he could command Him) just so in Heaven He still does all that he asks. This has also been the experience of other persons whom I have advised to commend themselves to him; and even to-day there are many who have great devotion to him through having newly experienced this truth.

I used to try to keep his feast with the greatest possible

3 [*Honra*. Cf. p. 70, n. 3.]

solemnity[4]; but, though my intentions were good, I would
observe it with more vanity than spirituality, for I always
wanted things to be done very meticulously and well. I had
this unfortunate characteristic that, if the Lord gave me
grace to do anything good, the way I did it was full of imperfections and extremely faulty. I was very assiduous and skilful in wrongdoing and in my meticulousness and vanity. May
the Lord forgive me. I wish I could persuade everyone to be
devoted to this glorious saint, for I have great experience of
the blessings which he can obtain from God. I have never
known anyone to be truly devoted to him and render him
particular services who did not notably advance in virtue, for
he gives very real help to souls who commend themselves to
him. For some years now, I think, I have made some request
of him every year on his festival and I have always had it
granted. If my petition is in any way ill directed, he directs
it aright for my greater good.

If I were a person writing with authority, I would gladly
describe, at greater length and in the minutest detail, the
favours which this glorious saint has granted to me and to
others. But in order not to do more than I have been commanded I shall have to write about many things briefly, much
more so than I should wish, and at unnecessarily great length
about others: in short, I must act like one who has little discretion in all that is good. I only beg, for the love of God,
that anyone who does not believe me will put what I say to
the test, and he will see by experience what great advantages
come from his commending himself to this glorious patriarch
and having devotion to him. Those who practise prayer should
have a special affection for him always. I do not know how
anyone can think of the Queen of the Angels, during the
time that she suffered so much with the Child Jesus, without giving thanks to Saint Joseph for the way he helped them.
If anyone cannot find a master to teach him how to pray, let
him take this glorious saint as his master and he will not go
astray. May the Lord grant that I have not erred in venturing
to speak of him; for though I make public acknowledgment
of my devotion to him, in serving and imitating him I have
always failed. He was true to his own nature when he cured

---

[4] In many Spanish convents at this time it was customary to allow
any nun who could afford to do so to pay the expenses of the
yearly festival of some one saint to whom she might be particularly
devoted. This custom obtained at the Incarnation.

my paralysis and gave me the power to rise and walk; and I am following my own nature in using this favour so ill.

Who would have said that I should fall so soon, after receiving so many favours from God, and after His Majesty had begun to grant me virtues which themselves aroused me to serve Him; after I had seen myself at death's door and in such great peril of damnation; after He had raised me up, in soul and in body, so that all who saw me were amazed to see me alive? What it is, my Lord, to have to live a life so full of perils! For here I am writing this, and it seems to me that with Thy favour and through Thy mercy I might say with Saint Paul, though not so perfectly as he: For it is not I now who live, but Thou, my Creator, livest in me.[5] For some years, so far as I can see, Thou hast held me by Thy hand, and I find I have desires and resolutions—tested to a certain extent, during these years, in many ways, by experience—to do nothing contrary to Thy will, however trifling it may be, though I must often have caused Thy Majesty numerous offences without knowing it. It seems to me, too, that nothing can present itself to me which I would not with great resolution undertake for love of Thee, and some of these things Thou hast helped me successfully to accomplish. I desire neither the world nor anything that is worldly, and nothing seems to give me pleasure unless it comes from Thee: everything else seems to me a heavy cross. I may well be mistaken and it may be that I have not the desire that I have described; but Thou seest, my Lord, that, so far as I can understand, I am not lying. I am afraid, and with good reason, that Thou mayest once more forsake me; for I know well how little my strength and insufficiency of virtue can achieve if Thou be not ever granting me Thy grace and helping me not to forsake Thee. May it please Thy Majesty that I be not forsaken by Thee even now, while I am thinking all this about myself. I do not know why we wish to live, when everything is so uncertain. I used to think, my Lord, that it was impossible to forsake Thee wholly; yet how many times have I forsaken Thee! I cannot but fear; for, when Thou didst withdraw from me but a little, I fell utterly to the ground. Blessed be Thou for ever! For, though I have forsaken Thee, Thou hast not so completely forsaken me as not to raise me up again by con-

[5] Galatians ii, 20.

tinually giving me Thy hand. Often, Lord, I would not take it, and often when Thou didst call me a second time I would not listen, as I shall now relate.

CHAPTER VII

Describes how she began to lose the favours which the Lord had granted her and how evil her life became. Treats of the harm that comes to convents from laxity in the observance of the rule of enclosure.

I began, then, to indulge in one pastime after another, in one vanity after another and in one occasion of sin after another. Into so many and such grave occasions of sin did I fall, and so far was my soul led astray by all these vanities, that I was ashamed to return to God and to approach Him in the intimate friendship which comes from prayer. This shame was increased by the fact that, as my sins grew in number, I began to lose the pleasure and joy which I had been deriving from virtuous things. I saw very clearly, my Lord, that this was failing me because I was failing Thee. The devil, beneath the guise of humility, now led me into the greatest of all possible errors. Seeing that I was so utterly lost, I began to be afraid to pray. It seemed to me better, since in my wickedness I was one of the worst people alive, to live like everyone else; to recite, vocally, the prayers that I was bound to say; and not to practise mental prayer or hold so much converse with God, since I deserved to be with the devils, and, by presenting an outward appearance of goodness, was only deceiving others. No blame for this is to be attributed to the house in which I lived, for I was clever enough to see to it that the nuns had a good opinion of me, though I did not do so deliberately, by pretending to be a good Christian, for in the matter of vainglory and hypocrisy—glory be to God!—I do not remember having even once offended Him, so far as I am aware. For if ever I perceived within myself the first motions of such a thing, it distressed me so much that the devil would depart confounded and I would be all the better for it; so he has very seldom tempted me much in this way. Perhaps, if God had permitted me to be tempted as severely in this respect as in others, I should have fallen here too, but so far His Majesty has kept me from this. May He be for ever blessed. In reality, therefore, I was very much troubled that they should have such a good opinion of me, as I knew what sort of person I was inwardly.

This belief which they had that I was not so wicked was the result of their seeing me, young though I was and exposed to so many occasions of sin, withdrawing myself frequently into solitude, saying my prayers, reading a great deal, speaking about God, liking to have pictures of Him in a great many places, wanting an oratory of my own, trying to get objects of devotion for it, refraining from evil-speaking and doing other things of that kind which gave me the appearance of being virtuous. I myself was vain and liked to be well thought of in the things wont to be esteemed by the world. On account of this they gave me as much liberty as is given to the oldest nuns, and even more, and they had great confidence in me. For I did no such things as taking liberties for myself or doing anything without leave—such as talking to people through crevices or over walls or by night—and I do not think I could ever have brought myself to talk in such a way with anyone in the convent, for the Lord held me by His hand. It seemed to me—for there were many things which I used to ponder deliberately and with great care—that it would be very wrong of me to compromise the good name of so many of the sisters when I was wicked and they were good: just as though all the other things that I did had been good! In truth, though I often acted very wrongly, my faults were never so much the result of a set purpose as those others would have been.

For that reason, I think it was a very bad thing for me not to be in a convent that was enclosed. The freedom which the sisters, who were good, might enjoy without becoming less so (for they were not obliged to live more strictly than they did as they had not taken a vow of enclosure) would certainly have led me, who am wicked, down to hell, had not the Lord, through very special favours, using means and remedies which are all His own, delivered me from this peril. It seems to me, then, that it is a very great danger for women in a convent to have such freedom: for those who want to be wicked it is not so much a remedy for their weaknesses as a step on the way to hell. But this is not to be applied to my convent, where there are so many who serve the Lord in very truth and with great perfection, so that His Majesty, in His goodness, cannot fail to help them. Nor is it one of those which are completely open, for all religious observances are kept in it: I am comparing it now with others which I know and have seen.

This seems to me, as I say, a great pity; for, when a convent follows standards and allows recreations which belong to the world, and the obligations of the nuns are so ill understood, the Lord has perforce to call each of them individually, and not once but many times, if they are to be saved. God grant that they may not all mistake sin for virtue, as I so often did! It is very difficult to make people see this and the Lord must needs take the matter right into His own hands. Parents seem to give little thought to the placing of their daughters where they may walk in the way of salvation, but allow them to run into more danger than they would in the world; nevertheless, if they will follow my advice, they will at least consider what concerns their honour. Let them be prepared to allow them to marry far beneath their stations rather than put them into convents of this kind, unless they are very devoutly inclined— and God grant that their inclinations may lead them into what is good! Otherwise they will do better to keep them at home; for there, if they want to be wicked, they cannot long hide their wickedness, whereas in convents it can be hidden for a very long time indeed, until, in the end, it is revealed by the Lord. They do harm not only to themselves but to everybody else; and at times the poor creatures are really not to blame, for they only do what they find others doing. Many of them are to be pitied: they wish to escape from the world, and, thinking that they are going to serve the Lord and flee from the world and its perils, they find themselves in ten worlds at once, and have no idea where to turn or how to get out of their difficulties. Youth, sensuality and the devil invite and incline them to do things which are completely worldly; and they see that these things are considered, as one might say, "all right". To me, in some ways, they resemble those unhappy heretics, who wilfully blind themselves and proclaim that what they do is good; and believe it to be so, yet without real confidence, for there is something within them which tells them they are doing wrong.

Oh, what terrible harm, what terrible harm is wrought in religious (I am referring now as much to men as to women) when the religious life is not properly observed; when of the two paths that can be followed in a religious house—one leading to virtue and the observance of the Rule and the other leading away from the Rule—both are frequented almost equally! No, I am wrong: they are not frequented equally, for our sins cause the more imperfect road to be more commonly taken; being the broader, it is the more generally favoured. The way of true religion is frequented so little that, if the friar and the nun are to begin to follow their vocation truly, they need to be more afraid of the religious in their own house than of all the devils. They must observe greater caution and dissimulation when speaking of the friendship which they would have with God than in speaking of other friendships and affections promoted in religious houses by the devil. I cannot think why we should be astonished at all the evils which exist in the Church, when those who ought to be models on which all may pattern their virtues are annulling the work wrought in the religious Orders by the spirit of the saints of old. May His Divine Majesty be pleased to find a remedy for this, as He sees needful. Amen.

Now when I began to indulge in these conversations, I did not think, seeing them to be so usual, that they would cause the harm and distraction to my soul which I found would be the case later. For I thought that, as in many convents it is such a common practice to receive visitors, I should take no more harm from it than would others whom I knew to be good. I did not realize that they were far better than I and that what was dangerous for me would not be so dangerous for others. Yet I have no doubt that the practice is never quite free from danger, if only because it is a waste of time. I was once in the company of a certain person, right at the beginning of my acquaintance with her, when the Lord was pleased to make me realize that these friendships were not good for me, and to warn me and enlighten my great blindness. Christ revealed Himself to me, in an attitude of great sternness, and showed me what there was in this that displeased Him.[1] I saw Him with the eyes of the soul more clearly than I could ever have seen Him with those of the body; and it made such an impression upon me that, although it is now more than twenty-six years ago, I seem to have Him present with me

[1] [The Saint wrote, no doubt inadvertently, "that did not displease Him".] P. Báñez corrected this to: "that He did not like".

still. I was greatly astonished and upset about it and I never wanted to see that person again.

It did me great harm not to know that it was possible to see anything otherwise than with the eyes of the body. It was the devil who encouraged me in this ignorance and made me think that anything else was impossible. He led me to believe that I had imagined it all, and that it might have been the work of the devil, and other things of that kind. I always had an idea that it was not due to my fancy but came from God. However, just because the vision did not please me, I forced myself to give the lie to my own instinct; and, as I dared not discuss it with anyone, and after a time great importunity was brought to bear on me, I entered into relations with that person once again. I was assured that there was no harm in my seeing such a person, and that by doing so I should not injure my good name[2] but rather enhance it. On subsequent occasions I got to know other people in the same way; and I spent many years in this pestilential pastime, which, whenever I was engaged in it, never seemed to me as bad as it really was, though sometimes I saw clearly that it was not good. But no one caused me as much distraction as did the person of whom I am speaking, for I was very fond of her.

On another occasion, when I was with that same person, we saw coming towards us—and others who were there saw this too—something like a great toad, but crawling much more quickly than toads are wont to do. I cannot imagine how such a reptile could have come from the place in question in broad daylight; it had never happened before, and the incident made such an impression on me that I think it must have had a hidden meaning, and I have never forgotten this either. O greatness of God! With what care and compassion didst Thou warn me in every way and how little did I profit by Thy warnings!

There was a nun in that convent, who was a relative of mine; she had been there a long time and was a great servant of God and devoted to the Rule of her Order. She, too, occasionally warned me; and not only did I disbelieve her but I was displeased with her, for I thought she was shocked without cause. I have mentioned this in order to make clear my

2 [*Honra.*]

wickedness and the great goodness of God and to show how by this great ingratitude of mine I had merited hell. I also mention it in order that, if it is the Lord's will and pleasure that it shall be read at any time by a nun, she may be warned by me. I beg all nuns, for the love of Our Lord, to flee from such pastimes as these. May His Majesty grant that some of those whom I have led astray may be set in the right path by me; I used to tell them that there was nothing wrong in this practice, and, blind that I was, reassure them about what was in reality a great danger. I would never have deliberately deceived them; but, through the bad example that I set them, as I have said, I was the cause of a great deal of wrongdoing without ever thinking I could be.

In those early days, during my illness, and before I knew how to take care of myself, I used to have the greatest desire to be of use to others. This is a very common temptation in beginners; in my case, however, its effects were good. I was so fond of my father that I longed for him to experience the benefit which I seemed to be deriving from the practice of prayer myself, for I thought that in this life there could be nothing greater. So by indirect methods, and to the best of my ability, I began to try to get him to practise it. To this end I gave him books to read. Being very virtuous, as I have said he was, he took so well to this exercise that in five or six years (I think it must have been[3]) he had made such progress that I praised the Lord greatly and was wonderfully encouraged. He had to bear the severest trials of many different kinds and he bore them with the greatest resignation. He often came to see me, for he derived great comfort from speaking of the things of God.

But now that I had fallen away so far, and no longer practised prayer, I could not bear him to think, as I saw he did, that I was still just as I used to be; so I had to undeceive him. For I had been a year or more without praying, thinking that to refrain from prayer was a sign of greater humility. This, as I shall afterwards explain, was the greatest temptation I had: it nearly brought about my ruin. For during the time I prac-

---

[3] [Hardly quite so long, as] it seems certain that Don Alonso died on December 24, 1543. His will is dated December 3, 1543, and his son and executor Lorenzo opened it on December 26 [P. Silverio reproduces documents which disprove Mir's date of 1545 for Don Alonso's death].

tised prayer, if I had offended God one day, I would recollect myself on the following days and withdraw farther from occasions of sin. When that dear good man came to visit me, it was very hard for me to see him under the false impression that I was still communing with God as I had been doing before. So I told him that I was no longer praying, without telling him the reason. I made my illnesses an excuse; for, though I had recovered from that very serious illness, I have suffered ever since from indispositions, and sometimes from grave ones, even to this day. For some time my complaints have been less troublesome, but they have by no means left me. In particular, for twenty years I suffered from morning sickness, so that I was not able to break my fast until after midday—sometimes not until much later. Now that I go oftener to Communion, I have to bring on the sickness at night, with feathers or in some other way, before I go to bed, which is much more distressing; but if I let it take its course I feel much worse. I think I can hardly ever be free from aches and pains, and sometimes very serious ones, especially in the heart, although the trouble which I once had continually now occurs only rarely, and I have been free for quite eight years from the paralysis and the feverish complaints from which I used often to suffer. Of these troubles I now make such little account that I often rejoice in them, thinking that to some extent they are pleasing to the Lord.

My father believed me when I told him that it was because of my health that I had ceased to pray, since he never told a lie himself, and, in view of the relations between us, there was no reason why I should have done so either. I told him, in order to make my story the more credible (for I well knew that I had no such excuse really), that it was as much as I could do to attend the choir offices. Not that this would be any sufficient reason for giving up something which needs no bodily strength, but only love and the formation of a habit; and the Lord always gives us an opportunity if we want one. I say always; for, though there may be times when we are prevented by various hindrances, and even by illness, from spending much time alone, there are plenty of others when we are in sufficiently good health to do so. And even despite illness, or other hindrances, we can still engage in true prayer, when there is love in the soul, by offering up that very impediment, remembering Him for Whom we suffer it and being resigned to it and to a thousand other things which may happen to us. It is here that love comes in; for we are not necessarily praying when we are alone, nor need we refrain from praying when we are not.

With a little care, great blessings can be acquired at times when the Lord deprives us of our hours of prayer by sending us trials; and this I had myself found to be the case when my conscience had been good. But my father, holding the opinion of me that he did and loving me as he did, believed everything I told him and in fact was sorry for me. As he had now reached such a high state of prayer he used not to stay with me for so long, but after he had seen me would go away, saying that he was wasting his time. As I was wasting mine on other vanities, this remark made little impression upon me. There were other persons, as well as my father, whom I tried to lead into the practice of prayer. Indulging in vanities myself though I was, when I saw people who were fond of saying their prayers, I would show them how to make a meditation and help them and give them books; for ever since I began to pray, as I have said, I had this desire that others should serve God. And now that I was no longer serving the Lord according to my ability, I thought that the knowledge which His Majesty had given me ought not to be lost and wanted others to learn to serve Him through me. I say this in order to show how great was my blindness, which allowed me to do such harm to myself and yet to try to be of profit to others.

It was at this time that my father was stricken by the illness of which he died. It lasted for some days. I went to look after him, more afflicted in soul than he in body, on account of my vanities, though, as far as I was aware, I was never in mortal sin during the whole of this wasted time of which I am speaking: if I had known myself to be so I would on no account have continued in it. I was greatly distressed by his illness and I believe I was able to return him some part of all he had done for me when I was ill myself. Distressed as I was, I forced myself into activity; and though in losing him I lost my greatest blessing and comfort, for he was always that to me, I was so determined not to let him see my grief for as long as he lived that I behaved as if I felt no grief at all. Yet so dearly did I love him that, when I saw his life was ending, I felt as if my very soul were being torn from me.

The Lord must be praised for the death which he died,

for his desire to die, for the advice which he gave us after receiving Extreme Unction, and for the way he charged us to commend him to God, to pray for mercy upon him and to serve God always, remembering how all things come to an end. He told us with tears how deeply grieved he was that he had not served God better: he would have liked to be a friar —and by that I mean to have joined one of the strictest Orders in existence. I am quite sure that a fortnight before his death the Lord had made him realize that he would not live much longer; for down to that time, ill though he was, he had not believed he would die. But during that last fortnight, though he got much better and the doctors told him so, he took no notice of them but occupied himself in putting his soul right with God.

His chief ailment was a most acute pain in the back, which never left him: at times it was so severe that it caused him great anguish. I said to him that, as he used to think so devoutly of the Lord carrying the Cross on His back, he must suppose His Majesty wished him to feel something of what He Himself had suffered under that trial. This comforted him so much that I do not think I ever heard him complain again. For three days he was practically unconscious; but, on the day of his death, the Lord restored his consciousness so completely that we were astonished, and he remained conscious until, half-way through the Creed, which he was repeating to himself, he died. He looked like an angel; and so he seemed to me, as one might say, both in his soul and in his disposition, for he was very good. I do not know why I have said this, unless it be to blame myself the more for my wicked life; for, after witnessing such a death and realizing what his life had been, I ought to have tried to do something to resemble such a father by growing better. His confessor, who was a Dominican[4] and a very learned man, used to say that he had not the least doubt he had gone straight to Heaven; he had been his confessor for some years and spoke highly of his purity of conscience.

This Dominican father, who was a very good man and had a great fear of God, was of the very greatest help to me. I made my confessions to him and he took great pains to lead my soul aright and make me realize how near I was to perdi-

4 P. Vicente Barrón [cf. p. 27, n. 2].

tion. He made me communicate once a fortnight; and gradually, as I got to know him, I began to tell him about my prayers. He told me never to leave these off, for they could not possibly do me anything but good. So I began to take them up once more (though I did not flee from occasions of sin) and I never again abandoned them. My life became full of trials, because by means of prayer I learned more and more about my faults. On the one hand, God was calling me. On the other, I was following the world. All the things of God gave me great pleasure, yet I was tied and bound to those of the world. It seemed as if I wanted to reconcile these two contradictory things, so completely opposed to one another—the life of the spirit and the pleasures and joys and pastimes of the senses. I suffered great trials in prayer, for the spirit was not master in me, but slave. I could not, therefore, shut myself up within myself (the procedure in which consisted my whole method of prayer) without at the same time shutting in a thousand vanities. I spent many years in this way, and now I am amazed that a person could have gone on for so long without giving up either the one or the other. I know quite well that by that time it was no longer in my power to give up prayer, because He who desired me for His own in order to show me greater favours held me Himself in His hand.

Oh, God help me! If only I could describe the occasions of sin during these years from which God delivered me, and tell how I plunged into them again and how He continually saved me from the danger of losing my entire reputation! I would show by my actions the kind of person I was; yet the Lord would hide the wrongs I did and reveal some small virtue, if I had any, and magnify it in the eyes of all, so that people invariably had a high opinion of me. For, although my vanities were sometimes crystal-clear, they would not believe them to be such when they observed other things in me which they considered good. This happened because He Who knows all things saw it to be necessary, in order that hereafter I might be given some credence when speaking of things that concern His service. His sovereign bounty regarded not my great sins but the desires which I so often had to serve Him and my grief at not having in myself the strength to turn the desires into actions.

O Lord of my soul! How can I magnify the favours which

Thou didst bestow upon me during these years? And how, at the very time when I was offending Thee most sorely, didst Thou suddenly prepare me, by the deepest repentance, to taste Thy favours and graces! In truth, my King, Thou didst choose the most delicate and grievous chastisement that I could possibly have to bear, for well didst Thou know what would cause me the greatest pain. Thou didst chastise my faults with great favours. And I do not believe I am speaking foolishly, though well might I become distraught when I recall to mind my ingratitude and wickedness. In the condition I was in at that time, it was much more painful for me, when I had fallen into grievous faults, to be given favours, than to be given punishments. A single one of these faults, I feel sure, troubled and confounded and distressed me more than many sicknesses and many other grievous trials all put together. For these last I knew that I deserved and thought that by them I was making some amends for my sins, although my sins were so numerous that everything I could do was very little. But when I find myself receiving new favours, after making so poor a return for those I have received already, I experience a kind of torture which is terrible to me, as I think it must be to all who have any knowledge or love of God. We can deduce our own unworthiness by imagining a state of real virtue. This accounts for my tears and vexation when I took stock of my own feelings, and realized that I was in such a state as to be on the point of falling again and again, though my resolutions and desires—at that time, I mean—were quite steadfast.

It is a great evil for a soul beset by so many dangers to be alone. I believe, if I had had anyone with whom to discuss all this, it would have helped me not to fall again, if only because I should have been ashamed in his sight, which I was not in the sight of God. For this reason I would advise those who practise prayer, especially at first, to cultivate friendship and intercourse with others of similar interests. This is a most important thing, if only because we can help each other by our prayers, and it is all the more so because it may bring us many other benefits. Since people can find comfort in the conversation and human sympathy of ordinary friendships, even when these are not altogether good, I do not know why anyone who is beginning to love and serve God in earnest should not be allowed to discuss his joys and trials with others

—and people who practise prayer have plenty of both. For, if the friendship which such a person desires to have with His Majesty is true friendship, he need not be afraid of becoming vainglorious: as soon as the first motion of vainglory attacks him, he will repel it, and, in doing so, gain merit. I believe that anyone who discusses the subject with this in mind will profit both himself and his hearers, and will be all the wiser for it; and, without realizing he is doing so, will edify his friends.

Anyone who could become vainglorious through discussing these matters would become equally so by hearing Mass with devotion in a place where people can see him, and by doing other things which he is obliged to do under pain of being no Christian at all: he cannot possibly refrain from doing these through fear of vainglory. This is also most important for souls which are not strengthened in virtue; they have so many enemies and friends to incite them to do what is wrong that I cannot insist upon it sufficiently. It seems to me that this scruple is an invention of the devil, who finds it extremely valuable. He uses it to persuade those who are anxious to try to love and please God to hide their good desires, while inciting others, whose wills are evilly inclined, to reveal their wrong intentions. This happens so frequently that people now seem to glory in it and the offences committed in this way against God are published openly.

I do not know if the things I am saying are nonsense: if so, Your Reverence must erase them; if not, I beg you to help my simplicity by adding to them freely. For people trouble so little about things pertaining to the service of God that we must all back each other up[5] if those of us who serve Him are to make progress. People think it a good thing to follow the pleasures and vanities of the world and there are few who look askance at these; but if a single person begins to devote himself to God, there are so many to speak ill of him that self-defence compels him to seek the companionship of others until he is strong enough not to be depressed by suffering. Unless he does this he will find himself in continual difficulties. It must have been for this reason, I think, that some of the saints were in the habit of going into the desert. It is a kind of humility for a man not to trust himself but to be-

[5] [The metaphor, *hacerse espaldas*, is St. Teresa's.]

lieve that God will help him in dealing with those with whom
he has intercourse. Charity grows when it is communicated
to others and from this there result a thousand blessings. I
should not dare to say this if I had not had a great deal of experience of its importance. It is true that of all who are born
I am the weakest and wickedest; but I believe that anyone,
however strong, who humbles himself and trusts not in himself but in someone who has experience, will lose nothing.
As regards myself, I can say that, if the Lord had not revealed
this truth to me and given me the means of speaking very
frequently with people who practise prayer, I should have
gone on rising and falling again until I fell right into hell. For
I had many friends who helped me to fall; but, when it came
to rising again, I found myself so completely alone that I
marvel now that I did not remain where I was, and I praise
the mercy of God, Who alone gave me His hand. May He
be blessed for ever. Amen.

CHAPTER VIII

Treats of the great benefit which she derived from not en-
tirely giving up prayer lest she should ruin her soul.
Describes the excellence of prayer as a help towards re-
gaining what one has lost. Urges all to practise it. Says
what great gain it brings and how great a benefit it is,
even for those who may later give it up, to spend some
time on a thing which is so good.

It is not without reason that I have dwelt upon this period
of my life at such length. I know well that nobody will derive
any pleasure from reading about anyone so wicked, and I
sincerely hope that those who read this will hold me in abhorrence, when they see that a soul which had received such
great favours could be so obstinate and ungrateful. I wish I
could be allowed to describe the many occasions on which I
failed God during this period through not having leaned
upon this strong pillar of prayer.

I spent nearly twenty years on that stormy sea, often falling
in this way and each time rising again, but to little purpose,
as I would only fall once more. My life was so far from per-

fection that I took hardly any notice of venial sins; as to mortal sins, although afraid of them, I was not so much so as I ought to have been; for I did not keep free from the danger of falling into them. I can testify that this is one of the most grievous kinds of life which I think can be imagined, for I had neither any joy in God nor any pleasure in the world. When I was in the midst of worldly pleasures, I was distressed by the remembrance of what I owed to God; when I was with God, I grew restless because of worldly affections. This is so grievous a conflict that I do not know how I managed to endure it for a month, much less for so many years. Nevertheless, I can see how great was the Lord's mercy to me, since, while I was still having intercourse with the world, He gave me courage to practise prayer. I say courage, because I know nothing in the world that needs more of this than to be dealing treacherously with the King and to know that He is aware of it and yet never to leave His presence. For, although we are always in the presence of God, it seems to me that those who practise prayer are specially so, because they can see all the time that He is looking at them; whereas others may be in God's presence for several days without ever remembering that He can see them.

It is true that, during these years, there were many months —once, I believe, there was as much as a whole year—in which I kept myself from offending the Lord, devoted myself earnestly to prayer and took various and very careful precautions not to offend Him. As all that I have written is set down in the strictest truth, I am saying this now. But I remember little about these good days, so there can have been few of them, whereas the bad ones must have been numerous. Yet not many days would pass without my spending long periods in prayer, unless I was very ill or very busy. When I was ill, I was nearer to God; and I contrived that the persons who were around me should be near Him too and I begged the Lord that this might be so and often spoke of Him. So, not counting the year I have referred to, more than eighteen of the twenty-eight years which have gone by since I began prayer have been spent in this battle and conflict which arose from my having relations both with God and with the world. During the remaining years, of which I have still to speak, the conflict has not been light, but its causes have changed; as I believe I have been serving God and have come to know the vanity inherent in the world, everything has gone smoothly, as I shall say later.

Now the reason why I have related all this is, as I have already said, to make evident God's mercy and my own ingratitude. Another reason is to show what great blessings God grants to a soul when He prepares it to love the practice of prayer, though it may not be as well prepared already as it should be; and how, if that soul perseveres, notwithstanding the sins, temptations and falls of a thousand kinds into which the devil leads it, the Lord, I am certain, will bring it to the harbour of salvation, just as, so far as can at present be told, He has brought me. May His Majesty grant that I may never again be lost.

The blessings possessed by one who practises prayer—I mean mental prayer—have been written of by many saints and good men. Glory be to God for this! If it were not so, I should not have assurance enough (though I am not very humble) to dare to speak of it. I can say what I know by experience—namely, that no one who has begun this practice, however many sins he may commit, should ever forsake it. For it is the means by which we may amend our lives again, and without it amendment will be very much harder. So let him not be tempted by the devil, as I was, to give it up for reasons of humility, but let him believe that the words cannot fail of Him Who says that, if we truly repent and determine not to offend Him, He will resume His former friendship with us and grant us the favours which He granted aforetime, and sometimes many more, if our repentance merits it.[1] And anyone who has not begun to pray, I beg, for love of the Lord, not to miss so great a blessing. There is no place here for fear, but only desire. For, even if a person fails to make progress, or to strive after perfection, so that he may merit the consolations and favours given to the perfect by God, yet he will gradually gain a knowledge of the road to Heaven. And if he perseveres, I hope in the mercy of God, Whom no one has ever taken for a Friend without being rewarded; and mental prayer, in my view, is nothing but friendly intercourse, and frequent solitary converse, with Him Who we know loves us. If love is to be true and friendship lasting, certain conditions are necessary: on the Lord's side

---

[1] [An apparent reference to Ezechiel xviii, 21.]

we know these cannot fail, but our nature is vicious, sensual and ungrateful. You cannot therefore succeed in loving Him as much as He loves you, because it is not in your nature to do so. If, then, you do not yet love Him, you will realize how much it means to you to have His friendship and how much He loves you, and you will gladly endure the troubles which arise from being[2] so much with One Who is so different from you.

O infinite goodness of my God! It is thus that I seem to see both myself and Thee. O Joy of the angels, how I long, when I think of this, to be wholly consumed in love for Thee! How true it is that Thou dost bear with those who cannot bear Thee to be with them! Oh, how good a Friend art Thou, my Lord! How Thou dost comfort us and suffer us and wait until our nature becomes more like Thine and meanwhile dost bear with it as it is! Thou dost remember the times when we love Thee, my Lord, and, when for a moment we repent, Thou dost forget how we have offended Thee. I have seen this clearly in my own life, and I cannot conceive, my Creator, why the whole world does not strive to draw near to Thee in this intimate friendship. Those of us who are wicked, and whose nature is not like Thine, ought to draw near to Thee so that Thou mayest make them good. They should allow Thee to be with them for at least two hours each day, even though they may not be with Thee, but are perplexed, as I was, with a thousand worldly cares and thoughts. In exchange for the effort which it costs them to desire to be in such good company (for Thou knowest, Lord, that at first this is as much as they can do and sometimes they can do no more at all) Thou dost prevent the devils from assaulting them so that each day they are able to do them less harm, and Thou givest them strength to conquer. Yea, Life of all lives, Thou slayest none of those that put their trust in Thee and desire Thee for their Friend; rather dost Thou sustain their bodily life with greater health and give life to their souls.

I do not understand the fears of those who are afraid to begin mental prayer: I do not know what they are afraid of.

___

[2] [Lit.: "the grief (pena) of being. . . ." "Discomfort," "embarrassment," "depression" would be modern equivalents of the substantive, but none of these is sufficiently comprehensive. St. Teresa is referring to all the varied reactions produced in man by the contact between his littleness and the greatness of God.]

The devil does well to instil fear into us so that he may do us real harm. By making me afraid he stops me from thinking of the ways in which I have offended God and of all I owe Him and of the reality of hell and of glory and of the great trials and griefs which He suffered for me. That was the whole extent of my prayer, and remained so for as long as I was subject to these perils, and it was about these things that I used to think whenever I could; and very often, over a period of several years, I was more occupied in wishing my hour of prayer were over, and in listening whenever the clock struck, than in thinking of things that were good. Again and again I would rather have done any severe penance that might have been given me than practise recollection as a preliminary to prayer. It is a fact that, either through the intolerable power of the devil's assaults or because of my own bad habits, I did not at once betake myself to prayer; and whenever I entered the oratory I used to feel so depressed that I had to summon up all my courage to make myself pray at all. (People say that I have little courage, and it is clear that God has given me much more than to most women, only I have made bad use of it.) In the end, the Lord would come to my help. Afterwards, when I had forced myself to pray, I would find that I had more tranquillity and happiness than at certain other times when I had prayed because I had wanted to.

Now if the Lord bore for so long with such a wicked creature as I—and it is quite clear that it was in this way that all my wrong was put right—what other person, however wicked he may be, can have any reason for fear? For, bad though he be, he will not remain so for all the years I did after having received so many favours from the Lord. Who can possibly despair, when He bore so long with me, merely because I desired and sought out some place and time for Him to be with me—and that often happened without my willing it because I forced myself to seek it, or rather the Lord Himself forced me? If, then, prayer is so good, and so necessary, for those who do not serve God, but offend Him, and if no one can possibly discover any harm that prayer can do him which would not be much greater if he did not practise it, why should those who serve and desire to serve God give it up? Really I cannot see any reason, unless it is that they want to endure the trials of life by adding more trials to them and to shut the door upon God so that He shall not give them the joy of prayer. I am indeed sorry for such people, for they are serving God at great cost to themselves. But when people practise prayer the Lord Himself bears the cost: in exchange for a little labour on their part, He gives them such consolation as will enable them to bear their trials.

As I shall have a great deal to say about these consolations which the Lord gives to those who persevere in prayer, I am saying nothing here: I will only observe that prayer is the door to those great favours which He has bestowed upon me. Once the door is closed, I do not see how He will bestow them; for, though He may wish to take His delight in a soul and to give the soul delight, there is no way for Him to do so, since He must have it alone and pure, and desirous of receiving His favours. If we place numerous hindrances in His path, and do nothing to remove them, how can He come to us? And yet we wish God to grant us great favours!

In order that it may be seen what mercy He showed me and what a great blessing it was for me that I did not give up prayer and reading, I will now describe something which it is very important should be understood—the assaults which the devil makes upon a soul in order to conquer it for his own, and the art and the loving-kindness with which the Lord endeavours to bring it back to Himself. My readers will then be on the watch for the perils for which I was not watchful myself. And, above all, I beg them, for the love of Our Lord, and for the great love wherewith He is continually seeking to bring us back to Himself, to be on the watch for occasions of sin; for, once we are in the midst of these, we have no cause for confidence, being attacked, as we are, by so many enemies and being so weak when it comes to defending ourselves.

I wish I knew how to describe the captivity of my soul at that time. I fully realized that I was a prisoner, and yet I could not see how, nor could I really believe that things which my confessors did not represent as being very serious were as wrong as in my soul I felt them to be. One of these confessors, when I went to him with a scruple, told me that, even if I were experiencing high contemplation, such intercourse and such occasions of sin were not doing me any harm. This was at the end of that period, when, by the grace of God, I was withdrawing farther and farther from grave perils, though I did not altogether flee from the occasions of them. When my confessors saw that I had good desires and was spending my time in prayer, they thought I was doing a great deal. But in my heart of hearts I knew that I was not doing what I was bound to do for Him to Whom I owed so much. I regret now all that my soul suffered and the scant help it had from anyone save God, and the numerous opportunities that were given it to indulge its pastimes and pleasures by those who said that these were lawful.

Sermons, again, caused me no small torture, for I was extremely fond of them, so that if I heard anyone preach a good, earnest sermon, I would conceive a special affection for him, without in any way trying to do so: I do not know to what this was due. A sermon rarely seemed to me so bad that I failed to listen to it with pleasure, even when others who heard it considered that the preaching was not good. If it were good, it was a very special refreshment to me. To speak of God, or to listen to others speaking of Him, hardly ever wearied me—this, of course, after I began to practise prayer. In one way I used to find great comfort in sermons; in another, they would torture me, because they would make me realize that I was not what I ought to be, or anything approaching it. I used to beseech the Lord to help me; but I now believe I must have failed to put my whole confidence in His Majesty and to have a complete distrust in myself. I sought for a remedy, and took great trouble to find one, but I could not have realized that all our efforts are unavailing useless we completely give up having confidence in ourselves and fix it all upon God. I wanted to live, for I knew quite well that I was not living at all but battling with a shadow of death; but there was no one to give me life and I was unable to take it for myself. He Who could have given it me was right not to help me, since He had so often brought me back to Himself and I had as often left Him.

CHAPTER IX

Describes the means by which the Lord began to awaken her soul and to give her light amid such great darkness, and to strengthen the virtues in her so that she should not offend Him.

By this time my soul was growing weary, and, though it desired to rest, the miserable habits which now enslaved it would not allow it to do so. It happened that, entering the oratory one day, I saw an image which had been procured for a certain festival that was observed in the house and had been taken there to be kept for that purpose. It represented Christ sorely wounded;[1] and so conducive was it to devotion that when I looked at it I was deeply moved to see Him thus, so well did it picture what He suffered for us. So great was my distress when I thought how ill I had repaid Him for those wounds that I felt as if my heart were breaking, and I threw myself down beside Him, shedding floods of tears and begging Him to give me strength once for all so that I might not offend Him.

I had a great devotion to the glorious Magdalen and often thought of her conversion, especially when I communicated, for, knowing that the Lord was certainly within me then, I would place myself at His feet, thinking that my tears would not be rejected. I did not know what I was saying; but in allowing me to shed those tears He was very gracious to me, since I so soon forgot my grief; and I used to commend myself to that glorious Saint so that she might obtain pardon for me.

But on this last occasion when I saw that image of which I am speaking, I think I must have made greater progress, because I had quite lost trust in myself and was placing all my confidence in God. I believe I told Him then that I would not rise from that spot until He had granted me what I was beseeching of Him. And I feel sure that this did me good, for from that time onward I began to improve. My method of prayer was this. As I could not reason with my mind, I would try to make pictures of Christ inwardly; and I used to think I felt better when I dwelt on those parts of His life when He was most often alone. It seemed to me that His being alone and afflicted, like a person in need, made it possible for me to approach Him. I had many simple thoughts of this kind. I was particularly attached to the prayer in the Garden, where I would go to keep Him company. I would think of the sweat and of the affliction He endured there. I wished I could have wiped that grievous sweat from His face,

---

[1] Tradition has it that this was an *Ecce Homo*, which is still venerated in the Convent of the Incarnation, though some writers have described it as a representation of Christ bound to the Column.

but I remember that I never dared to resolve to do so, for the gravity of my sins stood in the way. I used to remain with Him there for as long as my thoughts permitted it: I had many thoughts which tormented me.

For many years, on most nights before I fell asleep, when I would commend myself to God so as to sleep well, I used to think for a little of that scene—the prayer in the Garden—and this even before I was a nun, for I was told that many indulgences could be gained by so doing; and I feel sure that my soul gained a great deal in this way, because I began to practise prayer without knowing what it was, and the very habitualness of the custom prevented me from abandoning it, just as I never omitted making the sign of the Cross before going to sleep.

To return now to what I was saying about the torture caused me by my thoughts: this method of praying in which the mind makes no reflections means that the soul must either gain a great deal or lose itself—I mean by its attention going astray.[2] If it advances, it goes a long way, because it is moved by love. But those who arrive thus far will do so only at great cost to themselves, save when the Lord is pleased to call them very speedily to the Prayer of Quiet, as He has called a few people whom I know. It is a good thing for those who follow this method to have a book at hand, so that they may quickly recollect themselves. It used also to help me to look at a field, or water, or flowers. These reminded me of the Creator—I mean, they awakened me, helped me to recollect myself and thus served me as a book; they reminded me, too, of my ingratitude and sins. But when it came to heavenly things, or to any sublime subject, my mind was so stupid that I could never imagine them at all, until the Lord showed them to me in another way.

I had so little ability for picturing things in my mind that if I did not actually see a thing I could not use my imagination, as other people do, who can make pictures to themselves and so become recollected. Of Christ as Man I could only think: however much I read about His beauty and however often I looked at pictures of Him, I could never form any

[2] [The original has an untranslatable play upon words: *lit.*: "must be (*sic*) gained or lost a great deal—I mean (its) meditation (will be) lost."]

picture of Him myself. I was like a person who is blind, or in the dark: he may be talking to someone, and know that he is with him, because he is quite sure he is there—I mean, he understands and believes he is there—but he cannot see him. Thus it was with me when I thought of Our Lord. It was for this reason that I was so fond of pictures. Unhappy are those who through their own fault lose this blessing! It really looks as if they do not love the Lord, for if they loved Him they would delight in looking at pictures of Him, just as they take pleasure in seeing pictures of anyone else whom they love.

It was at this time that I was given the *Confessions of Saint Augustine*,[3] and I think the Lord must have ordained this, for I did not ask for the book nor had I ever seen it. I have a great affection for Saint Augustine, because the convent in which I had lived before becoming a nun belonged to his Order, and also because he had been a sinner. I used to find a great deal of comfort in reading about the lives of saints who had been sinners before the Lord brought them back to Himself. As He had forgiven them I thought that He might do the same for me. There was only one thing that troubled me, and this I have already mentioned: namely that, after the Lord had once called them, they did not fall again, whereas I had fallen so often that I was distressed by it. But when I thought of His love for me, I would take heart once more, for I never doubted His mercy, though I often doubted myself.

Oh, God help me! How amazed I am when I think how hard my heart was despite all the help I had received from Him! It really frightens me to remember how little I could do by myself and how I was so tied and bound that I could not resolve to give myself wholly to God. When I started to read the *Confessions*, I seemed to see myself in them and I began to commend myself often to that glorious Saint. When I got as far as his conversion and read how he heard that voice

[3] A Spanish translation of the *Confessions* was made by a Portuguese, P. Sebastián Toscano, and dedicated by him to Doña Leonor de Mascareñas, a great friend of St. Teresa (cf. *Foundations*, Chap. XVII: Vol. III, p. 81): the dedication is dated January 15, 1554. [If, as is likely, this was the edition given to the Saint, the incident supports a later date than 1554-5, which is the date commonly given, for her "second conversion".]

in the garden,[4] it seemed exactly as if the Lord were speaking in that way to me, or so my heart felt. I remained for a long time dissolved in tears, in great distress and affliction. Dear God, what a soul suffers and what torments it endures when it loses its freedom to be its own master! I am astonished now that I was able to live in such a state of torment. God be praised, Who gave me life to forsake such utter death!

I believe my soul gained great strength from the Divine Majesty: He must have heard my cries and had compassion on all my tears. I began to long to spend more time with Him, and to drive away occasions of sin, for, once they had gone, I would feel a new love for His Majesty. I knew that, so far as I could tell, I loved Him, but I did not know, as I should have done, what true love of God really means. I think I had not yet quite prepared myself to want to serve Him when His Majesty began to grant me favours again. It really seems that the Lord found a way to make me desire to receive what others strive to acquire with great labour—that is to say, during these latter years, He gave me consolations and favours. I never presumed to beg Him to give me either these things or tenderness in devotion: I only asked for grace not to offend Him and for the pardon of my grievous sins. Knowing how grievous they were, I never dared consciously to desire favours or consolations. His compassion, I think, worked in me abundantly, and in truth He showed me great mercy in allowing me to be with Him and bringing me into His presence, which I knew I should not have entered had He not so disposed it. Only once in my life—at a time when I was suffering from great aridity—do I remember having asked Him for consolations, and when I realized what I was doing I became so distressed that my very shame at finding myself so lacking in humility gave me what I had presumed to ask. I knew quite well that it was lawful to ask for it, but I thought it was only so for those who have done all in their power to obtain true devotion by not offending God and by being ready and determined to do all that is good. Those tears of mine, as they did not obtain for me what I desired, seemed to me effeminate and weak. But all the same I think they were of some benefit to me; for, as I say, especially after those two occasions when they caused me such compunction

4 [*Confessions*, Bk. VIII, Chap. XII.]

and such distress of heart, I began to devote myself more to prayer and to have less to do with things that were hurtful for me: these last I did not wholly abandon, but, as I say, God kept on helping me to turn from them. As His Majesty was only awaiting some preparedness on my part, His spiritual favours continually increased, in the way I shall describe. It is not usual for the Lord to give them save to those who have a greater purity of conscience.

CHAPTER X

Begins to describe the favours which the Lord granted her in prayer. Explains what part we ourselves can play here, and how important it is that we should understand the favours which the Lord is granting us. Asks those to whom she is sending this that the remainder of what she writes may be kept secret, since she has been commanded to describe in great detail the favours granted her by the Lord.

I used sometimes, as I have said, to experience in an elementary form, and very fleetingly, what I shall now describe. When picturing Christ in the way I have mentioned, and sometimes even when reading, I used unexpectedly to experience a consciousness of the presence of God, of such a kind that I could not possibly doubt that He was within me or that I was wholly engulfed in Him. This was in no sense a vision: I believe it is called mystical theology. The soul is suspended in such a way that it seems to be completely outside itself. The will loves; the memory, I think, is almost lost; while the understanding, I believe, though it is not lost, does not reason —I mean that it does not work, but is amazed at the extent of all it can understand; for God wills it to realize that it understands nothing of what His Majesty represents to it.

Previously to this, I had experienced a tenderness in devotion, some part of which, I think, can be obtained by one's own efforts. This is a favour neither wholly of sense nor wholly of spirit, but entirely the gift of God. It seems, however, that we can do a great deal towards the obtaining of it by reflecting on our lowliness and our ingratitude to God, on the great things that He has done for us, on His Passion, with its grievous pains, and on His life, which was so full of afflictions. We can also do much by rejoicing in the contemplation of His works, His greatness, His love for us, and a great deal more. Anyone really anxious to make progress often lights upon such things as these, though he may not be going about looking for them. If to this there be added a little love, the soul is comforted, the heart melts and tears begin to flow: sometimes we seem to produce these tears by force; at other times the Lord seems to be drawing them from us and we cannot resist Him. For the trifling pains we have taken His Majesty appears to be requiting us with the great gift of the comfort which comes to a soul from seeing that it is weeping for so great a Lord; and I do not wonder at this, for it has ample reason to be comforted. For here it finds encouragement, and here it finds joy.

The comparison which now suggests itself to me is, I think, a good one. These joys which come through prayer are something like what the joys of Heaven must be. As the souls in Heaven see no more than the Lord wills them to see, and as this is in proportion to their merits, and they realize how small their merits are, each of them is content with the place given to him, and yet there is the very greatest difference in Heaven between one kind of fruition and another—a difference much more marked than that between different kinds of spiritual joy on earth, though this is tremendous. When a soul is in its early stages of growth and God grants it this favour, it really thinks there is nothing more left for it to desire and counts itself well recompensed for all the service it has done Him. And it has ample reason for thinking so: a single one of these tears, which, as I say, we can cause to flow almost by ourselves (though nothing whatever can be done without God), cannot, I think, be purchased with all the labours in the world, so great is the gain which it brings us. And what greater gain is there than to have some evidence that we are pleasing God? Let anyone, then, who has arrived thus far give great praise to God and recognize how much he is in His debt. For it now seems that He wants him to be a member of His household and has chosen him for His kingdom, if he does not turn back.

Let him not trouble about certain kinds of humility, of which I propose to treat. We may think it humility not to realize that the Lord is bestowing gifts upon us. Let us understand very, very clearly, how this matter stands. God gives us these gifts for no merit of ours. Let us be grateful to His Majesty for them, for, unless we recognize that we are receiving them, we shall not be aroused to love Him. And it is a most certain thing that, if we remember all the time that we are poor, the richer we find ourselves, the greater will be the profit that comes to us and the more genuine our humility. Another mistake is for the soul to be afraid, thinking itself incapable of receiving great blessings, with the result that, when the Lord begins to grant them, it grows fearful, thinking that it is sinning through vainglory. Let us believe that, when the devil begins to tempt us about this, He Who gives us the blessings will also give us grace to realize that it is a temptation, and fortitude to resist it: I know God will do this if we walk before Him in simplicity, endeavouring to please Him alone and not men.

It is a very evident truth that we love a person most when we have a vivid remembrance of the kind actions he has done us. If, then, it is lawful, and indeed meritorious, for us to remember that it is from God that we have our being, and that He created us from nothing, and that He preserves us, and also to remember all the other benefits of His death and of the trials which He had suffered for all of us now living long before any of us was created, why should it not be lawful for me to understand, realize and consider again and again that, though once I was wont to speak of vanities, the Lord has now granted me the desire to speak only of Himself. Here is a jewel which, when we remember that it is given us, and that indeed we already possess it, invites and constrains us to love, and all this is the blessing that comes from prayer founded on humility. What, then, will it be when we find ourselves in possession of other and more precious jewels, which some servants of God have already received, such as contempt for the world and even for themselves? It is clear that such persons must think of themselves as still more in God's debt and under still greater obligations to serve Him. We must realize that nothing of all this comes from ourselves and acknowledge the bounteousness of the Lord, Who on a soul as poor and wretched and undeserving as mine—for whom the first of these jewels would have been enough, and more than enough—was pleased to bestow greater riches than I could desire.

We must seek new strength with which to serve Him, and endeavour not to be ungrateful, for that is the condition on which the Lord bestows His jewels. Unless we make good use of His treasures, and of the high estate to which He brings us, He will take these treasures back from us, and we shall be poorer than before, and His Majesty will give the jewels to some other person who can display them to advantage and to his own profit and that of others. For how can a man unaware that he is rich make good use of his riches and spend them liberally? It is impossible, I think, taking our nature into consideration, that anyone who fails to realize that he is favoured by God should have the courage necessary for doing great things. For we are so miserable and so much attracted by earthly things that only one who realizes that he holds some earnest of the joys of the next world will succeed in thoroughly abhorring and completely detaching himself from the things of this; for it is through these gifts that the Lord bestows upon us the fortitude of which our sins have deprived us. And a man is unlikely to desire the disapproval and abhorrence of all, or the other great virtues possessed by the perfect, unless he have some earnest of the love which God bears him and also a living faith. For our nature is so dead that we pursue what we see before us and so it is these very favours which awaken and strengthen faith. But it may well be that I am judging others by my wicked self, and that there may be some who need no more than the truths of the Faith to enable them to perform works of great perfection, whereas I, wretched woman, have need of everything.

Such as these must speak for themselves. I am describing my own experiences, as I have been commanded to do; if he to whom I send this does not approve of it, he will tear it up, and he will know what is wrong with it better than I. But I beseech him, for the love of the Lord, that what I have thus far said concerning my wicked life and sins be published. I give this permission, here and now, both to him and to all my confessors, of whom he who will receive this is one. If they like, they can publish it now, during my lifetime, so that I may no longer deceive the world and those who think there is some good in me. I am speaking the absolute and literal truth when I say that, as far as I understand myself at present, this will give me great comfort. But I do not make that permission applicable to what I shall say from now onwards; if this should be shown to anyone, I do not wish it to be stated to whom it refers, whose experience it recounts or who is its author; and for that reason I do not mention myself or anyone else by name. I shall write it all as well as I can, in order that my authorship may not be recognized. This I beg for the love of God. The authority of persons so learned and serious as my confessors suffices for the approval of any good thing that I may say, if the Lord gives me grace to say it, in which case it will not be mine but His; for I have no learning, nor have I led a good life, nor do I get my information from a learned man or from any other person whatsoever. Only those who have commanded me to write this[1] know that I am doing so, and at the moment they are not here. I am almost stealing the time for writing, and that with great difficulty, for it hinders me from spinning and I am living in a poor house and have numerous things to do. If the Lord had given me more ability, and a better memory, I might have profited by what I have heard or read, but I have little ability or memory of my own. If, then, I say any good thing, it will be because the Lord has been pleased, for some good purpose, that I should say it, while whatever is bad is my own work and Your Reverence will delete it. In neither case is there any advantage in giving my name. During my lifetime, of course, nothing good that I may have done ought to be talked about; and after my death there will be no point in mentioning me, for to do so would bring discredit on this good, to which no one would give credence if it were to be related of one so base and wicked as I.

And as I think that Your Reverence, and others who are to see this, will do what, for love of the Lord, I am asking you, I am writing quite freely. In any other case, I should have great scruples about writing at all, except to confess my sins, about doing which I have none. For the rest, the very thought that I am a woman is enough to make my wings droop—how much more, then, the thought that I am such a wicked one! So Your Reverence must take the responsibility

---

[1] These persons, according to a manuscript note by P. Gracián to be found in a copy of the first edition of St. Teresa's works, were "Master Fray Domingo Báñez and Fray García de Toledo".

for everything beyond the simple story of my life (since you have importuned me so earnestly to write some account of the favours which God grants me in prayer), if it be in accordance with the truths of our holy Catholic Faith; and if it be not, Your Reverence must burn it at once—I am quite willing for you to do that. I will describe my experiences, so that, if what I write is in accordance with these truths, it may be of some use to Your Reverence; if it be not, my soul will be disillusioned, and, if I am not gaining anything myself, as I trust I am, there will at least be no gain for the devil. The Lord well knows that, as I shall say later, I have always tried to seek out those who will enlighten me.

However clearly I may wish to describe these matters which concern prayer, they will be very obscure to anyone who has no experience of it. I shall describe certain hindrances, which, as I understand it, prevent people from making progress on this road, and also certain other sources of danger about which the Lord has taught me by experience. More recently I have discussed these things with men of great learning and persons who have led spiritual lives for many years; and they have seen that in the twenty-seven years during which I have been practising prayer, His Majesty has given me experiences, ill as I have walked and often as I have stumbled on this road, for which others need thirty-seven, or even forty-seven, in spite of having made steady progress and practised penitence and attained virtue. May His Majesty be blessed for everything, and may He, for His name's sake, make use of me. For my Lord well knows that I have no other desire than this, that He may be praised and magnified a little when it is seen that on so foul and malodorous a dunghill He has planted a garden of sweet flowers. May His Majesty grant that I may not root them up through my faults and become what I was before. This I beseech Your Reverence, for love of the Lord, to beg Him for me, for you know what I am more clearly than you have permitted me to say here.

CHAPTER XI

*Gives the reason why we do not learn to love God perfectly
in a short time. Begins, by means of a comparison, to
describe four degrees of prayer, concerning the first of
which something is here said. This is most profitable for
beginners and for those who are receiving no consolations
in prayer.*

I shall now speak of those who are beginning to be the servants of love—for this, I think, is what we become when we
resolve to follow in this way of prayer Him Who so greatly
loved us. So great a dignity is this that thinking of it alone
brings me a strange comfort, for servile fear vanishes at once
if while we are at this first stage we act as we should. O Lord
of my soul and my Good! Why, when a soul has resolved to
love Thee and by forsaking everything does all in its power
towards that end, so that it may the better employ itself in
the love of God, hast Thou been pleased that it should not at
once have the joy of ascending to the possession of this perfect love? But I am wrong: I should have made my complaint
by asking why we ourselves have no desire so to ascend, for it
is we alone who are at fault in not at once enjoying so great a
dignity. If we attain to the perfect possession of this true love
of God, it brings all blessings with it. But so niggardly and
so slow are we in giving ourselves wholly to God that we do
not prepare ourselves as we should to receive that precious
thing which it is His Majesty's will that we should enjoy only
at a great price.

I am quite clear that there is nothing on earth with which
so great a blessing can be purchased; but if we did what we
could to obtain it, if we cherished no attachment to earthly
things, and if all our cares and all our intercourse were centred in Heaven, I believe there is no doubt that this blessing
would be given us very speedily, provided we prepared ourselves for it thoroughly and quickly, as did some of the saints.
But we think we are giving God everything, whereas what we
are really offering Him is the revenue or the fruits of our land
while keeping the stock and the right of ownership of it in
our own hands. We have made a resolve to be poor, and that

is a resolution of great merit; but we often begin to plan and strive again so that we may have no lack, not only of necessaries, but even of superfluities; we try to make friends who will give us these, lest we should lack anything; and we take greater pains, and perhaps even run greater risks, than we did before, when we had possessions of our own. Presumably, again, when we became nuns, or previously, when we began to lead spiritual lives and to follow after perfection, we abandoned all thought of our own importance;[1] and yet hardly is our self-importance wounded[2] than we quite forget that we have surrendered it to God and we try to seize it again, and wrest it, as they say, out of His very hands, although we had apparently made Him Lord of our will. And the same thing happens with everything else.

A nice way of seeking the love of God is this! We expect great handfuls of it, as one might say, and yet we want to reserve our affections for ourselves! We make no effort to carry our desires into effect or to raise them far above the earth. It is hardly suitable that people who act in this way should have many spiritual consolations; the two things seem to me incompatible. So, being unable to make a full surrender of ourselves, we are never given a full supply of this treasure. May His Majesty be pleased to give it to us little by little, even though the receiving of it may cost us all the trials in the world.

The Lord shows exceeding great mercy to him whom He gives grace and courage to resolve to strive after this blessing with all his might. For God denies Himself to no one who perseveres but gradually increases the courage of such a one till he achieves victory. I say "courage" because of the numerous obstacles which the devil at first sets in his path to hinder him from ever setting out upon it, for the devil knows what harm will come to him thereby and that he will lose not only that one soul but many more. If by the help of God the beginner strives to reach the summit of perfection, I do not believe he will ever go to Heaven alone but will always take

[1] [*Honra.* Cf. p. 70, n. 3. This is an example of the use of the word to denote something reprehensible in nuns: elsewhere she adjures her sisters to think (in another sense) of their own *honra*, or reputation.]

[2] [*Lit.:* "hardly have they touched us in a point of honour." Cf. the use of "punto de honra" or "pundonor" in Spanish drama.]

many others with him: God treats him like a good captain, and gives him soldiers to go in his company. So many are the dangers and difficulties which the devil sets before him that if he is not to turn back he needs not merely a little courage but a very great deal, and much help from God.

To say something, then, of the early experiences of those who are determined to pursue this blessing and to succeed in this enterprise (I shall continue later with what I began to say about mystical theology, as I believe it is called): it is in these early stages that their labour is hardest, for it is they themselves who labour and the Lord Who gives the increase. In the other degrees of prayer the chief thing is fruition, although, whether at the beginning, in the middle or at the end of the road, all have their crosses, different as these may be. For those who follow Christ must take the way which He took, unless they want to be lost. Blessed are their labours, which even here, in this life, have such abundant recompense. I shall have to employ some kind of comparison, though, being a woman and writing simply what I am commanded, I should like to avoid doing so; but this spiritual language is so hard to use for such as, like myself, have no learning, that I shall have to seek some such means of conveying my ideas. It may be that my comparison will seldom do this successfully and Your Reverence will be amused to see how stupid I am. But it comes to my mind now that I have read or heard of this comparison: as I have a bad memory, I do not know where it occurred or what it illustrated, but it satisfies me at the moment as an illustration of my own.

The beginner must think of himself as of one setting out to make a garden in which the Lord is to take His delight, yet in soil most unfruitful and full of weeds. His Majesty uproots the weeds and will set good plants in their stead. Let us suppose that this is already done—that a soul has resolved to practise prayer and has already begun to do so. We have now, by God's help, like good gardeners, to make these plants grow, and to water them carefully, so that they may not perish, but may produce flowers which shall send forth great fragrance to give refreshment to this Lord of ours, so that He may often come into the garden to take His pleasure and have His delight among these virtues.

Let us now consider how this garden can be watered, so that we may know what we have to do, what labour it will cost us, if the gain will outweigh the labour and for how long this labour must be borne. It seems to me that the garden can be watered in four ways: by taking the water from a well, which costs us great labour; or by a water-wheel and buckets, when the water is drawn by a windlass (I have sometimes drawn it in this way: it is less laborious than the other and gives more water); or by a stream or a brook, which waters the ground much better, for it saturates it more thoroughly and there is less need to water it often, so that the gardener's labour is much less; or by heavy rain, when the Lord waters it with no labour of ours, a way incomparably better than any of those which have been described.

And now I come to my point, which is the application of these four methods of watering by which the garden is to be kept fertile, for if it has no water it will be ruined. It has seemed possible to me in this way to explain something about the four degrees of prayer to which the Lord, of His goodness, has occasionally brought my soul. May He also of His goodness grant me to speak in such a way as to be of some profit to one of the persons who commanded me to write this book,[3] whom in four months the Lord has brought to a point far beyond that which I have reached in seventeen years. He prepared himself better than I, and thus his garden, without labour on his part, is watered by all these four means, though he is still receiving the last watering only drop by drop; such progress is his garden making that soon, by the Lord's help, it will be submerged. It will be a pleasure to me for him to laugh at my explanation if he thinks it foolish.

Beginners in prayer, we may say, are those who draw up the water out of the well: this, as I have said, is a very laborious proceeding, for it will fatigue them to keep their senses recollected, which is a great labour because they have been accustomed to a life of distraction. Beginners must accustom themselves to pay no heed to what they see or hear, and they must practise doing this during hours of prayer; they must be alone and in their solitude think over their past life—all of us, indeed, whether beginners or proficients, must do this frequently. There are differences, however, in the degree to

[3] "P. Pedro Ibáñez", observes P. Gracián, in another manuscript note to the copy of the first edition of St. Teresa's works referred to above (p. 62).

which it must be done, as I shall show later. At first it causes distress, for beginners are not always sure that they have repented of their sins (though clearly they have, since they have so sincerely resolved to serve God). Then they have to endeavour to meditate upon the life of Christ and this fatigues their minds. Thus far we can make progress by ourselves—of course with the help of God, for without that, as is well known, we cannot think a single good thought. This is what is meant by beginning to draw up water from the well—and God grant there may be water in it! But that, at least, does not depend on us: our task is to draw it up and to do what we can to water the flowers. And God is so good that when, for reasons known to His Majesty, perhaps to our great advantage, He is pleased that the well should be dry, we, like good gardeners, do all that in us lies, and He keeps the flowers alive without water and makes the virtues grow. By water here I mean tears—or, if there be none of these, tenderness and an interior feeling of devotion.

What, then, will he do here who finds that for many days he experiences nothing but aridity, dislike, distaste and so little desire to go and draw water that he would give it up entirely if he did not remember that he is pleasing and serving the Lord of the garden; if he were not anxious that all his service should not be lost, to say nothing of the gain which he hopes for from the great labour of lowering the bucket so often into the well and drawing it up without water? It will often happen that, even for that purpose, he is unable to move his arms—unable, that is, to think a single good thought, for working with the understanding is of course the same as drawing water out of the well. What, then, as I say, will the gardener do here? He will be glad and take heart and consider it the greatest of favours to work in the garden of so great an Emperor; and, as he knows that he is pleasing Him by so working (and his purpose must be to please, not himself, but Him), let him render Him great praise for having placed such confidence in him, when He has seen that, without receiving any recompense, he is taking such great care of that which He had entrusted to him; let him help Him to bear the Cross and consider how He lived with it all His life long; let him not wish to have his kingdom on earth or ever cease from prayer; and so let him resolve, even if this aridity should persist his whole life long, never to let Christ fall beneath the

Cross. The time will come when he shall receive his whole reward at once. Let him have no fear that his labour will be lost. He is serving a good Master, Whose eyes are upon him. Let him pay no heed to evil thoughts, remembering how the devil put such thoughts into the mind of Saint Jerome in the desert.[4]

These trials bring their own reward. I endured them for many years; and, when I was able to draw but one drop of water from this blessed well, I used to think that God was granting me a favour. I know how grievous such trials are and I think they need more courage than do many others in the world. But it has become clear to me that, even in this life, God does not fail to recompense them highly; for it is quite certain that a single one of those hours in which the Lord has granted me to taste of Himself has seemed to me later a recompense for all the afflictions which I endured over a long period while keeping up the practice of prayer. I believe myself that often in the early stages, and again later, it is the Lord's will to give us these tortures, and many other temptations which present themselves, in order to test His lovers and discover if they can drink of the chalice and help Him to bear the Cross before He trusts them with His great treasures. I believe it is for our good that His Majesty is pleased to lead us in this way so that we may have a clear understanding of our worthlessness; for the favours which come later are of such great dignity that before He grants us them He wishes us to know by experience how miserable we are, lest what happened to Lucifer happen to us also.

What is there that Thou doest, my Lord, which is not for the greater good of the soul that Thou knowest to be already Thine and that places itself in Thy power, to follow Thee whithersoever Thou goest, even to the death of the Cross, and is determined to help Thee bear that Cross and not to leave Thee alone with it? If anyone finds himself thus determined, there is nothing for him to fear. No, spiritual people, there is no reason to be distressed. Once you have reached so high a state as this, in which you desire to be alone and to commune with God, and abandon the pastimes of the world, the chief

---

[4] The reference is to the twenty-second epistle of St. Jerome "Ad Eustochium", which describes how vividly there would come to him in the desert pictures of the pomps and vanities of pagan Rome.

part of your work is done. Praise His Majesty for this and trust in His goodness, which never yet failed His friends. Close the eyes of your thought and do not wonder: "Why is He giving devotion to that person of so few days' experience, and none to me after so many years?" Let us believe that it is all for our greater good; let His Majesty guide us whithersoever He wills; we are not our own, but His. It is an exceeding great favour that He shows us when it is His pleasure that we should wish to dig in His garden, and we are then near the Lord of the garden, Who is certainly with us. If it be His will that these plants and flowers should grow, some by means of the water drawn from this well and others without it, what matter is that to me? Do Thou, O Lord, what Thou wilt; let me not offend Thee and let not my virtues perish, if, of Thy goodness alone, Thou hast given me any. I desire to suffer, Lord, because Thou didst suffer. Let Thy will be in every way fulfilled in me, and may it never please Thy Majesty that a gift so precious as Thy love be given to people who serve Thee solely to obtain consolations.

It must be carefully noted—and I say this because I know it by experience—that the soul which begins to walk resolutely in this way of mental prayer and can persuade itself to set little store by consolations and tenderness in devotion, and neither to be elated when the Lord gives them nor disconsolate when He withholds them, has already travelled a great part of its journey. However often it may stumble, it need not fear a relapse, for its building has been begun on a firm foundation.[5] Yes, love for God does not consist in shedding tears, in enjoying those consolations and that tenderness which for the most part we desire and in which we find comfort, but in serving Him with righteousness, fortitude of soul and humility. The other seems to me to be receiving rather than giving anything.

As for poor women like myself, who are weak and lack fortitude, I think it fitting that we should be led by means of favours: this is the way in which God is leading me now, so that I may be able to suffer certain trials which it has pleased His Majesty to give me. But when I hear servants of God, men of weight, learning and intelligence, making such a fuss because God is not giving them devotion, it revolts me to

5 [The metaphors here follow the Spanish exactly.]

listen to them. I do not mean that, when God gives them such a thing, they ought not to accept it and set a great deal of store by it, because in that case His Majesty must know that it is good for them. But I do mean that if they do not receive it they should not be distressed: they should realize that, as His Majesty does not give it them, it is unnecessary; they should be masters of themselves and go on their way. Let them believe that they are making a mistake about this: I have proved it and seen that it is so. Let them believe that it is an imperfection in them if, instead of going on their way with freedom of spirit, they hang back through weakness and lack of enterprise.

I am not saying this so much for beginners (though I lay some stress upon it, even for these, because it is of great importance that they should start with this freedom and determination): I mean it rather for others. There must be many who have begun some time back and never manage to finish their course, and I believe it is largely because they do not embrace the Cross from the beginning that they are distressed and think that they are making no progress. When the understanding ceases to work, they cannot bear it, though perhaps even then the will is increasing in power, and putting on new strength,[6] without their knowing it. We must realize that the Lord pays no heed to these things: to us they may look like faults, but they are not so. His Majesty knows our wretchedness and the weakness of our nature better than we ourselves and He knows that all the time these souls are longing to think of Him and to love Him. It is this determination that He desires in us. The other afflictions which we bring upon ourselves serve only to disturb our souls, and the result of them is that, if we find ourselves unable to get profit out of a single hour, we are impeded from doing so for four. I have a great deal of experience of this and I know that what I say is true, for I have observed it carefully and have discussed it afterwards with spiritual persons. The thing frequently arises from physical indisposition, for we are such miserable creatures that this poor imprisoned soul shares in the miseries of the body, and variations of season and changes in the

---

[6] [*Lit.*: "is growing fat and taking strength." Fatness is often spoken of in Spain as synonymous with robustness and made a subject of congratulation.]

humours often prevent it from accomplishing its desires and make it suffer in all kinds of ways against its will. The more we try to force it at times like these, the worse it gets and the longer the trouble lasts. But let discretion be observed so that it may be ascertained if this is the true reason: the poor soul must not be stifled. Persons in this condition must realize that they are ill and make some alteration in their hours of prayer; very often it will be advisable to continue this change for some days.

They must endure this exile as well as they can, for a soul which loves God has often the exceeding ill fortune to realize that, living as it is in this state of misery, it cannot do what it desires because of its evil guest, the body. I said we must observe discretion, because sometimes the same effects will be produced by the devil; and so it is well that prayer should not always be given up when the mind is greatly distracted and disturbed, nor the soul tormented by being made to do what is not in its power. There are other things which can be done—exterior acts, such as reading or works of charity—though sometimes the soul will be unable to do even these. At such times the soul must render the body a service for the love of God, so that on many other occasions the body may render services to the soul. Engage in some spiritual recreation, such as conversation (so long as it is really spiritual), or a country walk, according as your confessor advises. In all these things it is important to have had experience, for from this we learn what is fitting for us; but let God be served in all things. Sweet is His yoke, and it is essential that we should not drag the soul along with us, so to say, but lead it gently, so that it may make the greater progress.

I repeat my advice, then (and it matters not how often I say this, for it is of great importance), that one must never be depressed or afflicted because of aridities or unrest or distraction of the mind. If a person would gain spiritual freedom and not be continually troubled, let him begin by not being afraid of the Cross and he will find that the Lord will help him to bear it; he will then advance happily and find profit in everything. It is now clear that, if no water is coming from the well, we ourselves can put none into it. But of course we must not be careless: water must always be drawn when there is any there, for at such a time God's will is that we should use it so that He may multiply our virtues.

CHAPTER XII

Continues to describe this first state. Tells how far, with the help of God, we can advance by ourselves and describes the harm that ensues when the spirit attempts to aspire to unusual and supernatural experiences before they are bestowed upon it by the Lord.

Although in the last chapter I digressed a good deal about other things, because they seemed to me very necessary, what I was trying to make clear was how much we can attain by our own power and how in this first stage of devotion we can do a certain amount for ourselves. For, if we examine and meditate upon the Lord's sufferings for us, we are moved to compassion, and this grief and the tears which proceed from it are very sweet. And then if we think about the glory we hope for, and the love which the Lord bore us, and His resurrection, we are moved to a rejoicing which is neither wholly spiritual nor wholly sensual, but is a virtuous joy; the grief also is of great merit. Of this nature are all the things which cause a devotion acquired in part by the understanding, though this can be neither merited nor attained unless it be given by God. It is best for a soul which has been raised no higher than this not to try to rise by its own efforts. Let this be noted carefully, for if the soul does try so to rise it will make no progress but only go backward.

In this state it can make many acts of resolution to do great things for God and it can awaken its own love. It can make other acts which will help the virtues to grow, as is explained in a book called *The Art of serving God*,[1] which is very good and suitable for persons in this state, because in it the understanding is active. The soul can picture itself in the presence of Christ, and accustom itself to become enkindled with great love for His sacred Humanity and to have Him ever with it and speak with Him, ask Him for the things it has need of, make complaints to Him of its trials, rejoice with Him in its joys and yet never allow its joys to make it forgetful of Him. It has no need to think out set prayers but

[1] By the Franciscan P. Alonso de Madrid: first published at Seville in 1521 and reprinted many times in the sixteenth century.

can use just such words as suit its desires and needs. This is an excellent way of making progress, and of making it very quickly; and if anyone strives always to have this precious companionship, makes good use of it and really learns to love this Lord to Whom we owe so much, such a one, I think, has achieved a definite gain.

For this reason, as I have said, we must not be troubled if we have no conscious devotion, but thank the Lord Who allows us to harbour a desire to please Him, although our deeds may be of little worth. This method of bringing Christ into our lives is helpful at all stages; it is a most certain means of making progress in the earliest stage, of quickly reaching the second degree of prayer, and, in the final stages, of keeping ourselves safe from the dangers into which the devil may lead us.

This, then, is what we can do. If anyone tries to pass beyond this stage and lift up his spirit so as to experience consolations which are not being given to him, I think he is losing both in the one respect and in the other. For these consolations are supernatural and, when the understanding ceases to act, the soul remains barren and suffers great aridity. And, as the foundation of the entire edifice is humility, the nearer we come to God, the greater must be the progress which we make in this virtue: otherwise, we lose everything. It seems to be a kind of pride that makes us wish to rise higher, for God is already doing more for us than we deserve by bringing us near to Him. It must not be supposed that I am referring here to the lifting up of the mind to a consideration of the high things of Heaven or of God, and of the wonders which are in Heaven, and of God's great wisdom. I never did this myself, for, as I have said, I had no ability for it, and I knew myself to be so wicked that even when it came to thinking of earthly things God granted me grace to understand this truth, that it was no small presumption in me to do so—how much more as to heavenly things! Other persons will profit in this way, especially if they are learned, for learning, I think, is a priceless help in this exercise, if humility goes with it. Only a few days ago I observed that this was so in certain learned men, who began but a short while since and have made very great progress; and this gives me great longings that many more learned men should become spiritual, as I shall say later.

When I say that people should not try to rise unless they are raised by God I am using the language of spirituality; anyone who has had any experience will understand me and if what I have already said cannot be understood I do not know how to explain it. In the mystical theology which I began to describe, the understanding loses its power of working, because God suspends it, as I shall explain further by and by if God grants me His help for that purpose. What I say we must not do is to presume or think that we can suspend it ourselves; nor must we allow it to cease working: if we do, we shall remain stupid and cold and shall achieve nothing whatsoever. When the Lord suspends the understanding and makes it cease from its activity, He gives it something which both amazes it and keeps it busy, so that, without reasoning in any way, it can understand more in a short space of time than we, with all our human efforts, in many years. To keep the faculties of the soul busy and to think that, at the same time, you can keep them quiet, is foolishness. And I say once more that, although the fact is not generally realized, there is no great humility in this: it may not be sinful, but it certainly causes distress, for it is lost labour, and the soul feels slightly frustrated, like a man who is just about to take a leap and then is pulled back, so that he seems to have put forth his strength and yet finds that he has not accomplished what he had expected to. Anyone who will consider the matter will detect, in the slightness of the gain achieved by the soul, this very slight lack of humility of which I have spoken. For that virtue has this excellent trait—that when an action is accompanied by it the soul is never left with any feeling of irritation. I think I have made this clear, though it may possibly be so only to me. May the Lord open the eyes of those who read this by granting them experience of it, and, however slight that experience may be, they will at once understand it.

I spent a good many years doing a great deal of reading and understanding nothing of what I read; for a long time, though God was teaching me, I could not utter a word to explain His teaching to others, and this was no light trial to me. When His Majesty so wills He can teach everything in a moment, in a way that amazes me. I can truthfully say this: though I used to talk with many spiritual persons, who would try to explain what the Lord was teaching me so that I might be able to speak about it, I was so stupid that I could not get the slightest profit from their instruction. Possibly, as His

Majesty has always been my teacher—may He be blessed for everything, for I am thoroughly ashamed at being able to say that this is the truth—, it may have been His will that I should be indebted to no one else for my knowledge. In any case, without my wishing it or asking for it (for I have never been curious about such things, as it would have been a virtue in me to be, but only about vanities), God suddenly gave me a completely clear understanding of the whole thing, so that I was able to speak about it in such a way that people were astounded. And I myself was more astounded even than my own confessors, for I was more conscious than they of my own stupidity. This happened only a short time ago. So I do not now attempt to learn what the Lord has not taught me, unless it be something affecting my conscience.

Once more I repeat my advice that it is very important that we should not try to lift up our spirits unless they are lifted up by the Lord: in the latter case we shall become aware of the fact instantly. It is specially harmful for women to make such attempts, because the devil can foster illusions in them, although I am convinced that the Lord never allows anyone to be harmed who strives to approach Him with humility: rather will he derive more profit and gain from the very experience through which the devil thought to send him to perdition. As this road is that most generally taken by beginners, and the counsels that I have given are of great importance, I have said a good deal about it. I confess that others have written about it much better elsewhere, and I have felt great confusion and shame in writing of it, though less than I should. May the Lord be blessed for it all, Whose will and pleasure it is that one such as I should speak of things that are His—things of such a nature as these and so sublime!

CHAPTER XIII

Continues to describe this first state and gives counsels for dealing with certain temptations which the devil is sometimes wont to prepare. This chapter is very profitable.

It has seemed to me appropriate to speak of certain temptations which, as I have observed, often attack beginners—I have had some of them myself—and to give counsels about matters which appear to me necessary. In the early stages, then, one should strive to feel happy and free. There are some people who think that devotion will slip away from them if they relax a little. It is well to have misgivings about oneself and not to allow self-confidence to lead one into occasions which habitually involve offences against God. This is most necessary until one becomes quite perfect in virtue; and there are not many who are so perfect as to be able to relax when occasions present themselves which tempt their own peculiar disposition. It is well that, all our lives long, we should recognize the worthlessness of our nature, if only for the sake of humility. Yet there are many circumstances in which, as I have said, it is permissible for us to take some recreation, in order that we may be the stronger when we return to prayer. In everything we need discretion.

We must have great confidence, for it is most important that we should not cramp our good desires, but should believe that, with God's help, if we make continual efforts to do so, we shall attain, though perhaps not at once, to that which many saints have reached through His favour. If they had never resolved to desire to attain this and to carry their desires continually into effect, they would never have risen to as high a state as they did. His Majesty desires and loves courageous souls if they have no confidence in themselves but walk in humility; and I have never seen any such person hanging back on this road, nor any soul that, under the guise of humility, acted like a coward, go as far in many years as the courageous soul can in few. I am astounded at how much can be done on this road if one has the courage to attempt great things; the soul may not have the strength to achieve these things at once but if it takes a flight it can make good progress, though, like a little unfledged bird, it is apt to grow tired and stop.

At one time I used often to bear in mind the words of Saint Paul, that everything is possible in God:[1] I realized quite well that in myself I could do nothing. This was a great help to me, as were also the words of Saint Augustine: "Give me, Lord, what Thou commandest me and command what

[1] [Presumably a reference to Philippians iv, 13, unless the author is attributing Our Lord's words in St. Matthew xix, 26 to St. Paul.]

Thou wilt."[2] I used often to reflect that Saint Peter had lost nothing by throwing himself into the sea, though after he had done so he was afraid.[3] These first resolutions are of great importance, although during this first stage we have to go slowly and to be guided by the discretion and opinion of our director; but we must see to it that he is not the kind of person to teach us to be like toads, satisfied if our souls show themselves fit only to catch lizards. We must always keep humility before us, so that we may realize that this strength cannot proceed from any strength of our own.

But it is necessary that we should realize what kind of humility this must be, for I believe the devil does a great deal of harm to those who practise prayer by encouraging misunderstandings about humility in them so as to prevent them from making much progress. He persuades us that it is pride which makes us have ambitious desires and want to imitate the saints and wish to be martyrs. Then he tells us, or induces us to believe, that we who are sinners may admire the deeds of the saints but must not copy them. I myself would agree with him to the extent that we must consider which of their deeds we are to admire and which to imitate. For it would not be a good thing for a person who was weak and ill to indulge in a great deal of fasting and in severe penances, or to go to a desert where he could not sleep or get anything to eat, or to attempt other things of that kind. But we must reflect that, with the help of God, we can strive to have a great contempt for the world, no regard for honour, and no attachment to possessions. For so ungenerous are we that we imagine the earth will go from under our feet if we try to forget the body a little and to cultivate the spirit. Or, again, we think that to have an abundance of all we need is a help to recollection because anxieties disturb prayer.

It distresses me to reflect that we have so little confidence in God, and so much love for ourselves, that anxieties like this upset us. When we have made so little spiritual progress, the smallest things will trouble us as much as important and weighty things will trouble others, and yet in our own minds we presume to think ourselves spiritual. Now to me it seems

[2] "Da quod jubes et jube quod vis" (*Confessions*, Bk. X, Chap. XXIX).

[3] St. Matthew xiv, 29.

that this kind of life is an attempt to reconcile body and soul, so that we may lose neither comfort in this world nor fruition of God in the world to come. We shall get along all right if we walk in righteousness and hold fast to virtue, but it will mean advancing at the pace of a hen and will never lead us to spiritual freedom. This is a procedure which seems to me quite good for people who are in the married state and have to live in accordance with their vocation; but in any other state I should not at all like to see such a method of progress nor will anyone persuade me to think it a good one. For I have tried it; and I should have been practising it still if the Lord in His goodness had not shown me another and a shorter road.

With regard to this matter of desires, my own were always ambitious, but I strove, as I have said, to practise prayer and yet to live according to my own pleasure. If there had been anyone to encourage me to soar higher, I think he might have brought me to a state in which these desires were carried into effect; but, for our sins, those who are not over-cautious in this respect are very few and far between, and that, I think, is sufficient reason why those who begin do not more quickly attain to great perfection. For the Lord never fails us and the fault is not His: it is we who are faulty and miserable.

We may also imitate the saints by striving after solitude and silence and many other virtues; such things will not kill these wretched bodies of ours, which want to have everything organized for their benefit in such a way as to disorganize the soul and which the devil does his best to incapacitate when he sees that we are getting fearful about them. That is quite enough for him: he tries at once to persuade us that all these habits of devotion will kill us, or ruin our health; he even makes us afraid that if we weep we shall go blind. I have experienced this, so I know it—and I also know that we can desire no better kind of sight or health than to lose both in so good a cause. As my own health is so bad, I was always impeded by my fears, and my devotion was of no value at all until I resolved not to worry any more about my body or my health; and now I trouble about them very little. For it pleased God to reveal to me this device of the devil; and so, whenever the devil suggested that I should ruin my health, I would reply: "Even if I die it is of little consequence." "Rest, indeed!" I would say. "I need no rest; what I need is crosses."

And so with other things. I saw clearly that in very many cases, although in fact I have very bad health, it was a temptation either of the devil or of my own weakness; and since I have been less self-regarding and indulgent my health has been very much better. It is of great importance, when we begin to practise prayer, not to let ourselves be frightened by our own thoughts. And you may take my word for this, for I have learned it by experience; this mere narration of my faults might be of use to others if they will take warning by me.

There is another temptation which is very common— namely to desire that everyone should be extremely spiritual when one is beginning to find what tranquillity, and what profit, spirituality brings. It is not wrong to desire this but it may not be right to try to bring it about unless we do so with such discretion and dissimulation that we give no impression of wanting to teach others. For if a person is to do any good in this respect he must be very strong in the virtues so as not to put temptation in others' way. This I found out for myself—and that is why I realize it. When, as I have said, I tried to get others to practise prayer, and when on the one hand they would hear me saying so much about the blessedness of prayer, while on the other they would observe that I, who practised it, was so poverty-stricken in virtue, it would lead them into temptations and various kinds of foolishness. And they had good reason on their side; for, as they have since told me, they could not see how one of these things could be compatible with the other. And so they came to believe that there was nothing wrong in what was intrinsically evil; for they saw that I sometimes did such things and at that time they had rather a good opinion of me.

This is the devil's doing. He seems to make use of the virtues which we have, and which are good, in order to give such authority as he can to the evil which he is trying to make us do: however trifling the evil may be, it must be of great value to him when it is done in a religious community—how much more, then, must he have gained from the evil which I did, for it was very great. So, over a period of many years, only three persons derived any profit from what I said to them;[4]

[4] According to P. Gracián, these persons were María de San Pablo, Ana de los Ángeles and Doña María de Cepeda. The same names

whereas, now that the Lord has made me stronger in virtue, many persons have derived such profit in the course of two or three years, as I shall afterwards relate. In addition, there is another great disadvantage in yielding to this temptation: namely, the harm caused to our own soul; for the utmost we have to do at first is to take care of our soul and to remember that in the entire world there is only God and the soul;[5] and this is a thing which it is very profitable to remember.

Another temptation comes from the distress caused by the sins and failings which we see in others, for we all have a zeal for virtue and so we must learn to understand ourselves and walk warily. The devil tells us that this distress arises solely from our desire that God should not be offended and from our concern for His honour and then we immediately try to set matters right. This makes us so excited that is prevents us from praying, and the greatest harm of all is that we think this to be a virtue, and a sign of perfection and of great zeal for God. I am not referring to the distress caused by public offences in a religious congregation, if they become habitual, or of wrongs done to the Church, such as heresies, through which, as we see, so many souls are lost; for distress caused by these is right, and, being right, causes us no excitement. Safety, then, for the soul that practises prayer will consist in its ceasing to be anxious about anything and anybody, and in its watching itself and pleasing God. This is most important. If I were to describe the mistakes I have seen people make because they trusted in their good intentions——!

Let us strive, then, always to look at the virtues and the good qualities which we find in others, and to keep our own grievous sins before our eyes so that we may be blind to their defects. This is a course of action which, though we may not become perfect in it all at once, will help us to acquire one

_____

are given by P. Gracián's sister, M. María de San José. (B.Nac., MS. 12,936.) [Lewis, however (p. 98, n. 6), aptly remarks that, as shown in Chap. VII (p. 101), one of the three must have been St. Teresa's father.]

[5] [While there are too many similarities between the writings of St. Teresa and St. John of the Cross for more than a very small proportion of them to be referred to, I cannot forbear quoting here the latter's well-known maxim: "Live in this world as though there were in it but God and thy soul, so that thy heart may be detained by naught that is human" (_St. John of the Cross_, III, 256).]

great virtue—namely, to consider all others better than ourselves. In this way we shall begin to profit, by God's help (which is always necessary, and, when it fails, our own efforts are useless), and we must beg Him to give us this virtue, which, if we exert our own efforts, He will deny to none. This counsel must also be remembered by those who use their intellects a great deal and from one subject can extract many ideas and conceptions. To those who cannot do this—and I used to be one—there is no need to offer any counsel, save that they must have patience until the Lord gives them occupation and enlightenment, for of themselves they can do so little that their intellect hinders rather than helps them.

Returning, then, to those who can make use of their reasoning powers, I advise them not to spend all their time in doing so; their method of prayer is most meritorious, but, enjoying it as they do, they fail to realize that they ought to have a kind of Sunday—that is to say, a period of rest from their labour. To stop working, they think, would be a loss of time, whereas my view is that this loss is a great gain; let them imagine themselves, as I have suggested, in the presence of Christ, and let them remain in converse with Him, and delighting in Him, without wearying their minds or fatiguing themselves by composing speeches to Him, but laying their needs before Him and acknowledging how right He is not to allow us to be in His presence. There is a time for one thing and a time for another; were there not, the soul would grow tired of always eating the same food. These foods are very pleasant and wholesome; and, if the palate is accustomed to their taste, they provide great sustenance for the life of the soul, and bring it many other benefits.

I will explain myself further, for these matters concerning prayer are difficult, and, if no director is available, very hard to understand. It is for this reason that, though I should like to write more briefly, and though merely to touch upon these matters concerning prayer would suffice for the keen intellect of him who commanded me to write of them, my own stupidity prevents me from describing and explaining in a few words a matter which it is so important to expound thoroughly. Having gone through so much myself, I am sorry for those who begin with books alone, for it is extraordinary what a difference there is between understanding a thing and knowing it by experience. Returning, then, to what I was saying, we begin to meditate upon a scene of the Passion—let us say upon the binding of the Lord to the Column. The mind sets to work to seek out the reasons which are to be found for the great afflictions and distress which His Majesty must have suffered when He was alone there. It also meditates on the many other lessons which, if it is industrious, or well stored with learning, this mystery can teach it. This method should be the beginning, the middle and the end of prayer for all of us: it is a most excellent and safe road until the Lord leads us to other methods, which are supernatural.

I say "for all of us," but there will be many souls who derive greater benefits from other meditations than from that of the Sacred Passion. For, just as there are many mansions in Heaven, so there are many roads to them. Some people derive benefit from imagining themselves in hell; others, whom it distresses to think of hell, from imagining themselves in Heaven. Others meditate upon death. Some, who are tenderhearted, get exhausted if they keep thinking about the Passion, but they derive great comfort and benefit from considering the power and greatness of God in the creatures, and the love that He showed us, which is pictured in all things. This is an admirable procedure, provided one does not fail to meditate often upon the Passion and the life of Christ, which are, and have always been, the source of everything that is good.

The beginner needs counsel to help him ascertain what benefits him most. To this end a director is very necessary; but he must be a man of experience, or he will make a great many mistakes and lead souls along without understanding them or without allowing them to learn to understand themselves; for the soul, knowing that it is a great merit to be subject to its director, dares not do other than what he commands it. I have come across souls so constrained and afflicted because of the inexperience of their director that I have been really sorry for them. And I have found some who had no idea how to act for themselves; for directors who cannot understand spirituality afflict their penitents both in soul and in body and prevent them from making progress. One person who spoke to me about this had been kept in bondage by her director for eight years; he would not allow her to aim at anything but self-knowledge, yet the Lord was already granting her the Prayer of Quiet, so she was suffering great trials.

At the same time, this matter of self-knowledge must never be neglected. No soul on this road is such a giant that it does not often need to become a child at the breast again. (This must never be forgotten: I may repeat it again and again, for it is of great importance.) For there is no state of prayer, however sublime, in which it is not necessary often to go back to the beginning. And self-knowledge with regard to sin is the bread which must be eaten with food of every kind, however dainty it may be, on this road of prayer: without this bread we could not eat our food at all. But bread must be taken in moderate proportions. When a soul finds itself exhausted and realizes clearly that it has no goodness of its own, when it feels ashamed in the presence of so great a King and sees how little it is paying of all that it owes Him, what need is there for it to waste its time on learning to know itself? It will be wiser to go on to other matters which the Lord sets before it, and we are not doing right if we neglect such things, for His Majesty knows better than we what kind of food is good for us.

It is of great importance, then, that the director should be a prudent man—of sound understanding, I mean—and also an experienced one: if he is a learned man as well, that is a very great advantage. But if all these three qualities cannot be found in the same man, the first two are the more important, for it is always possible to find learned men to consult when necessary. I mean that learning is of little benefit to beginners, except in men of prayer. I do not mean that beginners should have no communication with learned men, for I should prefer spirituality to be unaccompanied by prayer than not to be founded upon the truth. Learning is a great thing, for it teaches those of us who have little knowledge, and gives us light, so that, when we are faced with the truth of Holy Scripture, we act as we should. From foolish devotions may God deliver us!

I want to explain myself further, for I seem to be getting involved in a great many subjects. I have always had this failing—that I cannot explain myself, as I have said, except at the cost of many words. A nun begins to practise prayer: if her director is a simpleton and gets the idea into his head, he will give her to understand that it is better for her to obey him than her superior, and he will do this without any evil intention, thinking he is right. Indeed, if he is not a religious, it will probably seem right to him. If he is dealing with a married woman, he will tell her it is better for her to be engaged in prayer when she has work to do in her home, although this may displease her husband: he cannot advise her about arranging her time and work so that everything is done as true Christianity demands. Not being enlightened himself, he cannot enlighten others, even if he tries. And although learning may not seem necessary for this, my opinion has always been, and always will be, that every Christian should try to consult some learned person, if he can, and the more learned this person, the better. Those who walk in the way of prayer have the greater need of learning; and the more spiritual they are, the greater is their need.

Let us not make the mistake of saying that learned men who do not practise prayer are not suitable directors for those who do. I have consulted many such; and for some years past, feeling a greater need of them, I have sought them out more. I have always got on well with them; for, though some of them have no experience, they are not averse from spirituality, nor are they ignorant of its nature, for they study Holy Scripture, where the truth about it can always be found. I believe myself that, if a person who practises prayer consults learned men, the devil will not deceive him with illusions except by his own desire; for I think devils are very much afraid of learned men who are humble and virtuous, knowing that they will find them out and defeat them.

I have said this because some people think that learned men, if they are not spiritual, are unsuitable for those who practise prayer. I have already said that a spiritual director is necessary, but if he has no learning it is a great inconvenience. It will help us very much to consult learned men, provided they are virtuous; even if they are not spiritual they will do us good and God will show them what they should teach and may even make them spiritual so that they may be of service to us. I do not say this without proof and I have had experience of quite a number.[6] Anyone, I repeat, who surrenders his soul to a single director, and is subject to him alone, will be making a great mistake, if he is a religious, and has to be subject to his own superior, in not obtaining a director of this kind. For the director may be lacking in all the

---

[6] [*Lit.*: "of more than two"—but the expression is a figurative one.]

three things, and that will be no light cross for the penitent to bear without voluntarily submitting his understanding to one whose understanding is not good. For myself, I have never been able to bring myself to do this, nor do I think it right. If such a person be in the world, let him praise God that he is able to choose the director to whom he is to be subject and let him not give up such righteous freedom; let him rather remain without a director until he finds the right one, for the Lord will give him one if his life is founded upon humility and he has the desire to succeed. I praise God greatly, and we women, and those who are not learned, ought always to give Him infinite thanks, that there are persons who with such great labour have attained to the truth of which we ignorant people know nothing.

I am often amazed that learned men, and religious in particular, will give me the benefit of what they have gained with so much labour, and at no cost to myself save the labour of asking for it. And to think that there may be people who have no desire to reap such benefits! God forbid it be so! I see these learned fathers bearing the trials of the religious life, which are grievous ones—its penances, its poor food and its obligation to obey: really, I am sometimes downright ashamed to think of it. And then, the scant sleep they get: nothing but trials, nothing but crosses! I think it would be very wrong for anyone, through his own fault, to forfeit the benefits of such a life as that. It may be that some of us who are free from these trials—who are pampered, as they say— and live just as we like, think ourselves superior to those who undergo them, merely because we practise a little more prayer than they.

Blessed be Thou, Lord, Who has made me so incompetent and unprofitable! Most heartily do I praise Thee because Thou quickenest so many to quicken us! We should pray most regularly for those who give us light. What would become of us without them amid these great storms which the Church now has to bear? If some of them have been wicked, the good will shine the more. May it please the Lord to keep them in His hand and help them to help us. Amen.

I have wandered far from the aim with which I began, but for those who are beginners it is all to the point, and it will help them, as they set out upon so high a journey, to keep their feet planted upon the true road. Returning to what I was saying—the meditation upon Christ bound to the Column—it is well to reflect for a time and to think of the pains which He bore there, why He bore them, Who He is that bore them and with what love He suffered them. But we must not always tire ourselves by going in search of such ideas; we must sometimes remain by His side with our minds hushed in silence. If we can, we should occupy ourselves in looking upon Him Who is looking at us; keep Him company; talk with Him; pray to Him; humble ourselves before Him; have our delight in Him; and remember that He never deserved to be there. Anyone who can do this, though he may be but a beginner in prayer, will derive great benefit from it, for this kind of prayer brings many benefits: at least, so my soul has found. I do not know whether I have succeeded in what I have tried to say; but Your Reverence will know. May the Lord grant me always to succeed in pleasing Him. Amen.

CHAPTER XIV

Begins to describe the second degree of prayer, in which the Lord grants the soul experience of more special consolations. This description is made in order to explain the supernatural character of these consolations. It should be most carefully noted.

Having now spoken of the labour and manual effort with which this garden is watered when one draws water from the well, let us now speak of the second way of drawing it which is ordained by the Lord of the garden. By using a device of windlass and buckets the gardener draws more water with less labour and is able to take some rest instead of being continually at work. It is this method, applied to the prayer called the Prayer of Quiet, that I now wish to describe.

This state, in which the soul begins to recollect itself, borders on the supernatural, to which is could in no way attain by its own exertions. True, it sometimes seems to have been wearied by its work at the windlass—its labouring with the understanding and its filling of the buckets; but in this state the water is higher and thus much less labour is required than for the drawing of it from the well. I mean that the water is nearer to it, for grace reveals itself to the soul more clearly. This state is a recollecting of the faculties within the soul, so that its fruition of that contentment may be of greater delight. But the faculties are not lost, nor do they sleep. The will alone is occupied, in such a way that, without knowing how, it becomes captive. It allows itself to be imprisoned by God, as one who well knows itself to be the captive of Him Whom it loves. Oh, my Jesus and Lord, how much Thy love now means to us! It binds our own love so straitly that at that moment it leaves us no freedom to love anything but Thee.

The other two faculties help the will so that it may become more and more capable of enjoying so great a blessing, though sometimes it comes about that, even when the will is in union, they hinder it exceedingly. When that happens it should take no notice of them but remain in its fruition and quiet; for, if it tries to recollect them, both it and they will suffer. At such a time they are like doves which are not pleased with the food given them by the owner of the dovecot, without their having worked for it, and go in search of food elsewhere, but are so unsuccessful that they return. Just so these faculties come and go, to see if the will will give them some part of what it is enjoying. If this be the Lord's pleasure, it throws them food and they stop; if not, they return to their search. They must reflect that they are benefiting the will; or sometimes the memory or the imagination may do it harm by trying to present it with a picture of what it is enjoying. The will, then, must be careful in its dealings with them, as I shall explain.

Everything that now takes place brings the greatest consolation, and so little labour is involved that, even if prayer continues for a long time, it never becomes wearisome. For the understanding is now working very gradually and is drawing very much more water than it drew from the well. The tears which God bestows here flow joyfully; though the soul is conscious of them, it does nothing to induce them.

This water of great blessings and favours which the Lord gives in this state makes the virtues grow much more, beyond all comparison, than in the previous one; for the soul is already rising from its miserable condition and gaining some slight foreknowledge of the joys of glory. This, I believe, makes the virtues grow and also brings them nearer to that true Virtue from Whom all virtues spring—namely, God. For

His Majesty begins to communicate Himself to this soul and wishes it to be conscious of the method of His communication. As soon as it arrives at this state, it begins to lose its covetousness for the things of earth. And small merit to it, for it sees clearly that on earth it cannot have a moment of this joy; that there are no riches, or dominions, or honours, or delights which suffice to give it such satisfaction even for the twinkling of an eye; for this is true joy, and the soul realizes that it is this which gives genuine satisfaction. Those of us who are on earth, it seems to me, rarely understand where this satisfaction lies. It comes and goes. First it is with us; then it leaves us, and we find that it is all gone, and we cannot get it back again, having no idea how to do so. For even if we wear ourselves to pieces with penances and prayers and all kinds of other things, we can acquire but little if the Lord is not pleased to bestow it. God, of His greatness, desires the soul to realize that His Majesty is so near it that it need not send Him messengers,[1] but may speak with Him itself; nor need it cry aloud, because He is so near it that it has only to move its lips and He will understand it.

It seems beside the point to say this, as we know that God always understands us and is always with us. There is no possible doubt that this is so; but this Emperor and Lord of ours desires us now to realize that He understands us, and what is accomplished by His presence, and that He is about to begin a special work in the soul through the great satisfaction, both inward and outward, that He gives it, and through the difference which there is, as I have said, between this particular delight and contentment and others which we experience on earth, for He seems to be filling the void in our souls that we have caused by our sins. This satisfaction resides in the most intimate part of the soul, and the soul cannot tell whence or how it has come to it; often it knows neither what to do, nor to wish, nor to ask. It seems to find everything at once, yet not to know what it has found: I do not myself know how to explain this. For many purposes it is necessary to be learned; and it would be very useful to have some learning here, in order to explain what is meant by general or particular help (for there are many who do not know this) and how it is now the Lord's will that the soul

[1] [Cf. St. John of the Cross: *Spiritual Canticle*, Stanza VI.]

should see this particular help (as they say) with its own eyes; and learning would also serve to explain many other things about which mistakes may be made. However, as what I write is to be seen by persons who will know if I am wrong, I am going on without worrying about it. I know I have no need to worry from the point of view either of learning or of spirituality, as this is going into the possession of those who will be able to judge it and will cut out anything which may be amiss.

I should like, then, to explain this, because it is a fundamental matter, and, when the Lord begins to grant these favours, the soul itself does not understand them, or know what it ought to do. If God leads it, as He led me, by the way of fear, and there is no one who understands it, its trial will be a heavy one; and it will be very glad to read a description of itself which will show clearly that it is travelling on the right road. And it will be a great blessing for it to know what it has to do in order to continue to make progress in any of these states: I myself, through not knowing what to do, have suffered much and lost a great deal of time. I am very sorry for souls who reach this state and find themselves alone; for, although I have read many spiritual books which touch upon the matter, they explain very little; and if the soul has not had a great deal of practice in prayer it will have as much as it can do to understand its own case, however much the books may explain.

I wish very much that the Lord would help me to set forth the effects which these things produce in the soul and which are already verging on the supernatural, so that it may be known by the effects which they produce whether or no they proceed from the Spirit of God. Known, I mean, to the extent to which it is possible to know things on earth: it is always well that we should act with fear and caution, for, even if these things come from God, the devil may sometimes be able to transform himself into an angel of light.[2] If the soul has not had a great deal of experience it will not realize this, and so much experience is necessary that, in order to understand it, one must have reached the very summit of prayer. The little time I have makes it none too easy for me to explain this, for which reason it is necessary that His Majesty

_____

[2] [2 Corinthians xi, 14.]

should make the matter clear, for I have my work to do in the community and many other occupations (being now in a recently founded house, as will be seen later[3]) and so I can never settle down to what I write but have to do a little at a time. I wish I had more time, for, when the Lord gives inspiration, one can write better and more easily. I seem to be like one working with a pattern before her and copying it with her needle: I can perform my task, but if inspiration is wanting I can no more put my words together properly than if I were writing gibberish, as one might say, however many years I may have spent in prayer. And so I think it is a very great advantage to be immersed in prayer when I am writing. I realize clearly that it is not I who am saying this; for I am not putting it together with my own understanding and afterwards I cannot tell how I have managed to say it at all. This often happens to me.

Let us now return to our garden, or orchard, and see how these trees begin to take new life before putting forth flowers and afterwards giving fruit, and the flowers—carnations and so forth[4]—begin to give out their fragrance. I am pleased with this comparison, for often, when I was a beginner (and may the Lord grant that I have in fact even now begun to serve His Majesty—but I mean a beginner by comparison with what I shall say about my life hereafter), it used to give me great delight to think of my soul as a garden and of the Lord as walking in it. I would beg Him to increase the fragrance of the little buds of virtue which seemed to be beginning to appear, and to keep them alive so that they might bloom to His glory—for I wanted nothing for myself—and I would ask Him to prune away any of them He wished to, for I knew that the plants would be all the better if He did. I speak of pruning, for there come times when the soul feels like anything but a garden: everything seems dry to it and no water comes to refresh it, and one would think there had never been any kind of virtue in it at all. The soul suffers many trials,

[3] I.e., St. Joseph's, Ávila.
[4] [Lit.: "the flowers and carnations." No doubt carnations, with their strong fragrance, were flowers which particularly appealed to St. Teresa: she often lays special stress on some such thing when it catches her imagination.]

for the Lord wants the poor gardener to think that all the trouble he has taken in watering the garden and keeping it alive is lost. Then is the proper time for weeding and rooting out the smaller plants, and this must be done, however small they may be, if they are useless; for we know that no efforts of ours are availing if God withholds from us the water of grace, and we must despise ourselves as nothing and as less than nothing. By doing this we can gain great humility and then the flowers will begin to grow afresh.

O my Lord and my Good! I cannot say this without tears and great delight of soul that Thou, Lord, shouldst wish to be with us, and art with us, in the Sacrament. We may believe that this is so, in very truth, for so it is, and with the utmost truth we may make this comparison; and if our faults do not impede us we may rejoice in Thee and Thou wilt take Thy delight in us, since Thou sayest that Thy delight is to be with the children of men.[5] O my Lord! What is this? Whenever I hear these words they are a great comfort to me, as they were even when I had gone far astray. Is it possible, Lord, that there can be a soul which reaches a state in which Thou dost grant it such graces and favours and can realize that Thou takest Thy delight in it, and yet offends Thee again after Thou hast shown it so many favours and such signal marks of love that it cannot doubt them since it sees Thy work so clearly? Yes, there is indeed such a soul—there is myself. And I have done this not once, but often. May it please Thy goodness, Lord, that I may be alone in my ingratitude, that I may be the only one to have committed so great a wrong and been so excessively ungrateful. Yet even from me some good has been brought forth by Thine infinite goodness, and, the greater have been my sins, the more has the great blessing of Thy mercies shone forth in me. How many reasons have I for singing of them for ever! I beseech Thee, my God, that it may be so: may I sing of them, and that without end, since Thou hast seen good to work such exceeding great mercies in me that they amaze those who behold them, while as for me, I am drawn out of myself by them continually, that I may be the better able to sing Thy praise. For, so long as I am in myself, my Lord, and without Thee, I can do

[5] Proverbs viii, 31.

nothing but be cut off[6] like the flowers in this garden, and this miserable earth will become a dunghill again as before. Permit it not, Lord. Let it not be Thy will that a soul which Thou hast purchased with so many trials should be lost, when Thou hast so often redeemed it anew and hast snatched it from the teeth of the horrible dragon.

Your Reverence must forgive me for wandering from my subject: as I am speaking with a purpose in my mind you must not be surprised. I am writing what comes to my soul; and at times when, as I write, the greatness of the debt I owe Him rises up before me, it is only by a supreme effort that I can refrain from going on to sing praises to God. And I think Your Reverence will not be displeased by it, because I believe we can both sing the same song, though in a different way; for my debt to God is much the greater, since He has forgiven me more, as Your Reverence knows.

CHAPTER XV

Continues speaking of the same subject and gives certain counsels as to how the soul must behave in this Prayer of Quiet. Tells how there are many souls who attain to this prayer and few who pass beyond it. The things touched herein are very necessary and profitable.

Let us now return to our subject. This quiet and recollectedness in the soul makes itself felt largely through the satisfaction and peace which it brings to it, together with a very great joy and repose of the faculties and a most sweet delight. As the soul has never gone beyond this stage, it thinks there is no more left for it to desire and, like Saint Peter, it wishes that it could make its abode here.[1] It dares not move or stir, for it thinks that if it does so this blessing may slip from its grasp: sometimes it would like to be unable even to breathe. The poor creature does not realize that, having been unable

---

[6] [The verb *cortar*, here translated "cut off", is rendered "prune", "prune away" on p. 152. The sense is different here but the author seems to have the earlier passage in mind.]

[1] St. Matthew xvii, 4.

to do anything of itself to acquire that blessing, it will be still less able to keep it longer than the time for which the Lord is pleased that it shall possess it. I have already said that, in this first state of recollection and quiet, the faculties of the soul do not fail; but the soul has such satisfaction in God that, although the other two faculties may be distracted, yet, since the will is in union with God for as long as the recollection lasts, its quiet and repose are not lost, but the will gradually brings the understanding and memory back to a state of recollection again. For, although the will is not yet completely absorbed, it is so well occupied, without knowing how, that, whatever the efforts made by the understanding and memory, they cannot deprive it of its contentment and rejoicing: indeed, without any labour on its part, it helps to prevent this little spark of love for God from being quenched.

May His Majesty give me grace to explain this clearly, for there are many, many souls that reach this state and few that pass beyond it, and I do not know who is to blame for this. Most certainly it is not God; for, since His Majesty grants us the favour of advancing to this point, I do not believe that, unless there are faults on our part, He will fail to grant us many more favours. It is very important that the soul which arrives thus far should recognize the great dignity of its state and the greatness of the favours which the Lord has granted it, and how there is good reason why is should not belong to the earth, since, unless its own faults impede it, His goodness seems to be making it a citizen of Heaven. Alas for such a soul if it turns back! If it does so, I think it will begin to go downhill, as I should have done had not the Lord's mercy saved me. For, as a rule, I believe, it can be due only to grave faults: it is impossible to forfeit so great a blessing save through gross blindness caused by much evil.

And so, for love of the Lord, I beg the souls whom His Majesty has granted so great a favour as to attain to this state to learn to know themselves, and to hold themselves, with a humble and a holy presumption, in high esteem, so that they shall not return to the flesh-pots of Egypt. And if, through their weakness and wickedness and their miserable and wretched nature, they fall, as I did, let them ever bear in mind what a blessing they have lost, and preserve their misgivings and walk fearfully, as they have good reason to do, for unless they return to prayer they will go from bad to worse. I should call anything a real fall which made us hate the road that had led us to so great a blessing. In talking to these souls I do not say that they will not offend God and fall into sin; anyone who has begun to receive these favours would be right in guarding himself carefully against falling; for we are miserable sinners. What I strongly advise them to do is not to give up prayer, for prayer will enlighten them as to what they are doing, and the Lord will grant them repentance and strength to rise again. They must believe, and keep on believing, that if they cease from prayer they are running (or so I think) into danger. I am not sure if I understand what I am saying, because, as I have said, I am judging from my own experience.

This prayer, then, is a little spark of true love for the Lord which He begins to enkindle in the soul, and His will is that it should come to understand the nature of this love with its attendant joy. This quiet and recollection—this little spark—if it proceeds from the Spirit of God and is not a pleasure bestowed on us by the devil or sought by ourselves, is not a thing that can be acquired, as anyone who has experience of it must perforce realize immediately; but this nature of ours is so eager for delectable experiences that it tries to get all it can. Soon, however, it becomes very cold; for, hard as we may try to make the fire burn in order to obtain this pleasure, we seem only to be throwing water on it to quench it. This little spark, then, planted within us by God, small though it is, makes a loud noise; and if we do not quench it through some fault of our own, it is this that begins to kindle the great fire which (as I shall say in due course) sends forth the flames of that most ardent love of God with which His Majesty endows the souls of the perfect.

This spark is given to the soul by God as a sign or pledge that He is already choosing it for great things if it will prepare itself to receive them. It is a great gift, much greater than I can say. I am very sorry for this, for, as I have said, I know many souls who attain thus far; and I know, too, that those who go farther, as they ought to do, are so few that I am ashamed to confess it. I do not mean that they are really few, for there must be a great many of them, since God does not uphold us without a purpose. I am merely telling what I have seen. I should like very much to advise such persons to be careful not to hide their talent, for it would seem that God is pleased to choose them to the advantage of many, especially in these times when He needs His friends to be strong so that they may uphold the weak. Let those who recognize that they themselves have this grace look upon themselves as His friends if they can fulfil the obligations which even the world demands of faithful friendship. Otherwise, as I have just said, let them fear and tremble lest they be doing some harm to themselves—and please God it be to themselves alone!

What the soul has to do at these seasons of quiet is merely to go softly and make no noise. By noise, I mean going about with the understanding in search of many words and reflections with which to give thanks for this benefit and piling up its sins and imperfections so as to make itself realize that it does not deserve it. It is now that all this movement takes place: the understanding brings forward its representations and the memory becomes active—and sometimes I myself find these faculties really wearisome, for, weak though my memory is, I cannot subdue it. The will must be calm and discreet and realize that we cannot treat effectively with God by the might of our own efforts and that these are like great logs of wood being heaped up indiscriminately so that they will quench this spark. Let it recognize this and with all humility say: "Lord, what can I do here? What has the servant to do with her Lord? What has earth to do with Heaven?" Or let it utter any words of love which come to its mind, with the firm and sure knowledge that what it is saying is the truth; and let it take no notice of the understanding, which is merely making itself a nuisance. And if the will wishes to communicate its joy to the understanding, or strives to lead it into recollection (as will often happen in this union of the will and state of tranquillity), and the understanding is very much disturbed, it will do better to leave it alone than to run after it. Let it (the will, I mean) continue in the fruition of that favour, and be as recollected as the wise little bee, for if no bees entered the hive and they all went about trying to bring each other in, there would not be much chance of their making any honey.

The soul will lose a great deal if it is not careful about this, especially if it has a lively understanding, with the result that, when it begins to hold discourse with itself and think out reflections, it will soon begin to fancy it is doing something worth while if its discourses and reflections are at all clever. All that the reason has to do in this state is to understand that there is no reason, save His goodness alone, why God should grant us so great a favour, and to realize that we are very near Him, and to beg favours of His Majesty, and to pray to Him for the Church and for those who have been commended to us and for the souls in purgatory—not, however, with any noise of words, though with a hearty desire that He may hear us. This is a prayer that comprises a great deal and achieves more than any amount of meditation on the part of the understanding. Let the will, in order to quicken its love, arouse within itself certain reasons which reason itself will picture to it when it sees itself in so much better a state. Let it make certain acts of love, too, concerning what it will do for Him to Whom it owes so much, without allowing the understanding to make any noise, as I have said, in its search for these clever reflections. A few little straws laid down with humility (and they will be less than straws if it is we who lay them down) are more to the point here, and of more use for kindling the fire, than any amount of wood—that is, of the most learned reasoning—which, in our opinion, will put it out in a moment. This will be good advice for the learned men who are commanding me to write, for, by the goodness of God, all of them will reach this state, and it may be they will spend their time in making applications of verses from Scripture; but, although they will have no difficulty in making good use of their learning both before and after prayer, they will have little need for it, in my view, during their actual periods of prayer, when it will only make their will lukewarm; for at those times the understanding, through being so near the light, sees with the greatest clearness, so that even I, though the sort of person I am, seem to be quite different.

Thus, when in this state of Quiet, I, who understand hardly anything that I recite in Latin, particularly in the Psalter, have not only been able to understand the text as though it were in Spanish but have even found to my delight that I can penetrate the meaning of the Spanish. Let us leave out of account occasions when these learned men have to preach or teach, for then it will be well for them to make use of their learning, so as to help poor ignorant creatures like myself, for charity is a great thing, and so is a constant care for souls, when undertaken simply and purely for the sake of

God. In these periods of Quiet, then, let the soul repose in its rest; let them put their learning aside; the time will come when they will use it in the Lord's service and will esteem it so much that they would not have failed to acquire it for all the treasures imaginable, simply because they can serve His Majesty with it and for this purpose find it a great help. But in the sight of Infinite Wisdom, believe me, there is more value in a little study of humility and in a single act of it than in all the knowledge in the world. So in this state there is no room for argument but only for a plain recognition of what we are, a presenting of ourselves in our simplicity before God, Whose will is that the soul should become a fool, as in truth it is in His sight, for it is due to His Majesty's great humility,[2] we being what we are, that He suffers it to be near Him.

The understanding is also active now and gives thanks in set terms; but the will, in its tranquillity, is like the publican and dares not lift up its eyes, yet perhaps makes a better thanksgiving than the understanding can even when it has exhausted all its rhetoric. In short, mental prayer must not be completely given up, nor yet must vocal prayer, if we ever wish to turn to it and are able to do so; for, if the state of Quiet is intense, it becomes difficult to speak except with great distress. In my own opinion, it is possible to tell if this state comes from the Spirit of God or if, starting from devotion given us by God, we have attained to it by our own efforts. In the latter case, as I have said, we try of our own accord to pass on to this quiet of the will, and nothing comes of it; everything is quickly over and we are left in a state of aridity. If it comes from the devil, I think a practised soul will realize this, for it leaves behind it disquiet and very little humility and does little to prepare the soul for the effects produced by such prayer when it comes from God. It leaves neither light in the understanding nor steadfastness in the will.[3]

---

[2] Without altering the word "humility", P. Báñez wrote underneath it, in the original manuscript, "humanity". This emendation [if it was meant for one] has been adopted by none of the editions.

[3] The original has "truth" (*verdad*), not "will" (*voluntad*). [P. Silverio, while agreeing that *voluntad* is more logical, respects the clear reading of the autograph and gives *verdad*; but the context, I think, makes it quite clear that "will" is meant, and the two words,

The devil, in such a case, can do little or no harm if the soul directs the delight and sweetness which it now feels towards God and fixes its thoughts and desires upon Him, as it has already been advised to do. He can gain nothing; in fact, by Divine permission, the very delight which he causes in the soul will contribute to his frustration. For this delight will help the soul: thinking it to be of God, it will often come to its prayer with a desire for Him; and if it is a humble soul, and not curious or eager for joys, even for spiritual joys, but attached to the Cross, it will pay little attention to pleasure given by the devil, but will be unable to disregard that which comes from the Spirit of God, for this it will hold in high esteem. When the devil, being altogether a liar, sends the soul any pleasure or delight, and sees that this is causing it to humble itself (and it should try to be humble in all that concerns prayer and consolations), he will often see how he has been frustrated and refrain from trying again. For this and for many reasons, in writing of the first kind of prayer, and of the first water, I pointed out that it is most important for souls, when they begin to practise prayer, to start by detaching themselves from every kind of pleasure, and to enter upon their prayer with one sole determination, to help Christ bear His Cross. Anxious, like good knights, to serve their King without pay, since they are quite sure of their final reward, they will keep their eyes fixed upon the true and everlasting kingdom to which we are striving to attain.

It is a very great thing always to bear this in mind, especially at first; later, we realize it so clearly that we need to forget it, so that we may live out our lives, rather than to try to recall to our memory how brief is the duration of everything, and how nothing is of any value, and how such earthly rest as we have must be reckoned as no rest at all. This seems to be a very low ideal, and so indeed it is, and those who have reached a more advanced state, and a greater degree of perfection, would consider it a reproach and be ashamed if they thought that the reason they were renouncing the good things of this world was because these must pass away: even were such things everlasting, they would rejoice to give them

in the Spanish, are sufficiently alike to be confused by a writer as often inaccurate as St. Teresa. Lewis, p. 122, n., cites three Spanish commentators who have adopted *voluntad*, though he himself translates "truth".]

up for God. The nearer are these souls to perfection, the greater would be their joy, and the greater, too, would it be if these earthly blessings lasted longer.

In souls like these love is already highly developed and it is love which works in them. But for beginners this other consideration is of the greatest importance, and they must not look upon it as a low ideal, for the blessing that it brings is a great one, and for this reason I strongly commend it to them: even those who have reached great heights of prayer will find it necessary, when from time to time God is pleased to prove them and His Majesty seems to have forsaken them. For, as I have already said—and I should not like this to be forgotten —in this life of ours the soul does not grow in the way the body does, though we speak as if it did, and growth does in fact occur. But whereas a child, after attaining to the full stature of a man, does not diminish in size so that his body becomes small again, in spiritual matters the Lord is pleased that such diminution should take place—at least, according to my own observation, for I have no other means of knowing. This must be in order to humble us for our greater good, and so that we may not grow careless while we are in this exile; for, the higher a person has climbed, the more fearful he should be and the less he should trust himself. There come times when those whose will is so completely subjected to the will of God that they would let themselves be tortured rather than be guilty of one imperfection and die a thousand deaths rather than commit sins, find it necessary, if they are to be free from offending God, when they see themselves assaulted by temptations and persecutions, to make use of the primary weapons—that is, of prayer—and thus to recall to themselves that everything comes to an end, that there is a heaven and a hell, and other truths of the same kind.

Returning now to what I was saying, the great foundation which we must lay, if we are to be delivered from the snares and pleasures sent by the devil, is the initial determination not to desire these pleasures, but to walk from the first in the way of the Cross. For the Lord Himself showed us this way of perfection when He said: "Take up thy cross and follow Me."[4] He is our Pattern; and those who follow His counsels with the sole aim of pleasing Him have nothing to fear.

[4] St. Matthew xvi, 24.

They will know, by the improvement which they discern in themselves, that this is not the work of the devil. For, even though they keep falling, there is one sign that the Lord has been with them—namely, the speed with which they rise again. There are also other signs, which I shall now describe. When the Spirit of God is at work, there is no need to go about looking for ways of inducing humility and confusion; for the Lord Himself reveals these to us in a very different manner from any which we can find by means of our puny reflections, which are nothing by comparison with a true humility proceeding from the light given us in this way by the Lord. This produces a confusion which quite overwhelms us. The bestowal upon us of this knowledge by God so that we may learn that we ourselves have nothing good is a well-known experience, and the greater are the favours we receive from Him, the better we learn it. He gives us a burning desire to make progress in prayer, and not to abandon it, however great the trials it may bring us. We offer ourselves wholly to Him and we experience a security combined with humility and fear with respect to our salvation. This casts out from the soul all servile fear and implants in it a very much maturer fear which springs from faith. We realize that there is beginning to develop within us a love of God entirely devoid of self-interest and we desire periods of solitude in order to have the greater fruition of that blessing.

Let me end, lest I should grow weary, by saying that this prayer is the beginning of all blessings: the flowers have now reached a point at which they are almost ready to bloom. The soul is very conscious of this and at such a time it could not possibly decide that God was not with it; only when it becomes conscious once more of its failings and imperfections does it grow fearful of everything, as it is well that it should. There are souls, nevertheless, whose confidence that God is with them brings them benefits which are greater than all the fears that can beset them. For, if a soul is by nature loving and grateful, the remembrance of the favour which God has granted it causes it to turn to God despite all the punishments of hell which it can imagine. This, at any rate, was what happened to me, wicked as I am.

As I shall go on later to speak of the signs of true spiri-

tuality—and it has cost me much labour to apprehend them
clearly—I am not going to speak of them here and now. I
believe that, by God's help, I shall be able to do so with some
degree of success; for, quite apart from the experiences which
have done me so much good, I have been taught by certain
very learned men and very holy persons to whom it is right
that credence should be given, so that souls which by the
Lord's goodness reach this point may not become as fatigued
as I did.

CHAPTER XVI

*Treats of the third degree of prayer and continues to expound
very lofty matters, describing what the soul that reaches
this state is able to do and the effects produced by these
great favours of the Lord. This chapter is well calculated
to uplift the spirit in praises to God and to provide great
consolation for those who reach this state.*

Let us now go on to speak of the third water with which this
garden is watered—that is, of running water proceeding from
a river or a spring. This irrigates the garden with much less
trouble, although a certain amount is caused by the directing
of it. But the Lord is now pleased to help the gardener, so
that He may almost be said to be the gardener Himself, for
it is He Who does everything. This state is a sleep of the
faculties, which are neither wholly lost nor yet can understand how they work. The pleasure and sweetness and delight
are incomparably greater than in the previous state, for the
water of grace rises to the very neck of the soul, so that it is
unable to go forward, and has no idea how to do so, yet neither
can it turn back: it would fain have the fruition of exceeding
great glory. It is like a person holding the candle in his
hand,[1] who is soon to die a death that he longs for; and in
that agony it is rejoicing with ineffable joy. This seems to me
to be nothing less than an all but complete death to everything in the world and a fruition of God. I know no other

[1] [I have translated literally, but the phrase, a common one in
Spanish, is equivalent to "at the point of death."]

terms in which to describe it or to explain it, nor does the
soul, at such a time, know what to do: it knows not whether
to speak or to be silent, whether to laugh or to weep. This
state is a glorious folly, a heavenly madness, in which true
wisdom is acquired, and a mode of fruition in which the soul
finds the greatest delight.

It is now, I believe, some five, or perhaps six, years since
the Lord granted me this prayer in abundance, and granted
it me many times, yet I never understood it or knew how to
describe it. My intention, therefore, when I reached this point,
was to say very little about it, or even nothing at all. I fully
realized that it was not a complete union of all the faculties
and yet it was very obviously something higher than the previous state of prayer; but I confess that I could neither decide
nor understand the nature of this difference. I believe it is
because of Your Reverence's humility in consenting to be
helped by simplicity as great as mine that to-day, after I had
communicated, the Lord granted me this prayer, without allowing me to go beyond it, and set these comparisons before
me, and taught me how to express all this and to describe
what the soul in this state must do. I was certainly astonished,
for in a moment I understood everything. I used often to
commit follies because of this love, and to be inebriated with
it, yet I had never been able to understand its nature. I
realized that it came from God but I could not understand
the method of His working; for the truth is that the faculties
are in almost complete union, though not so much absorbed
as not to act. I am extremely pleased at having understood
it at last. Blessed be the Lord, Who has given me this consolation!

The faculties retain only the power of occupying themselves
wholly with God; not one of them, it seems, ventures to stir,
nor can we cause any of them to move except by trying to
fix our attention very carefully on something else, and even
then I do not think we could entirely succeed in doing so.
Many words are spoken, during this state, in praise of God,
but, unless the Lord Himself puts order into them, they have
no orderly form. The understanding, at any rate, counts for
nothing here; the soul would like to shout praises aloud, for it
is in such a state that it cannot contain itself—a state of
delectable disquiet. Already the flowers are opening: see, they
are beginning to send out their fragrance. The soul would

like everyone to see her now, and become aware of her glory, to the praise of God, and help her to sing His praises. She seems to me like the woman spoken of in the Gospel, who wanted to call (or did call) her neighbours.[2] Such as these, I think, must have been the wondrous feelings of the royal prophet David, when he played on the harp and sang in praise of God. I am very much devoted to this glorious king and I wish all were, especially those of us who are sinners.[3]

O God, what must that soul be like when it is in this state! It would fain be all tongue, so that it might praise the Lord. It utters a thousand holy follies, striving ever to please Him Who thus possesses it. I know a person who, though no poet, composed some verses in a very short time, which were full of feeling and admirably descriptive of her pain[4]: they did not come from her understanding, but, in order the better to enjoy the bliss which came to her from such delectable pain, she complained of it to her God. She would have been glad if she could have been cut to pieces, body and soul, to show what joy this pain caused her. What torments could have been set before her at such a time which she would not have found it delectable to endure for her Lord's sake? She sees clearly that, when the martyrs suffered their torments, they did hardly anything of themselves, for the soul is well aware that fortitude comes from somewhere outside itself. But what will the soul experience when it regains its senses and goes back to live in the world and has to return to the world's preoccupations and formalities? I do not think what I say is in the least exaggerated; I have rather fallen short of the truth in describing this kind of rejoicing which the Lord desires a soul to experience while in this exile. Blessed be Thou, Lord, for ever; let all things for ever praise Thee. Be pleased now, my King, I beseech Thee, to ordain that since, as I write this, I am, by Thy goodness and mercy, not yet recovered from this holy heavenly madness—a favour which Thou grantest me through no merits of my own—either those with whom I shall have to do may also become mad through Thy love or I my-

[2] St.Luke xv, 9.

[3] The feast of King David is to be found in the Carmelite calendar revised by the Chapter-General in 1564.

[4] The "person", as so often in St. Teresa, was the author herself. [The description of the poem is too vague for it to be identified.]

self may have no part in anything to do with the world or may be taken from it. This servant of Thine, my God, can no longer endure such trials as come when she finds herself without Thee; for, if she is to live, she desires no repose in this life nor would she have Thee give her any. This soul would fain see itself free: eating is killing it; sleep brings it anguish. It finds itself in this life spending its time upon comforts, yet nothing can comfort it but Thee: it seems to be living against nature, for it no longer desires to live to itself, but only to Thee.

O my true Lord and Glory, what a cross—light and yet most heavy—hast Thou prepared for those who attain to this state! Light, because it is sweet; heavy, because there come times when there is no patience that can endure it: never would the soul desire to be free from it save to find itself with Thee. When it remembers that as yet it has rendered Thee no service and that by living[5] it can still serve Thee, it would gladly take up a much heavier cross and never die until the end of the world. It sets no store by its own repose if by forfeiting this it can do Thee a small service. It knows not what to desire, but it well knows that it desires nothing else but Thee.

O my son! (He to whom this is addressed and who commands me to write it is so humble that he desires to be addressed thus).[6] May Your Reverence alone see some of these things in which I am transgressing my proper limits! For there is no reason strong enough to keep me within the bounds of reason when the Lord takes me out of myself. And since I communicated this morning I cannot believe that it is I who am speaking at all: I seem to be dreaming what I see and I wish all the people I see were suffering from the same complaint that I have now. I beseech Your Reverence, let us all be mad, for the love of Him Who was called mad for our sakes. Your Reverence says that you are attached to me: I want you to show it by preparing yourself for God to grant you this favour, for I see very few people who are not too worldly-wise to do what is incumbent upon them. I may of course be more so than anybody else: Your Reverence must

[5] [*Lit.*: "by seeing" (*viendo*), which reading P. Silverio adopts; but I think we may assume this to be an error for "by living" (*viviendo*).]
[6] The reference is to P. Pedro Ibáñez. The parenthetical sentence [which I have bracketed in the text] is scored through in the autograph, by some hand other than the Saint's—probably by P. Báñez.

not allow me to be. You are my confessor, my father,[7] and it is to you that I have entrusted my soul: undeceive me, then, by telling me the truth, for such truths as these are very seldom told.

I wish we five,[8] who now love each other in Christ, could make an agreement together. Just as others in recent times have been meeting secretly to contrive evil deeds and heresies against His Majesty,[9] so we might try to meet sometimes to undeceive one another and to advise one another as to ways in which we might amend our lives and be more pleasing to God; for there is no one who knows himself as well as he is known by those who see him if they observe him lovingly and are anxious to help him. I say "secretly", because it is no longer the fashion to talk in this way: even preachers nowadays phrase their sermons so as not to give offence.[10] No doubt their intention is good, and the work they do is good too, but they lead few people to amend their lives. How is it that there are not many who are led by sermons to forsake open sin? Do you know what I think? That it is because preachers have too much worldly wisdom. They are not like the Apostles, flinging it all aside and catching fire with love for God; and so their flame gives little heat: I do not say that their flame is as great as the Apostles' was, but I could wish it were stronger than I see it is. Does Your Reverence know what our great care ought to be? To hold our life in abhorrence and to consider our reputation as quite unimportant. Provided we say what is true and maintain it to the glory of God, we ought to be indifferent whether we lose everything

[7] After this word come three or four others, which have been so effectively scored through that they are indecipherable. No doubt they were words eulogizing P. Ibáñez.

[8] Probably the other four were P. Daza, Don Francisco de Salcedo, Doña Guiomar de Ulloa and P. Ibáñez.

[9] The reference is to clandestine meetings held at Valladolid by a group of people suspected of heresy, under the leadership of Dr. Agustín Cazalla, a Canon of Salamanca and a Chaplain to the Emperor Charles V. These meetings came to an end in 1559, when an *auto* was held which involved persons of high rank and caused a great sensation in the country. The unorthodox propaganda of the Cazallist group spread as far as Ávila and St. Teresa had herself come into contact with it.

[10] P. Báñez wrote in the margin of the autograph here: "Legant prædicatores."

or gain everything. For he who in all things is truly bold in God's service will be as ready to do the one as the other. I do not say I am that kind of person, but I wish I were.

Oh, what great freedom we enjoy! It makes us look upon having to live and act according to the laws of the world as captivity! It is a freedom which we obtain from the Lord; and there is not a slave who would not risk everything in order to get his ransom and return to his native country. And as this is the true road, there is no reason for lingering on it, for we shall never gain complete possession of that great treasure until our life is over. May the Lord give us His help to this end. Your Reverence must tear up what I have written if it seems good to you to do so; in that case consider it as a letter addressed to yourself and forgive me for having been so bold.

CHAPTER XVII

Continues the same subject, the exposition of this third degree of prayer. Concludes her exposition of the effects produced by it. Describes the hindrances caused in this state by the imagination and the memory.

A reasonable amount has been said concerning this mode of prayer and of what the soul must now do—or, more correctly, of what God does within it, for it is He Who now undertakes the work of the gardener and is pleased that the soul should be idle. The will has only to consent to those favours which it is enjoying and to submit to all that true Wisdom may be pleased to accomplish in it. And for this it needs courage, that is certain; for the joy is so great that sometimes the soul seems to be one the point of leaving the body—and what a happy death that would be!

In this state I think it is well, as Your Reverence has been told, for the soul to abandon itself wholly into the arms of God. If He is pleased to take it to Heaven, let it go; if to hell, it is not distressed, so long as it is going there with its Good. If its life is to come to an end for ever, that is its desire; if it is to live a thousand years, that is its desire also. Let His Majesty treat it as His own: it no longer belongs to itself; it is given wholly to the Lord; it can cease to worry altogether.

When God grants the soul prayer as sublime as that which belongs to this state, He can do all this and much more, for that is the effect it produces. The soul realizes that He is doing this without any fatiguing of its understanding; only I think it is, as it were, astonished to see what a good gardener the Lord is making, and to find that He does not desire the soul to undertake any labour, but only to take its delight in the first fragrance of the flowers. In any one of these visits, brief as its duration may be, the Gardener, being, as He is, the Creator of the water, gives the soul water without limit; and what the poor soul could not acquire, even if it laboured and fatigued its understanding for as much as twenty years, this heavenly Gardener achieves in a moment; the fruit grows and ripens in such a way that, if the Lord wills, the soul can obtain sufficient nourishment from its own garden. But He allows it to share the fruit with others only when it has eaten so much of it that it is strong enough not to consume it all by merely nibbling at it,[1] and not to fail to get profit from it, nor to omit to recompense Him Who has bestowed it, but to maintain others and give them food at its own cost while itself perhaps dying of hunger. This will be understood perfectly by persons of intelligence and they will be able to apply it more effectively than I can describe it, for I am growing tired.

The virtues, then, are now stronger than they were previously, in the Prayer of Quiet, for the soul sees that it is other than it was, and does not realize how it is beginning to do great things with the fragrance that is being given forth by the flowers. It is the Lord's will that these shall open so that the soul may see that it possesses virtues, though it also knows very well that it could not itself acquire them, and has in fact been unable to do so even after many years, whereas in this

[1] [*Tan fuerte . . . que no se le vaya en gostaduras.* A difficult phrase, which used to be interpreted by assuming *gastadura,* a presumedly archaic substantive from *gastar* (spend, waste, fail to profit from), for *gostadura,* of which the modern form is *gustadura,* and which denotes the action of tasting. But I greatly prefer *gostadura,* and, though the figure could not be pressed to its logical conclusion, the translation I suggest seems wholly in accord with St. Teresa's realistic way of looking at things, whereas the *gastadura* reading ("strong enough not to fritter it all away", ". . . not to waste it all") is by comparison conventional.]

short space of time they have been given to it by the heavenly Gardener. The humility, too, which remains in the soul is much greater and deeper than it was previously, for it sees more clearly that it has done nothing at all of itself save to consent that the Lord shall grant it favours and to receive them with its will.

This kind of prayer, I think, is quite definitely a union of the entire soul with God, except that His Majesty appears to be willing to give the faculties leave to understand, and have fruition of, the great things that He is now doing. It happens at certain seasons, very often indeed (I say this now so that Your Reverence may know that it can happen and recognize it when it happens to you: I myself was quite distracted by it), that, when the will is in union, the soul realizes that the will is captive and rejoicing, and that it alone is experiencing great quiet, while, on the other hand, the understanding and the memory are so free that they can attend to business and do works of charity. This may seem to be just the same as the Prayer of Quiet of which I spoke, but it is really different—partly because in that prayer the soul would fain neither stir nor move and is rejoicing in that holy repose which belongs to Mary, while in this prayer it can also be a Martha. Thus the soul is, as it were, occupied in the active and in the contemplative life at one and the same time: it is doing works of charity and also the business pertaining to its mode of life, as well as busying itself with reading. Those in this state, however, are not wholly masters of themselves and they know very well that the better part of the soul is elsewhere. It is as if we were speaking to one person while someone else was speaking to us: we cannot be wholly absorbed in either the one conversation or the other.

This is a thing which can be very clearly apprehended, and which, when experienced, gives great satisfaction and pleasure; it is also a most effective preparation for attainment to a very restful state of quiet, since it gives the soul a period of solitude or freedom from its business. It works in this way. A person may have so far satisfied his appetite that he has no need to eat; he feels quite well fed and would not look at ordinary food; yet he is not so replete that, if he sees something nice, he will not be glad to eat some of it. Just so here: the soul in this state is not satisfied by the pleasures of the world and has no desire for them because it has within it that which satisfies it more: greater joys in God and desires to satisfy its desire, to have greater fruition and to be with Him—that is what the soul seeks.

There is another kind of union, which, though not complete union, is more nearly so than the one which I have just described, but not so much so as the one which has been referred to in speaking of this third water. Your Reverence will be very glad, if the Lord grants them all to you (assuming that you do not possess them already), to have a written description of them and thus to be able to understand their nature. For it is one favour that the Lord should grant this favour; but quite another to understand what favour and what grace it is; and still another to be able to describe and explain it. And although only the first of these favours seems necessary for the soul to be able to proceed without confusion and fear and to walk in the way of the Lord with the greater courage, trampling underfoot all the things of the world, it is a great benefit and favour to understand it, and it is right that everyone who can do so, as well as everyone who cannot, should praise the Lord because His Majesty has granted it to a few people who are alive so that we may reap advantage from it. Now frequently this kind of union which I wish to describe comes about as follows (and this is specially true of myself, for God very often grants me this favour in this way). God constrains the will, and also, I think, the understanding, as it does not reason but occupies itself in the fruition of God, like one who, as he looks, sees so much that he does not know where to look next: as he sees one thing he loses sight of another so that he can give no description of anything. The memory remains free—both it and the imagination must be so—and when they find themselves alone one would never believe what a turmoil they make and how they try to upset everything. Personally, I get fatigued by it and I hate it, and often I beseech the Lord, if He must upset me so much, to let me be free from it at times like these. "My God," I say to Him sometimes, "when shall my soul be wholly employed in Thy praise, instead of being torn to pieces in this way, and quite helpless?" This makes me realize what harm is done to us by sin, which has bound us in this way so that we cannot do as we would—namely, be always occupied in God.

As I say, it happens at times—to-day has been one of them, so I have it clearly in mind—that I find my soul is becoming unwrought, because it wants to be wholly where the greater part of it is, yet it knows this to be impossible. Memory and imagination make such turmoil within it that they leave it helpless; and the other faculties, not being free, are unable to do anything, even harm. They do the soul extreme harm, of course, by disturbing it; but, when I say "unable to do harm", I mean that they have no strength and cannot concentrate. The understanding gives the soul no help whatever by what it presents to the imagination; it rests nowhere, but goes from one thing to another, like nothing so much as those restless, importunate little moths that fly by night: just so the understanding flies from one extreme to another. This comparison, I think, is extremely apt; for though the understanding has not the strength to do any harm, it importunes those who observe it. I do not know what remedy there is for this, for so far God has not revealed one to me. If He had, I would very willingly make use of it, for, as I say, I am often tormented in this way. Here we have a picture of our own wretchedness and a very clear one of God's great power; the faculty which remains free causes us all this fatigue and harm, whereas the others, which are with His Majesty, bring us rest.

The remedy which I finally discovered, after having caused myself much fatigue for many years, is the one I spoke of when describing the Prayer of Quiet: the soul must take no more notice of the will than it would of a madman, but leave it to its work, for God alone can set it free. In this state, in short, it is a slave. We must bear patiently with it as Jacob bore with Lia, for the Lord is showing us an exceeding great mercy if He allows us to enjoy Rachel. I say that it is a slave because, after all, however much it may try, it cannot attract to itself the other faculties; on the contrary, they often compel it to come to them and it does so without the smallest effort. Sometimes, seeing it so confused and restless because of its desire to be with the other faculties, God is pleased to have pity on it, and His Majesty allows it to burn in the fire of that Divine candle, which has already deprived the others of their natural form and reduced them to ashes: so great are the blessings they are enjoying that they have become almost supernatural.

In all these types of prayer which I have described in speaking of this last-mentioned kind of water, which comes from a spring, the glory and the repose of the soul are so great that the body shares in the soul's joy and delight, and this to a most marked extent, and the virtues are very highly developed in it, as I have said. It seems that the Lord has been pleased to describe these states in which the soul finds itself, and to do so as clearly, I believe, as in this life is possible. Your Reverence should discuss the matter with some spiritual person, who has himself reached this state and is a man of learning. If he tells you that it is all right, you may take his assurance as coming from God and be grateful for it to His Majesty. For, in due time, as I have said, you will rejoice greatly at having understood the nature of this, until He gives you grace to understand it fully, just as He is giving you grace to enjoy it. As His Majesty has granted you the first grace, you, with all your intellect and learning, will come to understand it as well. May He be praised for all things, for ever and ever. Amen.

CHAPTER XVIII

Treats of the fourth degree of prayer. Begins to describe in an excellent way[1] the great dignity conferred by the Lord upon the soul in this state. This chapter is meant for the great encouragement of those who practise prayer to the end that they may strive to reach this lofty state, which it is possible to attain on earth, though not through our merits but by the Lord's goodness. Let it be read with attention, for its exposition is most subtle and it contains most noteworthy things.[2]

May the Lord teach me words in which to say something about the fourth water. His help is very necessary, even more so than it was for describing the last water, for in that state the soul still feels that it is not completely dead—and we may use this word in speaking of it, since it is dead to the world. As I said, it retains sufficient sense to realize that it is in the world and to be conscious of its loneliness, and it makes use of exterior things for the expression of its feelings, even if this

---

[1] These four words were crossed out in the manuscript by the author.

[2] This sentence was also crossed out by the author.

is only possible by signs. In the whole of the prayer already described, and in each of its stages, the gardener is responsible for part of the labour; although in these later stages the labour is accompanied by such bliss and consolation that the soul's desire would be never to abandon it: the labour is felt to be, not labour at all, but bliss. In this state of prayer to which we have now come, there is no feeling, but only rejoicing, unaccompanied by any understanding of the thing in which the soul is rejoicing. It realizes that it is rejoicing in some good thing, in which are comprised all good things at once, but it cannot comprehend this good thing. In this rejoicing all the senses are occupied, so that none of them is free or able to act in any way, either outwardly or inwardly. Previously, as I have said, they were permitted to give some indication of the great joy that they feel; but in this state the soul's rejoicing is beyond comparison greater, and yet can be much less effectively expressed, because there is no power left in the body, neither has the soul any power, to communicate its rejoicing. At such a time everything would be a great hindrance and torment to it and a disturbance of its rest; so I assert that, if there is union of all the faculties, the soul cannot communicate the fact, even if it so desires (when actually experiencing it, I mean): if it can communicate it, then it is not union.

The way in which this that we call union comes, and the nature of it, I do not know how to explain. It is described in mystical theology, but I am unable to use the proper terms, and I cannot understand what is meant by "mind" or how this differs from "soul" or "spirit". They all seem the same to me, though the soul sometimes issues from itself, like a fire that is burning and has become wholly flame, and sometimes this fire increases with great force. This flame rises very high above the fire, but that does not make it a different thing: it is the same flame which is in the fire. This, with all your learning, Your Reverences will understand: there is nothing more that I can say of it.

What I do seek to explain is the feelings of the soul when it is in this Divine union. It is quite clear what union is—two different things becoming one. O my Lord, how good Thou art! Blessed be Thou for ever! Let all things praise Thee, my God, Who hast so loved us that we can truly say that Thou hast communication with souls even in this exile: even if they are good, this is great bounty and magnanimity. In a word, my Lord, it is a bounty and a magnanimity which are all Thine own, for Thou givest according to Thine own nature. O infinite Bounty, how magnificent are Thy works! Even one whose understanding is not occupied with things of the earth is amazed at being unable to understand such truths. Dost Thou, then, grant these sovereign favours to souls who have so greatly offended Thee? Truly my own understanding is overwhelmed by this, and when I begin to think about it I can make no progress. What progress, indeed, is there to be made which is not a turning back? As for giving Thee thanks for such great favours, there is no way of doing it, though sometimes I find it a help to utter foolishness.

When I have just received these mercies, or when God is beginning to bestow them on me (for while actually receiving them, as I have said, a person has no power to do anything), I am often wont to exclaim: "Lord, consider what Thou art doing; forget not so quickly the gravity of my evil deeds. Though Thou must have forgotten them before Thou couldst forgive me, I beseech Thee to remember them in order that Thou mayest set a limit to Thy favours. O my Creator, pour not such precious liquor into so broken a vessel, for again and again Thou hast seen how I have allowed it to run away. Put not such a treasure in a place where the yearning for the comforts of this life has not yet disappeared as it should, or it will be completely wasted. How canst Thou entrust this fortified city and the keys of its citadel to so cowardly a defender, who at the enemy's first onslaught allows him to enter? Let not Thy love, eternal King, be so great as to imperil such precious jewels. For it seems, my Lord, that men have an excuse for despising them if Thou bestowest them upon a creature so wretched, so base, so weak, so miserable and so worthless, who, though she may strive not to lose them, by Thy help (of which I have no small need, being what I am), cannot make use of them to bring profit to any. I am, in short, a woman, and not even a good one, but wicked.

"When talents are placed in earth as vile as this they seem to be not only hidden but buried. It is not Thy wont, Lord, to do such great things for a soul and to bestow such favours upon it save that it may profit many others. Thou knowest, my God, that I beseech this of Thee with all my heart and will, and that I have oftentimes besought it of Thee, and that

I count it a blessing to lose the greatest blessing which may be possessed upon earth, if Thou wilt bestow thy favours upon one who will derive greater profit from this blessing, to the increase of Thy glory." It has come to pass many times that I have said these things and others like them. And afterwards I have become conscious of my foolishness and want of humility; for the Lord well knows what is fitting for me and that my soul would have no power to attain salvation did not His Majesty bestow it on me with these great favours.

I propose also to speak of the graces and effects which remain in the soul, and of what it can do by itself, if it can do anything, towards reaching a state of such sublimity.

This elevation of the spirit, or union, is wont to come with heavenly love; but, as I understand it, the union itself is a different thing from the elevation which takes place in this same union. Anyone who has not had experience of the latter will think it is not so; but my own view is that, even though they may both be the same, the Lord works differently in them, so that the soul's growth in detachment from creatures is much greater in the flight of the spirit. It has become quite clear to me that this is a special grace, though, as I say, both may be, or may appear to be, the same; a small fire is as much fire as is a large one and yet the difference between the two is evident. In a small fire, a long time elapses before a small piece of iron can become red-hot; but if the fire be a large one, the piece of iron, though it may also be larger, seems to lose all its properties very quickly. So it is, I think, with these two kinds of favour from the Lord. Anyone who has attained to raptures will, I know, understand it well. If he has not experienced it, it will seem ridiculous to him, as well it may be: for a person like myself to speak of such a thing and to make any attempt to explain a matter which cannot even begin to be described in words may very well be ridiculous.

But I believe that the Lord will help me in this, since His Majesty knows that, next to doing what I am bidden, my chief aim is to cause souls to covet so sublime a blessing. I shall say nothing of which I have not myself had abundant experience. The fact is, when I began to write about this fourth water, it seemed to me more impossible to say anything about it than to talk Greek—and indeed it is a most difficult matter. So I laid it aside and went to Communion.

Blessed be the Lord, Who thus helps the ignorant! O virtue of obedience, that canst do all things! God enlightened my understanding, sometimes giving me words and sometimes showing me how I was to use them, for, as in dealing with the last kind of prayer, His Majesty seems to be pleased to say what I have neither the power nor the learning to express. What I am saying is the whole truth; and thus, if I say anything good, the teaching comes from Him, while what is bad, of course, comes from that sea of evil—myself. And so I say, if there are any persons (and there must be many) who have attained to the experiences in prayer which the Lord has granted to this miserable woman, and who think that they have strayed from the path and wish to discuss these matters with me, the Lord will help His servant to present His truth.

Speaking now of this rain which comes from Heaven to fill and saturate the whole of this garden with an abundance of water, we can see how much rest the gardener would be able to have if the Lord never ceased to send it whenever it was necessary. And if there were no winter, but eternal warm weather, there would never be a dearth of flowers and fruit and we can imagine how delighted he would be. But during this life, that is impossible, and, when one kind of water fails, we must always be thinking about obtaining another. This rain from Heaven often comes when the gardener is least expecting it. Yet it is true that at first it almost always comes after long mental prayer: as one degree of prayer succeeds another, the Lord takes this little bird and puts it into the nest where it may repose. Having watched it flying for a long time, striving with mind and will and all its strength to seek and please God, it becomes His pleasure, while it is still in this life, to give it its reward. And what a great reward that is! For even a moment of it suffices to recompense the soul for all the trials that it can possibly have endured.

While seeking God in this way, the soul becomes conscious that it is fainting almost completely away, in a kind of swoon, with an exceeding great and sweet delight. It gradually ceases to breathe and all its bodily strength begins to fail it: it cannot even move its hands without great pain; its eyes involuntarily close, or, if they remain open, they can hardly see. If a person in this state attempts to read, he is unable to spell out a single letter: it is as much as he can do to recognize one. He sees that letters are there, but, as the understanding gives him no help, he cannot read them even if he so wishes. He can hear, but he cannot understand what he hears. He can apprehend nothing with the senses, which only hinder his soul's joy and thus harm rather than help him. It is futile for him to attempt to speak: his mind cannot manage to form a single word, nor, if it could, would he have the strength to pronounce it. For in this condition all outward strength vanishes, while the strength of the soul increases so that it may the better have fruition of its bliss. The outward joy experienced is great and most clearly recognized.

This prayer, for however long it may last, does no harm; at least, it has never done any to me, nor do I ever remember feeling any ill effects after the Lord has granted me this favour, however unwell I may have been: indeed, I am generally much the better for it. What harm can possibly be done by so great a blessing? The outward effects are so noteworthy that there can be no doubt some great thing has taken place: we experience a loss of strength but the experience is one of such delight that afterwards our strength grows greater.

It is true that at first this happens in such a short space of time—so, at least, it was with me—that because of its rapidity it can be detected neither by these outward signs nor by the failure of the senses. But the exceeding abundance of the favours granted to the soul clearly indicates how bright has been the sun that has shone upon it and has thus caused the soul to melt away. And let it be observed that, in my opinion, whatever may be the length of the period during which all the faculties of the soul are in this state of suspension, it is a very short one: if it were to last for half an hour, that would be a long time—I do not think it has ever lasted so long as that with me. As the soul is not conscious of it, its duration is really very difficult to estimate, so I will merely say that it is never very long before one of the faculties becomes active again. It is the will that maintains the contact with God[3] but

---

[3] [Lit.: "Maintains the web." This curious phrase will be familiar to readers of St. John of the Cross ("Break the web of this sweet encounter": Living Flame of Love, Stanza I): cf. St. John of the Cross, III, 34–40, where the phrase is commented upon by its author. Here I think the reference is not to the web, or thread, of human life, but to that of Communion with God. Changing the metaphor, one might render: "It is the will that is the soul's stanchion." In the text, however, I have used a phrase which better suits the context.]

the other two faculties soon begin to importune it once more. The will, however, is calm, so they become suspended once again; but eventually, after another short period of suspension, they come back to life.

With all this happening, the time spent in prayer may last, and does last, for some hours; for, once the two faculties have begun to grow inebriated with the taste of this Divine wine, they are very ready to lose themselves in order to gain the more, and so they keep company with the will and all three rejoice together. But this state in which they are completely lost, and have no power of imagining anything—for the imagination, I believe, is also completely lost—is, as I say, of brief duration, although the faculties do not recover to such an extent as not to be for some hours, as it were, in disorder, God, from time to time, gathering them once more to Himself.

Let us now come to the most intimate part of what the soul experiences in this condition. The persons who must speak of it are those who know it, for it cannot be understood, still less described. As I was about to write of this (I had just communicated and had been experiencing this very prayer of which I am writing), I was wondering what it is the soul does during that time, when the Lord said these words to me: "It dies to itself wholly,[4] daughter, in order that it may fix itself more and more upon Me; it is no longer itself that lives, but I. As it cannot comprehend what it understands, it is an understanding which understands not." One who has experienced this will understand something of it; it cannot be more clearly expressed, since all that comes to pass in this state is so obscure. I can only say that the soul feels close to God and that there abides within it such a certainty that it cannot possibly do other than believe. All the faculties now fail and are suspended in such a way that, as I have said, it is impossible to believe they are active. If the soul has been meditating upon any subject,[5] this vanishes from its memory as if it had never thought of it. If it has been reading, it is unable to concentrate upon what it was reading or to remember it; and the

---

[4] [The Spanish is *deshacerse*: this verb, often used by St. Teresa, is the contrary of *hacer*, to do, and can generally be rendered "be consumed", "be destroyed", "be annihilated".]

[5] [*Paso*: incident, occurrence—here, no doubt, referring to some scene in the Gospels.]

same is true if it has been praying. So it is that this importunate little butterfly—the memory—is now burning its wings and can no longer fly. The will must be fully occupied in loving, but it cannot understand how it loves; the understanding, if it understands, does not understand how it understands, or at least can comprehend nothing of what it understands. It does not seem to me to be understanding, because, as I say, it does not understand itself. Nor can I myself understand this.

There was one thing of which at first I was ignorant: I did not know that God was in all things, and, when He seemed to me to be so very present, I thought it impossible. I could not cease believing that He was there, for it seemed almost certain that I had been conscious of His very presence. Unlearned persons would tell me that He was there only by grace; but I could not believe that, for, as I say, He seemed to me to be really present; and so I continued to be greatly distressed. From this doubt I was freed by a very learned man of the Order of the glorious Saint Dominic[6]: he told me that He was indeed present and described how He communicated Himself to us, which brought me very great comfort. It is to be noted and understood that this water from Heaven, this greatest of the Lord's favours, leaves the greatest benefits in the soul, as I shall now explain.

CHAPTER XIX

Continues the same subject. Begins to describe the effects produced in the soul by this degree of prayer. Exhorts souls earnestly not to turn back, even if after receiving this favour they should fall, and not to give up prayer. Describes the harm that will ensue if they do not follow this counsel. This chapter is to be read very carefully and will be of great comfort to the weak and to sinners.

The soul that has experienced this prayer and this union is left with a very great tenderness, of such a kind that it would

6 Probably P. Báñez, though P. Gracián and María de San José say that P. Barrón is meant.

gladly become consumed,[1] not with pain but in tears of joy. It finds itself bathed in these tears without having been conscious of them or knowing when or how it shed them. But it derives great joy from seeing the vehemence of the fire assuaged by water which makes it burn the more. This sounds like nonsense but none the less it is what happens. Sometimes, when I have reached the end of this prayer, I have been so completely beside myself that I have not known whether it has been a dream or whether the bliss that I have been experiencing has really come to me; and I have only known that it has not been a dream through finding myself bathed in tears, which have been flowing without causing me any distress and with such vehemence and rapidity that it has been as if they had fallen from a cloud in Heaven. This would happen to me in the early stages, when the condition soon passed away.

The soul is left so full of courage that it would be greatly comforted if at that moment, for God's sake, it could be hacked to pieces. It is then that it makes heroic resolutions and promises, that its desires become full of vigour, that it begins to abhor the world and that it develops the clearest realization of its own vanity. The benefits that it receives are more numerous and sublime than any which proceed from the previous states of prayer; and its humility is also greater, for it clearly sees how by no efforts of its own it could either gain or keep so exceeding and so great a favour. It also sees clearly how extremely unworthy it is—for in a room bathed in sunlight not a cobweb can remain hidden. It sees its own wretchedness. So far is vainglory from it that it cannot believe it could ever be guilty of such a thing. For now it sees with its own eyes that of itself it can do little or nothing, and that it hardly even gave its consent to what has happened to it, but that, against its own will, the door seemed to be closed upon all the senses so that it might have the greater fruition of the Lord. It is alone with Him: what is there for it to do but to love Him? It can neither see nor hear save by making a great effort and it can take little credit for that. Then its past life comes up before it and all the truth of God's great mercy is revealed. The understanding has no need to go out hunting; for its food is already prepared. The soul realizes that it has deserved to go to hell, yet its punishment is to taste glory.

[1] [*Deshacerse.* Cf. p. 179, n. 4.]

It becomes consumed[2] in praises of God as I would fain become now. Blessed be Thou, my Lord, Who from such filthy slime as I dost draw water so pure as to be meet for Thy table! Praised be Thou, O Joy of the angels, Who art thus pleased to raise up a worm so vile!

The benefits thus achieved remain in the soul for some time; having now a clear realization that the fruits of this prayer are not its own, it can start to share them and yet have no lack of them itself. It begins to show signs of being a soul that is guarding the treasures of Heaven and to be desirous of sharing them with others and to beseech God that it may not be alone in its riches. Almost without knowing it, and doing nothing consciously to that end, it begins to benefit its neighbours, and they become aware of this benefit because the flowers have now so powerful a fragrance as to make them desire to approach them. They realize that the soul has virtues, and, seeing how desirable the fruit is, would fain help it to partake of it. If the ground is well dug over by trials, persecutions, back-bitings and infirmities (for few can attain such a state without these), and if it is broken up by detachment from self-interest, the water will sink in so far that it will hardly ever grow dry again. But if it is just earth in the virgin state and as full of thorns as I was at first; if it is not yet free from occasions of sin and not so grateful as it should be after receiving such great favours: then it will once again become dry. If the gardener becomes careless, and the Lord is not pleased, out of His sheer goodness, to send rain upon it afresh, then you can set down the garden as ruined. This happened to me several times and I am really amazed at it: if I had not had personal experience of it, I could not believe it. I write this for the consolation of weak souls like myself, so that they may never despair or cease to trust in God's greatness. Even if, after reaching so high a point as this to which the Lord has brought them, they should fall, they must not be discouraged if they would not be utterly lost. For tears achieve everything: one kind of water attracts another.

This is one of the reasons why, though being what I am, I was encouraged to obey my superiors by writing this and giving an account of my wretched life and of the favours which the Lord has granted me, albeit I have not served Him but

2 [*Deshacerse.*]

offended Him. I only wish I were a person of great authority so that my words might be believed: I beseech the Lord that His Majesty may be pleased to grant me this. I repeat that no one who has begun to practise prayer should be discouraged and say: "If I am going to fall again, it will be better for me not to go on practising prayer." I think it will be if such a person gives up prayer and does not amend his evil life; but, if he does not give it up, he may have confidence that prayer will bring him into the haven of light. This was a matter about which the devil kept plaguing me, and I suffered so much through thinking myself lacking in humility for continuing prayer, when I was so wicked, that, as I have said, for a year and a half I gave it up—or at any rate for a year: I am not quire sure about the six months. This would have been nothing less than plunging into hell—nor was it: there was no need for any devils to send me there. Oh, God help me, how terribly blind I was! How well the devil succeeds in his purpose when he pursues us like this! The deceiver knows that if a soul perseveres in practising prayer it will be lost to him, and that, by the goodness of God, all the relapses into which he can lead it will only help it to make greater strides onward in His service. And this is a matter of some concern to the devil.

O my Jesus! What a sight it is to see a soul which has attained as far as this, and has fallen into sin, when Thou of Thy mercy stretchest forth Thy hand to it again and raisest it up! How conscious it becomes of the multitude of Thy wonders and mercies, and of its own wretchedness! Now indeed is it consumed with shame when it acknowledges Thy wonders. Now it dares not raise its eyes. Now it raises them only to acknowledge what it owes Thee. Now it devoutly beseeches the Queen of Heaven to propitiate Thee. Now it invokes the saints, who likewise fell after Thou hadst called them, that they may aid it. Now it feels all Thou givest it to be bounty indeed, for it knows itself to be unworthy even of the ground it treads upon. It has recourse to the Sacraments and a lively faith is implanted in it when it sees what virtues God has placed in them; it praises Thee for having left us such medicine and such ointment for our wounds, which, far from healing them superficially, eradicate them altogether. At this it is amazed—and who, Lord of my soul, can be other than amazed at mercy so great and favour so immense, at treason so foul and abominable? I cannot think why my heart does not break when I write this, wicked that I am.

With these few tears that I am here shedding, which are Thy gift (water, in so far as it comes from me, drawn from a well so impure), I seem to be making Thee payment for all my acts of treachery—for the evil that I have so continually wrought and for the attempts that I have made to blot out the favours Thou hast granted me. Do Thou, my Lord, make my tears of some efficacy. Purify this turbid stream, if only that I may not lead others to be tempted to judge me, as I have been tempted to judge others myself. For I used to wonder, Lord, why Thou didst pass by persons who were most holy, who had been piously brought up, who had always served Thee and laboured for Thee and who were truly religious and not, like myself, religious only in name: I could not see why Thou didst not show them the same favours as Thou showedst to me. And then, O my Good, it became clear to me that Thou art keeping their reward to give them all at once—that my weakness needs the help Thou bestowest on me, whereas they, being strong, can serve Thee without it, and that therefore Thou dost treat them as brave souls and as souls devoid of self-seeking.

But nevertheless Thou knowest, my Lord, that I would often cry out unto Thee, and make excuses for those who spoke ill of me, for I thought they had ample reason for doing so. This, Lord, was after Thou of Thy goodness hadst kept me from so greatly offending Thee and when I was turning aside from everything which I thought could cause Thee displeasure; and as I did this, Lord, Thou didst begin to open Thy treasures for Thy servant. It seemed that Thou wert waiting for nothing else than that I should be willing and ready to receive them, and so, after a short time, Thou didst begin, not only to give them, but to be pleased that others should know Thou wert giving them, to me.

When this became known, people began to have a good opinion of one of whose great wickedness all were not fully aware, though much of it was clearly perceptible. Then suddenly began evil-speaking and persecution, and I think with great justification, so I conceived enmity for none, but besought Thee to consider how far they were justified. They said that I wanted to become a saint, and that I was inventing newfangled practices, though in many respects I had not even achieved the full observance of my Rule, nor had I attained to the goodness and sanctity of nuns in my own house, and indeed I do not believe that I ever shall unless God brings this about of His own goodness. On the contrary, I was well on the way to giving up things that were good and adopting habits that were not so: at least I was adopting them to the best of my ability and I had a great deal of ability for doing wrong. So these people were not to blame when they blamed me. I do not mean only the nuns, but other people: they revealed things about me that were true because Thou didst permit it.

Once when, after having been tempted in this way for some time, I was reciting the Hours, I came to the verse which says: *"Justus es, Domine,* and Thy judgments. . . ."³ I began to think how very true this was; for the devil was never powerful enough to tempt me sufficiently to make me doubt that Thou, my Lord, hast all good things, or any other truth of the Faith; indeed, it seemed to me that the less of a natural foundation these truths had, the more firmly I held them and the greater was the devotion they inspired in me. Since Thou art almighty, I accepted all the wondrous works which Thou hadst done as most certain; and in this respect, as I say, I never harboured a doubt. While I was wondering how in Thy justice Thou couldst ordain that so many of Thy faithful handmaidens, as I have said, should not be given the graces and favours which Thou didst bestow on me, being such as I was, Thou didst answer me, Lord, saying "Serve thou Me, and meddle not with this". This was the first word which I ever heard Thee speak to me and so it made me very much afraid; but, as I shall describe this method of hearing later, together with certain other things, I will say nothing about it here, for that would be to digress from my purpose and I think I have digressed quite sufficiently as it is. I hardly know what I have said. It cannot be otherwise, and Your Reverence

³ Psalm cxviii, 137 [A.V., cxix, 137]. The Latin text is: "Justus es, Domine, et rectum judicium tuum." The remainder of the verse no doubt escaped the Saint's memory. [The Latin opening she would remember, because it comes at the beginning of one of the divisions of the psalm. This is an interesting illustration of her indifference to precision in her work. Even a hasty revision would have revealed the omission of the latter part of the verse: it is strange that P. Báñez did not supply it.]

must suffer these lapses; for, when I consider what God has borne with from me, and find myself in my present state, it is not surprising if I lose the thread of what I am saying and of what I still have to say. May it please the Lord that any foolishness I talk shall be of this kind and may His Majesty never allow me to have the power to resist Him in the smallest degree; rather than that, let Him consume me, just as I am, at this very moment.

It suffices as an illustration of His great mercies that He should have forgiven such ingratitude as mine, and this not once but many times. He forgave Saint Peter once; but me He has forgiven often. Good reason had the devil for tempting me, telling me not to aspire to a close friendship with One for Whom I was so publicly showing my enmity. How terribly blind I was! Where, my Lord, did I think I could find help save in Thee? What foolishness to flee from the light and to walk on all the time stumbling! What a proud humility did the devil find in me when I ceased to make use of the pillar and the staff whose support I so greatly need lest I should suffer a great fall! As I write I make the sign of the Cross: I do not believe I have ever passed through so grave a peril as when the devil put this idea into my head under the guise of humility. How, he asked me, could one who, after receiving such great favours, was still as wicked as I, approach God in prayer? It was enough for me, he would go on, to recite the prayers enjoined upon me, as all the nuns did, but I did not even do this properly: why, then, should I want to do more? It was showing small respect and indeed contempt for the favours of God. I was right to think about this and to try to realize it, but extremely wrong to put my thoughts into practice. Blessed be Thou, Lord, Who didst thus succour me!

This seems to me to be the principle on which the devil tempted Judas, except that he dared not tempt me so openly: none the less, he would gradually have brought me to the same fate. For the love of God, let all who practise prayer consider this. Let them be told that by far the worst life I ever led was when I abandoned prayer. Let them consider with what a fine remedy the devil provided me and with what a pretty humility he inspired me. It caused me a great deal of inward unrest. And how could my soul find any rest? Miserable creature that it was, it went farther and farther away from its rest. I was very conscious of the favours and graces I had received from Thee; for the pleasures of earth I felt a loathing: I am amazed that I was able to endure it all. Only hope enabled me to do so, for, as far as I can remember (and it must have been more than twenty-one years ago), I never swerved from my resolution to return to prayers—I was only waiting until I should be quite free from sins. Oh, how far this hope led me astray!

The devil would have encouraged me in it until the Day of Judgment, so that he might then carry me off to hell. But, though I had recourse to prayer and reading, and these revealed truths to me and showed me along what a disastrous road I was walking, and though I importuned the Lord, often with tears, I was so wicked that all this could avail me nothing. When I abandoned these practices, and gave myself up to pastimes which led me into many occasions of sin and helped me but little—I will even venture to say that the only thing they helped me to do was to fall—what could I expect but what I have already mentioned? I think much credit in the sight of God is due to a friar of the Order of Saint Dominic,[4] a very learned man, for it was he who awakened me from this sleep; it was he who, as I think I said, made me communicate once a fortnight, and do less that was wrong. I began to return to my senses, though I did not cease to offend the Lord, but, as I had not lost my way, I continued upon it, first falling and then rising again, and making very little progress; still, he who never ceases walking, and advances all the time, may reach his goal late, but does reach it all the same. To lose one's way seems to be the same thing as giving up prayer. May God, for His name's sake, deliver us from doing so.

From this it is evident (and for the love of the Lord let it be carefully noted) that, even if a soul should attain the point of receiving great favours from God in prayer, it must put no trust in itself, since it is prone to fall, nor must it expose itself to occasions of sin in any way whatsoever. This should be carefully considered, for it is most important: even though a favour may undoubtedly have come from God, the devil will later be able to practise a deception upon us by treacherously making such use as he can of that very favour against persons who are not strong in the virtues, or detached, or

4 P. Barrón.

mortified; for such persons, as I shall explain later, are not sufficiently strengthened to expose themselves to occasions of sin and other perils, however sincere may be their desires and resolutions. This is excellent doctrine, and it is not mine, but has been taught me by God, and so I should like people as ignorant as I am to know it. Even if a soul should be in this state, it must not trust itself so far as to sally forth to battle: it will have quite enough to do to defend itself. Arms are needed here for defence against devils: the soul is not yet strong enough to fight against them and to trample them under its feet as do those in the state which I shall describe later.

This is the deception by which the devil wins his prey. When a soul finds itself very near to God and sees what a difference there is between the good things of Heaven and those of earth, and what love the Lord is showing it, there is born of this love a confidence and security that there will be no falling away from what it is now enjoying. It seems to have a clear vision of the reward and believes that it cannot now possibly leave something which even in this life is so sweet and delectable for anything as base and soiled as earthly pleasure. Because it has this confidence, the devil is able to deprive it of the misgivings which it ought to have about itself; and, as I say, it runs into many dangers, and in its zeal begins to give away its fruit without stint, thinking that it has now nothing to fear. This condition is not a concomitant of pride, for the soul clearly understands that of itself it can do nothing; it is the result of its extreme confidence in God, which knows no discretion. The soul does not realize that it is like a bird still unfledged. It is able to come out of the nest, and God is taking it out, but it is not yet ready to fly, for its virtues are not yet strong and it has no experience which will warn it of dangers, nor is it aware of the harm done by self-confidence.

It was this that ruined me; and, both because of this and for other reasons, the soul has great need of a director and of intercourse with spiritual people. I fully believe that, unless a soul brought to this state by God completely abandons Him, His Majesty will not cease to help it nor will He allow it to be lost. But when, as I have said, the soul falls, let it look to it—for the love of the Lord, let it look to it—lest the devil trick it into abandoning prayer, in the way he tricked me, by inspiring it with a false humility, as I have said, and as I should like to repeat often. Let it trust in the goodness of God, which is greater than all the evil we can do. When, with full knowledge of ourselves, we desire to return to friendship with Him, He remembers neither our ingratitude nor our misuse of the favours that He has granted us. He might well chastise us for these sins, but in fact He makes use of them only to forgive us the more readily, just as He would forgive those who have been members of His household, and who, as they say, have eaten of His bread. Let them remember His words and consider what He has done to me, who wearied of offending His Majesty before He ceased forgiving me. Never does He weary of giving and never can His mercies be exhausted: let us, then, not grow weary of receiving. May He be blessed for ever, Amen, and may all things praise Him.

CHAPTER XX

Treats of the difference between union and rapture. Describes the nature of rapture and says something of the blessing that comes to the soul which the Lord, of His goodness, brings to it. Describes the effects which it produces. This chapter is particularly admirable.

I should like, with the help of God, to be able to describe the difference between union and rapture, or elevation, or what they call flight of the spirit, or transport—it is all one. I mean that these different names all refer to the same thing, which is also called ecstasy. It is much more beneficial than union: the effects it produces are far more important and it has a great many more operations, for union gives the impression of being just the same at the beginning, in the middle and at the end, and it all happens interiorly. But the ends of these raptures are of a higher degree, and the effects they produce are both interior and exterior. May the Lord explain this, as He has explained everything else, for I should certainly know nothing of it if His Majesty had not shown me the ways and manners in which it can to some extent be described.

Let us now reflect that this last water which we have described is so abundant that, were it not that the ground is incapable of receiving it, we might believe this cloud of great Majesty to be with us here on this earth. But as we are giving Him thanks for this great blessing, and doing our utmost to draw near to Him in a practical way, the Lord gathers up the soul, just (we might say) as the clouds gather up the vapours from the earth, and raises it up till it is right out of itself (I have heard that it is in this way that the clouds or the sun gather up the vapours)[1] and the cloud rises to Heaven and takes the soul with it, and begins to reveal to it things concerning the Kingdom that He has prepared for it. I do not know if the comparison is an exact one, but that is the way it actually happens.

In these raptures the soul seems no longer to animate the body, and thus the natural heat of the body is felt to be very sensibly diminished: it gradually becomes colder, though conscious of the greatest sweetness and delight. No means of resistance is possible, whereas in union, where we are on our own ground, such a means exists: resistance may be painful and violent but it can almost always be effected. But with rapture, as a rule, there is no such possibility: often it comes like a strong, swift impulse, before your thought can forewarn you of it or you can do anything to help yourself; you see and feel this cloud, or this powerful eagle, rising and bearing you up with it on its wings.

You realize, I repeat, and indeed see, that you are being carried away, you know not whither. For, though rapture brings us delight, the weakness of our nature at first makes us afraid of it, and we need to be resolute and courageous in soul, much more so than for what has been described. For, happen what may, we must risk everything, and resign ourselves into the hands of God and go willingly wherever we are carried away, for we are in fact being carried away, whether we like it or no. In such straits do I find myself at such a time that very often I should be glad to resist, and I exert all my strength to do so, in particular at times when it happens in public and at many other times in private, when I am afraid that I may be suffering deception. Occasionally I have been able to make some resistance, but at the cost of great exhaustion, for I would feel as weary afterwards as though I had been

[1] The bracketed sentence is found in the margin of the autograph in St. Teresa's hand.

fighting with a powerful giant. At other times, resistance has been impossible: my soul has been borne away, and indeed as a rule my head also, without my being able to prevent it: sometimes my whole body has been affected, to the point of being raised up from the ground.

This has happened only rarely; but once, when we were together in choir, and I was on my knees and about to communicate, it caused me the greatest distress. It seemed to me a most extraordinary thing and I thought there would be a great deal of talk about it; so I ordered the nuns (for it happened after I was appointed Prioress) not to speak of it. On other occasions, when I have felt that the Lord was going to enrapture me (once it happened during a sermon, on our patronal festival, when some great ladies were present),[2] I have lain on the ground and the sisters have come and held me down, but none the less the rapture has been observed. I besought the Lord earnestly not to grant me any more favours which had visible and exterior signs; for I was exhausted by having to endure such worries and after all (I said) His Majesty could grant me that favour without its becoming known. He seems to have been pleased of His goodness to hear me, for since making that prayer I have never again received any such favours: it is true, however, that this happened not long since.

When I tried to resist these raptures, it seemed that I was being lifted up by a force beneath my feet so powerful that I know nothing to which I can compare it, for it came with a much greater vehemence than any other spiritual experience and I felt as if I were being ground to powder. It is a terrible struggle, and to continue it against the Lord's will avails very little, for no power can do anything against His. At other times His Majesty is graciously satisfied with our seeing that He desires to show us this favour, and that, if we do not receive it, it is not due to Himself. Then, if we resist it out of humility, the same effects follow as if we had given it our entire consent.

These effects are very striking. One of them is the manifes-

2 [P. Silverio says that this happened at St. Joseph's, Ávila, "about the year 1565". But, as this book was only completed in 1565, and the incident is referred to in a phrase which suggests some lapse of time, his chronology would seem to have little meaning. Lewis (p. 162, n. 6) says "1564 or 1565", which is not much better.]

tation of the Lord's mighty power: as we are unable to resist His Majesty's will, either in soul or in body, and are not our own masters, we realize that, however irksome this truth may be, there is One stronger than ourselves, and that these favours are bestowed by Him, and that we, of ourselves, can do absolutely nothing. This imprints in us great humility. Indeed, I confess that in me it produced great fear—at first a terrible fear. One sees one's body being lifted up from the ground; and although the spirit draws it after itself, and if no resistance is offered does so very gently, one does not lose consciousness—at least, I myself have had sufficient to enable me to realize that I was being lifted up. The majesty of Him Who can do this is manifested in such a way that the hair stands on end, and there is produced a great fear of offending so great a God, but a fear overpowered by[3] the deepest love, newly enkindled, for One Who, as we see, has so deep a love for so loathsome a worm that He seems not to be satisfied by literally drawing the soul to Himself, but will also have the body, mortal though it is, and befouled as is its clay by all the offences it has committed.

This favour also leaves a strange detachment, the nature of which I cannot possibly describe, but I think I can say it is somewhat different—from that produced by these purely spiritual favours, I mean; for, although these produce a complete detachment of spirit, in this favour the Lord is pleased that it should be shared by the very body and it will thus experience a new estrangement from things of earth, which makes life much more distressing. Afterwards it produces a distress which we cannot ourselves bring about or remove once it has come. I should like very much to explain this great distress, but I am afraid I cannot possibly do so: still, I will say something about it if I can.

It is to be observed that these are my most recent experiences, more recent than all the visions and revelations of which I shall write and than the period during which I practised prayer and the Lord granted me such great consolations and favours. Though these have not ceased, it is this distress which I shall now describe that I more frequently and habitually experience at present. Sometimes it is more severe and sometimes less so. It is of its maximum severity that I

3 [*Envuelto*. See p. 92, n. 2.]

will now speak; for although I shall later describe those violent impulses which I used to experience when the Lord was pleased to grant me raptures, these, in my view, have no more connection with this distress than has an entirely physical experience with an entirely spiritual one, and in saying that I do not think I am greatly exaggerating. For, although the distress I refer to is felt by the soul, it is also felt by the body. Both seem to share in it, and it does not cause the same extreme sense of abandonment as does this. In producing the latter, as I have said, we can take no part, though very often a desire unexpectedly arises, in a way which I cannot explain. And this desire, which in a single moment penetrates to the very depths of the soul, begins to weary it so much that the soul soars upwards, far above itself and above all created things, and God causes it to be so completely bereft of everything that, however hard it may strive to do so, it can find nothing on earth to bear it company. Nor does it desire company; it would rather die in its solitude. Others may speak to it, and it may itself make every possible effort to speak, but all to no avail; do what it may, its spirit cannot escape from that solitude. God seems very far from the soul then, yet sometimes He reveals His greatness in the strangest way imaginable; this cannot be described—nor, I think, believed or understood—save by those who have experienced it. For it is a communication intended, not to comfort the soul but to show it the reason why it is wearied—namely, that it is so far away from the Good which contains all that is good within Itself.

In this communication the desire grows, and with it the extremity of loneliness experienced by the soul with a distress so subtle and yet so piercing that, set as it is in that desert, it can, I think, say literally, as the Royal Prophet said, when he was in the same state of loneliness (except that, being a saint, he may have been granted that experience by the Lord in a higher degree): *Vigilavi, et factus sum sicut passer solitarius in tecto.*[4] That verse comes to my mind at these times

---

[4] Psalm ci, 8. [A.V., cii, 7]: "I have watched, and am become as a sparrow all alone on the housetop." [St. Teresa's spelling of Latin is largely phonetic and always quaint. It will suffice to reproduce this one example of it: Vigilavi ed fatus sun sicud passer solitarius yn tecto. The orthography given in the text is here, and will normally be elsewhere, that of the Vulgate.]

in such a way that I feel it is fulfilled in myself; and it is a comfort to me to know that others, especially such a prophet as this, have experienced that great extremity of loneliness. The soul, then, seems to be, not in itself at all, but on the house-top, or the roof, of its own house, and raised above all created things; I think it is far above even its own very highest part.

On other occasions the soul seems to be going about in a state of the greatest need, and asking itself: "Where is thy God?"[5] I should point out here that I did not know the meaning of this verse in the vernacular, and that later, when I had learned it, it was a comfort to me to think that the Lord had brought it to my mind without any effort of my own. At other times I used to remember some words of Saint Paul, about his being crucified to the world.[6] I do not say that this is true of me—indeed, I know it is not—but I think it is true of the soul when no comfort comes to it from Heaven, and it is not in Heaven, and when it desires no earthly comfort, and is not on earth either, but is, as it were, crucified between Heaven and earth; and it suffers greatly, for no help comes to it either from the one hand or from the other. For the help which comes to it from Heaven is, as I have said, a knowledge of God so wonderful, and so far above all that we can desire, that it brings with it greater torment; for its desire grows in such a way that I believe its great distress sometimes robs it of consciousness, though such a state as that lasts only for a short time. It seems as though it were on the threshold of death, save that this suffering brings with it such great happiness that I know of nothing with which it may be compared. It is a martyrdom, severe but also delectable; for the soul will accept nothing earthly that may be offered it, even though it were the thing which it had been accustomed to enjoy most: it seems to fling it away immediately. It realizes clearly that it wants nothing save its God; but its love is not centred upon any particular attribute of Him: its desire is for the whole of God and it has no knowledge of what it desires. By "no knowledge", I mean that no picture is formed in the imagination; and, in my opinion, for a great part of the time

---

[5] Psalm xli, 4 [A.V., xlii, 3].
[6] Galatians vi, 14: ". . . by whom the world is crucified to me, and I to the world."

during which it is in that state, the faculties are inactive: they are suspended by their distress, just as in union and rapture they are suspended by joy.

O Jesus! I wish I could give Your Reverence a clear explanation of this, if only so that you might tell me what it is, for this is the state in which my soul now continually finds itself. As a rule, when not occupied, it is plunged into these death-like yearnings, and, when I am conscious that they are beginning, I become afraid, because they do not mean death. But when I am actually in that condition, I should like to spend the rest of my life suffering in that way, although the pain is so excessive that one can hardly bear it, and occasionally, according to those of my sisters who sometimes see me like this, and so now understand it better, my pulses almost cease to beat, my bones are all disjointed, and my hands are so stiff that sometimes I cannot clasp them together. Until the next day I have pains in the wrists, and in the entire body, as though my bones had been wrenched asunder.

Occasionally I really think that, if things are to go on like this, it must be the Lord's will to end them by putting an end to my life; for the distress I am in is severe enough to kill me, only I do not deserve that it should do so. All my yearning at such a time is to die: I do not think of purgatory, or of the great sins I have committed, for which I have deserved to go to hell. Such is my yearning to see God that I forget everything and the deserted and solitary state I am in seems better than all the world's companionship. If anything could comfort a person in this condition, it would be to speak with another who has passed through the same torment, for she finds that, despite her complaints of it, no one seems to believe her.

The soul in this state is also tormented because its distress has so greatly increased that it no longer desires solitude, as it did before, and the only companionship it seeks is with one to whom it can voice its complaint. It is like a person who has a rope around his neck, is being strangled and is trying to breathe. It seems to me, then, that this desire for companionship proceeds from human weakness; for, since this distress imperils our life, which it most certainly does (as I have said, I have several times found my own life imperilled by serious dangers and illnesses, and I think I might say that this particular peril is as grave as any), the desire that body and soul shall not be parted is like a voice crying out for help to breathe; and by speaking of it and complaining and distracting itself, the soul seeks a way to live quite contrarily to the will of the spirit, or of its own higher part, which would prefer not to escape from this distress.

I do not know if I am correct in what I say, or if I am expressing it properly, but to the best of my belief that is what happens. I ask Your Reverence, what rest can I have in this life, since the rest which I used to enjoy, and which consisted in prayer and solitude, wherein the Lord would comfort me, is habitually turned into this torment; and yet it is so delectable, and the soul is so conscious of its worth, that it desires it more than all the favours which it had been accustomed to enjoy. It believes it, too, to be a safer state, because it is the way of the Cross; and in my view it comprises a delight of exceeding worth, because the body gets nothing from it but distress, whereas the soul, even while suffering, rejoices alone in the joy and happiness which this suffering brings. I do not know how this can be, but so it is; and I believe I would not change this favour which the Lord is bestowing upon me (for it is certainly entirely supernatural and comes from His hand, and, as I have said, is in no way acquired by me) for any of the favours which I shall describe later: I do not say for all of them at once, but for any one of them taken by itself. And it must not be forgotten that this state, in which the Lord is now keeping me, has followed all the others described in this book: I mean that these violent impulses have followed the favours described here as having been bestowed upon me by the Lord.

At first I was afraid, as I almost always am when the Lord bestows a favour upon me, though His Majesty reassures me as I go on. He told me not to fear but to set greater store by this favour than by any other which He had granted me; for by this distress the soul was purified, worked upon and refined like gold in the crucible, so that He might the better set in it the enamel of His gifts: it was being cleansed now of the impurities of which it would need to be cleansed in purgatory. I had already quite clearly realized that it was a great favour, but this made me much more certain of the fact, and my confessor tells me that all is well. And although I was afraid, because I was so wicked, I could never believe that it was wrong; it was rather the sublimity of the blessing that made me afraid, when I remembered how ill I had deserved it. Blessed be the Lord, Who is so good! Amen.

I seem to have wandered from my subject, for I began by speaking of raptures, but what I have been describing is something even greater than a rapture and thus it leaves behind it the effects I have referred to.

Let us now return to raptures, and to their most usual characteristics. I can testify that after a rapture my body often seemed as light as if all weight had left it: sometimes this was so noticeable that I could hardly tell when my feet were touching the ground. For, while the rapture lasts, the body often remains as if dead and unable of itself to do anything: it continues all the time as it was when the rapture came upon it—in a sitting position, for example, or with the hands open or shut. The subject rarely loses consciousness: I have sometimes lost it altogether, but only seldom and for but a short time. As a rule the consciousness is disturbed; and, though incapable of action with respect to outward things, the subject can still hear and understand, but only dimly, as though from a long way off. I do not say that he can hear and understand when the rapture is at its highest point—by "highest point" I mean when the faculties are lost through being closely united with God. At that point, in my opinion, he will neither see, nor hear, nor perceive; but, as I said in describing the preceding prayer of union, this complete transformation of the soul in God lasts but a short time, and it is only while it lasts that none of the soul's faculties is able to perceive or know what is taking place. We cannot be meant to understand it while we are on earth—God, in fact, does not wish us to understand it because we have not the capacity for doing so. I have observed this myself.

Your Reverence will ask me how it is that the rapture sometimes lasts for so many hours. What often happens to me is that, as I said of the preceding state of prayer, it makes itself felt intermittently. The soul is often engulfed—or, to put it better, the Lord engulfs it in Himself—and, when He has kept it in this state for a short time, He retains the will alone. The movements of the other two faculties seem to me like the movement of the pointer on a sundial, which is never motionless; though if it pleases the Sun of Justice[7] to do so,

7 [Malachias iv, 2. A.V.: "Sun of Righteousness."]

He can make it stand still. What I am describing lasts only a short time; but, as the impulse and the uplifting of the spirit have been violent, the will is still engulfed even when the other two faculties begin to move again and produces that operation in the body as though it were its absolute mistress. For, although the two restless faculties try to disturb it, the will, thinking that the fewer enemies it has, the better, prevents the senses from doing so, and thus causes their suspension, which is the Lord's will. For the most part the eyes are closed, though we may not wish to close them; if, as I have already said, they are occasionally open, the subject neither perceives nor pays attention to what he sees.

There is very little, then, that a person in this condition can do, and this means that there will be little for him to do when the faculties come together again. Anyone, therefore, to whom the Lord grants this favour must not be discouraged at finding himself in this state, with the body unable to move for hours on end and the understanding and the memory sometimes wandering. True, they are generally absorbed in the praises of God or in an attempt to comprehend and realize what has happened to them. But even so they are not wide awake: they are like a person who has been asleep for a long time and has been dreaming and has not yet fully awakened.

The reason I am expounding this at such great length is that I know that there are persons now, in this very place, to whom the Lord is granting these favours; and if those who are directing such persons have not themselves experienced them—more especially if they have no learning—they may think that, when enraptured, they ought to be as if dead. It is a shame that such suffering should be caused by confessors who do not understand this, as I shall say later. Perhaps I do not know what I am saying; but, if my words are at all to the point, Your Reverence will understand it, for the Lord has already given you experience of it, though, as this happened only recently, you may not have considered the matter as fully as I. The position, then, is that, however hard I try, my body, for considerable periods, has not the strength to make it capable of movement: all its strength has been taken away by the soul. Often a person who was previously quite ill and troubled with severe pain finds himself in good health again, and even stronger than before, for what the soul receives in rapture is a great gift, and sometimes, as I say, the Lord is pleased that the body should have a share in it because of its obedience to the will of the soul. After the recovery of consciousness, if the rapture has been deep, the faculties may remain absorbed for a day or two, or even for as long as three days, and be as if in a state of stupor, so that they seem to be no longer themselves.

And now comes the distress of having to return to this life. Now the soul has grown new wings and has learned to fly. Now the little bird has lost its unformed feathers. Now in Christ's name the standard is raised on high; it would seem that what has happened is nothing less than that the captain of the fortress has mounted, or has been led up, to the highest of its towers, and has reared the standard aloft there in the name of God. From his position of security he looks down on those below. No longer does he fear perils; rather he desires them, for through them, as it were, he receives the assurance of victory. This becomes very evident in the little weight now given by the soul to earthly matters, which it treats as the worthless things that they are. He who is raised on high[8] attains many things. The soul has no desire to seek or possess any free-will, even if it so wished,[9] and it is for this that it prays to the Lord, giving Him the keys of its will. Behold, our gardener has become the captain of a fortress! He wants nothing save the will of the Lord; he wants to be neither his own master nor anybody else's; he wants not so much as an apple from this orchard. If there is anything of value in it, let His Majesty distribute it; henceforth, for himself, he wants nothing, and desires only that everything should be done to God's glory and in conformity with His will.

It is in this way, then, that these things actually happen, if the raptures are genuine, in which case there will remain in the soul the effects and advantages aforementioned. If they do not, I should doubt very much if they are from God; indeed, I should fear that they might be the frenzies described

8 [*Quien está de lo alto* . . . I give the most obvious translation of this rather unusual phrase (*lit.*: "he who is from the height"), but I suspect the omission of *mirando*: "He who is looking (down) from on high . . ." the reference being to the soul's attitude to the world.]

9 P. Báñez altered this phrase to: "It has no desire to seek or possess any will save that of Our Lord," and the change was followed in the *editio princeps*.

by Saint Vincent.[10] I know, for I have observed it in my own experience, that the soul, while enraptured, is mistress of everything, and in a single hour, or in less, acquires such freedom that it cannot recognize itself. It sees clearly that this state is in no way due to itself, nor does it know who has given it so great a blessing, but it distinctly recognizes the very great benefit which each of these raptures brings it. Nobody will believe this without having had experience of it; and so nobody believes the poor soul, knowing it to have been so wicked and seeing it now aspiring to such heroic acts; for it is no longer content with serving the Lord a little but must do so to the greatest extent in its power. They think this is a temptation and a ridiculous thing. If they knew that it arises, not from the soul, but from the Lord, to Whom the soul has given the keys of its will, they would not be so astounded.

I believe myself that a soul which attains to this state neither speaks nor does anything of itself, but that this sovereign King takes care of all that it has to do. Oh, my God, how clear is the meaning of that verse about asking for the wings of a dove[11] and how right the author was—and how right we shall all be!—to ask for them! It is evident that he is referring to the flight taken by the spirit when it soars high above all created things, and above itself first of all; but it is a gentle and a joyful flight and also a silent one.

What power is that of a soul brought hither by the Lord, which can look upon everything without being ensnared by it! How ashamed it is of the time when it was attached to everything! How amazed it is at its blindness! How it pities those who are still blind, above all if they are persons of prayer to whom God is still granting favours! It would like to cry aloud to them and show them how mistaken they are, and sometimes it does in fact do so and brings down a thousand persecutions upon its head. Men think it lacking in humility and suppose that it is trying to teach those from whom it

[10] St. Vincent Ferrer: *De Vita spirituali*, Chap. XIV: "Si dicerent tibi aliquid quod sit contra fidem, et contra Scripturam sacram, aut contra bonos mores, abhorreas eorum visionem et judicia, tanquam stultas dementias, et earum raptus, sicut rabiamenta." St. Teresa could have read this book in a Spanish version published at Toledo in 1510, and reprinted five years later, in a volume containing also the life of Blessed Angela de Foligno and the Rule of St. Clare.

[11] Psalm liv, 7 [A.V., lv, 6].

should learn, especially if the person in question is a woman. For this they condemn it, and rightly so, since they know nothing of the force by which it is impelled. Sometimes it cannot help itself nor endure failing to undeceive those whom it loves and desires to see set free from the prison of this life; for it is in a prison, nothing less—and it realizes that it is nothing less—that the soul has itself been living.

It is weary of the time when it paid heed to niceties concerning its own honour, and of the mistaken belief which it had that what the world calls honour is really so. It now knows that to be a sheer lie and a lie in which we are all living. It realizes that genuine honour is not deceptive, but true; that it values what has worth and despises what has none; for what passes away, and is not pleasing to God, is worth nothing and less than nothing.[12] It laughs at itself and at the time when it set any store by money and coveted it; though I do not believe I ever had to confess to being covetous of money—it was quite bad enough that I should have set any store by it at all. If the blessing of which I now see myself in possession could be purchased with money I should set tremendous store by it, but it is clear that this blessing is gained by abandoning everything.

What is there that can be bought with this money which people desire? Is there anything valuable? Is there anything lasting? If not, why do we desire it? It is but a miserable ease with which it provides us and one that costs us very dear. Very often it provides hell for us; it buys us eternal fire and endless affliction. Oh, if all would agree to consider it as useless dross, how well the world would get on, and how little trafficking there would be! How friendly we should all be with one another if nobody were interested in money and honour! I really believe this would be a remedy for everything.

The soul sees what blindness there is in the world where pleasures are concerned and how even in this life they purchase only trials and unrest. What disquiet! What discontent! What useless labour! Not only does the soul perceive the cobwebs which disfigure it and its own great faults, but so bright

---

12 [Cf. *St. John of the Cross*, I, 25: "All the creatures are nothing; and their affections, we may say, are less than nothing. . . . The soul that sets its affections upon the being of creation is likewise nothing in the eyes of God, and less than nothing." (*Ascent of Mount Carmel*, I, iv.)]

is the sunlight that it sees every little speck of dust, however small; and so, however hard a soul may have laboured to perfect itself, once this Sun really strikes it, it sees that it is wholly unclean. Just so the water in a vessel seems quite clear when the sun is not shining upon it; but the sun shows it to be full of specks. This comparison is literally exact. Before the soul had experienced that state of ecstasy, it thought it was being careful not to offend God and doing all that it could so far as its strength permitted. But once it reaches this stage, the Sun of Justice strikes it and forces it to open its eyes, whereupon it sees so many of these specks that it would fain close them again. For it is not yet so completely the child of that mighty eagle that it can look this Sun full in the face; nevertheless, during the short time that it can keep them open, it sees that it is wholly unclean. It remembers the verse which says: "Who shall be just in Thy presence?"[13]

When it looks upon this Divine Sun, the brightness dazzles it; when it looks at itself, its eyes are blinded by clay.[14] The little dove is blind. And very often it remains completely blind, absorbed, amazed, and dazzled by all the wonders it sees. From this it acquires true humility, which will never allow it to say anything good of itself nor will permit others to do so.[15] It is the Lord of the garden, and not the soul, that distributes the fruit of the garden, and so nothing remains in its hands, but all the good that is in it is directed towards God; if it says anything about itself, it is for His glory. It knows that it possesses[16] nothing here; and, even if it so wishes, it cannot ignore this; for it sees it by direct vision, and, willy-nilly, shuts its eyes to things of the world, and opens them to an understanding of the truth.

[13] [P. Silverio supposes this to refer to Psalm cxlii, 2 (A.V., cxliii, 2): "In thy sight no man living shall be justified." But the interrogative form suggests rather Job xxv, 4 ("Can man be justified compared with God?") or of Job iv, 17 ("Shall man be justified in comparison of God?").]

[14] [Barro: mud, clay. Often used in Spanish as a symbol of the earthly and material.]

[15] [Cf. St. John of the Cross, I, 62, § 9.]

[16] [This second "it" must refer to the soul (alma), which is feminine in Spanish. P. Silverio, however, has the masculine pronoun el; I follow earlier texts, which amend this to ella.]

CHAPTER XXI

Continues and ends the account of this last degree of prayer. Describes the feelings of the soul in this state on its return to life in the world and the light which the Lord sheds for it on the world's delusions. Contains good doctrine.

Concluding the matter under discussion, I remark that in this state there is no need for the soul to give its consent: it has given it already and knows that it has surrendered itself willingly into His hands and that He cannot deceive it because He knows all things. This is not as it is in the world, where life is full of delusions and deceits; you judge by the profession of friendship which a man makes that you have gained his good will, and then realize that the profession was a false one. No one can live amid such worldly trafficking, especially if he has himself any interest in the world. Blessed is the soul which the Lord brings to an understanding of the truth! Oh, what a state this would be for kings! How much better it would be for them if they strove after it rather than after great dominion! What uprightness there would be in their kingdoms! How many evils would be prevented—and might have been prevented already! Here no one fears to lose life or honour for the love of God. How great a blessing would such a state be for one who is more bound than those beneath him to consider the Lord's honour—kings will always lead and the people will follow! For the sake of the smallest increase in the number of the faithful and for the privilege of affording heretics the smallest glimmer of light, I would give up a thousand kingdoms, and rightly so. For it is a different thing to win a kingdom that shall have no end, because a single drop of the water of that kingdom gives him who tastes it a loathing for everything earthly. What will it be, then, when the soul is completely engulfed in such water?

O Lord, if Thou wert to give me the vocation to proclaim this aloud, I should be disbelieved, as are many who can speak of it in a way very different from mine. But at least I should myself have satisfaction. If I could make others understand a single one of these truths I think I should set little

store by my own life. I do not know what I should do afterwards, for I am entirely untrustworthy; despite my being the
sort of person I am, I keep experiencing strong and consum-
ing impulses to say this to persons in authority. But as I can
do no more, my Lord, I turn to Thee, to beg of Thee a remedy
for everything, and well dost Thou know that, provided I
remain in such a state as not to offend Thee, I would very
gladly strip myself of the favours Thou hast granted me and
give them to kings; for I know that, if they had them, it would
be impossible for them to permit things which they permit
now, or to fail to possess the greatest blessings.

O my God! Give them to understand how great are their
obligations. For Thou hast been pleased to single them out on
earth in such a way that, as I have heard, when Thou dost
remove one of them, Thou even showest signs in the heavens.
Enkindled indeed, is my devotion, O my King, when I reflect
that it is Thy will that this should teach them that they must
imitate Thee in their lives, since at their deaths there are such
signs in the heavens as there were when Thou Thyself didst
die.

I am being very bold. Your Reverence must destroy this
if you think it wrong. But, believe me, I should say it better
in the very presence of kings if I had the opportunity of doing so or thought they would believe me, for I commend
them earnestly to God and wish that I might be of some
profit to them. All this prompts one to risk one's life (and I
often wish I could lose mine): for the risk would be a small
one to run for so great a gain, and life becomes hardly possible when with one's own eyes one sees the great delusion in
which we are walking and the blind way in which we act.

When a soul has reached this state, it has not merely desires to serve God: His Majesty also gives it strength to carry
these desires into effect. No way in which it thinks it may
serve God can be set before it into which it will not fling itself; and yet it is doing nothing, because, as I say, it sees
clearly that nothing is of any value save pleasing God. The
trouble is that no such task presents itself to people who are
as worthless as I. May it be Thy pleasure, my God, that the
time may come in which I shall be able to pay at least a few
mites[1] of all I owe Thee; do Thou ordain it, Lord, according

---

[1] *Algún cornado.* The *cornado* was a small copper coin, worth
about as much as a *cuarto,* or 3/100 of a peseta. It had come in late

to Thy pleasure, that this Thy handmaiden may in some way serve Thee. There have been other women who have done heroic deeds for love of Thee. I myself am fit only to talk, and therefore, my God, it is not Thy good pleasure to test me by actions. All my will to serve Thee peters out in words and desires, and even here I have no freedom, for it is always possible that I may fail altogether.

Do Thou strengthen and prepare my soul first of all, Good of all good, my Jesus, and do Thou then ordain means whereby I may do something for Thee, for no one could bear to receive as much as I have done and pay nothing in return. Cost what it may, Lord, permit me not to come into Thy presence with such empty hands, since a man's reward must be in accordance with his works.[2] Here is my life; here is my honour and my will. I have given it all to Thee; I am Thine; dispose of me according to Thy desire. Well do I know, my Lord, of how little I am capable. But now that I have approached Thee, now that I have mounted this watch-tower whence truths can be seen, I shall be able to do all things provided Thou withdraw not from me. Withdraw Thou, and, for however short a time, I shall go where I have already been —namely, to hell.

Oh, what it is for a soul which finds itself in this state to have to return to intercourse with all, to look at this farce of a life and see how ill-organized it is, to spend its time in meeting the needs of the body, in sleeping and in eating. It is wearied by everything; it cannot run away; it sees itself chained and captive; and it is then that it feels most keenly the imprisonment into which we are led by our bodies and the misery of this life. It understands why Saint Paul besought God to deliver him from it;[3] it joins its cries to his; and, as I have said on other occasions, it begs God for freedom. But in this state it often cries with such vehemence that it seems as if the soul is desirous of leaving the body and going in search of that freedom, since no one is delivering it. It

---

in the thirteenth century and in St. Teresa's day was no longer current; but it was spoken of metaphorically, in the sense of "brass farthing" or "mite", much as the *cuarto* is now.

[2] [Probably a reminiscence of Apocalypse ii, 23: "And I will give to every one of you according to your works."]

[3] Romans vii, 24: "Unhappy man that I am, who shall deliver me from the body of this death?"

wanders about like one who has been sold into a strange land; its chief trouble is finding so few to join in its complaints and prayers, since as a rule men desire to live. Oh, were we but completely detached and were our happiness not fixed on things of earth, how the distress caused us by living all the time without God would temper our fear of death with the desire to enjoy true life!

I sometimes wonder, if a woman like myself, to whom the Lord has given this light, but whose charity is so lukewarm and whose works have not won for her any certainty of true rest, is nevertheless so often sad at finding herself in this exile, what the sorrow of the saints must have been. What must Saint Paul and the Magdalen have suffered, and others like them, in whom this fire of the love of God burned so vehemently? Their sufferings must have been one continuous martyrdom. I think any relief I obtain, and any desire I have for intercourse with others, is due to my finding people with these desires—I mean desires coupled with works. I say "with works" because there are people who think and proclaim themselves to be detached—and who must be so, for it is required by their vocation and certified by the many years that have passed since some of them began to walk in the way of perfection. Yet this soul of mine can distinguish from a long way off, and quite clearly, those who are detached only in word, and whose words are confirmed by their works; for it knows how little good is done by the one class and how much by the other; and this is a thing which can be very clearly discerned by anyone with experience.

We have now described the effects proceeding from raptures which come from the Spirit of God. It is true that some of these are greater and some less: by "less" I mean that, although these effects are produced, they are not at first expressed in works and it may not become evident that the soul has them. Perfection, too, has to grow; the cobwebs have to be brushed away from the memory; and this takes some time. And the more love and humility grow in the soul, the greater is the fragrance yielded by these flowers of the virtues for the benefit both of the soul itself and of others. The fact is that, during one of these raptures, the Lord can work in the soul in such a way that there remains little for it to do in order to acquire perfection. For, except by experience, no one will ever believe what the Lord bestows on the soul here; no efforts of ours, in my opinion, can acquire it. I do not mean that those who work hard for many years, in the ways described by writers on prayer, following their principles and using their methods, will not, after much labour, and with the help of the Lord, attain to detachment and perfection. But they will not do so as speedily as by means of raptures, in which the Lord works without our collaboration and draws the soul away from the earth and gives it dominion over all earthly things, although there may be no more merits in such a soul than there were in mine—and I cannot say more than that, for I had hardly any.

The reason His Majesty does this is that it is His will, and it is according as He wills that He does it; and, though the soul may not be prepared, His Majesty prepares it to receive the blessing which He is giving it. Although He most certainly never fails to comfort those who make proper preparation and strive after detachment, He does not always bestow blessings because the recipients have deserved them by cultivating their garden. It is sometimes His will, as I have said, to manifest His greatness in the worst kind of soil; He prepares it for every blessing, so that it seems almost as if it would be impossible for the soul to return to the life of sin against God which it had lived previously. Its mind is now so used to thinking upon eternal truth that anything else seems to it mere child's play. It sometimes enjoys a quiet laugh when it sees serious people—men of prayer, leading the religious life —making a great fuss about niceties concerning their honour, which it has long since trampled beneath its feet. They say that discretion demands this and that the more they have of the authority due to their positions the more good they can do. But the soul knows very well that if they subordinated the authority due to their positions to the love of God they would do more good in a day than they are likely to do as it is in ten years.

So the life of this soul continues—a troubled life, never without its crosses, but a life of great growth. Those with whom the soul has to do keep thinking it has reached its summit, but soon afterwards they find it higher still, for God is always giving it new favours. It is God Who is the soul of that soul; and, as He has it in His keeping, He sheds His light upon it. He seems to be continually watching over it, lest it should offend Him, and assisting and awakening it to serve Him. When my soul reached the point at which God began to grant me this great favour, my troubles ceased, and the Lord gave me strength to escape from them. Meeting occasions of sin and being with people who were wont to distract me had now no more effect upon me than if they had not been there. Indeed, what had previously been apt to harm me now became a help to me; everything was a means by which I was enabled to know and love God the better, to realize what I owed Him and to be grieved at having been what I once was.

I knew quite well that none of this was due to myself and that I had not won it by my own efforts, for there had not been time enough for me to do that. His Majesty had given me the needful strength out of His own goodness. From the time when the Lord began to grant me the favour of these raptures, until now, this strength has continued to increase, and God of His goodness has held me by His hand so that I should not turn back. This being so, I realize that I am doing hardly anything of myself; I understand clearly that it is all the work of the Lord. I think, therefore, that souls on whom the Lord bestows these favours, and who walk in humility and fear, ever realizing that all is due to the Lord Himself and in no wise to our efforts, may safely mix with any kind of company whatsoever. However distracting and vicious such company may be, it will have no effect on them nor will it in any way move them; on the contrary, as I have said, it will help them and be a means whereby they may derive the greater profit. It is strong souls that are chosen by the Lord to profit others, though their strength does not come from themselves. For, when the Lord brings a soul to this state, He gradually communicates to it very great secrets.

In this state of ecstasy occur true revelations, great favours and visions, all of which are of service in humbling and strengthening the soul and helping it to despise the things of this life and to gain a clearer knowledge of the reward which the Lord has prepared for those who serve Him. May it please His Majesty that the immense bounty with which He has treated this miserable sinner may do something to influence those who read this, so that they may find strength and courage to give up absolutely everything for God's sake! If

His Majesty requites us so amply that even in this life we have a clear vision of the reward and the gain of those who serve Him, what will He not do in the life to come?

CHAPTER XXII

Describes how safe a practice it is for contemplatives not to uplift their spirits to lofty things if they are not so uplifted by the Lord, and how the path leading to the most exalted contemplation must be the Humanity of Christ. Tells of an occasion on which she was herself deceived. This chapter is very profitable.

There is one thing that I want to say, if Your Reverence thinks it well that I should do so, as in my opinion it is important. It will serve as what may be necessary advice; for there are some books written about prayer which say that, although of itself the soul cannot reach this state, since the work wrought in it by the Lord is entirely supernatural, it can get some way towards it by raising the spirit above all created things and causing it to rise aloft in humility after it has spent some years in the Purgative life and made progress in the Illuminative. I do not know why they call it Illuminative but I understand it to mean the life of those who are making progress. And these books advise us earnestly to put aside all corporeal imagination and to approach the contemplation of the Divinity. For they say that anything else, even Christ's Humanity, will hinder or impede those who have arrived so far from attaining to the most perfect contemplation. They quote the words of the Lord on this subject to the Apostles with regard to the coming of the Holy Spirit[1]—I mean, after He had ascended into Heaven. But it seems to me that if they had then had faith, as they had after the Holy Spirit came, to believe that He was God and Man, it would have been no hindrance to them: for this was not said to the Mother of God, though

[1] [Presumably St. John xvi, 7–14 is meant. The Spanish has "at the time of" for "with regard to" and the "had" which follows is in the indicative mood: grammatically, therefore, the sense of the passage is that the words were spoken after the Holy Spirit had come. No doubt this was an inadvertence on the part of the author.]

she loved Him more than all the rest.[2] But these writers think that, as this work is entirely spiritual, anything corporeal may disturb or impede it, and that what contemplatives must contrive to do is to think of themselves as circumscribed, but of God as being everywhere, so that they may become absorbed in Him. It will be all right, I think, to do this sometimes, but I cannot bear the idea that we must withdraw ourselves entirely from Christ and treat that Divine Body of His as though it were on a level with our miseries and with all created things. May His Majesty grant me the ability to explain myself.[3]

I do not contradict this view, for it is held by learned and spiritual men, who know what they are saying, and God leads souls along many roads and by many ways, as He has led mine. It is of mine that I now wish to speak, without interfering with the souls of others, and of the danger in which I found myself through trying to fall into line with what I read. I can well believe that anyone who attains to union and goes no farther—I mean, to raptures and visions and other favours granted to souls by God—will think that view to be the best, as I did myself. But if I had acted upon it, I do not think I should ever have reached my present state, for I believe it to be mistaken. It may, of course, be I who am mistaken— but I will relate what happened to me.

As I had no director, I used to read these books, and gradually began to think I was learning something. I found out later that, if the Lord had not taught me, I could have learned little from books, for until His Majesty taught it me by experience what I learned was nothing at all; I did not even know what I was doing. When I began to gain some experience of supernatural prayer—I mean of the Prayer of Quiet—I tried to put aside everything corporeal, though I dared not lift up my soul, for, being always so wicked, I saw

---

[2] The passage "But it seems to me . . . all the rest" was inserted by the author in the margin of the autograph.

[3] This chapter, which dwells on the suitability of the Humanity of Christ as a subject for meditation, attacks an idea, very prevalent in St. Teresa's time, that at certain stages of mystical progress any such "corporeal" subject, even the mystery of Our Lord's Incarnation, should be rigidly excluded by the contemplative. All later Spanish mystics follow St. Teresa here and many specifically eulogize or embroider this exposition.

that to do this would be presumption. But I thought I was experiencing the presence of God, as proved to be true, and I contrived to remain with Him in a state of recollection. This type of prayer, if God has a part in it, is full of delight, and brings great joy. And in view of the advantage I was deriving from it and the pleasure it was bringing me, no one could have made me return to meditation on the Humanity —on the contrary, this really seemed to me a hindrance. O Lord of my soul and my Good, Jesus Christ crucified! Never once do I recall this opinion which I held without a feeling of pain: I believe I was committing an act of high treason, though I committed it in ignorance.

All my life I had been greatly devoted to Christ (for this happened quite recently: by "recently" I mean before the Lord granted me these favours—these raptures and visions),[4] so I remained of this opinion only for a very short time and then returned to my habit of continually rejoicing in the Lord. Especially when communicating, I would wish I had His portrait and image always before my eyes, since I could not have it as deeply engraven on my soul as I should like. Is it possible, my Lord, that for so much as an hour I could have entertained the thought that Thou couldst hinder my greatest good? Whence have all good things come to me save from Thee? I do not want to think that I was to blame for this, for I grieve greatly about it and it was certainly a matter of ignorance. So Thou, in Thy goodness, wert pleased to bring it to an end by giving me one who would cure me of this error,[5] and afterwards by permitting me often to see Thee, as I shall relate hereafter, so that I might clearly realize how great my error was and tell many people of it, as I have done, and set it all down here and now.

I believe myself that this is the reason why many souls, after succeeding in experiencing the Prayer of Union, do not make further progress and achieve a very great spiritual freedom. There are two reasons, I think, on which I can found my opinion; there may, of course, be nothing in it, but what I say I have observed in my own experience, for my soul was in a very bad way until the Lord gave it light: all the joys it

---

[4] "By 'recently' . . . visions" is a marginal addition in St. Teresa's hand.

[5] [Lewis (p. 187, n. 5) supposes this to be P. Juan de Prádanos: cf. p. 227, n. 11.]

had experienced had come in little sips, and, once these were over, it never experienced any companionship, as it did later, at times of trial and temptation. One of these reasons is that the soul is somewhat lacking in humility and that what it has is so completely disguised and hidden as not to be noticed. Who can there be, like myself, so miserably proud that, when he has laboured all his life long over every imaginable kind of penance and prayer and suffered every kind of persecution, he does not count himself very wealthy and very abundantly rewarded if the Lord allows him to stand with Saint John, at the foot of the Cross? I cannot imagine how it can enter anyone's head not to be contented with this; yet I myself was not, and I have lost in every respect where I ought to have gained.

It may be that our temperament, or some indisposition, will not always allow us to think of the Passion, because of its painfulness; but what can prevent us from being with Him in His Resurrection Body, since we have Him so near us in the Sacrament, where He is already glorified? Here we shall not see Him wearied and broken in body, streaming with blood, exhausted by journeying, persecuted by those to whom He was doing such good, disbelieved by the Apostles. Certainly it is not always that one can bear to think of such great trials as those which He suffered. But here we can behold Him free from pain, full of glory, strengthening some, encouraging others, ere He ascends to the Heavens. In the Most Holy Sacrament He is our Companion and it would seem impossible for Him to leave us for a moment. And yet it was possible for me to leave Thee, my Lord, in the hope that I might serve Thee better! True, when I offended Thee, I knew Thee not, but to think that, when I did know Thee, I could suppose it possible that in such a way I should gain more! How mistaken, Lord, was the path I followed! Indeed, I think I should be following no path at all hadst Thou not brought me back to it. For when I see Thee near me I have seen all blessings. No trial has come to me that I cannot gladly bear when I look at Thee as Thou stoodest before Thy judges. With so good a Friend, so good a Captain at our side, Who came forward first of all to suffer, one can bear everything. He helps us; He gives us strength; He never fails; He is a true Friend.

I can see clearly, and since that time have always seen, that it is God's will, if we are to please Him and He is to grant us great favours, that this should be done through His most sacred Humanity, in Whom, His Majesty said, He is well pleased. Very, very many times have I learned this by experience: the Lord has told it me. I have seen clearly that it is by this door that we must enter if we wish His Sovereign Majesty to show us great secrets. Therefore, Sir,[6] even if you reach the summit of contemplation Your Reverence must seek no other way: that way alone is safe. It is through this Lord of ours that all blessings come. He will show us the way; we must look at His life—that is our best pattern. What more do we need than to have at our side so good a Friend, Who will not leave us in trials and tribulations, as earthly friends do? Blessed is he who loves Him in truth and has Him always at his side. Let us consider the glorious Saint Paul, from whose lips the name of Jesus seems never to have been absent, because He was firmly enshrined in his heart. Since realizing this, I have looked carefully at the lives of a number of saints who were great contemplatives and I find that they followed exactly the same road. Saint Francis, with his stigmata, illustrates this, as does Saint Anthony of Padua with the Divine Infant. Saint Bernard, too, delighted in Christ's Humanity, and so did Saint Catherine of Siena and many others of whom Your Reverence will know better than I.

This withdrawal from the corporeal must doubtless be good, since it is advised by such spiritual people, but my belief is that it must be practised only when the soul is very proficient: until then, it is clear, the Creator must be sought through the creatures. All this has to do with the grace which the Lord bestows on every soul: into that matter I will not enter. What I should like to make clear is that Christ's most sacred Humanity must not be reckoned among these corporeal objects. Let that point be clearly understood: I wish I knew how to explain it.

When God is pleased to suspend all the faculties, as we have seen that He does in the modes of prayer already described, it is clear that, though we may not desire it to be so,

6 She seems to be addressing P. García de Toledo here and the addition of "Sir" may be due to the fact that he was the son of the Count of Oropesa. She uses the same word when writing to the aristocratic Don Álvaro de Mendoza, Bishop of Ávila.

this Presence is taken from us. At such a time as that, let this be done. Blessed is such a loss, since it brings with it the enjoyment of more than we seem to have sacrificed; for the soul can then employ itself wholly in loving One Whom the understanding has been striving hard to know; it loves what it has not comprehended and rejoices in that of which it could not have such great fruition save by losing itself, in order, as I say, the better to gain itself. But that we should exert care and skill to accustom ourselves not to endeavour with all our strength to have always before us—and the Lord grant it be always!—this most sacred Humanity, it is that, I say, which seems to me not to be right. The soul is left, as the phrase has it, in the air; for it has nothing to lean upon, however full it may think itself to be of God. It is a great thing for us, while we live as human beings, to have before us Christ's Humanity. This is that other inconvenience to which I have already referred. The first, which I was beginning to speak about earlier, is a certain lack of humility, a desire on the soul's part to rise before the Lord raises it, a dissatisfaction with merely meditating on something so precious, and a longing to be Mary before one has laboured with Martha. When the Lord wishes one to be Mary, there is no need for fear, even on the very first day, but we must go carefully about it, as I believe I have said already. This little mote of deficient humility, though it seems to be of no importance, does a great deal of harm to those who wish to make progress in contemplation.

To come now to the second point: we are not angels and we have bodies. To want to become angels while we are still on earth, and as much on earth as I was, is ridiculous. As a rule, our thoughts must have something to lean upon, though sometimes the soul may go out from itself and very often may be so full of God that it will need no created thing to assist it in recollection. But this is not very usual: when we are busy, or suffering persecutions or trials, when we cannot get as much quiet as we should like, and at seasons of aridity, we have a very good Friend in Christ. We look at Him as a Man; we think of His moments of weakness and times of trial; and He becomes our Companion. Once we have made a habit of thinking of Him in this way, it becomes very easy to find Him at our side, though there will come times when it is impossible to do either the one thing or the other. For that reason it is advisable to do as I have already said: we must not show ourselves to be striving after spiritual consolations; come what may, the great thing for us to do is to embrace the Cross. The Lord was deprived of all consolation; they left Him alone in His trials. Let us not leave Him; for His hand will help us to rise more effectually than our own efforts; and He will withdraw Himself when He sees that it is good for us and when He is pleased to draw the soul out of itself, as I have said.

God is well pleased to see a soul humbly taking His Son as Mediator, and yet loving Him so much that, even if His Majesty is pleased to raise it to the highest contemplation, as I have said, it realizes its unworthiness, and says with Saint Peter: "Depart from me, Lord, for I am a sinful man."[7] I have proved this, for it is in this way that God has led my soul. Others, as I have said, will take another and a shorter road. What I have learned is this: that the entire foundation of prayer must be established in humility, and that, the more a soul abases itself in prayer, the higher God raises it. I do not remember that He has ever granted me any of the outstanding favours of which I shall speak later save when I have been consumed with shame by realizing my own wickedness; and His Majesty has even managed to help me to know myself by revealing to me things which I myself could not have imagined. I believe myself that, when a soul does anything to further its own progress in this Prayer of Union, it may seem to be deriving some immediate benefit but will very quickly fall again, because it has not laid the proper foundations. Indeed, I fear it will never attain to true poverty of spirit, which consists in seeking, not comfort or pleasure in prayer (for it has already abandoned earthly comforts and pleasures), but consolation in trials for the love of Him Who suffered trials all His life long; and we must endure these trials, and be calm amidst aridities, though we may feel some regret at having to suffer them. They should not cause us the unrest and distress which they cause some people who think that, if they are not for ever labouring with the understanding and striving after feelings of devotion, they are going completely astray, as if by so labouring they were meriting some great blessing. I do not mean that these things should not be sought after, or that we should not be careful how we ap-

[7] St. Luke v, 8.

proach the presence of God, but merely that, as I have said elsewhere, we must not worry ourselves to death if we cannot think one single good thought. We are unprofitable servants:[8] what do we suppose it is in our power to accomplish?

But it is the Lord's will that we should know this and be like the little donkeys that draw the above-described water-wheel. Though their eyes are shut and they have no idea what they are doing, these donkeys will draw more water than the gardener can with all his efforts. After placing ourselves in the hands of God, we must walk along this road quite freely. If His Majesty is pleased to promote us to be among those of His chamber and privy council, we must go with Him willingly; if He is not, we must serve Him in lowly offices and not sit down in the best places, as I have said elsewhere. God cares for us better than we can care for ourselves and He knows of what each of us is capable. What is the use of governing oneself if one has surrendered one's whole will to God? In my view this is much less tolerable here than in the first degree of prayer and does much greater harm: these blessings are supernatural. If a man has a bad voice, however often he forces himself to sing, he will never make it a good one; whereas, if God is pleased to give him a good one, he has no need to practise singing.[9] Let us, then, continually beseech Him to grant us favours, resigned in spirit and yet trusting in God's greatness. Since the soul is given leave to sit at Christ's feet, let it contrive not to stir thence; let it remain where it will; and let it imitate the Magdalen, and, when it is strong, God will lead it into the desert.

Your Reverence must be satisfied with this until you find someone who has more experience and more knowledge of the matter than I. When people tell you that they are beginning to taste of God, do not believe them if they think they are making more progress and receiving more consolations by making efforts of their own. Oh, how well God can reveal Himself, when it is His will to do so, without these puny

8 [St. Luke xvii, 10.]

9 [The exact sense of this clause is doubtful. *Dar voces* means to cry or shout aloud and the meaning may well be "he has no need to make a fuss about it". I translate "practise singing" only out of deference to the context. P. Silverio has "He" for "he": if we adopt this, we must read: "He (God) has no need to proclaim the fact." But this seems to me a definitely inferior interpretation.]

efforts of ours! Do what we may, He transports the spirit as easily as a giant might take up a straw, and it is useless for us to resist Him. What a strange kind of belief is this, that, when God has willed that a toad should fly, He should wait for it to do so by its own efforts. And it seems to me that for our spirits to be lifted up is a more difficult and troublesome matter even than this if God does not lift them up for us. For they are weighed down by the earth and by a thousand impediments, and the fact that they want to fly is of no help to them; for, though flying comes more naturally to them than to a toad, they are so completely sunk in the mire that through their own fault they have lost the ability.

I will conclude, then, by saying that, whenever we think of Christ, we should remember with what love He has bestowed all these favours upon us, and how great is the love which God has revealed to us in giving us such a pledge of the love which He bears us; for love begets love. And though we may be only beginners, and very wicked, let us strive ever to bear this in mind and awaken our own love, for, if once the Lord grants us the favour of implanting this love in our hearts, everything will be easy for us and we shall get things done in a very short time and with very little labour. May His Majesty give us this love, since He knows how much we need it, for the sake of the love which He bore us and through His glorious Son, Who revealed it to us at such great cost to Himself. Amen.

One thing which I should like to ask Your Reverence is this. How is it, when the Lord begins to grant a soul such sublime favours as that of bringing it to perfect contemplation, that it does not, as by rights it should, become perfect all at once? By rights there is no doubt that it should, for anyone who receives so great a favour ought not to seek any further comforts on earth. Why is it, then, that raptures, and the soul's growing habituation to the receiving of favours, seem to produce results of great and growing sublimity—and the more detached the soul becomes the sublimer they are—when the Lord might leave the soul completely sanctified in the same moment that He comes to it? How is it that it is only later, as time goes on, that the same Lord leaves it perfect in the virtues? I want to know the reason of this, for I am quite ignorant of it. What I do know is that there is a great difference between the degree of fortitude bestowed by God in the early stages of rapture, when this favour lasts no longer than the twinkling of an eye and, save for the effects which it leaves, is hardly noticed, and in the later stages, when it is bestowed in more bountiful measure. And I often think that the reason may be that the soul does not at once completely prepare itself for this, but that the Lord gradually trains it, and gives it determination and manly strength so that it may trample everything under its feet. It was thus that He dealt with the Magdalen, doing His work in her very quickly; and it is thus that He deals with other people, according to the way in which they allow His Majesty to work. We cannot bring ourselves to realize that even in this life God rewards us a hundredfold.

I have also been thinking of the comparison which follows. Assuming that what is given to the most advanced soul is the same as what is given to beginners, it is like food shared by many people; those who eat very little of it experience the pleasant taste only for a short time; those who eat more derive some sustenance from it; while those who eat a great deal derive life and strength. It is possible to eat of this food of life so frequently and with such satisfaction as to derive no pleasure from eating any other. For the soul sees how much good it is deriving from it and its palate is now so completely accustomed to its sweetness that it would rather not live than have to eat any other food, for that would do nothing but spoil the pleasant taste left by the good food. Again, the companionship of good people does not afford us such profitable conversation in one day as in many; and if we have the help of God and are long enough in their company, we may become like them. In fact, everything depends upon His Majesty's good pleasure and upon the person on whom He wishes to bestow this favour. But it is very important that anyone who is beginning to receive it should resolve to detach himself from everything else and hold it in due esteem.

I think, too, that His Majesty goes about seeking to prove who the people are that love Him—whether this person does, or that person—and reveals Himself to us with the sublimest joy, so as to quicken our faith, if it is dead, concerning what He will give us. "See," He says, "this is but a drop in a vast sea of blessings"; for He leaves nothing undone for those He loves, and, when He sees that they accept His gifts, He gives —and gives Himself. He loves every one who loves Him—and

how well loved He is[10] and how good a Friend! Oh, Lord of
my soul, if only one had words to explain what Thou givest
to those that trust in Thee, and what is lost by those who
reach this state and yet do not give themselves to Thee![11] It
is not Thy will, Lord, that this should be so, for Thou doest
more than this when Thou comest to a lodging as wretched
as mine. Blessed be Thou for ever and ever!

I beseech Your Reverence once more, if you discuss these
things that I have written about prayer with spiritual persons,
to be sure they are really spiritual. For if they know only one
path, or have gone half-way and then remained where they
are, they will not be able to discover what it all means. There
are some, of course, whom God leads by a very exalted road;
and these think that others can make progress in the same
way—by quieting the understanding and making no use of
corporeal aids to devotion—but if such persons act thus they
will remain as dry as sticks. There are others who have attained a certain degree of quiet and at once think that, as they
have done this, they can do everything else. But, instead of
gaining in this way, they will lose, as I have said. So experience and discretion are necessary in everything. May the Lord
give us these of His goodness.

CHAPTER XXIII

*Resumes the description of the course of her life and tells
how and by what means she began to aim at greater
perfection. It is of advantage for persons who are concerned in the direction of souls that practise prayer to
know how they must conduct themselves in the early
stages. The profit that she herself gained thereby.*

I will now return to the place where I left off the description
of my life, for I have digressed—longer, I think, than I ought
—in order that what is to come may be the better understood.
From this point onward, I am speaking of another and a new
book—I mean, of another and a new life. Until now the life

10 [Or: "and how well loved is he who loves Him . . . !"]
11 [*Lit.*: "and keep themselves (to themselves)."]

I was describing was my own; but the life I have been living since I began to expound these matters concerning prayer is the life which God has been living in me—or so it has seemed to me. For I believe it to be impossible in so short a time to escape from such wicked deeds and habits. Praised be the Lord, Who has delivered me from myself!

Now when I began to avoid occasions of sin and to devote myself more to prayer, the Lord began to bestow favors upon me and it looked as though He were desirous that I should wish to receive them. His Majesty began to grant me quite frequently the Prayer of Quiet, and often, too, the Prayer of Union, which lasted for a long time. As there have been cases recently in which women have been subjected by the devil to serious illusions and deceptions,[1] I began to be afraid, for the delight and the sweetness which I felt were so great and often I could not help feeling them. But on the other hand I was conscious of a very deep inward assurance that this was of God, especially when I was engaged in prayer, and I found that I was the better for it and developed greater fortitude. But as soon as I became a little distracted, I would grow afraid again and begin to wonder if it was the devil who wanted to suspend my understanding, and make me believe it was a good thing, so that he might deprive me of mental prayer, and prevent me from thinking of the Passion and making use of my understanding. It seemed to me that I was losing rather than gaining, but I did not understand the matter properly.

As His Majesty, however, was now pleased to give me light so that I should not offend Him and should understand how much I owed Him, my fear increased, to such an extent that it made me seek diligently after spiritual persons with whom to discuss this. I already knew of some, for the Fathers of the Company of Jesus had come here,[2] and, though I was unacquainted with any of them, I was attracted to them by my knowledge of their method of life and prayer alone. But I

[1] Such were the notorious Sor Magdalena de la Cruz of Córdoba [and María de la Visitación, the Lisbon prioress who was credited with having received the stigmata: cf. S.S.M., I, 37–8].

[2] It was in 1554 that the Society of Jesus founded the College of St. Giles (San Gil) at Ávila, to which foundation St. Teresa owed a great deal of the spiritual help which she received from the Jesuit Fathers.

did not consider myself worthy to speak to them or strong enough to obey them, and this made me still more afraid; for I felt that it would be unthinkable[3] for me to discuss these matters with them and yet remain as I was.

I went on for some time in this way, until, after experiencing much inward strife and many fears, I determined to have a talk with a spiritual person, to ask him what that kind of prayer was which I was practising and to make it clear to me if I was going astray. I also determined to do all I could not to offend God, for, as I have said, my lack of fortitude, of which I was so conscious, made me very timid. God help me, what a great mistake I was making by giving up what was good when I wanted to be good all the time! The devil must think this very important at the outset of a soul's growth in virtue, for I was quite unable to take myself in hand.[4] He knows that the great means of progress for a soul is converse with friends of God, and thus it was for this reason that I could not come to a decision. First of all, I waited till I had amended my life, just as I had done when I gave up prayer. It may be that I should never have amended it, for I was such a slave to my little bad habits that I could not bring myself to realize that they were bad at all: I needed the help of others, who would take me by the hand and raise me up. Blessed be the Lord that, in the end, the first hand to raise me was His!

When I found that my fear was getting such a hold over me, because I was progressing in the practice of prayer, it seemed to me that there must either be something very good about this or something terribly bad; for I was quite sure that my experiences were supernatural because sometimes I was unable to resist them, nor could I come by them whenever I wanted to. I thought to myself that there was nothing I could do but keep a clear conscience and avoid all occasions of even venial sin; for, if it was the Spirit of God at work, I was obviously the gainer, whereas, if it was the devil, he could do me little harm provided I strove to please the Lord and not to offend Him—in fact, the devil could not fail to be the loser. Having resolved upon this, and begging God all the time to

3 [*Cosa recia. Lit.*: "a stout (tough, hard) thing." As we might say in conversation: "A little *too* strong."]

4 [*Acabarlo conmigo*. A stronger rendering, such as "put an end to it all", would not be out of place.]

help me, I strove for some days to live in this way, but found that my soul was not strong enough by itself to achieve such a high degree of perfection; for I was attached in certain ways to things which, though not wrong in themselves, were sufficient to spoil all my efforts.

They told me of a learned cleric who lived in that place, and whose goodness and holy life the Lord was beginning to make known among the people.[5] I got to know him through a saintly gentleman who lived there also.[6] This gentleman is married, but his life is so exemplary and virtuous, and so outstanding in prayer and charity, that everything he does is resplendent with his goodness and perfection. And with good reason, for many souls have been greatly benefited by him: such great talents has he that, although his being married is anything but a help to him, he cannot do otherwise than use them. He is a man of great intelligence, and very gentle with everybody; and his conversation is never wearisome, but so pleasant and gracious, not to say upright and holy, that it gives great delight to those with whom he has to do. He directs all he does to the great good of the souls with whom he holds converse and he seems to have no other aim than to do whatever he can for everyone he meets and to give everyone pleasure.

Well, so diligent on my behalf was this blessed and holy man that he seems to me to have been the beginning of my soul's salvation. The humility he has shown me is astounding; for he has practised prayer, I believe, for nearly forty years—perhaps two or three years less—and the life he lives, I think, is as nearly perfect as his married state permits. His wife, too, is so great a servant of God and so charitable a woman that she is no hindrance to him: indeed, she was chosen to be the wife of one who God knew would be a great servant of His.

Some of their relatives were married to some of mine[7] and

---

[5] This was Gaspar Daza, a pious and learned priest who for some time was St. Teresa's confessor and helped her a great deal with the foundation of St. Joseph's. He died in 1592.

[6] Don Francisco de Salcedo, an Ávilan gentleman whose wife, Doña Mencía del Águila, was a cousin of the wife of Don Pedro de Cepeda, St. Teresa's uncle (cf. p. 80). He had studied theology at the Dominican College of St. Thomas, in Ávila, and after the death of his wife, took Holy Orders. He died in 1580.

[7] One of these links is mentioned in the preceding note.

I also had a good deal to do with another great servant of God who was married to one of my cousins. It was in this way that I arranged for this cleric who, as I say, was such a servant of God to come to speak with me: he was a great friend of this gentleman and I thought of having him as my confessor and director. When he had brought him to talk to me, I, in the greatest confusion at finding myself in the presence of so holy a man, spoke to him about my soul and my method of prayer, but he would not hear my confession, saying that he was very much occupied, as indeed he was. He began with the holy determination to treat me as if I were strong (and so I ought to have been, considering the extent to which, as he saw, I practised prayer), so that I should give no offence of any kind to God. But when I saw how determinedly he was attacking these little habits of mine which I have already mentioned, and that I had not courage enough to live more perfectly, I became distressed, and, realizing that he was treating me in spiritual matters as though I were going to become perfect immediately, I saw that I should have to be much more careful.

In due course I realized that I should not improve by using the means which he employed with me, for they were meant for a soul which was much more perfect, and I, though advanced in Divine favours, was, as regards virtues and mortification, still quite a beginner. Really, if I had had nobody else to consult, I think my soul would never have shown any improvement, for the distress which it caused me to find that I was not doing what he told me, and felt unable to do so, was sufficient to make me lose hope and give up the whole thing. I sometimes marvel that, though he was a person with a particular gift for leading beginners to God, it was not God's will that he should understand my own soul or desire to take it into his charge. But I see now that it was all for my good, so that I should get to know and consult people as holy as those of the Company of Jesus.

So I made an arrangement with this saintly gentleman that he should sometimes come to see me. It showed what great humility he had, that he should have been willing to have to do with anyone as wicked as I. He began to pay me visits and to encourage me and to tell me not to think that I could get rid of all my troubles in a day but to be sure that God would help me to get rid of them by degrees. He himself, he said, had for many years been troubled by some quite trivial imperfections, which he had never been able to get rid of. O humility, what great blessings dost thou bring to those who possess thee and also to those who have to do with the humble-minded! This saint (for so I think I can rightly call him) would tell me about his own weaknesses—or what his humility led him to think of as such—so that he might help me. Considered in relation to his state of life, they were neither faults nor imperfections, though they would be great faults in the life of a religious like myself. I am not saying this without a reason; I seem to be enlarging upon small points, and yet these are most important if a soul which is not yet fledged, as they say, is to begin to make progress and learn to fly, though no one will believe this who has not experienced it. And as I hope in God that Your Reverence will benefit many souls, I say this here, for my whole salvation was due to the fact that this gentleman knew how to treat me and had the humility and charity necessary for dealing with me and could put up with me when he saw that in some respects I was not amending my life. Gradually and discreetly he showed me ways of vanquishing the devil. So great was the love which I began to bear him that I found nothing more restful than seeing him, though there were few days when I was able to do so. Whenever a long time passed without a visit from him I would at once become very much worried, thinking that he was not coming to see me because I was so wicked.

When he began to realize the seriousness of my imperfections, which may even have been sins (though I improved after I got to know him), and when, in order to obtain light from him, I told him of the graces which God was bestowing upon me, he warned me that these two things were not consistent, that such favours were given to persons who were very far advanced and greatly mortified, and that he could not help having misgivings lest in some of these matters an evil spirit might be at work in me, though he was not sure. But he told me to think well over my experiences in prayer, so far as I understood them, and to tell him about them. But that was the difficulty: I simply could not describe these experiences; it is only quite recently that God has granted me the grace of being able to understand their nature and to describe them.

When he said this to me, fearful as I already was, I was greatly distressed and wept sorely; for I really desired to please God and I could not persuade myself that this was the work of the devil, but I was afraid lest on account of my great sins God might be blinding me so that I could not realize it. Looking through books to see if I could learn how to describe my method of prayer, I found in one, called *The Ascent of the Mount*,[8] which describes the union of the soul with God, all the symptoms I had when I was unable to think of anything. It was exactly this that I was always saying—that when I was experiencing that type of prayer I could think of nothing. So I marked the relevant passages and gave him the book, in order that he and that other cleric to whom I have referred, a holy man and a servant of God, should look at it and tell me what I ought to do. If they thought it well, I would give up prayer altogether, for why should I run into these dangers? If after almost twenty years' experience of prayer I had gained nothing, but had been deluded by the devil, surely it was better for me not to pray at all—though this would also have been very difficult, for I had already discovered what my soul was like without prayer. Whichever way I looked, then, I was beset by trials. I was like a person who has fallen into a river: whatever the direction he takes, he is afraid the danger will be greater and yet he is almost drowning. This is a very great trial, and I have experienced many such, as I shall say later: it may seem unimportant but it may possibly be of great advantage to learn how spirituality is to be tested.

And certainly this is a grievous trial to experience and one needs to be careful—women especially so, since we are very weak, and may come to great harm if we are told in so many words that we are being deluded by the devil. The matter should be very carefully considered and women protected from all possible dangers. They should be advised to keep their experiences very secret and it is well that their advisers should observe secrecy too. I speak of this from knowledge, for I have been caused great distress by the indiscretion of certain persons with whom I have discussed my experiences in prayer. By talking about them to each other they have done me great harm, divulging things which should have been

---

[8] [She refers to the *Ascent of Mount Sion*, published at Seville, in 1535, by a Franciscan lay-brother, Bernardino de Laredo. An account of Laredo and his book will be found in *S.S.M.*, II, 41–76.]

kept very secret, for they are not meant for everyone to know, and it looked as though I were publishing them myself. The fault, I believe, was not theirs: the Lord permitted it so that I might suffer. I do not mean that they divulged what I had told them in confession, but none the less, as they were people whom I had consulted about my fears, so that I might obtain light from them, I thought they ought to have kept silence. In spite of this, however, I never dared to hide anything from such persons. I think, then, that women should be counselled with great discretion, and encouraged, and the right moment should be awaited, at which the Lord will help them as He has helped me: had He not done so, I should have come to great harm, so timorous was I and so fearful. Considering the serious heart trouble from which I was suffering, I am amazed that this did not greatly harm me.

Well, when I had given him the book, together with the best general account of my life and sins that I could (not in confession, as he was a layman, but I made it very clear to him how wicked I was), these two servants of God[9] considered with great charity and love what would be best for me. At length they gave me the reply which I had awaited with such dread. During the intervening days I had begged many persons to commend me to God and had prayed continually. But, when this gentleman came to me, it was to tell me with great distress that to the best of their belief my trouble came from the devil, and the wisest thing for me to do would be to discuss it with a Father of the Company of Jesus, who would come to see me if I asked him to do so and told him what I needed. I could then give him a perfectly clear description of my whole life and spiritual state in the form of a general confession; and through the virtue of the Sacrament of Confession God would give him more light on my case: these Fathers were men of great experience in spiritual matters. I ought not, they said, to depart in the very least from whatever he might say, because if I had no one to direct me I was in great peril.

This caused me such distress and fear that I did not know what to do: I could only weep. But while I was in an oratory, in great affliction, and not knowing what was to become of me, I read in a book, which it seemed as if the Lord had put

9 Salcedo and Daza.

into my hands, those words of Saint Paul, that God is very
faithful and never allows people who love Him to be deluded
by the devil.[10] This was the greatest comfort to me. I began
to think over my general confession and to write down all my
good and bad points and prepare the clearest account of my
life that I possibly could, leaving nothing unsaid. I remember
that, after writing it, I found so many bad points and so little that was good that it caused me the greatest distress and
affliction. I was also troubled that my sisters in the convent
should see me consulting such saintly people as those of the
Company of Jesus; for I was afraid of my wickedness and
thought that I should now be obliged to abandon it and to
give up my pastimes, and that if I did not do so I should
grow worse; and so I arranged with the sacristan and portress
that they should not talk about it to anyone. However, this
was of little use, because when I was sent for there was someone at the door who talked about it all over the convent.
What a lot of obstacles and fears the devil sets before those
who are anxious to approach God!

I told that servant of God[11] all about my soul (and he was
indeed a servant of God and a very prudent one, too); and,
being well versed in the subject, he told me what was wrong
and greatly encouraged me. He said that I was very evidently
being led by the Spirit of God and that I needed to return to
my prayer: I was not working upon a good foundation, nor
had I begun to understand the nature of mortification (which
was true: I do not believe I even understood the meaning of
the word). I must on no account give up prayer; on the contrary, since God was granting me such special favours, I must
work hard at it. How did I know, he asked me, that the Lord
was not desirous of using me in order to help a great number
of people and perhaps to do other things (it seems now that
he was prophesying what the Lord afterwards did with me)?
I should be very much to blame, he added, if I were not re-
sponsive to the favours that God was showing me. Throughout, as it seemed to me, the Holy Spirit was speaking through

[10] 1 Corinthians x, 13. "And God is faithful, who will not suffer
you to be tempted above that which you are able: but will make
also with temptation issue, that you may be able to bear it."
[11] This was P. Juan de Prádanos, who was St. Teresa's confessor
for two months and probably the first Jesuit confessor she ever had.
He died at Valladolid, in 1597.

him, for the good of my soul, to judge from the way that his words impressed themselves upon it.

He made me very much ashamed; and led me along paths which seemed to make me quite a different person. What a great thing it is to understand a soul! He told me that my daily prayer should be based upon one of the incidents of the Passion, and that I should get all I could out of that incident, think only of Christ's Humanity and as far as possible resist the desire for recollection and consolations; these I was not to indulge again until he gave me further instructions.

He left me comforted and strengthened. The Lord helped us both, enabled him to understand my spiritual condition and showed him how to direct me. I made a determination not to depart in any way from what he commanded me and to that determination I have remained true until this day. Praised be the Lord, Who has given me grace to obey my confessors, however imperfectly! These have almost always been chosen from the blessed Fathers of the Company of Jesus, although, as I say, I have followed them imperfectly. My soul began to grow notably better, as I shall now relate.

CHAPTER XXIV

Continues the subject already begun. Describes how her soul profited more and more after she began to obey, how little it availed her to resist the favours of God and how His Majesty went on giving them to her in increasing measure.

After I had made this confession my soul became so amenable that I thought there could be nothing which I should not be prepared to do; and so I began to make many changes in my habits, although my confessor did not press me to do so and in fact seemed to trouble about it all very little. But this moved me the more, for he led me by the way of love for God, which brought me, not oppression, as it would if I had not done it out of love, but freedom. I remained in that state for nearly two months, doing all I could to resist the favours and graces of God. The change in me was manifest even superficially, for the Lord was already beginning to encourage me to suffer things which persons who knew me, and even the nuns in my own house,[1] considered and described as extreme. And they were right: these things were indeed extreme by comparison with what I had been doing before. But they fell short of the obligations of my habit and profession.

By resisting the consolations and favours of God I gained this—that His Majesty Himself taught me. For previously I had thought that, if I was to receive favours in prayer, I must go apart by myself a great deal, and so I had hardly dared to stir. Then I began to see how little this had to do with it; the more I tried to think of other things, the more completely the Lord enveloped me in that sweetness and glory until I felt so completely surrounded by it that I could not flee from it in any direction; and thus matters continued. I was so much concerned about this that it caused me distress. The Lord, however, was much more concerned, during those two months, to grant me favours and to reveal Himself to me more than He had been wont to do, so that I might the better understand that resistance was no longer in my power. I began to conceive a new love for the most sacred Humanity. My prayers now began to take shape like an edifice with solid foundations, and I grew fonder of penances, which I had neglected because of my frequent indispositions.

That holy man[2] who heard my confessions told me that there were certain things which could not hurt me; and suggested that God might perhaps be giving me ill-health just because I did not perform penances—that is, that His Majesty was being pleased to give me the penances Himself. My confessor ordered me to practise certain mortifications which I did not find very agreeable. But I performed them all, because his commands seemed to me to come from the Lord, and I thanked him for giving them to me so that I could obey Him. Any offence, however slight, which I might commit against God I would feel in my soul so deeply that if I had anything I did not need[3] I could not become recollected again until it had been taken away. I prayed earnestly that the Lord would hold me by His hand, and, now that I was in touch with His servants, would grant me grace not to turn

[1] The Convent of the Incarnation, Ávila.

[2] P. Juan de Prádanos.

[3] [Lit.: "any superfluous thing"—presumably referring to small comforts or luxuries.]

back. For to do this, I thought, would be a great failing, since it would detract from their credit.

During this period the town was visited by Father Francis, who was Duke of Gandía but some years before had given up everything and entered the Company of Jesus.[4] My confessor and the gentleman I have spoken of arranged for him to come and see me so that I might talk to him and tell him about my experiences in prayer, as they knew him to be very proficient in this and to be receiving great favours and graces from God, as rewards in this life for all that he had given up for Him. When he had heard my story, he told me that I was being led by the Spirit of God and that he thought I should not be doing right to resist Him further. It had been right to do so, he said, until now; but he suggested that I should always begin my prayers with a meditation on one of the incidents of the Passion, and, if the Lord should then transport my spirit, I should not resist Him but should allow His Majesty to have it and make no effort to keep it back. He gave me this medicine and counsel as one who had himself made great progress: in this matter there is much potency in experience. He said that it would be a mistake for me to resist any longer. I was greatly comforted and so was this gentleman: he was delighted that the Father had said I was being led by God and he continued to help and advise me to the best of his ability, which was very great.

About this time my confessor was transferred elsewhere. I was very sorry for this, for I thought I should be bound to grow wicked again, not supposing that it would be possible to find another like him. My soul was as if in a desert; I grew most disconsolate and fearful; and I did not know what would become of me. But a relative of mine arranged for me to go and stay with her and I at once set about getting another confessor from the Company. It was the Lord's good pleasure

---

[4] St. Francis Borgia [Sp., Borja] had been appointed Commissary of the Society of Jesus in Spain and it was in this capacity that, on several occasions, he visited the College of St. Giles at Ávila. The visit on which he made the acquaintance of St. Teresa took place in 1557. The Duchess of Gandía, who was one of the witnesses when evidence was being taken previously to her beatification, deposed that she had "often heard the Duke of Gandía, Father Francis of Borja, who became General of the Society of Jesus, speak of the spirituality, life and sanctity of the Mother Teresa of Jesus."

that I should become friendly with a widowed lady of good family,[5] who was much given to prayer, and had a great deal to do with these Fathers. She arranged for me to make my confessions to her own confessor and I stayed in her house for some days; she lived quite near. I was delighted at getting into close touch with the Fathers, for the mere realization of the holiness of their way of life brought my soul great benefit.

This Father[6] began to lead me to greater perfection. He told me that I ought to leave nothing undone so as to become entirely pleasing to God, and he treated me with great skill, yet also very gently, for my soul was not at all strong, but very sensitive, especially as regards abandoning certain friendships which were not actually leading me to offend God. There was a great deal of affection beneath these and it seemed to me that if I abandoned them I should be sinning through ingratitude; so I asked him why it was necessary for me to be ungrateful if I was not offending God. He told me to commend the matter to God for a few days, and to recite the hymn *Veni, Creator*, and I should be enlightened as to which was the better thing to do. So I spent the greater part of one whole day in prayer; and then, beseeching the Lord that He would help me to please Him in everything, I began the hymn. While I was reciting it, there came to me a transport so sudden that it almost carried me away: I could make no mistake about this, so clear was it. This was the first time that the Lord had granted me the favour of any kind of rapture. I heard these words: "I will have thee converse now, not with

[5] Doña Guiomar (or Jerónima) de Ulloa. Both her parents, Don Pedro de Ulloa and Doña Aldonza de Guzmán, bore illustrious names. Left a widow at the age of twenty-five, she devoted herself to a life of virtue, and helped St. Teresa, whom she first met in 1557, with her early work in connection with the Discalced Reform. Cf. St. Teresa's testimony to her in a letter to her brother Lorenzo, dated December 31, 1561 (*Letters* [St.], I, 4), where she describes their friendship as closer than one between sisters.

[6] P. Baltasar Álvarez, who was one of the best directors St. Teresa ever had, though at times, as we shall see in Chap. XXVIII, he was somewhat hesitating and timid in his treatment of her. He acted as her confessor from 1559 to 1564, and in 1567, while at Medina del Campo, was of great use to her in connection with the foundation which she made there. He died on July 25, 1580, at the age of only forty-seven.

men, but with angels." This simply amazed me, for my soul was greatly moved and the words were spoken to me in the depths of the spirit. For this reason they made me afraid, though on the other hand they brought me a great deal of comfort, which remained with me after the fear caused by the strangeness of the experience had vanished.

The words have come true: never since then have I been able to maintain firm friendship save with people who I believe love God and try to serve Him, nor have I derived comfort from any others or cherished any private affection for them. It has not been in my own power to do so; and it has made no difference if the people have been relatives or friends. Unless I know that a person loves God or practises prayer, it is a real cross to me to have to do with him. I really believe this is the absolute truth.

Since that day I have been courageous enough to give up everything for the sake of God, Who in that moment—for I think it happened in no more than a moment—was pleased to make His servant another person. So there was no need for my confessor to give me any further commands. When he had found me so much attached to these friendships, he had not ventured to tell me definitely to abandon them. He had to wait until the Lord took it in hand, as He did. I did not think at first that I could ever give them up, for I had tried it already, and it had caused me such great distress that I had put the idea aside, as the friendships did not appear unseemly. But now the Lord set me free and gave me strength to carry my resolution into practice. So I told my confessor this and gave up everything, exactly as he had instructed me to do. And when the persons with whom I had been intimate saw how determined I was it caused them great edification.

Blessed for ever be God, Who in one moment gave the freedom which, despite all the efforts I had been making for so many years, I had never been able to attain, though sometimes I had done such violence to myself that it badly affected my health. As it was the work of One Who is almighty and the true Lord of all, it caused me no distress.

CHAPTER XXV

*Discusses the method and manner in which these locutions
bestowed by God on the soul are apprehended without
being heard and also certain kinds of deception which
may occur here and the way to recognize them. This
chapter is most profitable for anyone who finds himself
at this stage of prayer because the exposition is very
good and contains much teaching.*

It will be well, I think, to explain the nature of the locutions
which God bestows upon the soul, and the soul's experiences
on receiving them, so that Your Reverence may understand
this. For, since the occasion I have described[1] on which the
Lord granted me this favour, it has become quite a common
experience even to this day, as will be seen in what is to come.
Though perfectly formed, the words are not heard with the
bodily ear; yet they are understood much more clearly than if
they were so heard, and, however determined one's resistance,
it is impossible to fail to hear them. For when, on the natural
plane, we do not wish to hear, we can close our ears, or attend to something else, with the result that, although we may
hear, we do not understand. But when God talks in this way
to the soul, there is no such remedy: I have to listen, whether
I like it or no, and my understanding has to devote itself so
completely to what God wishes me to understand that
whether I want to listen or not makes no difference. For, as
He Who is all-powerful wills us to understand, we have to do
what He wills; and He reveals Himself as our true Lord. I
have long experience of this; I was so much afraid of it that
I kept up my resistance for almost two years and sometimes
I still try to resist, though with little success.

I should like to describe the different kinds of deception
which may occur here, though I think anyone who has much
experience will seldom, if ever, be deceived. But, as considerable experience is necessary before this state can be reached,
I will explain the difference between locutions coming from
good spirits and from evil ones and how, as may happen, the

[1] Chap. XIX (p. 186). The date of this first locution can be fixed
only approximately, between 1555 and 1557.

apprehension can be caused by the understanding itself or by the spirit conversing with itself (I do not know if that is possible, but I was thinking that it was, this very day). With regard to cases in which the locution is of God, I have a great deal of evidence, as I have heard such voices two or three years beforehand and all that they have said has come true—not a single one of them so far has proved deceptive. And there are other things in which the Spirit of God can be clearly perceived, as will be said later.

Sometimes, I think, a person who has commended some matter to God with great affection and concern will believe he hears something telling him if it will be granted him or not—that is quite possible—though, once he has really heard anything of the kind, he will recognize it immediately, for there is a great difference between true and false. If it is something invented by the understanding, subtle as the invention may be, he realizes that it is the understanding which is making up the words and uttering them, for it is just as if a person were making up a speech or as if he were listening to what someone else was saying to him. The understanding will realize that it is not listening, but being active; and the words it is inventing are fantastic and indistinct and have not the clarity of true locutions. In such a case we have the power to divert our attention from them, just as we are able to stop speaking and become silent, whereas with true locutions no such diversion is possible. A further indication, which is surer than any other, is that these false locutions effect nothing, whereas, when the Lord speaks, the words are accompanied by effects, and although the words may be, not of devotion, but rather of reproof, they prepare the soul and make it ready and move it to affection, give it light and make it happy and tranquil; and, if it has been afflicted with aridity and turmoil and unrest, the Lord frees it as with His own hand, or more effectively even than that; for He appears to wish it to realize His power and the efficacy of His words.

It seems to me that the difference is like that between speaking and listening—neither greater nor less. For while I am speaking, as I have said, my understanding is composing what I am saying, whereas, if I am being spoken to, I am doing nothing but listen and it costs me no labour. In the one case it is as if the thing is there but we cannot be sure what it is, any more than if we were half asleep. In the other case there is a voice which is so clear that not a syllable of what it says is lost. And sometimes it happens that the understanding and the soul are so perturbed and distracted that they could not put together a single sentence and yet the soul hears long set speeches addressed to it which it could not have composed, even if completely recollected. And at the first word, as I say, it is completely changed. How, especially if it is in rapture and the faculties are suspended, can the soul understand things that had never come into its mind before? How can they come at a time when the memory is hardly working and the imagination is, as it were, in a stupor?

It should be noted that we never, I think, see visions or hear these words at a time when the soul is in union during an actual state of rapture, for then, as I have already explained (I think it was in writing of the Second Water), all the faculties are wholly lost, and at that time I do not believe there is any seeing, hearing or understanding at all. For the soul is wholly in the power of another, and during that period, which is very short, I do not think the Lord leaves it freedom for anything. It is of when this short period has passed, and the soul is still enraptured, that I am speaking; for the faculties, though not lost, are in such a state that they can do practically nothing; they are, as it were, absorbed and incapable of coherent reasoning. There are so many reasoning processes by which we may tell the difference between these types of locution that, although we may be mistaken once, we shall not be so often.

I mean that, if a soul is experienced and alert, it will see the difference very clearly; for, apart from other characteristics which prove the truth of what I have said, human locutions produce no effect upon the soul and it does not accept them (as it has to accept Divine locutions, even against its will) or give them credence: on the contrary, it recognizes them as ravings of the mind and will take no more notice of them than of a person whom it knows to be mad. But to Divine locutions we listen as we should to a person of great holiness, learning and authority who we know will not lie to us. Indeed, even this is an inadequate comparison, for sometimes these words are of such majesty that, without our knowing from whom they come, they make us tremble if they are words of reproof and if they are words of love fill us with a love that is all-consuming. Further, as I have said, they are things of which the memory has no recollection, and sometimes they are such lengthy speeches and are uttered so quickly that it would take us a long time to make them up ourselves and in that case I am sure we could not be unaware that we had composed them. So there is no reason for my dwelling any longer upon this, for, unless he deliberately courted deception, I think it would be extraordinary if any experienced person were deceived.

I have often been doubtful, and failed to believe what was said to me, and wondered if I had been imagining it (after the experience was over, I mean, for at the time doubt is impossible); and then, after a long interval has elapsed, I have found it all fulfilled. For the Lord impresses His words upon the memory so that it is impossible to forget them, whereas the words that come from our own understanding are like the first movement of thought, which passes and is forgotten. The Divine words resemble something of which with the lapse of time a part may be forgotten but not so completely that one loses the memory of its having been said. Only if a long time has passed, or if the words were words of favour or of instruction, can this happen; words of prophecy, in my opinion, cannot possibly be forgotten—at least, I can never forget them myself, and my memory is a poor one.

I repeat, then, that, unless a soul should be so impious as to want to pretend to have received this favour, and to say it has understood something when it has not, which would be very wrong, there seems to me no possibility of its failing to know quite well if it is making up these words and addressing them to itself. This is assuming that it has once heard the Spirit of God: if it has not, it may continue to be deceived all its life long, and think it is understanding what is being said to it, though I do not know how it can do so. Either this soul wishes to understand or it does not: if it is sorely troubled at what it hears and has not the slightest desire to hear because of its many fears and many other reasons it may have for desiring to be quiet in its times of prayer and not to have these experiences, how can its understanding have time enough for the making up of these speeches? For time is essential for this. The Divine words, on the other hand, instruct us at once, without any lapse of time, and by their means we can understand things which it would probably take us a month to make up ourselves. And at some of the things which they understand, the understanding and the soul are astounded.

That is the position; and anyone who has experience of it will know that all I have said is literally true. I praise God that I have been able so to explain it. And I will end by saying that, if all locutions came from the understanding, we could hear them whenever we liked and we could think we heard them whenever we prayed. But with Divine locutions this is not the case. I may listen for many days; and, although I may desire to hear them, I shall be unable to do so; and then, at other times, when I have no desire to hear them, as I have said, I am compelled to. It seems to me that anyone who wishes to deceive people by saying that he has heard from God what comes from himself might equally well say that he heard it with his bodily ears. It is certainly a fact that I never thought there was any other way of hearing or understanding until I had this experience myself, and so, as I have said, it has cost me a great deal of trouble.

When a locution comes from the devil, it not only fails to leave behind good effects but leaves bad ones. This has happened to me, though only on two or three occasions, and each time I have immediately been warned by the Lord that the locution came from the devil. Besides being left in a state of great aridity, the soul suffers a disquiet such as I have experienced on many other occasions when the Lord has allowed me to be exposed to many kinds of sore temptation and spiritual trial; and though this disquiet continually tortures me, as I shall say later, it is of such a nature that one cannot discover whence it comes. The soul seems to resist it and is perturbed and afflicted without knowing why, for what the devil actually says is not evil, but good. I wonder if one kind of spirit can be conscious of another.

The pleasures and joys which the devil bestows are, in my opinion, of immense diversity. By means of these pleasures he might well deceive anyone who is not experiencing, or has not experienced, other pleasure given by God.

I mean what I say when I describe them as pleasures, for they consist of a refreshment which is sweet, invigorating, lasting in its effects, delectable and tranquil. Mild feelings of devotion which come to the soul and which issue in tears and other brief emotional outlets are merely frail flowerets blasted at the first breath of persecution: they are a good beginning, and the emotions they engender are holy ones, but I do not call them true devotion at all and they are useless as means of distinguishing between a good spirit and an evil one. So it is well for us always to proceed with great caution, for persons who experience visions or revelations and are no farther advanced in prayer than this might easily be deceived. I myself had never experienced anything of the kind until God, of His goodness alone, granted me the Prayer of Union, unless it were on the first occasion of which I have spoken, when, many years ago, I saw Christ.[2] How I wish His Majesty had been pleased for me to realize then that this was a genuine vision, as I have since realized it was: it would have been no small blessing to me. After experiencing Satanic locutions,[3] the soul is not in the least docile but seems both bewildered and highly discontented at the same time.

I consider it quite certain that the devil will not deceive, and that God will not permit him to deceive, a soul which has no trust whatever in itself, and is strengthened in faith and knows full well that for one single article of the Faith it would suffer a thousand deaths. With this love for the Faith, which God immediately infuses into it, and which produces a faith that is living and strong, the soul strives ever to act in conformity with a doctrine of the Church, asking for instruction from this person and from that, and acts as one already strongly established in these truths, so that all the revelations it could imagine, even were it to see the heavens opened, would not cause it to budge an inch from the Church's teachings. If it should ever feel its thoughts wavering about this, or find itself stopping to say "If God says this to me, it may quite well be true, just as what He said to the Saints is true", I will not assert that it necessarily believes what it is saying, but the devil is certainly taking the first step towards tempting it. To stop and say this is clearly wrong; but often, I believe, even this first step will have no effect if the soul is so strong in this respect (as the Lord makes the soul to whom He grants these things), that it feels able to pulverize the devils in its defence of one of the smallest of the truths which the Church holds.

[2] Chap. VII (p. 99).
[3] [This phrase is not in the original, but appears to be understood.]

I mean by this that, if the soul does not find itself in possession of this great strength, and is not helped by devotion or by visions, it must not consider its strength to be secure. For, though it may not be aware of any immediate harm, great harm might be caused it by slow degrees; for, as far as I can see and learn by experience, the soul must be convinced that a thing comes from God only if it is in conformity with Holy Scripture; if it were to diverge from that in the very least, I think I should be incomparably more firmly convinced that it came from the devil than I previously was that it came from God, however sure I might have felt of this. There is no need, in that case, to go in search of signs, or to ask from what spirit it comes; for this is so clear a sign that it is of the devil that, if the whole world assured me it came from God, I should not believe it. The position is that, when it comes from the devil, all that is good is hidden from the soul, and flees from it, and the soul becomes restless and peevish and the effects produced cannot possibly be good. It may have good desires, but they are not strong ones, and the humility left in it is false humility, devoid of tranquillity and gentleness. Anyone, I think, who has experience of the good spirit will understand this.

None the less, the devil can play many tricks; and so there is nothing so certain as that we must always preserve our misgivings about this, and proceed cautiously, and choose a learned man for our director, and hide nothing from him. If we do this, no harm can befall us, although a great deal has befallen me through these excessive fears which some people have. This was particularly so on one occasion, at a meeting between a number of people in whom I had great confidence, and rightly so. Though my relations were with only one of them, he ordered me to speak freely with the rest; I did so, and they had long talks together about helping me, for they had a great affection for me and feared I was deluded. I, too, was terribly afraid of this except when at prayer, for at these times I was immediately reassured whenever the Lord bestowed any favour upon me. I think there were five or six of these people, all of them great servants of God, and my confessor told me that they had all decided I was being deceived by the devil and that I must communicate less frequently and try to find distractions so that I should not be alone. I was extremely fearful, as I have said, and my heart trouble made things worse, with the result that I seldom dared to remain alone in a room by day. When I found that they all affirmed this, but that I myself could not believe it, I developed a most serious scruple, and believed myself lacking in humility. These men, I said, were all leading incomparably better lives than I, and they were also learned men: how, then, could I do other than believe them? So I made every possible effort to believe what they said, realizing how wicked my life was, and supposing that, in view of this, they must be right in what they said about me.

With this affliction oppressing me, I left the church and went into an oratory. For many days I had refrained from communicating and from being alone, which was my great comfort; and I had had no one with whom to discuss this matter, for everyone was against me. Some of them, I thought, were mocking me when I spoke to them about it, as if I were imagining it all. Others warned my confessor to be on his guard against me. Others said that it was clearly a deception of the devil. Only my confessor consistently comforted me, and, as I afterwards found out, he was siding with them in order to test me. He used to tell me that, provided I did not offend God, my prayer could do me no harm even if it came from the devil, and that in that case I should be delivered from it and must pray frequently to God. He and all his penitents did the same continually, with many others; and I myself, like many more whom I knew to be servants of God, spent the whole of the time which I set apart for prayer in begging His Majesty to lead me by another path. This went on for perhaps two years, during the whole of which time I made this petition to the Lord.

Nothing was any comfort to me when I reflected that words which I heard might so often be coming from the devil. As I never now spent hours of solitude in prayer, the Lord caused me to be recollected in conversation. He would say what He pleased to me and I could do nothing against Him: much as it troubled me to do so, therefore, I had to listen.

Now when I was alone, and had no one in whose company I could find relaxation, I was unable to pray or read, but was like a person stunned by all this tribulation and fear that the devil might be deceiving me, and quite upset and worn out, with not the least idea what to do. I have sometimes—often, indeed—found myself in this kind of affliction, but never, I think, have I been in such straits as I was then. I was like this for four or five hours, and neither in Heaven nor on earth was there any comfort for me: the Lord permitted my fears of a thousand perils to cause me great suffering. O my Lord, how true a Friend Thou art, and how powerful! For Thou canst do all Thou wilt and never dost Thou cease to will if we love Thee.[4] Let all things praise Thee, Lord of the world. Oh, if someone would but proclaim throughout the world how faithful Thou art to Thy friends! All things fail, but Thou, Lord of them all, failest never. Little is the suffering that Thou dost allow to those who love Thee. O my Lord, how delicately and skilfully and delectably canst Thou deal with them! Oh, would that we had never stayed to love any-one save Thee! Thou seemest, Lord, to give severe tests to those who love Thee, but only that in the extremity of their trials they may learn the greater extremity of Thy love.

O my God, had I but understanding and learning and new words with which to exalt Thy works as my soul knows them! All these, my Lord, I lack, but if Thou forsakest me not, I shall never fail Thee.[5] Let all learned men rise up against me, let all created things persecute me, let the devils tor-ment me, but fail Thou me not, Lord, for I have already ex-perience of the benefits which come to him who trusts only in Thee and whom Thou deliverest. When I was in this ter-rible state of exhaustion—for at that time I had not yet had a single vision—these words alone were sufficient to remove it and give me complete tranquillity: "Be not afraid, daughter, for it is I and I will not forsake thee: fear not."

In the state I was in at that time, I think it would have needed many hours to persuade me to be calm and no single person would have sufficed to do so. Yet here I was, calmed by nothing but these words, and given fortitude and courage and conviction and tranquillity and light, so that in a mo-ment I found my soul transformed and I think I would have maintained against the whole world that this was the work of God. Oh, what a good God! Oh, what a good Lord! What a powerful Lord! He gives not only counsel but solace. His

---

[4] [The verb translated "wilt", "will" and "love" is *querer*: the play upon words cannot be satisfactorily rendered.]

[5] [The verb is *faltar*, translated "lack" and "fail" in this half-punning sentence, and "fail" below. One might render: "All these, my Lord, I lack, but . . . Thou shalt never lack me."]

words are deeds. See how He strengthens our faith and how our love increases!

This is very true, and I would often recall how when a storm arose the Lord used to command the winds that blew over the sea to be still, and I would say to myself: "Who is this, that all my faculties thus obey Him[6]—Who in a moment sheds light upon such thick darkness, softens a heart that seemed to be made of stone, and sends water in the shape of gentle tears where for so long there had seemed to be aridity? Who gives these desires? Who gives this courage? What have I been thinking of? What am I afraid of? What is this? I desire to serve the Lord; I aim at nothing else than pleasing Him. I seek no contentment, no rest, no other blessing but to do His will." I felt I was quite sure about this and so could affirm it.

"Well, now," I went on, "if this Lord is powerful, as I see He is, and know He is, and if the devils are His slaves (and of that there can be no doubt, for it is an article of the Faith), what harm can they do me, who am a servant of this Lord and King? How can I fail to have fortitude enough to fight against all hell?" So I took a cross in my hand and it really seemed that God was giving me courage: in a short time I found I was another person and I should not have been afraid to wrestle with devils, for with the aid of that cross I believed I could easily vanquish them all. "Come on, now, all of you," I said: "I am a servant of the Lord and I want to see what you can do to me."

It certainly seemed as if I had frightened all these devils, for I became quite calm and had no more fear of them—in fact, I lost all the fears which until then had been wont to trouble me. For, although I used sometimes to see the devils, as I shall say later, I have hardly ever been afraid of them again—indeed, they seem to be afraid of me. I have acquired an authority over them, bestowed upon me by the Lord of all, so that they are no more trouble to me now than flies. They seem to me such cowards—as soon as they see that anyone despises them they have no strength left. They are enemies who can make a direct attack only upon those whom they see giving in to them, or on servants of God whom, for their

[6] [Evidently a reference to the miracle recorded in St. Matthew viii, 23–7, St. Mark iv, 35–40 and St. Luke viii, 22–5.]

greater good, God allows to be tried and tormented. May His Majesty be pleased to make us fear Him Whom we ought to fear[7] and understand that one venial sin can do us greater harm than all the forces of hell combined—for that is really true.

These devils keep us in terror because we make ourselves liable to be terrorized by contracting other attachments—to honours, for example, and to possessions and pleasures. When this happens, they join forces with us—since, by loving and desiring what we ought to hate, we become our own enemies—and they will do us much harm. We make them fight against us with our own weapons, which we put into their hands when we ought to be using them in our own defence. That is the great pity of it. If only we will hate everything for God's sake and embrace the Cross and try to serve Him in truth, the devil will fly from these truths as from the plague. He is a lover of lies and a lie himself.[8] He will have no truck with anyone who walks in truth. When he sees that such a person's understanding is darkened, he gaily assists him to become completely blind; for if he sees anyone blind enough to find comfort in vanities—and such vanities! for the vanities of this world are like children's playthings—he sees that he is indeed a child, and treats him as one, making bold to wrestle with him, first on some particular occasion and then again and again.

Please God I be not one of these! May His Majesty help me to find comfort in what is really comfort, to call honour what is really honour and to take delight in what is really delight—and not the other way round. Not a fig[9] shall I care then for all the devils in hell: it is they who will fear me. I do not understand these fears. "Oh, the devil, the devil!" we say, when we might be saying "God! God!" and making the devil tremble. Of course we might, for we know he cannot move a finger unless the Lord permits it. Whatever are we thinking of? I am quite sure I am more afraid of people who are themselves terrified of the devil than I am of the devil

[7] [An apparent reference to St. Matthew x, 28.]

[8] [Clearly St. Teresa has here in mind St. John viii, 44.]

[9] [The fig, or "fico", is a contemptuous motion which we should make by a "snap of the fingers" but which in sixteenth-century Spain was made by holding up the closed fist with the thumb showing between the first and the second finger (*dar higas*). Cf. p. 270.]

himself. For he cannot harm me in the least, whereas they, especially if they are confessors, can upset people a great deal, and for several years they were such a trial to me that I marvel now that I was able to bear it. Blessed be the Lord, Who has been of such real help to me!

CHAPTER XXVI

Continues the same subject. Goes on with the description and explanation of things which befell her and which rid her of her fears and assured her that it was the good spirit that was speaking to her.

This courage which the Lord gave me for my fight with the devils I look upon as one of the great favours He has bestowed upon me; for it is most unseemly that a soul should act like a coward, or be afraid of anything, save of offending God, since we have a King Who is all-powerful and a Lord so great that He can do everything and makes everyone subject to Him. There is no need for us to fear if, as I have said, we walk truthfully in His Majesty's presence with a pure conscience. For this reason, as I have said, I should desire always to be fearful so that I may not for a moment offend Him Who in that very moment may destroy us. If His Majesty is pleased with us, there is none of our adversaries who will not wring his hands in despair.[1] This, it may be said, is quite true, but what soul is upright enough to please Him altogether? It is for this reason, it will be said, that we are afraid. Certainly there is nothing upright about my own soul: it is most wretched, useless and full of a thousand miseries. But the ways of God are not like the ways of men. He understands our weaknesses and by means of strong inward instincts the soul is made aware if it truly loves Him; for the love of those who reach this state is no longer hidden, as it was when they were beginners, but is accompanied by the most vehement impulses and the desire to see God, which I shall describe later and have described already. Everything

[1] [The Spanish idiom is literally: "who will not clap his hands to his head".]

wearies such a soul; everything fatigues it; everything torments it. There is no rest, save that which is in God, or comes through God, which does not weary it, for it feels its true rest to be far away, and so its love is a thing most evident, which, as I say, cannot be hidden.

On various occasions it happened that I found myself greatly tried and maligned about a certain matter, to which I shall refer later, by almost everyone in the place where I am living and by my Order. I was greatly distressed by the numerous things which arose to take away my peace of mind. But the Lord said to me: "Why dost thou fear? Knowest thou not that I am all-powerful? I will fulfil what I have promised thee." And shortly afterwards this promise was in fact completely fulfilled. But even at that time I began at once to feel so strong that I believe I could have set out on fresh undertakings, even if serving Him had cost me further trials and I had had to begin to suffer afresh. This has happened so many times that I could not count them. Often He has uttered words of reproof to me in this way, and He does so still when I commit imperfections, which are sufficient to bring about a soul's destruction. And His words always help me to amend my life, for, as I have said, His Majesty supplies both counsel and remedy. At other times the Lord recalls my past sins to me, especially when He wishes to grant me some outstanding favour, so that my soul feels as if it is really at the Judgment; with such complete knowledge is the truth presented to it that it knows not where to hide. Sometimes these locutions warn me against perils to myself and to others, or tell me of things which are to happen three or four years hence: there have been many of these and they have all come true—it would be possible to detail some of them. There are so many signs, then, which indicate that these locutions come from God that I think the fact cannot be doubted.

The safest course is that which I myself follow: if I did not, I should have no peace—not that it is right for women like ourselves to expect any peace, since we are not learned, but if we do what I say we cannot run into danger and are bound to reap great benefit, as the Lord has often told me. I mean that we must describe the whole of our spiritual experiences, and the favours granted us by the Lord, to a confessor who is a man of learning, and obey him. This I have often done. I had a confessor who used to mortify me a great deal and would sometimes distress and try me greatly by unsettling my mind: yet I believe he is the confessor who has done me most good.[2] Though I had a great love for him, I was several times tempted to leave him, for I thought that the distress he caused me disturbed my prayer. But each time I determined to do so, I realized at once that I must not and I received a reproof from God which caused me more confusion than anything done by my confessor. Sometimes, what with the questions on the one hand and the reproofs on the other, I would feel quite exhausted. But I needed them all, for my will was not bent to obedience. Once the Lord told me that I was not obeying unless I was determined to suffer. I must fix my eyes on all that He had suffered and I should find everything easy.

A confessor to whom I had gone in my early days once advised me, now that my experiences were proved to be due to the good spirit, to keep silence and say nothing about them to anyone, as it was better to be quiet about such things. This seemed to me by no means bad advice, for whenever I used to speak about them to the confessor, I would be so distressed and feel so ashamed that sometimes it hurt me more to talk about these favours, especially if they were outstanding ones, than to confess grievous sins, for I thought my confessors would not believe me and would make fun of me. This distressed me so much that it seemed to me I was treating the wonders of God irreverently by talking about them, and for that reason I wanted to keep silence. I then found out that I had been very badly advised by that confessor and that when I made my confession I must on no account keep back anything: if I obeyed that rule I should be quite safe, whereas otherwise I might sometimes be deceived.

Whenever the Lord gave me some command in prayer and the confessor told me to do something different, the Lord Himself would speak to me again and tell me to obey Him; and His Majesty would then change the confessor's mind so that he came back and ordered me to do the same thing. When a great many books written in Spanish were taken from us and we were forbidden to read them,[3] I was very

[2] P. Baltasar Álvarez.
[3] In 1559, Don Fernando de Valdés, Grand Inquisitor of Spain, published an Index of books of which he forbade the reading, and

sorry, for the reading of some of them gave me pleasure and I could no longer continue this as I had them only in Latin. Then the Lord said to me: "Be not distressed, for I will give thee a living book." I could not understand why this had been said to me, for I had not then had any visions.[4] But a very few days afterwards, I came to understand it very well, for what I saw before me gave me so much to think about and so much opportunity for recollection, and the Lord showed me so much love and taught me by so many methods, that I have had very little need of books—indeed, hardly any. His Majesty Himself has been to me the Book in which I have seen what is true. Blessed be such a Book, which leaves impressed upon us what we are to read and do, in a way that is unforgettable! Who can see the Lord covered with wounds and afflicted with persecutions without embracing them, loving them and desiring them for himself? Who can see any of the glory which He gives to those who serve Him without recognizing that anything he himself can do and suffer is absolutely nothing compared with the hope of such a reward? Who can behold the torments suffered by the damned without feeling that the torments of earth are by comparison pure joy and realizing how much we owe to the Lord for having so often delivered us from damnation?

As, by the help of God, I shall say more about some of these things, I will now go on with the account of my life. May it have pleased the Lord to enable me to make clear what I have said. I truly believe that anyone who has had experience of it will understand it and see that I have succeeded in describing some of it; but I shall not be at all surprised if those who have not think it all nonsense. The fact that it is I who have said it will be enough to clear them from blame, and I myself shall blame no one who may so speak of it. May the Lord grant me duly to carry out His will. Amen.

---

this included not only heretical works, but also a great many devotional books written in Spanish which he thought might do simple souls harm.

[4] [Unless the author is mistaken about this, her first imaginary vision (see p. 259) cannot have taken place before January 25, 1560.]

CHAPTER XXVII

Treats of another way in which the Lord teaches the soul and in an admirable manner makes His will plain to it without the use of words. Describes a vision and a great favour, not imaginary, granted her by the Lord. This chapter should be carefully noted.

Returning to the account of my life, I have already described my great distress and affliction and the prayers that were being made for me that the Lord would lead me by another and a surer way, since, as they told me, there was so much doubt about this one. The truth is that, though I was beseeching God to do this, and though I wished very much I could desire to be led by another way, yet, when I saw how much my soul was already benefiting, I could not possibly desire it, except occasionally when I was troubled by the things that were being said to me and the fears with which I was being inspired. Still, I kept on praying for it. I realized that I was completely different; so I put myself into God's hands, for I could do nothing else: He knew what was good for me and it was for Him to fulfil His will in me in all things. I saw that this road was leading me towards Heaven, whereas formerly I had been going in the direction of hell. I could not force myself to desire this change or to believe that I was being led by the devil; I did my best to believe this, and to desire the change, but it was simply impossible. To this end I offered up all my actions, in case any of them might be good. I begged the Saints to whom I was devoted to deliver me from the devil. I made novenas and commended myself to Saint Hilarion and to Saint Michael the Angel, for whom, with this in view, I conceived a fresh devotion, and I importuned many other Saints so that the Lord might show me the truth—I mean so that they might prevail with His Majesty to this purpose.

At the end of two years, during the whole of which time both other people and myself were continually praying for what I have described—that the Lord would either lead me by another way or make plain the truth: and these locutions which, as I have said, the Lord was giving me were very frequent—I had the following experience. I was at prayer on a festival of the glorious Saint Peter when I saw Christ at my side—or, to put it better, I was conscious of Him, for neither with the eyes of the body nor with those of the soul did I see anything. I thought He was quite close to me and I saw that it was He Who, as I thought, was speaking to me. Being completely ignorant that visions of this kind could occur, I was at first very much afraid, and did nothing but weep, though, as soon as He addressed a single word to me to reassure me, I became quiet again, as I had been before, and was quite happy and free from fear. All the time Jesus Christ seemed to be beside me, but, as this was not an imaginary vision,[1] I could not discern in what form: what I felt very clearly was that all the time He was at my right hand, and a witness of everything that I was doing, and that, whenever I became slightly recollected or was not greatly distracted, I could not but be aware of His nearness to me.

Sorely troubled, I went at once to my confessor, to tell him about it. He asked me in what form I had seen Him. I told him that I had not seen Him at all. Then he asked me how I knew it was Christ. I told him that I did not know how, but that I could not help realizing that He was beside me, and that I saw and felt this clearly; that when in the Prayer of Quiet my soul was now much more deeply and continuously recollected; that the effects of my prayer were very different from those which I had previously been accustomed to experience; and that the thing was quite clear to me. I did nothing, in my efforts to make myself understood, but draw comparisons—though really, for describing this kind of vision, there is no comparison which is very much to the point, for it is one of the highest kinds of vision possible. This was told me later by a holy man of great spirituality called Fray Peter of Alcántara,[2] to whom I shall afterwards refer, and other distinguished and learned men have told me the same thing. Of all kinds of vision it is that in which the devil has the least power of interference, and so there are no ordinary terms by which we women, who have so little knowledge, can

[1] [On various types of vision, see Vol. II, p. 279, n.]

[2] This Franciscan saint [of whom an account will be found in S.S.M., II, 99–120] had in 1540 initiated a Discalced Reform in his Order not unlike that afterwards begun by St. Teresa. Cf. pp. 255–7, 276–80.

describe it: learned men will explain it better. For, if I say that I do not see Him with the eyes either of the body or of the soul, because it is not an imaginary vision, how can I know and affirm that He is at my side, and this with greater certainty than if I were to see Him? It is not a suitable comparison to say that it is as if a person were in the dark, so that he cannot see someone who is beside him, or as if he were blind. There is some similarity here, but not a great deal, because the person in the dark can detect the other with his remaining senses, can hear him speak or move, or can touch him. In this case there is nothing like that, nor is there felt to be any darkness—on the contrary, He presents Himself to the soul by a knowledge brighter than the sun. I do not mean that any sun is seen, or any brightness is perceived, but that there is a light which, though not seen, illumines the understanding so that the soul may have fruition of so great a blessing. It brings great blessings with it.

It is not like another kind of consciousness of the presence of God which is often experienced, especially by those who have reached the Prayer of Union and the Prayer of Quiet. There we are on the point of beginning our prayer when we seem to find Him Whom we are about to address and we seem to know that He is hearing us by the spiritual feelings and effects of great love and faith of which we become conscious, and also by the fresh resolutions which we make with such deep emotion. This great favour comes from God: and he to whom it is granted should esteem it highly, for it is a very lofty form of prayer. But it is not a vision. The soul recognizes the presence of God by the effects which, as I say, He produces in the soul, for it is by that means that His Majesty is pleased to make His presence felt: but in a vision the soul distinctly sees that Jesus Christ, the Son of the Virgin, is present. In that other kind of prayer there come to it influences from the Godhead; but in this experience, besides receiving these, we find that the most sacred Humanity becomes our Companion and is also pleased to grant us favours.

My confessor then asked me who told me it was Jesus Christ. "He often tells me so Himself", I replied; "but, before ever He told me so, the fact was impressed upon my understanding, and before that He used to tell me He was there when I could not see Him." If I were blind, or in pitch darkness, and a person whom I had never seen, but only heard of, came and spoke to me and told me who he was, I should believe him, but I could not affirm that it was he as confidently as if I had seen him. But in this case I could certainly affirm it, for, though He remains unseen, so clear a knowledge is impressed upon the soul that to doubt it seems quite impossible. The Lord is pleased that this knowledge should be so deeply engraven upon the understanding that one can no more doubt it than one can doubt the evidence of one's eyes—indeed, the latter is easier, for we sometimes suspect that we have imagined what we see, whereas here, though that suspicion may arise for a moment, there remains such complete certainty that the doubt has no force.

It is the same with another way in which God teaches the soul, and addresses it without using words, as I have said. This is so celestial a language that it is difficult to explain it to mortals, however much we may desire to do so, unless the Lord teaches it to us by experience. The Lord introduces into the inmost part of the soul what He wishes that soul to understand, and presents it, not by means of images or forms of words, but after the manner of this vision aforementioned. Consider carefully this way in which God causes the soul to understand what He wills, and also great truths and mysteries; for often what I understand, when the Lord expounds to me some vision which His Majesty is pleased to present to me, comes in this way; for the reasons I have given, I think this is the state in which the devil has the least power of interference. If the reasons are not good ones, I must be suffering from deception.

This kind of vision and this kind of language are such spiritual things that I believe no turmoil is caused by them in the faculties, or in the senses, from which the devil can pluck any advantage. They occur only from time to time and are quickly over; at other times, as I think, the faculties are not suspended, nor is the soul bereft of its senses, but these remain active, which in contemplation is not always the case —it happens, indeed, very seldom. When it is the case, I believe that we ourselves do nothing and accomplish nothing —the whole thing seems to be the work of the Lord. It is as if food has been introduced into the stomach without our having eaten it or knowing how it got there. We know quite well that it is there, although we do not know what it is or who put it there. In this experience, I do know Who put it there, but not how He did so, for my soul saw nothing and cannot understand how the operation took place; it had never been moved to desire such a thing, nor had it even come to my knowledge that it was possible.

In the locutions which we described previously, God makes the understanding attentive, even against its will, so that it understands what is said to it, for the soul now seems to have other ears with which it hears and He makes it listen and prevents it from becoming distracted. It is like a person with good hearing, who is forbidden to stop his ears when people near him are talking in a loud voice: even if he were unwilling to hear them, he could not help doing so. As a matter of fact he does play a part in the process, because he is attending to what they are saying. But in this experience the soul does nothing, for even the mere insignificant ability to listen, which it has possessed until now, is taken from it. It finds all its food cooked and eaten: it has nothing to do but to enjoy it. It is like one who, without having learned anything, or having taken the slightest trouble in order to learn to read, or even having ever studied, finds himself in possession of all existing knowledge; he has no idea how or whence it has come, since he has never done any work, even so much as was necessary for the learning of the alphabet.

This last comparison, I think, furnishes some sort of explanation of this heavenly gift, for the soul suddenly finds itself learned, and the mystery of the Most Holy Trinity, together with other lofty things, is so clearly explained to it that there is no theologian with whom it would not have the boldness to contend in defence of the truth of these marvels. So astounded is the soul at what has happened to it that a single one of these favours suffices to change it altogether and make it love nothing save Him Who, without any labour on its part, renders it capable of receiving such great blessings, and communicates secrets to it and treats it with such friendship and love as is impossible to describe. For some of the favours which He bestows upon it, being so wonderful in themselves and granted to one who has not deserved them, may be regarded with suspicion, and they will not be believed save by one who has a most lively faith. So unless I am commanded to say more I propose to refer only to a few of those which the Lord has granted me; I shall confine myself to certain visions an account of which may be of some use to others, may stop anyone to whom the Lord gives them from thinking them impossible, as I used to do, and may explain to such a person the method and the road by which the Lord has led me, for that is the subject on which I am commanded to write.

Now, returning to this method of understanding, the position seems to me to be that the Lord's will is for the soul to have at any rate some idea of what is happening in Heaven, and, just as souls in Heaven understand one another without speaking (which I never knew for certain till the Lord in His goodness willed me to see it and revealed it to me in a rapture), even so it is here. God and the soul understand each other, simply because this is His Majesty's will, and no other means is necessary to express the mutual love of these two friends. Just so, in this life, two persons of reasonable intelligence, who love each other dearly, seem able to understand each other without making any signs, merely by their looks. This must be so here, for, without seeing each other, we look at each other face to face as these two lovers do: the Spouse in the Songs, I believe, says this to the Bride: I have been told that it occurs there.[3]

O wondrous loving-kindness of God, Who permittest Thyself to be looked upon by eyes which have looked on things as sinfully as have the eyes of my soul! After this sight, Lord, may they never more accustom themselves to look on base things and may nothing content them but Thee. O ingratitude of mortal men! How far will it go? I know by experience that all I am saying now is true and that what it is possible to say is the smallest part of what Thou doest with a soul that Thou leadest to such heights as this. O souls that have begun to pray and that possess true faith, what blessings can you find in this life to equal the least of these, to say nothing of the blessings you may gain in eternity?

Reflect—for this is the truth—that to those who give up everything for Him God gives Himself. He is not a respecter of persons.[4] He loves us all: no one, however wicked, can be

[3] Canticles vi, 2 or vi, 4 is probably meant, but the reminiscence is a vague one and several other phrases in the same book might have been in St. Teresa's mind.

[4] [Lit.: "accepter" (acetador), but the context suggests a reference to Acts x, 34. (D.V.: "God is not a respecter of persons.")]

excluded from His love since He has dealt in such a way with me and brought me to so high a state. Reflect that what I am saying is barely a fraction of what there is to say. I have only said what is necessary to explain the kind of vision and favour which God bestows on the soul; but I cannot describe the soul's feelings when the Lord grants it an understanding of His secrets and wonders—a joy so far above all joys attainable on earth that it fills us with a just contempt for the joys of life, all of which are but dung. It is loathsome to have to make any such comparison, even if we might enjoy them for ever. And what are these joys that the Lord gives? Only a single drop of the great and abundant river which He has prepared for us.

It makes one ashamed, and certainly I am ashamed of myself: if it were possible to be ashamed in Heaven, I should be more so than anyone else. Why must we desire so many blessings and joys, and everlasting glory, all at the cost of the good Jesus? If we are not helping Him to carry His Cross with the Cyrenean, shall we not at least weep with the daughters of Jerusalem?[5] Will pleasures and pastimes lead us to the fruition of what He won for us at the cost of so much blood? That is impossible. And do we think that by accepting vain honours we shall be following Him Who was despised so that we might reign for ever? That is not the right way. We are going astray, far astray: we shall never reach our goal. Proclaim these truths aloud, Your Reverence, since God has denied me the freedom to do so myself. I should like to proclaim them for ever, but, as will be seen from what I have written, it was so long before God heard me and I came to know Him that it makes me very much ashamed to speak of it and I prefer to keep silence; so I shall only speak of something about which I meditate from time to time.

May it please the Lord to bring me to a state in which I can enjoy this blessing. What will be the accidental glory and what the joy of the blessed who already have fruition of it when they see that, late as they were, they left nothing undone that they could possibly do for God, and kept back nothing, but gave to Him in every possible way, according to their power and their position; and the more they had, the more they gave! How rich will he find himself who has for-

[5] [St. Luke xxiii, 26, 28.]

saken all his riches for Christ! What honour will be paid to those who for His sake desired no honour but took pleasure in seeing themselves humbled! What wisdom will be attributed to the man who rejoiced at being accounted mad, since madness was attributed to Him Who is Wisdom itself. How few such, through our sins, are there now! Alas, alas! No longer are there any whom men account mad because they see them perform the heroic deeds proper to true lovers of Christ. O world, world! How much of thy reputation dost thou acquire because of the few there are who know thee!

For we believe that God is better pleased when we are accounted wise and discreet. That may be so: it all depends on what we mean by discretion. We at once assume that we are failing to edify others if each one of us in his calling does not comport himself with great circumspection and make a show of authority. Even in the friar, the cleric and the nun we think it very strange and a scandal to the weak if they wear old, patched clothes, or even (to such a pass has the world come and so forgetful are we of the vehement longings which the saints had for perfection) if they are greatly recollected and given to prayer. The world is bad enough nowadays without being made worse by things like this.[6] No scandal would be caused to anyone if religious put into practice what they say about the little esteem in which the world should be held, for the Lord turns any such scandals as these to great advantage. If some were scandalized, too, others would be struck with remorse; and we should at least have a picture of what was suffered by Christ and His Apostles, which we need now more than ever.

And what a grand picture of it has God just taken from us in the blessed Fray Peter of Alcántara![7] The world is not yet in a fit state to bear such perfection. It is said that people's health is feebler nowadays and that times are not what they were. But it was in these present times that this holy man lived; and yet his spirit was as robust as any in the days of old, so that he was able to keep the world beneath his feet.

[6] [This sentence is a free translation of one of the most obscure and ungrammatical sentences in St. Teresa. One can only guess at its precise meaning, but there is no doubt as to its general sense.]

[7] St. Peter of Alcántara died on October 18, 1562 [a fact which would be useful in helping to fix the date of this book were there not references to later events below].

And, although everyone does not go about unshod[8] or perform such severe penances as he did, there are many ways, as I have said on other occasions, of trampling on the world and these ways the Lord teaches to those in whom He sees courage. And what great courage His Majesty gave to this holy man to perform those severe penances, which are common knowledge, for forty-seven years! I will say something about this, for I know it is all true.

He told this to me, and to another person from whom he concealed little[9]—the reason he told me was his love for me, for the Lord was pleased to give him this love so that he might stand up for me and encourage me at a time of great need, of which I have spoken and shall speak further. I think it was for forty years that he told me he had slept only for an hour and a half between each night and the next day, and that, when he began, the hardest part of his penance had been the conquering of sleep, for which reason he was always either on his knees or on his feet. What sleep he had he took sitting down, with his head resting against a piece of wood that he had fixed to the wall. Sleep lying down he could not, even if he had so wished, for his cell, as is well known, was only four and a half feet long. During all these years, however hot the sun or heavy the rain, he never wore his hood, or anything on his feet, and his only dress was a habit of sackcloth, with nothing between it and his flesh, and this he wore as tightly as he could bear, with a mantle of the same material above it. He told me that, when it was very cold, he would take off the mantle, and leave the door and window of his cell open, so that, when he put it on again and shut the door, he could derive some physical satisfaction from the increased protection. It was a very common thing for him to take food only once in three days. He asked me why I was so surprised at this and said that, when one got used to it, it was quite possible. A companion of his told me that sometimes he would go for a week without food. That must have been when he was engaged in prayer, for he used to have great

8 [*Lit.*: naked.]

9 This was his penitent María Díaz, a well-to-do woman of great saintliness who lived a life of Franciscan poverty and charity in Ávila and to whom St. Teresa alludes by name more than once [e.g., *Letters*, 10, 403], describing her as a saint.

raptures and violent impulses of love for God, of which I was myself once a witness.

His poverty was extreme, and so, even when he was quite young, was his mortification: he told me that he once spent three years in a house of his Order and could not have recognized a single friar there, except by his voice, for he never raised his eyes, and so, when he had to go to any part of the house, could only do so by following the other friars. It was the same thing out of doors. At women he never looked at all and this was his practice for many years. He told me that it was all the same to him now whether he saw anything or not; but he was very old when I made his acquaintance[10] and so extremely weak that he seemed to be made of nothing but roots of trees. But with all this holiness he was very affable, though, except when answering questions, a man of few words. When he did speak it was a delight to listen to him, for he was extremely intelligent. There are many other things which I should like to say about him but I am afraid Your Reverence will ask why I am starting on this subject—indeed, I have been afraid of that even while writing. So I will stop here, adding that he died as he had lived, preaching to, and admonishing, his brethren. When he saw that his life was drawing to a close, he repeated the psalm "Laetatus sum in hic quae dicta sunt mihi",[11] and knelt down and died.

Since his death it has been the Lord's good pleasure that I should have more intercourse with him than I had during his life and that he should advise me on many subjects. I have often beheld him in the greatest bliss. The first time he appeared to me he remarked on the blessedness of the penance that had won him so great a prize, and he spoke of many other things as well. One of his appearances to me took place a year before his death. I was away at the time; and, knowing he was soon to die, I told him so, when he was some leagues from here. When he expired, he appeared to me and said that he was going to rest. I did not believe this, but repeated it to a number of people and in a week came the news that he was dead—or, to put it better, that he had entered upon eternal life.

10 [Actually he was fifty-nine.]
11 Psalm cxxi, 1 [A.V., cxxii, 1]: "I rejoiced at the things that were said to me: We shall go into the house of the Lord."

See, then, how this austere life has ended in great glory. He is a much greater comfort to me, I think, than when he was on earth. The Lord once told me that no one should ask Him for anything in his name and not be heard. Many things which I have commended to him so that he should ask the Lord for them I have seen granted. Blessed be He for ever! Amen.

But what a lot I have been saying in order to incite Your Reverence to pay no esteem to the things of this life, as though you did not know this already and had not already determined to forsake everything and put your determination into practice. I see so many people in the world going to perdition that, although when I speak in this way I may succeed only in tiring myself by writing, it is a comfort to me, for everything I say tells against myself. May the Lord forgive me for anything in which I have offended Him in this matter, and may Your Reverence also forgive me, for I am wearying you to no purpose. It looks as if I want to make you do penance for the sins which I have myself committed.

CHAPTER XXVIII

Treats of the great favours which the Lord bestowed upon her, and of His first appearance to her. Describes the nature of an imaginary vision. Enumerates the important effects and signs which this produces when it proceeds from God. This chapter is very profitable and should be carefully noted.

Returning to our subject: I spent some days, though only a few, with that vision continually in my mind, and it did me so much good that I remained in prayer unceasingly and contrived that everything I did should be such as not to displease Him Who, as I clearly perceived, was a witness of it. And, although I was given so much advice that I sometimes became afraid, my fear was short-lived, for the Lord reassured me. One day, when I was at prayer, the Lord was pleased to reveal to me nothing but His hands, the beauty of which was so great as to be indescribable. This made me very fearful, as does every new experience that I have when the Lord is beginning to grant me some supernatural favour. A few days later I also saw that Divine face, which seemed to leave me completely absorbed. I could not understand why the Lord revealed Himself gradually like this since He was later to grant me the favour of seeing Him wholly, until at length I realized that His Majesty was leading me according to my natural weakness. May He be blessed for ever, for so much glory all at once would have been more than so base and wicked a person could bear: knowing this, the compassionate Lord prepared me for it by degrees.

Your Reverence may suppose that it would have needed no great effort to behold those hands and that beauteous face. But there is such beauty about glorified bodies that the glory which illumines them throws all who look upon such supernatural loveliness into confusion. I was so much afraid, then, that I was plunged into turmoil and confusion, though later I began to feel such certainty and security that my fear was soon lost.

One year, on Saint Paul's Day,[1] when I was at Mass, I saw a complete representation of this most sacred Humanity, just as in a picture of His resurrection body, in very great beauty and majesty; this I described in detail to Your Reverence in writing, at your very insistent request. It distressed me terribly to have to do so, for it is impossible to write such a description without a disruption of one's very being, but I did the best I could and so there is no reason for me to repeat the attempt here. I will only say that, if there were nothing else in Heaven to delight the eyes but the extreme beauty of the glorified bodies there, that alone would be the greatest bliss. A most especial bliss, then, will it be to us when we see the Humanity of Jesus Christ; for, if it is so even on earth, where His Majesty reveals Himself according to what our wretchedness can bear, what will it be where the fruition of that joy is complete? Although this vision is imaginary, I never saw it, or any other vision, with the eyes of the body, but only with the eyes of the soul.

Those who know better than I say that the type of vision

1 [P. Silverio dates this occurrence January 25, 1558, but a reference in Chap. XXVI (p. 247) suggests that it was subsequent to 1559. A further allusion (pp. 270–1) would indicate June 29 or 30 rather than January 25.]

already described[2] is nearer perfection than this, while this in its turn is much more so than those which are seen with the eyes of the body. The last-named type, they say, is the lowest and the most open to delusions from the devil. At that time I was not aware of this, and wished that, as this favour was being granted me, it could have been of such a kind as was visible to the eyes of the body, and then my confessor would not tell me I was imagining it. And no sooner had the vision faded—the very moment, indeed, after it had gone—than I began to think the same thing myself—that I had imagined it—and was worried at having spoken about it to my confessor and wondered if I had been deceiving him. Here was another cause for distress, so I went to him and consulted him about it. He asked me if I had told him what the vision really looked like to me or if I had meant to deceive him. I said I had told him the truth, for I felt sure I had not been lying or had had any such intention; I would not think one thing and say another for the whole world. This he well knew, and so he managed to calm me. It worried me so much to have to go to him about these things that I cannot imagine how the devil could ever have suggested to me that I must be inventing them and thus be torturing myself. But the Lord made such haste to grant me this favour and to make its reality plain that my doubt about its being fancy left me immediately and since then it has become quite clear to me how silly I was. For, if I were to spend years and years imagining how to invent anything so beautiful, I could not do it, and I do not even know how I should try, for, even in its whiteness and radiance alone, it exceeds all that we can imagine.

It is not a radiance which dazzles, but a soft whiteness and an infused radiance which, without wearying the eyes, causes them the greatest delight; nor are they wearied by the brightness which they see in seeing this Divine beauty. So different from any earthly light is the brightness and light now revealed to the eyes that, by comparison with it, the brightness of our sun seems quite dim and we should never want to open our eyes again for the purpose of seeing it. It is as if we were to look at a very clear stream, in a bed of crystal, reflect-

---

[2] [I.e., the intellectual vision. By "this", of course, is meant the imaginary vision.]

ing the sun's rays, and then to see a very muddy stream, in an earthy bed and overshadowed by clouds. Not that the sun, or any other such light, enters into the vision: on the contrary, it is like a natural light and all other kinds of light seem artificial. It is a light which never gives place to night, and, being always light, is disturbed by nothing. It is of such a kind, indeed, that no one, however powerful his intellect, could, in the whole course of his life, imagine it as it is. And so quickly does God reveal it to us that, even if we needed to open our eyes in order to see it, there would not be time for us to do so. But it is all the same whether they are open or closed: if the Lord is pleased for us to see it, we shall do so even against our will. There is nothing powerful enough to divert our attention from it, and we can neither resist it nor attain to it by any diligence or care of our own. This I have conclusively proved by experience, as I shall relate.

I should like now to say something of the way in which the Lord reveals Himself through these visions. I do not mean that I shall describe how it is that He can introduce this strong light into the inward sense and give the understanding an image so clear that it seems like reality. That is a matter for learned men to explain. The Lord has not been pleased to grant me to understand how it is; and I am so ignorant, and my understanding is so dull that, although many attempts have been made to explain it to me, I have not yet succeeded in understanding how it can happen. There is no doubt about this: I have not a keen understanding, although Your Reverence may think I have; again and again I have proved that my mind has to be spoon-fed, as they say, if it is to retain anything. Occasionally my confessor used to be astounded at the depths of my ignorance, and it never became clear to me how God did this and how it was possible that He should; nor, in fact, did I want to know, so I never asked anyone about it, though, as I have said, I have for many years been in touch with men of sound learning. What I did ask them was whether certain things were sinful or no: as for the rest, all I needed was to remember that God did everything and then I realized that I had no reason to be afraid and every reason to praise Him. Difficulties like that only arouse devotion in me, and, the greater they are, the greater is the devotion.

I will describe, then, what I have discovered by experience. How the Lord effects it, Your Reverence will explain better than I and will expound everything obscure of which I do not know the explanation. At certain times it really seemed to me that it was an image I was seeing; but on many other occasions I thought it was no image, but Christ Himself, such was the brightness with which He was pleased to reveal Himself to me. Sometimes, because of its indistinctness, I would think the vision was an image, though it was like no earthly painting, however perfect, and I have seen a great many good ones. It is ridiculous to think that the one thing is any more like the other than a living person is like his portrait: however well the portrait is done, it can never look completely natural: one sees, in fact, that it is a dead thing. But let us pass over that, apposite and literally true through it is.

I am not saying this as a comparison, for comparisons are never quite satisfactory: it is the actual truth. The difference is similar to that between something living and something painted, neither more so nor less. For if what I see is an image it is a living image—not a dead man but the living Christ. And He shows me that He is both Man and God—not as He was in the sepulchre, but as He was when He left it after rising from the dead. Sometimes He comes with such majesty that no once can doubt it is the Lord Himself; this is especially so after Communion, for we know that He is there, since the Faith tells us so. He reveals Himself so completely as the Lord of that inn, the soul, that it feels as though it were wholly dissolved and consumed in Christ. O my Jesus, if one could but describe the majesty with which Thou dost reveal Thyself! How completely art Thou Lord of the whole world, and of the heavens, and of a thousand other worlds, and of countless worlds and heavens that Thou hast created! And the majesty with which Thou dost reveal Thyself shows the soul that to be Lord of this is nothing for Thee.

Here it becomes evident, my Jesus, how trifling is the power of all the devils in comparison with Thine, and how he who is pleasing to Thee can trample upon all the hosts of hell. Here we see with what reason the devils trembled when Thou didst descend into Hades: well might they have longed for a thousand deeper hells in order to flee from such great Majesty! I see that Thou art pleased to reveal to the soul the greatness of Thy Majesty, together with the power of this most sacred Humanity in union with the Divinity. Here is a clear picture of what the Day of Judgment will be, when we

shall behold the Majesty of this King and see the rigour of
His judgment upon the wicked. Here we find true humility,
giving the soul power to behold its own wretchedness, of
which it cannot be ignorant. Here is shame and genuine repentance for sin; for, though it sees God revealing His love
to it, the soul can find no place to hide itself and thus is
utterly confounded. I mean that, when the Lord is pleased to
reveal to the soul so much of His greatness and majesty, the
vision has such exceeding great power that I believe it would
be impossible to endure, unless the Lord were pleased to
help the soul in a most supernatural way by sending it into a
rapture or an ecstasy, during the fruition of which the vision
of that Divine Presence is lost. Though it is true that afterwards the vision is forgotten, the majesty and beauty of
God are so deeply imprinted upon the soul that it is impossible to forget these—save when the Lord is pleased for the
soul to suffer the great loneliness and aridity that I shall describe later; for then it seems even to forget God Himself.
The soul is now a new creature: it is continuously absorbed
in God; it seems to me that a new and living love of God is
beginning to work within it to a very high degree; for, though
the former type of vision which, as I said, reveals God without presenting any image of Him, is of a higher kind, yet, if
the memory of it is to last, despite our weakness, and if
the thoughts are to be well occupied, it is a great thing that
so Divine a Presence should be presented to the imagination
and should remain within it. These two kinds of vision almost invariably occur simultaneously, and, as they come in
this way, the eyes of the soul see the excellence and the
beauty and the glory of the most holy Humanity. And in the
other way which has been described it is revealed to us how
He is God, and that He is powerful, and can do all things,
and commands all things, and rules all things, and fills all
things with His love.

This vision is to be very highly esteemed, and, in my view,
there is no peril in it, as its effects show that the devil has no
power over it. Three or four times, I think, he has attempted
to present the Lord Himself to me in this way, by making a
false likeness of Him. He takes the form of flesh, but he
cannot counterfeit the glory which the vision has when it
comes from God. He makes these attempts in order to destroy the effects of the genuine vision that the soul has ex-

perienced; but the soul, of its own accord, resists them: it
then becomes troubled, despondent and restless; loses the
devotion and joy which it had before; and is unable to pray.
At the beginning of my experiences, as I have said, this happened to me three or four times. It is so very different from
a true vision that I think, even if a soul has experienced only
the Prayer of Quiet, it will become aware of the difference
from the effects which have been described in the chapter on
locutions. The thing is very easy to recognize; and, unless a
soul wants to be deceived, I do not think the devil will deceive it if it walks in humility and simplicity. Anyone, of
course, who has had a genuine vision from God will recognize the devil's work almost at once; he will begin by giving
the soul consolations and favours, but it will thrust them
from it. And further, I think, the devil's consolations must
be different from those of God: there is no suggestion in
them of pure and chaste love and it very soon becomes easy
to see whence they come. So, in my view, where a soul has
had experience, the devil will be unable to do it any harm.

Of all impossibilities, the most impossible is that these
true visions should be the work of the imagination. There is
no way in which this could be so: by the mere beauty and
whiteness of a single one of the hands which we are shown
the imagination is completely transcended. In any case, there
is no other way in which it would be possible for us to see
in a moment things of which we have no recollection, which
we have never thought of, and which, even in a long period of
time, we could not invent with our imagination, because, as I
have already said, they far transcend what we can comprehend on earth. Whether we could possibly be in any way responsible for this will be clear from what I shall now say. If,
in a vision, the representation proceeded from our own understanding, quite apart from the fact that it would not bring
about the striking effects which are produced when a vision is
of God, or, indeed, any effects at all, the position would be
like that of a man who wants to put himself to sleep but stays
awake because sleep has not come to him. He needs it—perhaps his brain is tired—and so is anxious for it; and he settles
down to doze, and does all he can to go off to sleep, and sometimes thinks he is succeeding, but if it is not real sleep it will
not restore him or refresh his brain—indeed, the brain some-

times grows wearier. Something like that will be the case here: instead of being restored and becoming strong, the soul will grow wearier and become tired and peevish. It is impossible for human tongue to exaggerate the riches which a vision from God brings to the soul: it even bestows health and refreshment on the body.

I used to put forward this argument, together with others, when they told me, as they often did, that I was being deceived by the devil and that it was all the work of my imagination. I also drew such comparisons as I could and as the Lord revealed to my understanding. But it was all to little purpose, because there were some very holy persons in the place, by comparison with whom I was a lost creature; and, as God was not leading these persons by that way, they were afraid and thought that what I saw was the result of my sins. They repeated to one another what I said, so that before long they all got to know about it, though I had spoken of it only to my confessor and to those with whom he had commanded me to discuss it.

I once said to the people who were talking to me in this way that if they were to tell me that a person whom I knew well and had just been speaking to was not herself at all, but that I was imagining her to be so, and that they knew this was the case, I should certainly believe them rather than my own eyes. But, I added, if that person left some jewels with me, which I was actually holding in my hands as pledges of her great love, and if, never having had any before, I were thus to find myself rich instead of poor, I could not possibly believe that this was delusion, even if I wanted to. And, I said, I could show them these jewels—for all who knew me were well aware how my soul had changed: my confessor himself testified to this, for the difference was very great in every respect, and no fancy, but such as all could clearly see. As I had previously been so wicked, I concluded, I could not believe that, if the devil were doing this to delude me and drag me down to hell, he would make use of means which so completely defeated their own ends by taking away my vices and making me virtuous and strong; for it was quite clear to me that these experiences had immediately made me a different person.

My confessor, who, as I have said, was a very holy Father

of the Company of Jesus,[3] gave them—so I learned—the same reply. He was very discreet and a man of deep humility, and this deep humility brought great trials upon me; for, being a man of great prayer and learning, he did not trust his own opinion, and the Lord was not leading him by this path. Very great trials befell him on my account, and this in many ways. I knew they used to tell him that he must be on his guard against me, lest the devil should deceive him into believing anything I might say to him, and they gave him similar examples of what had happened with other people. All this worried me. I was afraid that there would be no one left to hear my confession, and that everyone would flee from me: I did nothing but weep.

By the providence of God this Father consented to persevere with me and hear me: so great a servant of God was he that for His sake he would have exposed himself to anything. So he told me that I must not offend God or depart from what he said to me, and if I were careful about that I need not be afraid that He would fail me. He always encouraged me and soothed me. And he always told me not to hide anything from him, in which I obeyed him. He would say that, if I did this, the devil—assuming it to be the devil—would not hurt me, and that in fact, out of the harm which he was trying to do my soul, the Lord would bring good. He did his utmost to lead my soul to perfection. As I was so fearful, I obeyed him in every way, though imperfectly. For the three years and more during which he was my confessor,[4] I gave him a great deal of trouble with these trials of mine, for during the grievous persecutions which I suffered and on the many occasions when the Lord allowed me to be harshly judged, often undeservedly, all kinds of tales about me were brought to him and

[3] P. Baltasar Álvarez. As this Father was only twenty-five years of age when he became St. Teresa's director, it is not surprising that he was disinclined to trust his own opinion, the more so as his Rector, P. Dionisio Vázquez, was a man of a rigid and inflexible temperament. P. Luis de la Puente [who was under him at Medina and wrote his biography: cf. *S.S.M.*, II, 310–13] tells us that he himself was very conscious of his deficiencies in this respect. Cf. La Puente: *Vida del Padre Baltasar Álvarez*, etc., Madrid, 1615, Chap. XIII.

[4] The period was actually of six years, but the author naturally dwells most upon the first three, which were the most difficult for her.

he would be blamed on my account when he was in no way blameworthy.

Had he not been a man of such sanctity, and had not the Lord given him courage, he could not possibly have endured so much, for he had to deal with people who did not believe him but thought I was going to destruction and at the same time he had to soothe me and deliver me from the fears which were oppressing me, though these he sometimes only intensified. He had also to reassure me; for, whenever I had a vision involving a new experience, God allowed me to be left in great fear. This all came from my having been, and my still being, such a sinner. He would comfort me most compassionately, and, if he had had more trust in himself, I should have had less to suffer, for God showed him the truth about everything and I believe the Sacrament itself gave him light.

Those of God's servants who were not convinced that all was well would often come and talk to me. Some of the things I said to them I expressed carelessly and they took them in the wrong sense. To one of them I was very much attached: he was a most holy man and my soul was infinitely in his debt and I was infinitely distressed at his misunderstanding me when he was so earnestly desirous that I should advance in holiness and that the Lord should give me light. Well, as I have said, I spoke without thinking what I was saying and my words seemed to these people lacking in humility. When they saw any faults in me, and they must have seen a great many, they condemned me outright. They would ask me certain questions, which I answered plainly, though carelessly; and they then thought I was trying to instruct them and considered myself a person of learning. All this reached the ears of my confessor (for they were certainly anxious to improve me), whereupon he began to find fault with me.

This state of things went on for a long time and I was troubled on many sides; but, thanks to the favours which the Lord granted me, I endured everything. I say this so that it may be realized what a great trial it is to have no one with experience of this spiritual road; if the Lord had not helped me so much, I do not know what would have become of me. I had troubles enough to deprive me of my reason, and I sometimes found myself in such a position that I could do nothing but lift up my eyes to the Lord. For though the opposition of good people to a weak and wicked woman like myself, and a timid one

THE LIFE OF TERESA OF JESUS

at that, seems nothing when described in this way, it was one of the worst trials that I have ever known in my life, and I have suffered some very severe ones. May the Lord grant me to have done His Majesty a little service here; for I am quite sure that those who condemned and arraigned me were doing Him service and that it was all for my great good.

CHAPTER XXIX

Continues the subject already begun and describes certain great favours which the Lord showed her and the things which His Majesty said to her to reassure her and give her answers for those who opposed her.

I have strayed far from any intention, for I was trying to give the reasons why this kind of vision cannot be the work of the imagination. How could we picture Christ's Humanity by merely studying the subject or form any impression of His great beauty by means of the imagination? No little time would be necessary if such a reproduction was to be in the least like the original. One can indeed make such a picture with one's imagination, and spend time in regarding it, and considering the form and the brilliance of it; little by little one may even learn to perfect such an image and store it up in the memory. Who can prevent this? Such a picture can undoubtedly be fashioned with the understanding. But with regard to the vision which we are discussing there is no way of doing this: we have to look at it when the Lord is pleased to reveal it to us—to look as He wills and at whatever He wills. And there is no possibility of our subtracting from it or adding to it, or any way in which we can obtain it, whatever we may do, or look at it when we like or refrain from looking at it. If we try to look at any particular part of it, we at once lose Christ.

For two years and a half things went on like this and it was quite usual for God to grant me this favour. It must now be more than three years since He took it from me as a continually recurring favour,[1] by giving me something else of a

[1] [If the first imaginary vision occurred on January 25, 1560 (cf. pp. 247, 259, but also p. 270), this would mean that St. Teresa

higher kind, which I shall describe later. Though I saw that He was speaking to me, and though I was looking upon that great beauty of His, and experiencing the sweetness with which He uttered those words—sometimes stern words—with that most lovely and Divine mouth, and though, too, I was extremely desirous of observing the colour of His eyes, or His height, so that I should be able to describe it, I have never been sufficiently worthy to see this, nor has it been of any use for me to attempt to do so; if I tried, I lost the vision altogether. Though I sometimes see Him looking at me compassionately, His gaze has such power that my soul cannot endure it and remains in so sublime a rapture that it loses this beauteous vision in order to have the greater fruition of it all. So there is no question here of our wanting or not wanting to see the vision. It is clear that the Lord wants of us only humility and shame, our acceptance of what is given us and our praise of its Giver.

This refers to all visions, none excepted. There is nothing that we can do about them; we cannot see more or less of them at will; and we can neither call them up nor banish them by our own efforts. The Lord's will is that we shall see quite clearly that they are produced, not by us but by His Majesty. Still less can we be proud of them: on the contrary, they make us humble and fearful, when we find that, just as the Lord takes from us the power of seeing what we desire, so He can also take from us these favours and His grace, with the result that we are completely lost. So while we live in this exile let us always walk with fear.

Almost invariably the Lord showed Himself to me in His resurrection body, and it was thus, too, that I saw Him in the Host. Only occasionally, to strengthen me when I was in tribulation, did He show me His wounds, and then He would appear sometimes as He was on the Cross and sometimes as in the Garden. On a few occasions I saw Him wearing the crown of thorns and sometimes He would also be carrying the Cross—because of my necessities, as I say, and those of others—but always in His glorified flesh. Many are the affronts and trials that I have suffered through telling this and many are the fears and persecutions that it has brought me. So sure

was writing this chapter in the summer of 1565, which (cf. pp. 59–60) is about correct. To date the first vision in January 1558 would bring the writing of the chapter to 1563, which is almost certainly too early.]

were those whom I told of it that I had a devil that some of them wanted to exorcize me. This troubled me very little, but I was sorry when I found that my confessors were afraid to hear my confessions or when I heard that people were saying things to them against me. None the less, I could never regret having seen these heavenly visions and I would not exchange them for all the good things and delights of this world. I always considered them a great favour from the Lord, and I think they were the greatest of treasures; often the Lord Himself would reassure me about them. I found my love for Him growing exceedingly: I used to go to Him and tell Him about all these trials and I always came away from prayer comforted and with new strength. I did not dare to argue with my critics, because I saw that that made things worse, as they thought me lacking in humility. With my confessor, however, I did discuss these matters; and whenever he saw that I was troubled he would comfort me greatly.

As the visions became more numerous, one of those who had previously been in the habit of helping me and who used sometimes to hear my confessions when the minister was unable to do so, began to say that it was clear I was being deceived by the devil. So, as I was quite unable to resist it, they commanded me to make the sign of the Cross whenever I had a vision, and to snap my fingers at it[2] so as to convince myself that it came from the devil, whereupon it would not come again: I was not to be afraid, they said, and God would protect me and take the vision away. This caused me great distress: as I could not help believing that my visions came from God, it was a terrible thing to have to do; and, as I have said, I could not possibly wish them to be taken from me. However, I did as they commanded me. I besought God often to set me free from deception; indeed, I was continually doing so and with many tears. I would also invoke Saint Peter and Saint Paul, for the Lord had told me (it was on their festival that He had first appeared to me)[3] that they would prevent

[2] Dar higas—i.e., make the sign of contempt described on p. 243, n. 9.

[3] [This phrase would seem to indicate that the first vision was on June 29 (or possibly on June 30: the Commemoration of St. Paul) and not on January 25 (see p. 268). If this deduction and my dating of the year as 1560 are both correct, this part of the book was not written until the very end of 1565. Cf. pp. 58–9.]

me from being deluded; and I used often to see them very clearly on my left hand, though not in an imaginary vision. These glorious Saints were in a very real sense my lords.

To be obliged to snap my fingers at a vision in which I saw the Lord caused me the sorest distress. For, when I saw Him before me, I could not have believed that the vision had come from the devil even if the alternative were my being cut to pieces. So this was a kind of penance to me, and a heavy one. In order not to have to be so continually crossing myself, I would carry a cross in my hand. This I did almost invariably; but I was not so particular about snapping my fingers at the vision, for it hurt me too much to do that. It reminded me of the way the Jews had insulted Him, and I would beseech Him to forgive me, since I did it out of obedience to him who was in His own place, and not to blame me, since he was one of the ministers whom He had placed in His Church. He told me not to worry about it and said I was quite right to obey, but He would see that my confessor learned the truth. When they made me stop my prayer He seemed to me to have become angry, and He told me to tell them that this was tyranny. He used to show me ways of knowing that the visions were not of the devil; some of these I shall describe later.

Once, when I was holding in my hand the cross of a rosary, He put out His own hand and took it from me, and, when He gave it back to me, it had become four large stones, much more precious than diamonds—incomparably more so, for it is impossible, of course, to make comparisons with what is supernatural, and diamonds seem imperfect counterfeits beside the precious stones which I saw in that vision. On the cross, with exquisite workmanship, were portrayed the five wounds.[4] He told me that henceforward it would always look to me like that, and so it did: I could never see the wood of which it was made, but only these stones. To nobody, however, did it look like this except to myself. As soon as they had begun to order me to test my visions in this way, and to resist them, the favours became more and more numerous. In my efforts to divert my attention from them, I never ceased from prayer; even

[4] This cross was later given by St. Teresa's sister Juana to Doña María Enríquez de Toledo, Duchess of Alba. After the Duchess's death the Carmelites claimed possession of it and until the end of the eighteenth century it was preserved in their Valladolid convent. It was lost during the religious persecutions of 1835.

when asleep I used to seem to be praying, for this made me
grow in love. I would address my complaints to the Lord, telling Him I could not bear it. Desire and strive to cease thinking of Him as I would, it was not in my power to do so. In
every respect I was as obedient as I could be, but about this
I could do little or nothing, and the Lord never gave me leave
to disobey. But, though He told me to do as I was bidden, He
reassured me in another way, by teaching me what I was to
say to my critics; and this He does still. The arguments with
which He provided me were so conclusive that they made me
feel perfectly secure.

Shortly after this, His Majesty began to give me clearer
signs of His presence, as He had promised me to do. There
grew within me so strong a love of God that I did not know
who was inspiring me with it, for it was entirely supernatural
and I had made no efforts to obtain it. I found myself dying
with the desire to see God and I knew no way of seeking that
life save through death. This love came to me in vehement
impulses, which, though less unbearable, and of less worth,
than those of which I have spoken previously, took from me
all power of action. For nothing afforded me satisfaction
and I was incapable of containing myself: it really seemed as
though my soul were being torn from me. O sovereign artifice
of the Lord, with what subtle diligence dost Thou work upon
Thy miserable slave! Thou didst hide Thyself from me, and
out of Thy love didst oppress me with a death so delectable
that my soul's desire was never to escape from it.

No one who has not experienced these vehement impulses
can possibly understand this: it is no question of physical
restlessness within the breast, or of uncontrollable devotional
feelings which occur frequently and seem to stifle the spirit.
That is prayer of a much lower kind, and we should check
such quickenings of emotion by endeavouring gently to turn
them into inward recollection and to keep the soul hushed
and still. Such prayer is like the violent sobbing of children:
they seem as if they are going to choke, but if they are given
something to drink their superabundant emotion is checked
immediately. So it is here: reason must step in and take the
reins, for it may be that this is partly accountable for by the
temperament. On reflection comes a fear that there is some
imperfection, which may in great part be due to the senses.

So this child must be hushed with a loving caress which will move it to a gentle kind of love; it must not, as they say, be driven at the point of the fist. Its love must find an outlet in interior recollection and not be allowed to boil right over like a pot to which fuel has been applied indiscriminately. The fire must be controlled at its source and an endeavour must be made to quench the flame with gentle tears, not with tears caused by affliction, for these proceed from the emotions already referred to and do a great deal of harm. I used at first to shed tears of this kind, which left my brain so distracted and my spirit so wearied that for a day or more I was not fit to return to prayer. Great discretion, then, is necessary at first so that everything may proceed gently and the operations of the spirit may express themselves interiorly; great care should be taken to prevent operations of an exterior kind.

These other impulses are very different. It is not we who put on the fuel; it seems rather as if the fire is already kindled and it is we who are suddenly thrown into it to be burned up. The soul does not try to feel the pain of the wound caused by the Lord's absence. Rather an arrow is driven into the very depths of the entrails, and sometimes into the heart, so that the soul does not know either what is the matter with it or what it desires. It knows quite well that it desires God and that the arrow seems to have been dipped in some drug which leads it to hate itself for the love of this Lord so that it would gladly lose its life for Him. No words will suffice to describe the way in which God wounds the soul and the sore distress which He causes it, so that it hardly knows what it is doing. Yet so delectable is this distress that life holds no delight which can give greater satisfaction. As I have said, the soul would gladly be dying of this ill.

This distress and this bliss between them bewildered me so much that I was never able to understand how such a thing could be. Oh, what it is to see a wounded soul—I mean when it understands its condition sufficiently to be able to describe itself as wounded for so excellent a cause! It sees clearly that this love has come to it through no act of its own, but that, from the exceeding great love which the Lord bears it, a spark seems suddenly to have fallen upon it and to have set it wholly on fire. Oh, how often, when in this state, do I remember that verse of David: *Quemadmodum desiderat cervus ad fontes aquarum*,[5] which I seem to see fulfilled literally in myself!

When these impulses are not very strong they appear to calm down a little, or, at any rate, the soul seeks some relief from them because it knows not what to do. It performs certain penances, but is quite unable to feel them, while the shedding of its blood causes it no more distress than if its body were dead. It seeks ways and means whereby it may express something of what it feels for the love of God; but its initial pain is so great that I know of no physical torture which can drown it. There is no relief to be found in these medicines: they are quite inadequate for so sublime an ill.[6] A certain alleviation of the pain is possible, which may cause some of it to pass away, if the soul begs God to grant it relief from its ill, though it sees none save death, by means of which it believes it can have complete fruition of its Good. At other times the impulses are so strong that the soul is unable to do either this or anything else. The entire body contracts and neither arm nor foot can be moved. If the subject is on his feet, he remains as though transported and cannot even breathe: all he does is to moan—not aloud, for that is impossible, but inwardly, out of pain.

It pleased the Lord that I should sometimes see the following vision. I would see beside me, on my left hand, an angel in bodily form—a type of vision which I am not in the habit of seeing, except very rarely. Though I often see representations of angels, my visions of them are of the type which I first mentioned. It pleased the Lord that I should see this angel in the following way. He was not tall, but short, and very beautiful, his face so aflame that he appeared to be one of the highest types of angel who seem to be all afire. They must be those who are called cherubim:[7] they do not tell me their names but I am well aware that there is a great difference between certain angels and others, and between these and others still, of a kind that I could not possibly explain. In his hands I saw a long golden spear and at the end of the iron

---

[5] Psalm xli, 1 [A.V., xlii, 1]: "As the hart panteth after the fountains of water, so my soul panteth after thee, O God."

[6] [*Lit.*: "too low for so high an ill."]

[7] St. Teresa wrote "Cherubims", but P. Báñez added the marginal note: "it seems more like those which are called Seraphims", and Fray Luis de León, in his edition, adopted this form.

tip I seemed to see a point of fire. With this he seemed to pierce my heart several times so that it penetrated to my entrails. When he drew it out, I thought he was drawing them out with it and he left me completely afire with a great love for God. The pain was so sharp that it made me utter several moans; and so excessive was the sweetness caused me by this intense pain that one can never wish to lose it, nor will one's soul be content with anything less than God. It is not bodily pain, but spiritual, though the body has a share in it—indeed, a great share. So sweet are the colloquies of love which pass between the soul and God that if anyone thinks I am lying I beseech God, in His goodness, to give him the same experience.[8]

During the days that this continued, I went about as if in a stupor. I had no wish to see or speak with anyone, but only to hug my pain, which caused me greater bliss than any that can come from the whole of creation. I was like this on several occasions, when the Lord was pleased to send me these raptures, and so deep were they that, even when I was with other people, I could not resist them; so, greatly to my distress, they began to be talked about. Since I have had them, I do not feel this pain so much, but only the pain of which I spoke somewhere before—I do not remember in what chapter.[9] The latter is, in many respects, very different from this, and of greater worth. But, when this pain of which I am now speaking begins, the Lord seems to transport the soul and to send it into an ecstasy, so that it cannot possibly suffer or have any pain because it immediately begins to experience fruition. May He be blessed for ever, Who bestows so many favours on one who so ill requites such great benefits.

[8] [P. Silverio dates this occurrence "about 1562" but gives no evidence for the date, and I see none. An earlier year (1559–60) is more usually given.] Carmelite tradition has it that St. Teresa received the same favour again while Prioress of the Incarnation, between 1571 and 1574. The heart of the Saint has not unnaturally been the subject of the most extraordinary inventions. [Some of these are described by P. Silverio.] On May 25, 1726, Pope Benedict XIII appointed a festival and office for the Transverberation, which is observed on August 27. First instituted for the Discalced Carmelites, it was extended to Spain as a whole by Clement XII on December 11, 1733.

[9] Chap. XX.

CHAPTER XXX

Takes up the course of her life again and tells how the Lord granted her great relief from her trials by bringing her a visit from the holy man Fray Peter of Alcántara, of the Order of the glorious Saint Francis. Discusses the severe temptations and interior trials which she sometimes suffered.

Now when I saw that I could do little or nothing to stop myself from experiencing these violent impulses, I began to be afraid of them, for I could not understand how distress and contentment could go together. I already knew that it was quite possible for physical distress and spiritual contentment to exist together in the same person but it bewildered me to experience such excessive spiritual distress and with it such intense joy. Though I still did not cease striving to resist, I could do so little that it sometimes fatigued me. I used to seek the protection of the Cross and to try to defend myself against Him Who through the Cross became the Protector of us all. I saw that no one understood me, though I understood it very clearly myself; I did not dare, however, to speak of it save to my confessor, for to have done so would certainly have been to proclaim that I had no humility.

The Lord was pleased to grant me relief from a great part of my trials, and, for the time being, from all of them, by bringing to this place the blessed Fray Peter of Alcántara, whom I mentioned earlier when I said something about his penitential life: among other things, I have been assured that for twenty years he continuously wore a shirt made of iron.[1] He is the author of some little books on prayer, written in Spanish,[2] which are being used a great deal nowadays; as he was a man with great experience of prayer, his writings are very profitable for those who practise it. He kept the Primitive Rule of the blessed Saint Francis in all its rigour, as well as doing those other things of which something has already been said.

---

[1] [*Hoja de lata. Lit.*: "tinplate."]

[2] [The only one of these "little books" still extant is the *Treatise of Prayer and Meditation: S.S.M.*, II, 106.]

In due course that servant of God—the widow of whom I have spoken and who was a friend of mine[3]—learned that this great man was here. She knew of my necessities, for she was a witness of my afflictions and used to afford me great consolation, her faith being so strong that she could not but believe that what most people said was of the devil was really the work of the Spirit of God; and, as she is a person of very great intelligence and is also most discreet and was receiving many favours from the Lord in prayer, His Majesty was pleased to enlighten her upon matters of which learned men were ignorant. My confessors gave me permission to relieve my mind by talking to her about certain things, because for a multitude of reasons she was a suitable person for such confidences. She sometimes shared in the favours which the Lord was granting me and would receive counsels which were of great benefit to her soul. Well, when she learned that this holy man was here, she said nothing to me but obtained leave from my Provincial for me to stay with her for a week so as to give me a better opportunity of consulting him. So on this occasion of his first visit I had many talks with him, both in her house and in several churches, and later I had a great deal to do with him on many occasions. I gave him a summary account of my life and method of prayer with the greatest clarity of which I was capable; for I have always acted on the principle of speaking with the utmost clarity and truth to those whom I consult about my soul. I would always try to reveal to them its very first motions and tell them even the most dubious and suspicious things about myself: indeed, in discussing these matters with them I would put forward arguments which told against me. I was able, therefore, to reveal my soul to Fray Peter without duplicity or concealment.

Almost from the beginning, I saw that, out of his own experience, he understood me. And that was all I needed; for I did not understand myself then as I do now, and I could not describe what I was experiencing. Since that time God has granted me the ability to understand and describe the favours which His Majesty sends me. But just then I needed someone who had gone through it all himself, for such a person alone could understand me and interpret my experiences. He enlightened me wonderfully about them. I had been unable, at

---

[3] Doña Guiomar de Ulloa.

least as regards the visions which were not imaginary, to understand what they could all mean: I did not see how I could
understand the nature of visions which I saw with the eyes of
the soul, for, as I have said, I had thought that only visions
which can be seen with the bodily eyes are of any importance,
and of these I had none.

This holy man enlightened me about the whole matter,
explained it all to me and told me not to be distressed but to
praise God and be quite certain that it was the work of the
Spirit; with the exception of the Faith, he said, there could be
nothing truer, and nothing in which I could more confidently
believe. He derived great happiness from what I said to him,
was helpful and kind to me in every way and ever afterwards
took a great interest in me and told me about his own affairs
and undertakings. When he saw that I had desires which he
himself had already carried into effect—for the Lord had bestowed very resolute desires upon me—and when he found,
too, that I was so full of courage, he delighted in talking to
me about these things. For if the Lord brings anyone to this
state he will find no pleasure or comfort equal to that of meeting with another whom he believes He has brought along the
first part of the same road—for at this time I could not, I
think, have gone much farther than that: please God I may
still be as far advanced as I was then.

He had the greatest compassion on me. He told me that
the trial I had been suffering—that is to say, the opposition of
good people—was one of the severest in the world and that
there would be many more such trials awaiting me. I should
therefore have continual need of someone who understood me
and there was no such person in this city, but he would speak
to the priest to whom I made my confessions, and also to one
of those who caused me the deepest distress—namely, that
married man of whom I have already spoken. The latter, just
because he bore me the greatest goodwill, opposed me more
than anyone else: being a holy and God-fearing[4] soul, and having so recently seen how wicked I was, he could not bring
himself to have any confidence about me. The saintly man did
as he had said he would: he spoke to them both and put rea-

_____

[4] [This word, _temerosa_, might also be translated "timorous",
"timid" but St. Teresa's use of "and", rather than of "but", to con-
nect it with "holy" seems to indicate the meaning given in the text.]

sons and arguments before them as to why they should be reassured about me and not cause me any more disquiet. My confessor hardly needed the advice. This gentleman, however, even when he had heard it, was not completely convinced, but it was sufficient to prevent him from frightening me as much as he had been doing.

We arranged—Fray Peter and I—that from that time onward I should write and tell him of anything that happened to me and that we should commend each other earnestly to God; for so great was his humility that he thought that there was value in the prayers of this miserable creature, which made me very much ashamed. He left me greatly comforted and very happy, telling me to continue confidently in prayer and not to doubt that the prayer came from God. For my greater security, I was to report any doubts I might have to my confessor; and, provided I did this, I should feel safe all my life. I was unable, however, to experience this feeling of complete security, for the Lord was leading me by the road of fear, with the result that, whenever I was told that the devil was deceiving me, I would believe it. In reality, none of my advisers was able to make me feel either afraid enough or secure enough to believe in him rather than in the feelings which the Lord implanted in my soul. So, although Fray Peter comforted and calmed me, I had not sufficient trust in him to be wholly without fear, especially when the Lord left me with the spiritual trials which I shall now describe. But, on the whole, as I say, I was greatly comforted. I was never weary of giving thanks to God and to my glorious father Saint Joseph, who seemed to me to have brought Fray Peter here, as he was Commissary General of the Custody[5] of Saint Joseph, to whom, as to Our Lady, I used often to commend myself. I had sometimes to endure—and still have, though to a lesser degree—the sorest spiritual trials, together with bodily pains and tortures, so severe that I could do nothing to ease them. At other times I suffered from more grievous bodily ills, and, if I had no spiritual distress, I bore these with great joy. It was when both kinds of distress came upon me together that my trials were so great and caused me such deep depression. I would forget all the favours that the Lord had bestowed

5 [The Franciscan term for a group of religious houses not large enough to form a province.]

upon me: nothing would remain with me but the mere recollection of them, like the memory of a dream, and this was a great distress to me. For, when a person is in this condition, the understanding becomes stupid; and so I was tormented by a thousand doubts and suspicions. I thought that I had not understood it properly, and that it might have been my fancy, and that it was bad enough for me to be deluded myself, without deluding good men as well. I felt I was so evil that I began to think that all the evils and heresies that had arisen were due to my sins.

This is a false humility; and it was invented by the devil so that he might unsettle me and see if he could drive my soul to despair. I have had so much experience by now of the devil's work that he sees I know his tricks and so he troubles me much less with this kind of torture than he used to. His part in it is evident from the disquiet and unrest with which it begins, from the turmoil which he creates in the soul for so long as his influence lasts, and from the darkness and affliction into which he plunges it, causing it an aridity and an ill-disposition for prayer and for everything that is good. He seems to stifle the soul and to constrain the body, and thus to render both powerless. For, though the soul is conscious of its own wretchedness and it distresses us to see what we are and our wickedness seems to us to be of the worst possible kind—as bad as that which has just been described—and we feel it very deeply, yet genuine humility does not produce inward turmoil, nor does it cause unrest in the soul, or bring it darkness or aridity: on the contrary, it cheers it and produces in it the opposite effects—quietness, sweetness and light. Though it causes us distress, we are comforted to see what a great favour God is granting us by sending us that distress and how well the soul is occupied. Grieved as it is at having offended God, it is also encouraged by His mercy. It is sufficiently enlightened to feel ashamed, but it praises His Majesty, Who for so long has borne with it. In that other humility, which is the work of the devil, the soul has not light enough to do anything good and thinks of God as of one who is always wielding fire and sword. It pictures God's righteousness, and, although it has faith in His mercy, for the devil is not powerful enough to make it lose its faith, yet this is not such as to bring me consolation, for, when my soul considers

God's mercy, this only increases its torment, since I realize that it involves me in greater obligations.[6]

This is an invention of the devil, and one of the most grievous and subtle and dissembling that I have found in him, and so I should like to warn Your Reverence of it, so that, if he should tempt you in this way, you may have some light, and may recognize his hand, if he leaves you sufficient understanding for doing so. Do not suppose that learning and knowledge have anything to do with this, for I am wholly destitute of both, and yet, after escaping from the devil's wiles, I see quite clearly that this is folly. What I have learned is that the Lord is pleased to give him permission and leave to tempt us, just as He gave him leave to tempt Job, although, being so wicked, I am not myself tempted as severely as that.

I have, however, been tempted in this way—once, I remember, on the day before the vigil of Corpus Christi, a festival to which I am devoted, though not so much so as I ought to be. On that occasion the temptation lasted only until the day of the festival: on other occasions it has lasted for a week or a fortnight, or even perhaps for three weeks, or it may have been even longer. In particular it used to come during Holy Week, a time when I would derive great comfort from prayer. What happens on such occasions is that the devil suddenly lays hold on my understanding, sometimes by making use of things so trifling that at any other time I should laugh at them. He confuses the understanding and does whatever he likes with it, so that the soul, fettered as it is and no longer its own mistress, can think of nothing but the absurdities which he presents to it—things of no importance, which neither keep the soul in bondage nor allow it to be free, and enslave it only in the sense that they stupefy it until its control over itself is gone. It has sometimes seemed to me, indeed, that the devils behave as though they were playing ball with the soul, so incapable is it of freeing itself from their power. Its sufferings at such a time are indescribable. It goes about in search of relief and God allows it to find none; it has only the reasoning power derived from its free-will, and it is unable to reason clearly. I mean that its eyes seem to be almost blindfolded: it is like someone who has gone along a particular road

---

[6] [The sudden and characteristic change of person is reproduced exactly from the original.]

again and again, so that, even if it is night, and quite dark, he knows by the instinct which comes from experience where he is likely to stumble, for he has seen the road by day and is therefore on his guard against that danger. Just so the soul, in avoiding giving offence to God, seems to be walking by habit. This explanation, however, leaves out of account the fact that the Lord has it in His keeping, which is the thing that matters.

At such a time, faith, like all the other virtues, is quite numbed and asleep. It is not lost, for the soul has a firm belief in what is held by the Church; but, though it can testify with the mouth, it seems in other respects to be oppressed and stupefied, and it feels as if it knows God only as something of which it has heard from afar off. So lukewarm does its love become that, if it hears Him spoken of, it listens, believing that He is Who He is, because this is held by the Church, but it retains no memory of its own experiences of Him. To go and say its prayers, or to be alone, only causes it greater anguish, for the inward torture which it feels, without knowing the source of it, is intolerable; and, in my opinion, bears some slight resemblance to hell. Indeed this is a fact, for the Lord revealed it to me in a vision: the soul is inwardly burning, without knowing who has kindled the fire, nor whence it comes, nor how to flee from it, nor with what to put it out. In vain does it seek a remedy in reading: it might as well be unable to read at all. Once I chanced to take up the Life of a saint, to see if I could become absorbed in the reading of it and find comfort in thinking of the saint's sufferings. But I read four or five lines as many times, and, though they were in Spanish, I understood less of them at the end than at the beginning; so I gave it up. This happened to me on many occasions but I have a particular recollection of that one.

To engage in conversation with anyone is worse still, for the devil then makes me so peevish and ill-tempered that I seem to want to snap everyone up. I cannot help this, but if I can keep myself in hand I feel I am doing something, or rather that the Lord is doing something when His hand restrains anyone in this condition from saying or doing anything which may harm his neighbour or offend God. Then again, it is certainly useless to go to one's confessor. I will tell you what often happened to me. Saintly as were those whom I was consulting at that time, and am consulting still, they would say such things to me, and reprove me with such asperity that, when I spoke to them about it later, they were astonished at it themselves but said that they had been unable to do otherwise. For, although they had previously made up their minds not to speak to me like this, and afterwards would be sorry they had done so, and even feel scruples about it because of these bodily and spiritual trials which I was suffering, the resolutions they had made to comfort me with words of compassion would fall to the ground.

The words they used were not wrong—not offensive, I mean, to God—but they were the strongest words of displeasure permissible in a confessor. Their aim must have been to mortify me, and, although at other times I delighted in mortification and was well able to bear it, it was now pure torture to me. Then, too, I used to think I was deceiving them, so I would go and warn them most earnestly to be on their guard against me in case I might be doing so. I knew quite well that I would not deceive them intentionally, or tell them a lie, but I was thoroughly afraid. One of them, realizing how I was being tempted, once told me not to be distressed, for, even if I tried to deceive him, he had discernment enough not to allow himself to be deceived.[7] This was a great comfort to me.

Sometimes—almost habitually, indeed, or at least very frequently—I would find relief after communicating. There were times, in fact, when the very act of approaching the Sacrament would at once make me feel so well, both in soul and in body, that I was astounded. I would feel as if all the darkness in my soul had suddenly been dispersed and the sun had come out and shown me the stupidity of the things I had been saying and doing. At other times, if the Lord spoke only one word to me (if, for example, as on the occasion I have already described, He said no more than "Be not troubled: have no fear"), that one word completely cured me, or, if I were to see some vision, it was as if there had been nothing wrong with me. I rejoiced in God and made my complaint to Him, asking Him how He could allow me to suffer such tortures, but telling Him that I was well rewarded for them, since, when they were over, I almost invariably received favours in great abundance. My soul seemed to emerge from the crucible like gold, both brighter and purer, to find the Lord within

7 P. Baltasar Álvarez, according to Gracián.

it. So trials like these, unbearable as they may seem, eventually become light, and the soul becomes anxious to suffer again if by so doing it can render the Lord greater service. And, however numerous may be our troubles and persecutions, if we endure them without offending the Lord, but rejoice to suffer for His sake, they all work together for our greater gain—though I do not myself bear them as they should be borne, but in a way which is most imperfect.

On other occasions these temptations came to me in another fashion, as they do still. At such times as these I seem to have been totally deprived of the possibility of thinking a single good thought or of desiring to put it into practice. My soul and body seem to be completely useless and merely a burden to me. But I do not then have these other temptations and discomforts: only a feeling of dissatisfaction—with what, I do not know—so that there is nothing in which my soul can take pleasure. I used to try to occupy myself with the outward performance of good works, and I would half force myself to do these, and I know well how little a soul can do when it is without grace. This did not cause me great distress, for I derived some satisfaction from realizing my own baseness. At other times I find myself unable to formulate a single definite thought, other than quite a fleeting one, about God, or about anything good, or to engage in prayer, even when I am alone; yet none the less I feel that I know Him.

It is the understanding and the imagination, I think, which are doing me harm here. My will, I believe, is good, and well-disposed to all good things; but this understanding is so depraved that it seems to be nothing but a raving lunatic—nobody can repress it and I have not myself sufficient control of it to keep it quiet for a moment. Sometimes I laugh at myself and realize what a miserable creature I am and then I keep an eye on my understanding and leave it alone to see what it will do; and for a wonder—glory be to God!—it never occupies itself with evil things, but only with indifferent ones, looking round for things to think about here, there and everywhere. I then become more conscious of the exceeding great favour which the Lord bestows on me when He keeps this lunatic bound and allows me to enjoy perfect contemplation. I sometimes reflect on what would happen if people who think of me as good were to see me in this condition of distraction. I am deeply grieved when I find that my soul is in such bad company. I want to see it free, so I say to the Lord:

"When, my God, shall I at last see all the faculties of my soul united in Thy praise and having fruition of Thee? Permit my soul no longer, Lord, to be dispersed in fragments, with each fragment seeming to go its own way." This is an experience I often have, but sometimes I know quite well that my poor bodily health is having a great deal to do with it. I often think of the harm wrought in us by original sin; it is this, I believe, that has made us incapable of enjoying so much good all at once, and added to this are my own sins, for, had I not committed so many, I should have been more nearly perfect in goodness.

There was another great trial, too, which I suffered. I used to think I understood all the books dealing with prayer which I read, and that, as the Lord had bestowed this gift of prayer upon me, I no longer needed them. So I left off reading them and read only lives of saints, for, as I find myself falling so far short of the saints in the service which they rendered to God, such reading helps me and spurs me on to do better. Then it would occur to me that it showed a great lack of humility to suppose that I had received that gift of prayer, and, as I could not succeed in persuading myself of the contrary, I was greatly distressed, until learned men, and the blessed Fray Peter of Alcántara, told me not to let it trouble me. I realize perfectly that, although in granting me favours His Majesty treats me as He does many good people, I have not yet begun to serve Him, and that I am nothing but imperfection except in desire and love, with regard to which I know well the Lord has helped me so that I may render Him some service. I do really believe I love Him, but my actions and the many imperfections which I find in myself discourage me.

At other times my soul is troubled by what I should call a kind of foolishness: I seem to be doing neither good nor evil, but to be following the crowd, as they say, without experiencing either suffering or bliss. I care not whether I live or die, nor whether I experience pleasure or pain: I seem to feel nothing. The soul appears to me to be like a little ass, feeding and sustaining its life by means of the food which is given it and which it eats almost unconsciously. For the soul in this state cannot do otherwise than feed on some of God's great favours; it does not mind living this miserable life and bears its existence with equanimity, but it is quite unconscious of any motions or effects which might help it to understand its condition.

This, it now seems to me, is like sailing with a very calm wind: one makes great headway, but without knowing how, whereas in these other experiences the effects are so noticeable that the soul almost immediately becomes conscious of its improvement, for the desires begin at once to be aroused and the soul is never fully satisfied. This is the result of the violent impulses of love, which I have already mentioned, in those to whom God gives them. It reminds me of little springs which I have seen gushing up and which keep on incessantly stirring up the sand all around them. This, I think, is a very lifelike illustration or comparison to apply to souls which attain to this state. Love is continually bubbling up in them and thinking of the things it will do: it cannot remain where it is, just as the spring-water seems unable to remain in the earth, but issues forth from it. Just so, as a general rule, is it with the soul: such is the love it has that it can find no rest, nor can it contain itself, and it has already saturated the earth around. It would like others to drink of its love, since it has itself no lack of it, so that they might help it to praise God. Oh, how often do I remember the living water of which the Lord spoke to the woman of Samaria! I am so fond of that Gospel. I have loved it ever since I was quite a child—though I did not, of course, understand it properly then, as I do now—and I used often to beseech the Lord to give me that water. I had a picture of the Lord at the well, which hung where I could always see it, and bore the inscription: "Domine, da mihi aquam."[8]

This love is also like a great fire, which has always to be fed lest it should go out. Just so with the souls I am describing: cost them what it might, they would always want to be bringing wood, so that this fire should not die. For my own part, I am the sort of person who would be satisfied if she had even straw to throw upon it, and it is sometimes—often, indeed—like that with me. Now I am laughing; now I am greatly troubled. An inward impulse moves me to serve God in some way, but I am useless except for decking images

---

[8] St. John iv, 15: "Sir, give me this water." These words, which form part of the Gospel for the Friday after the third Sunday in Lent, the Saint could have read as a child beneath a picture of the scene in the Gospel. On her father's death the picture was given to the Convent of the Incarnation, where it is still preserved.

with branches of trees and flowers, or for sweeping or tidying an oratory or doing other trifling things which I am ashamed of. If I did anything in the way of penance, it was all so insignificant that, unless the Lord would take the will for the deed, I realized how completely worthless it was and scoffed at my own self. It is no small trial, then, for souls to whom God in His goodness grants an abundance of this fire of His love, that they should lack bodily strength to enable them to do anything for Him. It is a very great grief; for, when a soul lacks the strength to throw any wood on this fire, and is frightened to death lest it should go out, I think it becomes consumed itself and turns into ashes, or melts into tears, and is burned up; and this, though delectable, is severe torture.

Let the soul give great praise to the Lord when it has progressed as far as this, and when He has granted it bodily strength to enable it to do penance, or given it learning and talent and freedom to preach, hear confessions and bring souls to God. It has no knowledge or understanding of the blessing it possesses if it has not learned by experience what it is to be able to do nothing in the Lord's service and always to be receiving so much from Him. May He be blessed for all things and may the angels glorify Him. Amen.

I do not know if I am doing right to say so much about trifles. As Your Reverence has again sent me a message telling me not to mind writing at length and to omit nothing, I am continuing to give a true and clear description of everything that I remember. But I cannot help omitting a great deal, for otherwise I should have to devote much more time to this (and, as I said, I have so little time) without perhaps doing any good by it.

CHAPTER XXXI

Treats of certain outward temptations and representations made to her by the devil and of tortures which he caused her. Discusses likewise several matters which are extremely useful for people to know if they are walking on the road to perfection.

Having described certain secret and inward disturbances and temptations inflicted upon me by the devil I shall now speak of others which he brought upon me almost in public and in which it was impossible not to detect his hand.

Once, when I was in an oratory, he appeared on my left hand in an abominable form; as he spoke to me, I paid particular attention to his mouth, which was horrible. Out of his body there seemed to be coming a great flame, which was intensely bright and cast no shadow. He told me in a horrible way that I had indeed escaped out of his hands but he would get hold of me still. I was very much afraid and made the sign of the Cross as well as I could, whereupon he disappeared, but immediately returned again. This happened twice running and I did not know what to do. But there was some holy water there, so I flung some in the direction of the apparition, and it never came back. On another occasion the devil was with me for five hours, torturing me with such terrible pains and both inward and outward disquiet that I do not believe I could have endured them any longer. The sisters who were with me were frightened to death and had no more idea of what to do for me than I had of how to help myself.

When the pains and the bodily suffering are quite intolerable, my custom is to make interior acts as well as I can, and to beseech the Lord, if it be His Majesty's good pleasure, to give me patience—if only I have that I can keep on suffering in this way until the very end of the world. So, when on this occasion I found myself suffering so severely, I took to these acts and resolutions, using them as means which would enable me to bear the pain. The Lord evidently meant me to realize that this was the work of the devil, for I saw beside me a most hideous little negro, snarling as if in despair at having lost what he was trying to gain. When I saw him, I laughed and was not afraid. Some of the sisters who were with me were helpless and had no idea how to relieve such torture; for the devil had made me pound the air[1] with my body, head and arms and I had been powerless to resist him. But the worst thing had been the interior disquiet: I could find no way of regaining my tranquillity. I was afraid to ask for holy water, lest I should frighten my companions and they should discover what was wrong.

From long experience I have learned that there is nothing

[1] [*Lit.*: "had made me give great blows."]

like holy water to put devils to flight and prevent them from coming back again. They also flee from the Cross, but return; so holy water must have great virtue. For my own part, whenever I take it, my soul feels a particular and most notable consolation. In fact, it is quite usual for me to be conscious of a refreshment which I cannot possibly describe, resembling an inward joy which comforts my whole soul. This is not fancy, or something which has happened to me only once: it has happened again and again and I have observed it most attentively. It is, let us say, as if someone very hot and thirsty were to drink from a jug of cold water: he would feel the refreshment throughout his body. I often reflect on the great importance of everything ordained by the Church and it makes me very happy to find that those words of the Church are so powerful that they impart their power to the water and make it so very different from water which has not been blessed.

Well, as my tortures did not cease, I said: "If you wouldn't laugh at me, I should ask for some holy water." So they brought me some and sprinkled me with it but it did me no good. Then I sprinkled some in the direction of the place where the little negro was standing and immediately he disappeared and all my troubles went, just as if someone had lifted them from me with his hand, except that I was as tired as if I had been dealt a great many blows. It edified me greatly to find that, when the Lord gives him permission, the devil can do so much harm to a soul and a body which are not his. For what, then, I thought, will he not do when he has them in his possession? And I felt a renewed desire to be freed from such pernicious companionship.

On another occasion, quite recently, the same thing happened to me, though it did not last so long and I was alone. I asked for holy water, and, after the devils had gone away, the next persons to come in (two nuns who may safely be believed, for they would not tell a lie for anything) noticed a very bad smell, like brimstone. I could not detect it myself but it had remained there long enough for them to have noticed it. On another occasion I was in choir when I felt a vehement impulse towards recollection. I went out, so that the sisters should not observe it, but all who were near me heard sounds where I was, like the noise of heavy blows, and I myself heard voices near me as though people were discussing something. I could not hear what they were saying, however: so deeply immersed was I in prayer that I heard nothing at all and I was not in the least afraid. This happened nearly always at times when the Lord was granting me the favour of allowing some soul, through my agency, to be making progress. What I am now going to describe is something which actually happened to me; and there are many people who will bear witness to this, in particular my present confessor,[2] who saw a written account of the occurrence in a letter. I did not tell him who the author of the letter was, but he knew quite well.

A person came to me who for two and a half years had been living in mortal sin—one of the most abominable sins that I had ever heard of—and during the whole of that time he neither confessed it nor amended his life, and yet went on saying Mass. And, though he confessed his other sins, when it came to that one, he would ask himself how he could possibly confess such a dreadful thing. He had a great desire to give it up but could not bring himself to do so. I was terribly sorry for him and very much distressed to find that God was being offended in such a way. I promised him that I would pray earnestly to God that He would help him and that I would get other people better than myself to do so too, and I wrote to a certain person who, he said, would be able to distribute the letters. And, lo and behold, at the first possible moment, he confessed; for through the many most saintly persons who at my request had prayed to Him on his behalf God was pleased to bestow this mercy upon his soul, and I, miserable though I am, had done what I could and taken the greatest pains about it. He wrote to me and said that he was now so much better that days passed without his falling into this sin, but he was suffering such tortures from temptation that his distress made him feel as if he were already in hell; and he asked me to commend him to God. I spoke about it again to my sisters, through whose prayers the Lord must have granted me this favour, and they took it very much to heart. (None of them could guess who he was.)[3] I begged

---

[2] This would be either P. Báñez or P. García de Toledo, who were the Saint's confessors from about 1563 to 1566.

[3] [The brackets here are mine. The sentence is an excellent example (and there are many others in the *Life*) of St. Teresa's incon-

His Majesty that these tortures and temptations might be assuaged and the devils be sent to torture me instead, provided I gave no offence to the Lord. This led me to suffer a month of the severest tortures and it was during that time that the two incidents happened which I have described.

It was the Lord's good pleasure that the devils should leave him; this I learned from letters, for I wrote to tell him what had been happening to me during the past month. His soul took new strength and he remained completely free from his sin and was never tired of giving thanks to the Lord and to me, as if I had done anything for him, unless he was helped by his belief that the Lord was granting me favours. He said that, when he found himself sorely oppressed, he would read my letters, and the temptation would leave him, and added that he was astounded to hear of what I had suffered and of how he had been delivered. I was astounded myself, for that matter, and I would have gone through as much for many years longer to set that soul free. May He be praised for everything, for the prayers of those who serve the Lord can do a great deal and I believe the sisters in this house do indeed serve Him. But the devils must have loosed most of their wrath on me because all this happened through my agency and the Lord permitted me to suffer on account of my sins.

One night, too, about this time, I thought the devils were stifling me; and when the nuns had sprinkled a great deal of holy water about I saw a huge crowd of them running away as quickly as though they were about to fling themselves down a steep place. So often have these accursed creatures tormented me and so little am I afraid of them, now that I see they cannot stir unless the Lord allows them to, that I should weary Your Reverence, and weary myself too, if I were to talk about them any further.

May what I have said help the true servant of God to make little account of these horrors, which the devils present us with in order to make us afraid. Let him realize that, every time we pay little heed to them, they lose much of their power and the soul gains much more control over them. We always derive some great benefit from these experiences, but

___

sequent way of writing. An idea comes into her head and at once she writes it down, even if (which is not the case here) doing so completely dislocates her sentence.]

of this benefit I will say nothing lest I should write too fully. I will only describe something that happened to me one night of All Souls. I was in an oratory: I had said one nocturn and was repeating some very devotional prayers which follow it—they are extremely devotional: we have them in our office-book—when actually the devil himself alighted on the book, to prevent me from finishing the prayer. I made the sign of the Cross and he went away. I then began again and he came back. I think I began that prayer three times and not until I had sprinkled some holy water on him could I finish it. At the same moment I saw several souls coming out of purgatory: their time there must have been nearly up and I thought that perhaps the devil was trying to impede their deliverance. I have seldom seen him in bodily shape, but I have often seen him without any form, as in the kind of vision I have described, in which no form is seen but the object is known to be there.

I want also to describe the following incident, which caused me great alarm. One Trinity Sunday, I was in the choir of a certain convent, and, while in a rapture, I saw a great battle between devils and angels. I could not understand the meaning of that vision, but before a fortnight had passed it had become clear that it referred to a conflict that had taken place between some persons who practised prayer and others who did not, which did the house great harm. It was a conflict which lasted a long time and caused a great deal of commotion. On other occasions I saw around me a great multitude of devils, and yet I seemed to be enveloped by a great light, which prevented them from coming nearer. I realized that God was guarding me so that they should not come near me and thus make me offend Him. From what I sometimes saw in myself, I knew the vision was a genuine one. The fact is, I realize so clearly now how little power the devils have, if I am not fighting against God, that I am hardly afraid of them at all: for their strength is nothing unless they find souls surrendering to them and growing cowardly, in which case they do indeed show their power. Sometimes, during the temptations I have already described, I would feel as if all my vanities and weaknesses of times past were re-awakening in me, and then I certainly had to commend myself to God. Until my confessor set my fears at rest, I was tormented by the idea that, because these thoughts came into my mind, I must be wholly possessed by the devil. For it seemed to me that not even the first impulse towards an evil thought ought to come to one on whom the Lord had bestowed so many favours. At other times I was greatly tormented—and I still am even now—by finding myself thought so much of, especially by people of importance, and so much good said of me. I have suffered a great deal from this, and suffer from it still. At such times I turn straight to the life of Christ and to the lives of the saints and realize that I am travelling in the opposite direction from that which they took, for they experienced nothing but contempt and insults. This makes me proceed very fearfully and as one who dares not lift her head, for I do not want to seem to be doing what I am not.

When I am undergoing persecutions, my body suffers and I am afflicted in other ways, but my soul is completely mistress of itself to an extent that I should not have thought possible. But that is how it is: on such occasions the soul seems to be in its own kingdom and to have all things under its feet. This happened to me several times and lasted for quite a number of days: it seemed to be a kind of virtue, and humility, but I can now see quite well that it was a temptation. A Dominican friar, who was a very learned man, gave me a clear explanation of this. When I thought that a knowledge of these favours which the Lord is granting me might become public, my torture grew so excessive that it greatly disturbed my soul. Such a pitch did it reach that, when I dwelt on the matter, I decided I would rather be buried alive than endure this. So, when these raptures or these periods of deep recollection began, and I could not resist them, even in public, I would become so ashamed after they were over as to want not to appear where anyone would see me.

Once, when I was very much troubled about this, the Lord asked me what I was afraid of, for only two things could happen—people would either speak ill of me or praise Him. He meant that those who believed it was His work would praise Him, and those who did not would condemn me without my having done wrong, and that either course would be advantageous to me and therefore I must not be troubled. This calmed me a great deal and whenever I think of it it still comforts me. The temptation reached such a point that I wanted to leave this place and go and take my dowry to another convent, much more strictly enclosed than the one I was then in, which I had heard remarkably well spoken of. It belonged to my own Order and was a long way away; it is the distance that would have given me the greatest relief, for I should have been where nobody knew me.[4] But my confessor never allowed me to go.

These fears robbed me of much freedom of spirit; later I came to see that all this restlessness on my part was not real humility. And the Lord revealed this truth to me: that if I believed resolutely and with conviction that anything good in me was not mine at all but came from God, then, just as I was not troubled at hearing other people praised but rather rejoiced and took comfort at seeing that God was showing His power in them, so, too, I should not be troubled if He were to show His works in me.

I also fell victim to another excess of zeal, which was to beseech God, and to make it my special prayer, that when a person thought there was any good in me, His Majesty would reveal my sins to him, so that he might see how utterly undeserving I was of these favours—which is always my great desire. My confessor told me not to do this; but I continued to do it almost down to this day. If I observed that someone was thinking very well of me, I would manage, indirectly or in any way that I could, to make him aware of my sins. That seemed to bring me relief. My sins have made me very scrupulous about this.

This, however, I think, was not the result of humility, but often proceeded from a temptation. It seemed to me that I was deceiving everybody; and, though it is true that it was their own belief that there was some good in me which was deceiving them, I had no desire to deceive them, nor did I ever try to do so: for some reason the Lord permitted it. So, unless I saw that such a course was necessary, I said nothing about these things even to my confessors, for to do so would have caused me grave scruples. I realize now that all these little fears and troubles and this apparent humility were sheer

[4] P. Federico de S. Antonio (*Vita della Santa Madre Teresa di Gesú*, Bk. I, Chap. XXII) thinks the Saint had contemplated going to a convent in Flanders or Brittany. The Parisian Carmelites (*Oeuvres de Sainte Thérèse*, Vol. I, p. 409) suggest that she had in mind a convent established near Nantes, in 1477, by B. Françoise d'Amboise. But there seems no reason to assume that she ever thought of going to a house outside Spain.

imperfection, due to my lack of mortification. For a soul left in the hands of God cares nothing whether good or evil is spoken of it if it has a right understanding. And, when the Lord is pleased to grant it the grace of understanding, it must understand clearly that it has nothing of its own. Let it trust its Giver and it will learn why He reveals His gifts, and let it prepare itself for persecution, which at a time like the present is sure to come to a person when the Lord is pleased for it to be known that He is granting him such favours as these. For upon a soul like this are fixed a thousand eyes, whereas upon a thousand souls of baser texture there will not be fixed a single one.

In truth, there is no small reason here for being afraid, and I certainly ought to have been so—I was being, not humble, but pusillanimous. For a soul which God allows to walk in this way in the sight of the whole world may well prepare itself to be martyred by the world, for, if it will not die to the world of its own free will, the world itself will kill it. Really, I can see nothing in the world that seems to me good save its refusal to allow that good people can ever do wrong and the way it perfects them by speaking ill of them. I mean that more courage is necessary for following the way of perfection, if one is not perfect, than for suddenly becoming a martyr; for perfection cannot be acquired quickly, except by one to whom by some particular privilege the Lord is pleased to grant this favour. When the world sees anyone setting out on that road it expects him to be perfect all at once and detects a fault in him from a thousand leagues' distance; yet in that particular person the fault may be a virtue, and his critic, in whom it is a vice, may be judging him by himself. They will not allow him to eat or sleep—they will hardly let him breathe, as we say: the more highly they think of him, the more they seem to forget that he is still in the body. For, however perfect his soul may be, he is still living on earth, and however resolutely he may trample earth's miserable limitations beneath his feet, he is still subject to them. And so, as I say, he needs great courage. His poor soul has not yet begun to walk, and men expect it to fly. He has not yet conquered his passions, and men expect him to rise to great occasions and be as brave as they read the saints were after they had been confirmed in grace. What happens here gives us cause for praising the Lord and also for great sorrow of heart, since so many poor souls turn back because they have no idea what to do to help themselves. And I believe my soul would have been like them had not the Lord Himself had such compassion on me and done everything for me. Until He of His goodness had done everything, I myself did nothing, as Your Reverence will know, but fall and rise again.

I wish I knew how to express this, for many souls, I believe, go wrong here and want to fly before God gives them wings. I think I have made this comparison somewhere before, but it is very much to the point, so I will attempt it again, for I find that some souls are very much distressed by this. They begin with good desires, and fervour, and determination to advance in virtue, and some of them give up all external things for God. Then they see in others who are more fully grown in grace many notable fruits, in the shape of virtues given them by the Lord—for we cannot acquire these ourselves. They see in all the books written on prayer and contemplation a description of things which we must do in order to rise to that dignity. And, as they themselves cannot manage to do all these things, they lose courage. I refer to such things as not caring if people speak ill of us, but being more pleased than when they speak well; holding our own reputation in little esteem; cultivating detachment from our kindred, and, unless they be persons of prayer, not desiring converse with them but finding it wearisome; and many other things of that kind. These, I think, must be bestowed upon us by God, for they seem to me to be supernatural blessings, contradicting our natural inclinations. They must not be troubled, but hope in the Lord; for what they now are in desire His Majesty will, if they pray and do what they can for themselves, make them to be in very deed. It is most necessary that this weak nature of ours should have great confidence, and not be dismayed or think that, if we do our utmost, we can fail to come out victorious.

As I have a great deal of experience here, I will say something to Your Reverence by way of counsel. Do not think, even though it may seem so to you, that anyone has acquired a virtue when he has not tested it by its corresponding vice. We must always guard our misgivings, and never, all our lives long, grow careless, for much of the world will cling to us, if, as I say, God has not given us the grace fully to understand the nature of everything; and there is never anything in this life which is not attended by many dangers. A few years ago, I believed, not merely that I was not attached to my relatives, but that they were wearisome to me, and this was certainly true, for I could not endure their conversation. Then a matter of great importance cropped up and I had to go and stay with a sister of mine of whom, in the past, I had been extremely fond.[5] Though she is a better woman than I am, I could not get on with her at all in conversation; for as she is married, and therefore lives a different kind of life, we could not always be talking of the things I should have liked, and all I could do was to try to be alone. But I found that when she was distressed it affected me much more than when my neighbours were; sometimes, in fact, I would be quite concerned about her. In short, I discovered that I was not as free from attachment as I had supposed and indeed that I needed to avoid occasions of sin, so that this virtue, which the Lord had begun to implant in me, might grow; and with His help I have done my utmost to cultivate it ever since.

When the Lord begins to implant a virtue in us, it must be esteemed very highly and we must on no account run the risk of losing it. So it is in matters concerning our reputation[6] and in many others. Your Reverence can be quite sure that we are not all completely detached when we think we are and it is essential that we should never be careless about this. If any person wishing to make progress in spiritual matters finds that he is becoming punctilious about his reputation, let him believe what I say and put this attachment right behind him, for it is a chain which no file can sever: only God can break it, with the aid of prayer and great effort on our part. It seems to me to be an impediment on this road and I am amazed at the harm it does. I see some people whose actions are very holy and who do such wonderful things that everyone is astonished at them. God bless me, then! Why are

[5] This reference is probably to a stay which St. Teresa made with her younger sister, Juana, and her husband, Don Juan de Ovalle. From letters which the Saint wrote to her brother, Don Lorenzo, it is clear that lack of means, together with Don Juan's difficult temperament, made Doña Juana's married life anything but a smooth one. The two came from Alba to Ávila, for reasons connected with the foundation of St. Joseph's, in August 1561.

[6] [*Honra*; and so throughout this and the following paragraphs. Cf. p. 70, n. 3.]

such souls still on earth? How is it that they have not reached the summit of perfection? What is the reason for this? What can it be that is impeding one who is doing so much for God? Why, simply his punctiliousness about his reputation! And the worst of it is that this sort of person will not realize that he is guilty of such a thing, the reason sometimes being that the devil tells him that punctiliousness is incumbent upon him.

Let such persons believe me, then: for the love of the Lord let them believe this little ant, for she speaks because it is the Lord's will that she should do so. If they fail to remove this caterpillar, it may not hurt the whole tree, for some of the other virtues will remain, but they will all be worm-eaten. The tree will not be beautiful: it will neither prosper itself nor allow the trees near it to do so, for the fruit of good example which it bears is not at all healthy and will not last for long. I repeat this: however slight may be our concern for our reputation, the result of it will be as bad as when we play a wrong note, or make a mistake in time, in playing the organ—the whole passage will become discordant. Such concern is a thing which harms the soul whenever it occurs; but in the life of prayer it is pestilential.

You are trying to attain to union with God. We want to follow the counsels of Christ, on Whom were showered insults and false witness. Are we, then, really so anxious to keep intact our own reputation and credit? We cannot do so and yet attain to union, for the two ways diverge. When we exert our utmost efforts and try in various ways to forgo our rights, the Lord comes to the soul. Some will say: "I have nothing to forgo: I never get an opportunity of giving up anything." But if anyone has this determination I do not believe the Lord will ever allow him to lose so great a blessing. His Majesty will arrange so many ways in which he may gain this virtue that he will soon have more than he wants. I would urge you, then, to set to work and root out things which are of little or no consequence, just as I used to do when I began—or, at least, some of them. They are mere straws; and, as I have said, I throw them on the fire. I am incapable of doing more than that, but the Lord accepts it: may He be blessed for ever.

One of my faults was this: I knew very little of my office-book, and of what I ought to do in choir, and of how to behave, simply because I was careless and absorbed in other vanities. I saw other novices who could have taught me these things, but I did not ask them to do so, lest they should become aware how little I knew. But good example soon prevails: that, at least, is the general rule. Once God opened my eyes a little, I would ask the other girls' opinion[7] even when I knew something but was the slightest bit in doubt about it; and my doing so damaged neither my honour[8] nor my credit—in fact I think the Lord has been pleased since then to give me a better memory. I was bad at singing and I felt it very deeply if I had not studied what was entrusted to me: not for my shortcomings in the Lord's eyes—that would have been virtue—but because of all the nuns who were listening to me. Merely out of concern for my own honour I was so much perturbed that I did much worse than I need have done. Later, when I did not know my part very well, I made a point of saying so. At first, this hurt me terribly but after a time I began to take pleasure in it. And when I ceased caring if my ignorance were known or not, I got on much better. So this miserable concern for my honour prevented me from being able to do what I really regarded as an honour, for everyone interprets the word "honour" to mean what he chooses.

By means of these nothings, which after all actually are nothing (and I, too, am certainly nothing, to be hurt by a thing like this), one's actions gradually become worthier. And if we take trouble over such trifling things, to which God attaches importance because they are done for Him, His Majesty helps us to do greater ones. And so it was with me in matters concerning humility; seeing that all the nuns except myself were making progress (for I myself was always a good-for-nothing) I would collect their mantles when they left the choir. I felt that by doing this I was serving angels who were praising God there, until—I do not know how—they came to hear of it, which made me not a little ashamed. For my virtue had not reached the point of desiring them to know of these things—not out of humility, but lest they should laugh at me over something so unimportant.

[7] ["Girls'," may seem an unduly colloquial word, but the Spanish is even more unexpected: *niñas*, "young girls", "children".]

[8] [Cf. p. 70, n. 3. "Reputation" would be a better word here, but the wordplay in the last sentence of the paragraph requires "honour".]

O my Lord, how ashamed I am at having to confess all this wickedness! I go on counting these little grains of sand, which as yet were not being stirred up in the river-bed for Thy service, but were embedded in all kinds of filth.[9] The water of Thy grace was not yet flowing beneath all this sand to stir it up. O my Creator, if only amid so many things that are evil I had a few that were worthy of enumeration, to set beside the great favours that I have received from Thee! But thus it is, my Lord, and I know not how my heart can bear it or how anyone who reads this can fail to abhor me when he sees how ill I have requited such exceeding great favours and that despite all this I am not ashamed to reckon any services that I may have rendered Thee as my own. In reality, my Lord, I am ashamed to do so, but the fact that I have nothing else of my own to enumerate makes me speak of such mean beginnings so that those who began better may be hopeful that, as the Lord has taken notice of these, He will take notice of theirs still more. May it please His Majesty to give me grace so that I may not always remain a beginner. Amen.

CHAPTER XXXII

Tells how the Lord was pleased to carry her in spirit to a place in hell which she had merited for her sins. Describes a part of what was shown her there. Begins to tell of the way and means whereby the convent of Saint Joseph was founded in the place where it now is.

A long time after the Lord had granted me many of the favours which I have described, together with other very great ones, I was at prayer one day when suddenly, without knowing how, I found myself, as I thought, plunged right into hell. I realized that it was the Lord's will that I should see the place which the devils had prepared for me there and which I had merited for my sins. This happened in the briefest space of time, but, even if I were to live for many years, I

---

[9] [This is evidently a reminiscent reference to p. 286. The application of the figure, however, it will be seen, is slightly different.]

believe it would be impossible for me to forget it. The entrance, I thought, resembled a very long, narrow passage, like a furnace, very low, dark and closely confined; the ground seemed to be full of water which looked like filthy, evil-smelling mud, and in it were many wicked-looking reptiles. At the end there was a hollow place scooped out of a wall, like a cupboard, and it was here that I found myself in close confinement. But the sight of all this was pleasant by comparison with what I felt there. What I have said is in no way an exaggeration.

My feelings, I think, could not possibly be exaggerated, nor can anyone understand them. I felt a fire within my soul the nature of which I am utterly incapable of describing. My bodily sufferings were so intolerable that, though in my life I have endured the severest sufferings of this kind—the worst it is possible to endure, the doctors say, such as the shrinking of the nerves during my paralysis[1] and many and divers more, some of them, as I have said, caused by the devil—none of them is of the smallest account by comparison with what I felt then, to say nothing of the knowledge that they would be endless and never-ceasing. And even these are nothing by comparison with the agony of my soul, an oppression, a suffocation and an affliction so deeply felt, and accompanied by such hopeless and distressing misery, that I cannot too forcibly describe it. To say that it is as if the soul were continually being torn from the body is very little, for that would mean that one's life was being taken by another; whereas in this case it is the soul itself that is tearing itself to pieces. The fact is that I cannot find words to describe that interior fire and that despair, which is greater than the most grievous tortures and pains. I could not see who was the cause of them, but I felt, I think, as if I were being both burned and dismembered; and I repeat that that interior fire and despair are the worst things of all.

In that pestilential spot, where I was quite powerless to hope for comfort, it was impossible to sit or lie, for there was no room to do so. I had been put in this place which looked like a hole in the wall, and those very walls, so terrible to the sight, bore down upon me and completely stifled me. There was no light and everything was in the blackest darkness. I do

1 [See p. 87.]

not understand how this can be, but, although there was no light, it was possible to see everything the sight of which can cause affliction. At that time it was not the Lord's will that I should see more of hell itself, but I have since seen another vision of frightful things, which are the punishment of certain vices. To look at, they seemed to me much more dreadful; but, as I felt no pain, they caused me less fear. In the earlier vision the Lord was pleased that I should really feel those torments and that affliction of spirit, just as if my body had been suffering them. I do not know how it was, but I realized quite clearly that it was a great favour and that it was the Lord's will that I should see with my own eyes the place from which His mercy had delivered me. It is nothing to read a description of it, or to think of different kinds of torture (as I have sometimes done, though rarely, as my soul made little progress by the road of fear): of how the devils tear the flesh with their pincers or of the various other tortures that I have read about—none of these are anything by comparison with this affliction, which is quite another matter. In fact, it is like a picture set against reality, and any burning on earth is a small matter compared with that fire.

I was terrified by all this, and, though it happened nearly six years ago, I still am as I write: even as I sit here, fear seems to be depriving my body of its natural warmth. I never recall any time when I have been suffering trials or pains and when everything that we can suffer on earth has seemed to me of the slightest importance by comparison with this; so, in a way, I think we complain without reason. I repeat, then, that this vision was one of the most signal favours which the Lord has bestowed upon me: it has been of the greatest benefit to me, both in taking from me all fear of the tribulations and disappointments of this life and also in strengthening me to suffer them and to give thanks to the Lord, Who, as I now believe, has delivered me from such terrible and never-ending torments.

Since that time, as I say, everything has seemed light to me by comparison with a single moment of such suffering as I had to bear during that vision. I am shocked at myself when I think that, after having so often read books which give some idea of the pains of hell, I was neither afraid of them nor rated them at what they are. What could I have been thinking of? How could anything give me satisfaction which was driving me to so awful a place? Blessed be Thou, my God, for ever! How plain it has become that Thou didst love me, much more than I love myself! How often, Lord, didst Thou deliver me from that gloomy prison and how I would make straight for it again, in face of Thy will!

This vision, too, was the cause of the very deep distress which I experience because of the great number of souls who are bringing damnation upon themselves—especially of those Lutherans, for they were made members of the Church through baptism. It also inspired me with fervent impulses for the good of souls: for I really believe that, to deliver a single one of them from such dreadful tortures, I would willingly die many deaths. After all, if we see anyone on earth who is especially dear to us suffering great trial or pain, our very nature seems to move us to compassion, and if his sufferings are severe they oppress us too. Who, then, could bear to look upon a soul's endless sufferings in that most terrible trial of all? No heart could possibly endure it without great affliction. For even earthly suffering, which after all, as we know, has a limit and will end with death, moves us to deep compassion. And that other suffering has no limit: I do not know how we can look on so calmly and see the devil carrying off as many souls as he does daily.

This also makes me wish that in so urgent a matter we were not ourselves satisfied with anything short of doing all that we can. Let us leave nothing undone; and to this end may the Lord be pleased to grant us His grace. I recall that, wicked creature though I was, I used to take some trouble to serve God and refrain from doing certain things which I see tolerated and considered quite legitimate in the world; that I had serious illnesses, and bore them with great patience, which the Lord bestowed on me; that I was not given to murmuring or speaking ill of anyone, nor, I think, could I ever have wished anyone ill; that I was not covetous and never remember having been envious in such a way as grievously to offend the Lord; and that I abstained from certain other faults, and, despicable though I was, lived in the most constant fear of God. And yet look at the place where the devils had prepared a lodging for me! It is true, I think, that my faults had merited a much heavier punishment; but none the less, I repeat, the torture was terrible, and it is a perilous thing for a soul to indulge in its own pleasure or to be placid and contented when at every step it is falling into mortal sin. For the love of God, let us keep free from occasions of sin and the Lord will help us as He has helped me. May it please His Majesty not to let me out of His hand lest I fall once more, now that I have seen the place to which that would lead me. May the Lord forbid this, for His Majesty's sake. Amen.

After I had seen this vision, and other great things and secrets which, being what He is, the Lord was pleased to show me, concerning the bliss reserved for the good and the affliction for the wicked, I desired to find some way and means of doing penance for all my evil deeds and of becoming in some degree worthy to gain so great a blessing. I desired, therefore, to flee from others and to end by withdrawing myself completely from the world. My spirit was restless, yet the restlessness was not disturbing but pleasant: I knew quite well that it was of God and that His Majesty had given my soul this ardour to enable me to digest other and stronger meat than I had been in the habit of eating.

I would wonder what I could do for God, and it occurred to me that the first thing was to follow the vocation for a religious life which His Majesty had given me by keeping my Rule with the greatest possible perfection. And although in the house where I was living[2] there were many servants of God, and He was well served in it, yet, as it was very needy, we nuns would often leave it for other places where we could live honourably and keep our vows. Furthermore, the Rule was not observed in its primitive rigour but, as throughout the Order, according to the Bull of Mitigation.[3] There were also other disadvantages, such as the excessive amount of comfort which I thought we had, for the house was a large and pleasant one. But this habit of frequently going away (and I was one who did it a great deal) was a serious drawback to me, for there were certain persons, to whom my superiors could refuse nothing, who liked to have me with them, and so, when importuned by these persons, they would order me to go and visit them. So things went on until I was able to be in the convent very little; the devil must have had something to do with my being away so much, though at the same time I was in the habit of repeating to some of the nuns the things

[2] The Convent of the Incarnation, Ávila.
[3] A Bull published by Pope Eugenius IV on February 15, 1432.

taught me by the people I met and these did them a great deal of good.

One day it happened that a person to whom I was talking,[4] with some other sisters, asked me why we should not become Discalced nuns,[5] for it would be quite possible to find a way of establishing a convent. I had had desires of this kind myself, so I began to discuss the matter with a companion—that widowed lady who, as I have said before, had the same desire. She began to think out a way to find the money for such a house; I see now that that would not have got us very far, though our desire to achieve our object made us think that it would. But, for my own part, I was most happy in the house where I was, for I was very fond both of the house and of my cell, and this held me back. None the less, we agreed to commend the matter very earnestly to God.

One day, after Communion, the Lord gave me the most explicit commands to work for this aim with all my might and made me wonderful promises—that the convent would not fail to be established; that great service would be done to Him in it; that it should be called Saint Joseph's; that He[6] would watch over us at one door and Our Lady at the other; that Christ would go with us; that the convent would be a star giving out the most brilliant light; and that, although the Rules of the religious Orders were mitigated, I was not to think He was very little served in them, for what would become of the world if it were not for religious? I was to tell

[4] María de Ocampo, daughter of Don Diego de Cepeda and Doña Beatriz de la Cruz y Ocampo, who were St. Teresa's cousins. She herself took the Discalced habit at Ávila in 1563.

[5] Another account of this conversation [cit. P. Silverio, I, 268, n.] says that it arose out of a discussion on the hermit-saints. Some of the nuns suggested the establishment of a small convent in which a few of them could lead a more penitential life. St. Teresa then said they ought to restore the primitive Rule and one nun offered her financial help if she would found a convent of the kind described. At this point, Doña Guiomar de Ulloa (the "widowed lady" of the text) arrived, and, on being told of the conversation, said that she too would help in the good work.

[6] [I translate "He" in deference to P. Silverio's capitalization of the pronoun, but a likelier reading seems to me "he" (St. Joseph). Sixteenth-century manuscripts do not capitalize pronouns which refer to God, so the matter must remain one for conjecture.]

my confessor this[7] and to say that it was He Who was giving me this command and that He asked him not to oppose it nor to hinder me in carrying it out.

So great was the effect upon me of this vision and such was the nature of these words which the Lord addressed to me that I could not doubt that it was He Who had uttered them. This caused me the deepest distress, because I had a fairly good idea of the serious disturbances and trials which the work would cost me. I was very happy, too, in that house, and, though in the past I had been accustomed to speak of such a foundation, it had not been with any great degree of determination or certainty that the thing would be done. I felt now that a great burden was being laid upon me, and, when I saw that I was at the beginning of a very disturbing time, I became doubtful what I should do. But the Lord appeared and spoke to me about it again and again, and so numerous were the motives and arguments which He put before me, in such a way that I saw that they were valid and that the project was His will, that I dared not do otherwise than speak to my confessor about it and give him a written account of everything that took place.

He did not venture to tell me expressly to give up the idea, but he saw that, humanly speaking, there was no way of putting it into practice, since my companion, who was to be the person to effect this, had no resources at all, or very scanty ones. He told me to talk it over with my Superior, and to do what he advised. I did not discuss these visions with the Superior, but the lady who was desirous of founding this convent had a talk with him, and the Provincial,[8] who is well-disposed to the religious Orders, took to the idea very well, gave her all necessary help and told her he would give the house his sanction. They discussed the revenue which the convent would need, and we decided that, for many reasons, the number of nuns in the convent ought never to exceed thirteen. Before beginning to discuss the matter we had written to the holy Fray Peter of Alcántara and told him all that was happening. He advised us not to desist from our work and gave us his opinion about the whole matter.

[7] P. Baltasar Álvarez.

[8] This was not, as is often said, P. Ángel de Salazar, but P. Gregorio Fernández, who was Provincial from 1551 to 1553 and again from 1559 to the end of 1561.

Hardly had news of the project begun to be known here than there descended upon us a persecution so severe that it is impossible in a few words to describe it: people talked about us, laughed at us and declared that the idea was ridiculous. Of me, they said that I was all right in the convent where I was living, while my companion was subjected to such persecution that it quite exhausted her. I did not know what to do, for up to a certain point I thought these people were right. Worn out with it all as I was, I commended myself to God and His Majesty began to give me consolation and encouragement. He told me that I could now see what those saints who had founded religious Orders had suffered: they had had to endure much more persecution than any I could imagine and we must not allow ourselves to be troubled by it. He told me certain things which I was to say to my companion, and to my absolute amazement we at once felt comforted by what had happened and courageous enough to resist everybody. And it is a fact that, at that time, both among people of prayer and in the whole place, there was hardly anyone who was not against us and did not consider our project absolutely ridiculous.[9]

There was so much commotion and talk of this kind in my own convent that the Provincial thought it would be hard for him to set himself against everybody; so he changed his mind and refused to sanction the plan. He said that the revenue was not assured, that in any case there would be too little of it, and that the plan was meeting with considerable opposition. In all this he appeared to be right. So he dropped the matter and refused to sanction the new convent. We, on whom the first blows now seemed to have fallen, were very much distressed at this, and I myself was particularly so at finding the Provincial against me, for his previous approval of the plan

[9] The Saint's niece Teresita related [cf. P. Silverio, I, 270, n.] that the proposed reform was even publicly denounced from Ávilan pulpits. On one occasion, she says, St. Teresa and her sister Doña Juana went to hear a sermon at St. Thomas's and to Doña Juana's discomfiture the preacher ("a religious of a certain Order") began to inveigh against "nuns who left their convents to go and found new Orders". But when she turned indignantly to see how St. Teresa was taking it, she found that she was having a quiet laugh (con gran paz se estaba riendo). [Cf. p. 312, ll. 29–30.] The identity of the preacher has been guessed at, but is not known.

had justified me in the eyes of all. My companion was refused absolution unless she would give up the idea; it was incumbent on her, she was told, to remove the scandal.

She went to talk the matter over with a very learned man, a most devout servant of God, of the Order of Saint Dominic,[10] and to him she detailed the whole story. This she did even before the Provincial withdrew his support from us, for we had no one in the whole place who would advise us in the matter; and it was for that reason that they said the whole thing had come out of our own heads. The lady gave this holy man an account of everything and told him how much revenue she derived from her estate; she hoped very much that he would help us, since at that time he was the most learned man in the place, and there are few more learned than he in his entire Order. I myself told him all that we were proposing to do and some of the reasons for it. I said nothing to him about any of the revelations I had had, but only described the reasons, other than supernatural, which were prompting me, for it was these alone that I wanted him to take into account when giving us his opinion. He told us that we must allow him a week to think the matter over before answering and asked if we were definitely going to act upon whatever he said. I told him we were; but although I said this, and I think I would have acted upon it,[11] I never for a moment lost my confidence that the foundation would be made. My companion had more faith; and, whatever people might say to her, nothing would persuade her to abandon it.

For my own part, although, as I say, the abandonment of the project seemed to me impossible, I believed the revelation to be true only in the sense that it was not contrary to what is in Holy Scripture or to the laws of the Church which we are obliged to keep; for, despite my belief that it really came from God, if that learned man had told me that we could not act upon it without offending Him and that we were acting against our conscience, I think I should at once have abandoned the plan and sought some other way. But the Lord showed me no other way than this. Later, this servant of God told me that at one point he had definitely decided to

[10] P. Pedro Ibáñez, one of the Saint's chief supporters in the early days of her Reform, of which, however, he saw very little, for he died in 1565.

[11] A line is obliterated here, presumably by P. Báñez.

urge us to give the project up, because his attention had been directed to the popular clamour, and also because to him, as to everyone else, it had seemed folly; that a certain gentleman, on hearing that we had gone to him, had sent to advise him to be careful what he did and not to help us; but that, when he had begun to consider what he should say to us, to think over the matter, and to reflect upon the intentions that were prompting us, the way we were setting to work and our concern for our Order, he became convinced that we should be rendering God a great service and that the scheme must not be abandoned. And so his answer was that we should make haste to carry it out; he told us by what ways and methods this should be done; and, although our income was small, we must be prepared to some extent to trust God. Anyone, he said, who offered further opposition should be referred to him for an answer; and he always helped us in this way, as I shall show later.

We were greatly comforted by this, and also by the fact that several saintly persons, who had previously been against us, were now better disposed and some of them actually helped us. One of these was the saintly gentleman whom I have already mentioned. He now felt that the project, being founded, as in fact it was, on prayer, would lead to great perfection, and though he thought it would be difficult and impracticable to find the necessary means for making the foundation, he gave up his former view and decided that the idea might be from God, in which decision the Lord Himself must have inspired him. He also inspired that Master, the cleric and servant of God to whom, as I said, I had spoken first of all, who is a pattern to the whole place and a person whom God keeps there for the help and profit of many souls.[12] He, too, came forward to help me in the matter. And while things were in that position, and many people were continually helping us by their prayers, we practically completed the negotiations for purchasing the house. It was a small one, but that did not trouble me in the least, for the Lord had told me to start work as well as I could and in due course I should see what His Majesty would do for us. (And how

[12] Master Gaspar Daza. [The title of "Master" was conferred by the Orders upon certain religious in virtue of teaching posts held by them, or as a distinction.]

clearly I have seen it!) And so, though I realized our income would be small, I believed that the Lord would have other ways of arranging things for us and would give us His help.

CHAPTER XXXIII

Proceeds with the same subject—the foundation of the convent of the glorious Saint Joseph. Tells how she was commanded not to continue it, how for a time she gave it up, how she suffered various trials and how in all of them she was comforted by the Lord.

It was when matters had reached this position and were so near completion that the deeds were to be signed on the following day that the attitude of our Father Provincial suddenly changed. I believe, and it has since become apparent, that this change was by Divine appointment; for, while all these prayers were being offered for us, the Lord was perfecting His work and arranging for it to be accomplished in another way. As the Provincial would not now sanction the foundation, my confessor at once forbade me to go on with it, though the Lord knows what sore trials and afflictions it had cost me to bring it to its present state. When the project was given up, and remained unaccomplished, people became still more certain that it was all some ridiculous women's idea, and the evil-speaking against me increased, though until then I had been acting on my Provincial's orders.

I was now very unpopular throughout my convent for having wanted to found a convent more strictly enclosed. The nuns said that I was insulting them; that there were others there who were better than myself, and so I could serve God quite well where I was; that I had no love for my own convent; and that I should have done better to get money for that than for founding another. Some said I ought to be thrown into the prison-cell;[1] others came out on my side, though of these there were very few. I saw quite well that in

[1] The prison-cell of the Incarnation still exists. It was quite common in those days for religious communities to imprison their recalcitrant members.

many respects they were right and I could sometimes make allowances for them; although, as I could not tell them the principal thing—namely, that I had been obeying the Lord's command—I did not know what to do and so was silent. At other times God was so gracious to me that none of this worried me in the slightest; I gave up the project as easily and happily as though it had cost me nothing. This nobody could believe, not even the very persons, given to prayer as they were, with whom I had to do: they supposed I must be very much distressed and ashamed—even my confessor could not really believe that I was not. It seemed to me that I had done all I possibly could to fulfil the Lord's command and that therefore I had no further obligation. So I remained in my own house, quite content and happy. I could not, however, give up my belief that the task would be duly accomplished, and, though I was unable to forecast the means and knew neither how nor when the work would be done, I was quite sure that it would be done in time.

What troubled me a great deal was that on one occasion my confessor[2] wrote me a letter of a kind which suggested that I had in some way been acting against his wishes. It must have been the Lord's will that I should not be immune from trials coming from the source which would cause me the greatest pain. For, amid this multitude of persecutions, my confessor, whom I had expected to console me, wrote that I must now have realized that all that had happened was just a dream and that henceforth I must lead a better life and not try to do anything more of the kind or talk about it any further, since I now saw what scandal it had occasioned. He said other things, too, all of them very distressing. This troubled me more than everything else put together, for I wondered if I had myself been an occasion of sin to others, if it had been my fault that offence had been given to God, if these visions were illusory, if all my prayer had been a deception and if I was sorely deluded and lost. These thoughts oppressed me to such an extent that I was quite upset by them and plunged into the deepest affliction. But the Lord, Who never failed me, and in all these trials which I have enumerated often comforted and strengthened me, in a way that need not here be described, told me at once not to distress

2 P. Baltasar Álvarez.

myself and said that I had not offended Him in the matter at
all but had rendered Him great service. He told me to do
what my confessor ordered me and to keep silence for the
present and until the time came for the project to be resumed.
This brought me such comfort and satisfaction that all the
persecution which I was undergoing seemed nothing at all.

The Lord now showed me what a signal blessing it is to
suffer trials and persecutions for His sake, for so great was
the growth in my soul of love for God and of many other
graces that I was astounded, and this made me incapable of
ceasing to desire trials. The other people thought I was very
much ashamed—as indeed I should have been had the Lord
not helped me in these straits by granting me such great
favours. It was now that I began to experience the increasingly
strong impulses of the love of God which I have described,
and also deeper raptures, although I was silent on this subject and never spoke to anyone of what I had gained. The
saintly Dominican[3] did not cease to share my certainty that
the project would be accomplished; and, as I myself would
take no further part in it, lest I should run contrary to the
obedience which I owed my confessor, he discussed it with
my companion and they wrote to Rome and sought a way
out.

And now the devil began to contrive that one person after
another should hear that I had received some kind of revelation about this matter, and people came to me in great concern to say that these were bad times and that it might be
that something would be alleged against me and I should
have to go before the Inquisitors. But they only amused me
and made me laugh, because I never had any fear about this.
I knew quite well that in matters of faith no one would ever
find me transgressing even the smallest ceremony of the
Church, and that for the Church or for any truth of Holy
Scripture I would undertake to die a thousand deaths. So I
told them not to be afraid, for my soul would be in a very
bad way if there were anything about it which could make me
fear the Inquisition. If ever I thought there might be, I
would go and pay it a visit of my own accord; and if anything
were alleged against me the Lord would deliver me and I
should be very much the gainer. I discussed this with my

[3] P. Pedro Ibáñez.

Dominican Father, who, as I say, was a very learned man, so that I knew I could rely on anything he might say to me. I told him, as clearly as I could, all about my visions, my way of prayer and the great favours which the Lord was granting me, and I begged him to think it all over very carefully, to let me know if there was anything in them contrary to Holy Scripture and to tell me his feelings about the whole matter. He reassured me a great deal and I think it was a help to him too; for, although he was very good, from that time onward he devoted himself much more to prayer, and retired to a monastery of his Order where there is great scope for solitude, so that he might the better practise prayer; and here he stayed for over two years.[4] He was then commanded under obedience to leave, which caused him great regret, but he was such an able man that they needed him.

In one way, I was very sorry when he went, because I too needed him badly. But I did nothing to unsettle him, for I realized that the gain was his; and, when I was feeling very much grieved at his departure, the Lord told me to take comfort and not be distressed, because he was being led in the right way. When he came back, his soul had made such progress and his spiritual growth had been so great that he told me after his return that he would not have missed going for anything. And I too could say the same thing; for previously he had been reassuring and comforting me only by his learning, whereas now he did so as well by the ample spiritual experience which he had acquired of things supernatural. And God brought him back just at the right time, for His Majesty saw that he would be needed to help with this convent, the foundation of which was His Majesty's will.

For five or six months I remained silent, taking no further steps with regard to the plan and never even speaking about it, and the Lord gave me not a single command. I had no idea what was the reason for this, but I could not get rid of my belief that the foundation would be duly made. At the end of that time, the priest who had been Rector of the Company of Jesus having left, His Majesty brought a successor

[4] At Trianos, in the province of León. Actually he died there, at about the time when St. Teresa was completing this book, so his return to Ávila, referred to in the text below, can have been only temporary.

to him here who was a very spiritual man, of great courage, intelligence and learning, at a time when I was in dire need.[5] For the priest who at that time was hearing my confessions had a superior over him, and in the Company they are extremely particular about the virtue of never doing the slightest thing save in conformity with the will of those who are over them. So, although he thoroughly understood my spirit and desired its progress, there were certain matters about which, for very good reasons, he dared not be at all definite. My spirit, which was now experiencing the most vehement impulses, was greatly troubled at being constrained in this way; I did not, however, depart from his orders.

One day, when I was in great affliction, thinking that my confessor did not believe me, the Lord told me not to be worried, for my distress would soon be over. I was very glad, supposing His meaning to be that I was soon going to die, and whenever I thought of this I was very happy. Later I realized that He was referring to the arrival of this Rector whom I have mentioned; for I never had any reason to feel so distressed again, because the new Rector placed no restrictions upon the minister who was my confessor, but told him that, as there was no cause for fear, he should comfort me and not lead me by so strait a path, but allow the Spirit of the Lord to work in me, for sometimes it seemed as if these strong spiritual impulses prevented my soul even from breathing.

This Rector came to see me and my confessor told me to consult him with the utmost frankness and freedom. I used to dislike very much speaking about the matter, and yet, when I went into the confessional, I felt something in my spirit which I do not recall having felt in the presence of anyone else, either before or since. I cannot possibly describe its

[5] The Rector who left Ávila was P. Dionisio Vázquez, confessor of St. Francis Borgia and famous in the history of the Society of Jesus for his negotiations with Philip II, the Inquisition and the Holy See, the aim of which was to remove the Spanish houses of the Society from the jurisdiction of the General in Rome. He was succeeded, in 1561, by P. Gaspar de Salazar. Disagreements which arose between St. Giles' College and Don Álvaro de Mendoza, Bishop of Ávila, led to P. Salazar's removal early in 1562: he had gone when St. Teresa returned from her visit to Toledo. She had a great regard for him and speaks highly of him in a number of her letters.

nature or compare it with anything whatsoever. For it was a spiritual joy: my soul knew that here was a soul that would understand and be in harmony with mine, although, as I say, I do not know how this happened. If I had ever spoken to him or had been told great things about him, it would not have been strange that I should have felt happy and been sure that he would understand me; but I had never spoken a word to him before, nor had he to me, nor was he a person about whom I had ever previously heard anything. Later I discovered that my instinct had not been wrong, and my contact with him has in every way been of great benefit to me and to my soul; for he knows how to treat persons whom the Lord seems to have brought to an advanced state: he makes them run, not walk a step at a time. His method is to train them in complete detachment and mortification, and for this, as for many other things, the Lord has given him the greatest aptitude.

When I began to have dealings with him, I realized at once what type of director he was, and saw that he had a pure and holy soul and a special gift from the Lord for the discernment of spirits. From this I derived much comfort. Soon after I came under his direction, the Lord began to lay it upon me again that I must take up the matter of the convent and put all my reasons and aims before my confessor and this Rector so that they should not hinder me. Some of the things I said made them afraid, but this Father Rector never doubted that I was being led by the Spirit of God, having studied and thought very carefully about the effects which would be produced by the foundation. In short, after hearing these numerous reasons, they did not dare to risk hindering me.

My confessor now gave me leave once more to take up the work again with all my might. I saw clearly with what a task I was burdening myself, since I was quite alone and there was so very little that I could do. We agreed that the work should be done in all secrecy, and so I arranged that a sister of mine,[6] who lived outside the town, should buy the house and furnish it, as if it were to be for herself, the Lord having given us money, from various sources, for its purchase. It would take a long time to tell how the Lord continued to

[6] Doña Juana who lived at Alba. Cf. p. 297, n. 5.

provide for us. I thought it of great importance to do nothing against obedience, but I knew that, if I told my superiors about it, everything would be ruined, just as it was on the last occasion, and this time things might be even worse. Getting the money, finding a convent, arranging for its purchase and having it furnished cost me many trials, some of which I had to suffer quite alone; my companion did what she could, but that was little—so little as to be hardly anything beyond allowing the work to be done in her name and with her approval. All the most difficult part of the work was mine and there were so many different things to do that I wonder now how I was able to go through with it. Sometimes in my distress I would say: "My Lord, how is it that Thou commandest me to do things which seem impossible? If only I were free, woman though I am—! But being bound in so many ways, without money or means of procuring it, either for the Brief or for anything else, what can I do, Lord?"

Once, when I was in a difficulty and could not think what to do, or how I was going to pay some workmen, Saint Joseph, my true father and lord, appeared to me and gave me to understand that money would not be lacking and I must make all the necessary arrangements. I did so, though I had not a farthing, and the Lord, in ways which amazed people when they heard of them, provided the money.[7] I thought the house very small, so small that it seemed impossible to turn it into a convent.[8] I wanted to buy another, but had not the wherewithal, so there was no way of buying it, and I could not think what to do. There was a house near our own, but it was also too small to make into a church. One day,

[7] The benefactor was St. Teresa's brother Lorenzo, who had emigrated to America, settled in what to-day is the capital of Ecuador and married a daughter of one of the *conquistadores* of Peru. He came back to Spain a wealthy man and did a great deal of good with his money. See *Letters*, 2.

[8] The house, which St. Teresa bought through the agency of her brother-in-law Don Juan de Ovalle, was indeed so small that all her biographers have compared it to the "little porch of Bethlehem" (cf. *Foundations*: Vol. III, p. 66). Julián de Ávila (*Vida de Santa Teresa*, Part II, Chap. VIII) describes the chapel as "hardly more than ten paces in length". The diminutive bell used in this first convent was restored in 1868 to Ávila from Pastrana, where it was taken in 1634, and now hangs beside the great bell which calls the religious to offices.

after I had communicated, the Lord said to me: "I have already told you to go in as best you can," and then added a kind of exclamation: "Oh, the greed of mankind! So you really think there will not be enough ground for you![9] How often did I sleep all night in the open air because I had not where to lay My head!" This amazed me, but I saw that He was right. So I went to look at the little house, and worked things out, and found that it would just make a convent, though a very small one. I thought no more then about buying another site but arranged to have this house furnished so that we could live in it. Everything was very rough and it had only enough done to it not to make it injurious to the health. And that is the principle that should be followed everywhere.

On Saint Clare's day, as I was going to Communion, that Saint appeared to me in great beauty and told me to put forth all my efforts and proceed with what I had begun and she would help me. I conceived a great devotion for her and her words turned out to be the exact truth, for a convent of her Order, which is near our own, is helping to maintain us. What is more, she has gradually brought this desire of mine to such perfection that the poverty observed by the blessed Saint in her own house is being observed in this and we live upon alms. It has cost me no little trouble to get this principle quite definitely and authoritatively approved by the Holy Father—this, of course, being essential—so that we shall never have any income.[10] And—at the request, it may be, of this blessed Saint—the Lord is doing still more for us. Without any demand on our part His Majesty is providing amply for all our needs. May He be blessed for it all. Amen.

At this same period, on the festival of the Assumption of Our Lady, I was in a monastery of the Order of the glorious

[9] [The second personal pronouns in this quotation are in the singular, but the phraseology is markedly colloquial, and to bring this out I have used "you" in preference to "thou".]

[10] The original Brief (February 7, 1562), addressed to Doña Aldonza de Guzmán and her daughter Doña Guiomar de Ulloa, authorized them to hold property in common, as the Saint had not at that time decided to forgo an endowment. A Rescript dated December 5, 1562, however, confirmed by Brief of July 17, 1565, granted the Convent permission to live on public charity, without a fixed revenue.

Saint Dominic, thinking of the many sins which in times past I had confessed in that house and of other things concerning my wicked life, when there came upon me a rapture so vehement that it nearly drew me forth out of myself altogether.[11] I sat down and I remember even now that I could neither see the Elevation nor hear Mass being said, and later this caused me a certain amount of scruple. While in this state, I thought I saw myself being clothed in a garment of great whiteness and brightness. At first I could not see who was clothing me, but later I saw Our Lady on my right hand and my father Saint Joseph on my left, and it was they who were putting that garment upon me. I was given to understand that I was now cleansed of my sins. When the clothing was ended, and I was experiencing the greatest joy and bliss, I thought that Our Lady suddenly took me by the hands and told me that I was giving her great pleasure by serving the glorious Saint Joseph and that I might be sure that all I was trying to do about the convent would be accomplished and that both the Lord and they two would be greatly served in it. I was not to fear that there would be any failure whatever about this, although the nature of the obedience which it would have to render might not be to my liking. They would keep us safe and her Son had already promised to go with us: as a sign that that was true, she said, she would give me this jewel. Then she seemed to throw round my neck a very beautiful gold collar, to which was fastened a most valuable cross. The gold and stones were so different from earthly things of the kind that no comparison between them is possible: their beauty is quite unlike anything that we can imagine and the understanding cannot soar high enough to comprehend the nature of the garment or to imagine the brightness of the vision which it was the Lord's will to send me, and by comparison with which everything on earth looks, as one might say, like a smudge of soot.

The beauty which I saw in Our Lady was wonderful, though I could discern in her no particularly beautiful detail of form: it was her face as a whole that was so lovely and the whiteness and the amazing splendour of her vestments,

[11] This rapture is believed to have come to the Saint in 1561, in the chapel known as that of the Santísimo Cristo in the Dominican church of St. Thomas, Ávila.

though the light was not dazzling, but quite soft. The glorious Saint Joseph I did not see so clearly, though I could see plainly that he was there, as in the visions to which I have already referred and in which nothing is seen. Our Lady looked to me quite like a child. When they had been with me for a short time and caused me the greatest bliss and happiness—more, I believe, than I had ever before experienced, so that I wished I need never lose it—I seemed to see them ascending to Heaven with a great multitude of angels. I remained quite alone, but so greatly comforted and exalted and recollected in prayer, and so full of tender devotion, that I stayed for some time where I was, without moving, and unable to speak, quite beside myself. I was left with a vehement impulse to melt away in love for God, and with other feelings of a like kind, for everything happened in such a way that I could never doubt that this was of God, however hard I tried. It left me greatly comforted and full of peace.

As to what the Queen of the Angels said about obedience, the point of it is that it was a grief to me not to make over the convent to the Order, but the Lord had told me that it would not be wise for me to do so. He gave me reasons for which it would be extremely unwise and told me to send to Rome, and to follow a certain procedure, which He also described to me. He would see to it that that procedure should bring security. And so it came about. I sent as the Lord had told me—had I not, we should never have concluded the negotiations—and it turned out very well. As to the things which have happened since, it proved a very wise arrangement that we should be under the Bishop's obedience, but at the time I did not know this, nor did I even know who that prelate would be. But the Lord was pleased that he should be good and helpful to this house, as has been necessary, in view of all the opposition it has met with, which I shall recount later, and in order to bring it to the state it is now in.[12] Blessed be He Who has brought all this to pass! Amen.

[12] The Bishop, when the foundation was made, was Don Álvaro de Mendoza (p. 314, n. 5, above), who had taken possession of his office on December 4, 1560. He was greatly devoted to St. Teresa and a strong supporter of her Reform.

CHAPTER XXXIV

Describes how about this time she had to leave the place, for a reason which is given, and how her superior ordered her to go and comfort a great lady who was in sore distress. Begins the description of what happened to her there, of how the Lord granted her the great favour of being the means whereby His Majesty aroused a great person to serve Him in real earnest and of how later she obtained help and protection from Him. This chapter should be carefully noted.

Despite all the care I took that nothing should be known of all this work that I was doing, it could not be done so secretly but that a few people heard of it: of these, some believed in it, while others did not. I was sorely afraid that they would say something about it to the Provincial when he came, and that he might then order me to stop, in which case all would be up with it. The Lord provided against this as follows. It happened that, in a large city,[1] more than twenty leagues from here, there was a lady in great distress because of the death of her husband: her grief had reached such a pitch that there were fears for her health.[2] She had heard about this poor sinner—for the Lord had ordained that people should speak well to her about me for other good purposes which resulted from this. This lady was well acquainted with the Provincial, and as she was an important person and knew that I lived in a convent where the nuns were allowed to leave the house, the Lord gave her a very great desire to see me: she thought that I might bring her comfort, which she could not find herself. So she began at once to use all possible means to get me to visit her, sending a great distance, for that purpose, to the Provincial. He sent me an order to go at once, under obedience, with a single companion. This message I received on Christmas night.

It disturbed me a little and distressed me a great deal to

[1] Toledo.

[2] This lady was Doña Luisa de la Cerda, widow of Don Arias Pardo de Saavedra, who died in 1561, and daughter of the Duke of Medinaceli, who was in the direct line of descent from Alfonso X.

think that she wanted me to come to her because she believed there was some good in me: knowing myself to be so wicked, I could not bear this. I commended myself earnestly to God; and, during the whole of Matins, or for a great part of it, I was in a deep rapture. The Lord told me I must go without fail and must not listen to people's opinions, as there were few who would advise me otherwise than rashly: to go might bring trials upon me, but God would be greatly served, and, as far as the convent was concerned, it would be as well if I were absent until the Brief arrived, because the devil had organized a great plot against the arrival of the Provincial; I was to fear nothing, however, for He would help me in this. I found this assurance a great strength and comfort. I told the Rector about it. He told me to go by all means, whereas others were telling me that I should not stand it, that it was an invention of the devil to bring some evil upon me there, and that I ought to send word about it to the Provincial.

I obeyed the Rector, and, after what I had learned in prayer, went without any fear, though not without the greatest confusion when I saw the reason of their sending for me and knew all the time how completely they were mistaken. This made me beseech the Lord still more earnestly that He would not abandon me. It was a great comfort to me that there was a house of the Company of Jesus in the place where I was going[3]: I thought I should feel fairly safe if I continued to be subject to their direction, as I was here. The Lord was pleased that the lady should be so much comforted that she began at once to grow markedly better: she felt more comforted every day. This was a notable achievement, for, as I have said, her distress was causing her great depression: the Lord must have brought it about in response to the many prayers for the success of my enterprise which had been offered by the good people whom I knew. She was a most God-fearing lady and so good that her most Christian spirit made up for what was lacking in me. She conceived a great affection for me, as I also did for her when I saw how good she was. But almost everything was a cross for me: the comforts in her house were a real torment and when she made so much

---

[3] A Jesuit house had been founded at Toledo in 1558 by St. Francis Borgia. Its first Superior, P. Pedro Domenech, later became St. Teresa's confessor.

of me I was filled with fear. My soul had such misgivings that I dared not be careless, and the Lord was not careless of me, for while I was there He showed me the most signal favours[4] and these made me feel so free and enabled me so to despise all I saw—and the more I saw, the more I despised it—that I never treated those great ladies, whom it would have been a great honour to me to serve, otherwise than with the freedom of an equal. From this I derived great profit, and I told my lady so. I saw that she was a woman, and as subject to passions and weaknesses as I was myself. I learned, too, how little regard ought to be paid to rank, and how, the higher is the rank, the greater are the cares and the trials that it brings with it. And I learned that people of rank have to be careful to behave according to their state, which hardly allows them to live: they must take their meals out of the proper time and order, for everything has to be regulated, not according to their constitutions but according to their position; often the very food which they eat has more to do with their position than with their liking.

So it was that I came to hate the very desire to be a great lady. God deliver me from this sinful fuss—though I believe that, despite her being one of the most important in the kingdom, there are few humbler and simpler people than this woman. I was sorry for her, and I still am when I think how often she has to act against her own inclination in order to live up to her position. Then, with regard to servants, though hers were good, one can really place very little trust in them. It is impossible to talk more to one of them than to another; otherwise the favoured one is disliked by the rest. This is slavery; and one of the lies which the world tells is that it calls such persons masters, whereas in a thousand ways, I think, they are nothing but slaves. The Lord was pleased that, during the time I spent in that house, its inmates should come to render His Majesty better service, though I was not free from trials, or from certain jealousies on the part of some of them, on account of the great love which my lady had for me. They must surely have thought that I was working for some interest of my own. The Lord must have allowed such things to try me to some extent so that I should not become ab-

---

[4] Some of these favours are described in the *Relations* (cf. pp. 315–16).

sorbed in the comforts which I was enjoying there, and He
was pleased to free me from all this to my soul's profit.

While I was there, it chanced that a religious arrived with
whom for many years I had been in communication on various occasions and who was a person of great importance.[5]
When I was at Mass in a monastery of his Order, which was
near the house where I was staying,[6] the desire came to me to
know about the state of his soul, for I wished him to be a
great servant of God; so I got up in order to go to speak to
him. But then, as I was already recollected in prayer, this
seemed to me a waste of time. What right, I thought, had I
to interfere with him? So I sat down again. This happened,
I believe, no less than three times, but finally my good angel
got the better of my evil angel and I went to ask for him and
he came to one of the confessionals to speak to me. I began
to question him about his past life, and he to question me
about mine, for we had not seen one another for many years.
I began to tell him that mine had been a life of many spiritual trials. He urged me to tell him what the trials were. I
said that they were not such as could be told and that I ought
not to say anything about them. He replied that, as the
Dominican Father to whom I have alluded[7] knew of them,
and was a great friend of his, he would tell him about them
at once, so that I need not mind doing so myself.

The truth is, he could not help importuning me, any more,
I think, than I could help talking to him; for, despite all the
regret and shame which I used to feel when I discussed these

[5] Ribera, Yepes and St. Teresa's early biographers in general suppose this religious to have been P. Vicente Barrón, but modern
editors follow Gracián, who, in the notes already referred to (pp.
62–3), identifies him as P. García de Toledo. Of aristocratic stock
(p. 213, n. 6) this Dominican went to the Indies as a child with the
Viceroy of Mexico, and professed in the capital of the Viceroyalty in
1535. Returning to Spain, he became Superior of the Ávilan monastery in 1555. Later, he accompanied his cousin, who was appointed
Viceroy of Peru, to that country, returning shortly before St. Teresa's
death.

[6] This monastery, dedicated to St. Peter Martyr, was in fact near
the palace of the Duke of Medinaceli, which has been a Discalced
Carmelite convent since 1607, and is not far from the Puerta del
Cimbrón.

[7] P. Pedro Ibáñez.

things with him and with the Rector whom I have mentioned,[8] I was not now in the least distressed—in fact, I found it a great comfort. I told him everything under the seal of confession. I had always taken him for a man of great intelligence, but now he seemed to me shrewder than ever. I thought what great talents and gifts he had and what a deal of good he could do with them if he gave himself wholly to God. For some years now I have felt like this—I never see a person whom I like very much without immediately wishing that I could see him wholly given to God, and sometimes this yearning of mine is so strong that I am powerless against it. Though I want everybody to serve God, my desire that those whom I like may do so is particularly vehement, and so I become extremely importunate for them with the Lord. This is what happened in the case of the religious I am referring to.

He asked me to commend him often to God: he had no need to do so, for my state of mind was such that I could not do otherwise, so I went to the place where I am in the habit of praying in solitude, and, with extreme recollection, began to speak to the Lord in that silly way in which I often speak to Him without knowing what I am saying; for it is love that speaks, and my soul is so far transported that I take no notice of the distance that separates it from God. For the love which it knows His Majesty has for it makes it forget itself and it thinks it is in Him, and that He and it are one and the same thing without any division, and so it talks nonsense. I shed copious tears, and begged Him that that soul might really give itself up to His service, for, good as I thought him, I was not satisfied but wanted him to be better still. And after praying in that way, I remember saying these words: "Lord, Thou must not refuse me this favour. Think what a good person he is for us to have as our friend."

Oh, the great goodness and humaneness of God, Who regards not the words but the desires and the good-will with which they are uttered! To think that His Majesty should allow such a person as myself to speak to Him thus boldly! May He be blessed for ever and ever.

That night, I remember, I was greatly troubled during those hours of prayer, wondering if I had incurred the enmity of

[8] P. Gaspar de Salazar.

God. I could not be sure if I were in grace or no—not that I wanted to be sure, but I wanted to die, so as to find myself no longer in a life in which I was not sure if I were dead or alive. For there could be no worse death for me than to think I had offended God and my distress about this caused me great depression: then I felt quite happy again, and, dissolving into tears, besought Him not to permit such a thing. I soon learned that I might safely take comfort and be certain[9] that I was in grace, since my love for God was so strong and His Majesty was working these favours in my soul and, of His compassion, giving it feelings which He would never give to a soul that was in mortal sin. I became confident that the Lord must surely do for this person what I begged of Him. He told me to say certain things to him. I was troubled about this, as I had no idea how to say them, and the thing I most dislike, as I have said, is having to take messages to a third person, especially if I am not sure how he will receive them or even that he will not make fun of me. So I was sorely distressed. But in the end I was quite persuaded that I must do it without fail, and I believe I promised God that I would, but I was so shy about it that I wrote down the message and handed it to him.

The effect which it produced upon him showed clearly that it came from God, for he made a most earnest resolve to give himself to prayer, though he did not fulfil that resolve immediately. As the Lord desired to have him for Himself, He had sent through my instrumentality to tell him certain truths which, without my knowing it, were so apposite that he was astounded. The Lord must have prepared him to believe that they came from His Majesty. And for my part, miserable creature though I am, I kept beseeching the Lord to bring him right back to Himself and make him hate the pleasures and affairs of this life. And—praised be God for ever!—so he did, to such an extent that, every time he speaks to me, he astounds me. If I had not seen it for myself, I should have thought it doubtful that in so short a time God could have shown him such increased favours, and led him to become so

9 Luis de León substituted "trust" (*confiar*) for the "be certain" (*estar cierta*) of the original manuscript, and other editors have followed him. But St. Teresa felt that the joint witness of a good conscience and her interior locutions gave her the moral certainty which she describes.

completely immersed in Him that, so far as things of earth are concerned, he no longer seems to be alive. May His Majesty hold him in His hand, for he has such profound self-knowledge that, if he advances farther, as I hope in the Lord he may, he will be one of the most notable of His servants and bring many souls great advantage. For in spiritual things he has had a great deal of experience in a short time, these being gifts bestowed by God when He wills and as He wills and having nothing to do either with time or with service. I do not mean that these latter things are unimportant but that often the Lord grants to one person less contemplation in twenty years than to others in one: His Majesty knows why. We are wrong if we think that in the course of years we are bound to understand things that cannot possibly be attained without experience, and thus, as I have said, many are mistaken if they think they can learn to discern spirits without being spiritual themselves. I do not mean that, if a man is learned but not spiritual, he may not direct a person of spirituality. But in both outward and inward matters which depend upon the course of nature, his direction will of course be of an intellectual kind, while in supernatural matters he will see that it is in conformity with Holy Scripture. In other matters he must not worry himself to death, or think he understands what he does not, or quench the spirits, for these souls are being directed by another Master, greater than he, so that they are not without anyone over them.

He must not be astonished at this or think such things are impossible: everything is possible to the Lord. He must strive to strengthen his faith and humble himself, because the Lord is perhaps making some old woman better versed in this science than himself, even though he be a very learned man. If he has this humility, he will be of more use both to other souls and to himself than if he tries to become a contemplative without being so by nature. I repeat, then, that if he has neither experience nor the deepest humility which will reveal to him how little he understands and show him that a thing is not impossible because he cannot understand it, he will gain little himself and the people who have to do with him will gain less. But, if he is humble, he need not fear that the Lord will allow either him or them to fall into error.

Now this Father of whom I am speaking, and to whom in many ways the Lord has granted humility, has studied these matters and done his utmost to discover all that study can reveal. For he is a very good scholar, and when he has no experience of a thing he consults those who have; and, as the Lord also helps him by granting him great faith, he has rendered a great deal of service both to himself and to certain souls, of which mine is one. For, as the Lord knew of the trials I had to endure, His Majesty, having seen good to call to Himself some who were directing me,[10] seems to have provided others who have helped me in numerous trials and done me a great deal of good. The Lord has almost completely transformed this religious, until, as one might say, he hardly knows himself. Though formerly he had poor health, He has given him physical strength, so that he can do penance, and has made him valiant in all that is good, and has done other things for him as well. He seems, then, to have received a very special vocation from the Lord. May He be blessed for ever.

All this good, I believe, has come to him from the favours which the Lord has granted him in prayer, for there is no mistaking their reality. The Lord has already been pleased to test him in a number of situations, and from all these he has emerged like one who has amply proved the reality of the merit which we gain by suffering persecutions. I hope the Lord in His might will grant that much good may come through him to various members of his Order and to that Order itself. This is already beginning to be understood. I have seen great visions and the Lord has told me a number of very wonderful things about him and about the Rector of the Company of Jesus, whom I have already mentioned,[11] and about two other religious of the Order of Saint Dominic:[12] especially about one of them, to whom, for his own profit, the Lord has taught certain things which He[13]

---

[10] Probably St. Peter of Alcántara (d. October 18, 1562) and P. Ibáñez (d. February 2, 1565). [If P. Ibáñez is included, the reference has a bearing upon the date of this book: cf. p. 58 and pp. 366–7.]

[11] P. Gaspar de Salazar.

[12] PP. Pedro Ibáñez and Domingo Báñez, especially the first-named.

[13] [P. Silverio reads "he", as though St. Teresa could have learned things from the Dominican which the Lord taught him later! The pluperfect and the word "previously" (antes) seem to settle the matter.]

had previously taught me. From this Father of whom I am now speaking I have learned a great deal.

To one of my experiences with him I will refer here. I was with him once in the locutory, and so great was the love that my soul and spirit felt to be burning within him that I became almost absorbed, as I thought of the wonders of God, Who had raised a soul to so lofty a state in so short a time. It filled me with confusion to see him listening so humbly to what I was telling him about certain things concerning prayer. There was little enough humility in me that I could talk in this way with such a person, but the Lord must have borne with me because of the earnest desire that I had to see him make great progress. It helped me so much to be with him that he seemed to have left my soul ablaze with a new fire of longing to begin to serve the Lord all over again. O my Jesus, how much a soul can do when ablaze with Thy love! What great value we ought to set on it and how we should beseech the Lord to allow it to remain in this life! Anyone who has this love should follow after such souls if he is able.

For one who has this sickness it is a great thing to find another stricken by it too. It is a great comfort to him to see that he is not alone: the two are of mutual help in their sufferings and their deservings. They stand shoulder to shoulder, ready for God's sake to risk a thousand lives and longing for a chance to lose them. They are like soldiers who, in order to win booty and grow rich upon it, are spoiling for war, realizing that without fighting they can never become rich at all. Toiling in this way, in fact, is their profession. Oh, what a great thing it is, when the Lord gives this light, to know how much we are gaining in suffering for His sake! But we cannot properly understand this until we have given up everything; for, if there is a single thing to which a man clings, it is a sign that he sets some value upon it; and if he sets some value upon it, it will naturally distress him to give it up, and so everything will be imperfection and loss. "He who follows what is lost is himself lost": that saying is appropriate here. And what greater loss, what greater blindness, what greater misfortune is there than to set a great price on what is nothing?

Returning, then, to what I was saying: As I looked at that soul I rejoiced exceedingly and I think the Lord was desirous that I should have a clear view of the treasures He had laid

up in it. So when I became aware of the favour which He
had done me in bringing this to pass through my interven-
tion, I realized how unworthy I was of it. I prized the favours
which the Lord had bestowed upon him and considered them
more my own than if they had actually been granted to me,
and I praised the Lord repeatedly when I found that His Majesty was fulfilling my desires and had heard my prayer that
He would awaken such persons as this. And then my soul, in
such a state that it could not endure so much joy, went out
from itself, and lost itself for its own greater gain. It abandoned its meditations, and, as it heard that Divine language,
which seems to have been that of the Holy Spirit, I fell into a
deep rapture, which caused me almost to lose my senses,
though it lasted but for a short time. I saw Christ, in the
greatest majesty and glory, manifesting His great satisfaction
at what had been taking place. This He told me, and said
that He wanted me to realize clearly that He was always
present at conversations of this kind, for He was very pleased
when people found their delight in talking of Him.

At another time, when I was a long way from here,[14] I saw
him being carried up to the angels in great glory.[15] By this
vision I understood that his soul was making great progress,
as indeed it was. For a cruel slander against his reputation
had been started by a person whom he had helped a great
deal and to whose reputation and to whose soul he had rendered a great service; and he had endured this very happily
and had done other things which tended greatly to the service
of God and had undergone other persecutions. I do not think
it suitable to say more about this just now, but Your Reverence knows about it all, and in the future, if you think well,
it can all be set down to the glory of the Lord. All the prophe-
cies about this house to which I have already referred, and
others of which I shall speak later, concerning both this house
and other matters, have been fulfilled. Some the Lord made
to me three years before they became known; others, before
that time, and others, again, since. And I always mentioned
them to my confessor and to that widow who was a friend of
mine, and with whom, as I said before, I was permitted to
discuss them. She, I have learned, repeated them to other peo-

---

[14] I.e., from Ávila.
[15] According to Gracián, this was P. García de Toledo.

ple, who know that I am not lying. God grant that I may never, in any matter, speak anything but the whole truth, especially on so serious a subject as this!

Once, when I was in great distress because a brother-in-law of mine[16] had died suddenly without being careful[17] to make his confession, I was told in prayer that my sister, too, would die in the same way and that I must go to see her and get her to prepare for death. I told my confessor about this, but he would not let me go; I then heard the same thing several times more. When he found that this was so, he told me to go, as no harm could possibly come of it. She lived in a village,[18] and I went there without telling her the reason but giving her what light I could about everything. I got her to go to confession very frequently and always to think of her soul's profit. She was very good and did as I said. Some four or five years after she had adopted these habits and begun to pay great heed to her conscience, she died in such circumstances that nobody could come to see her or hear her confession. So it was a fortunate thing that, following her usual custom, she had made her last confession little more than a week previously. When I heard of her death, it made me very happy to think that she had done so. She remained only a very short time in purgatory.

It could hardly have been a week later when, just after I had communicated, the Lord appeared to me and was pleased to let me see her as He was taking her to glory. During all those years between the time when the Lord spoke to me and the time of her death, neither my companion[19] nor I forgot what I had been told, and, when she died, my companion came to me in amazement at the way in which it had all been fulfilled. God be praised for ever, Who takes such care of souls so that they are not lost!

[16] Don Martín de Guzmán y Barrientos, husband of the Saint's half-sister María (p. 79).

[17] Thus St. Teresa in the autograph; but P. Báñez emended the phrase so that it read: "without having had the opportunity." The early editions follow the author, but later editors have tended to adopt the emendation.

[18] Cf. p. 74, n. 3.

[19] Doña Guiomar de Ulloa.

CHAPTER XXXV

Continues the same subject—the foundation of this house of our glorious father Saint Joseph. Tells how the Lord brought it about that holy poverty should be observed there and why she left that lady, and describes several other things that happened to her.

While I was with this lady whom I have mentioned, and with whom I stayed for over six months,[1] the Lord brought it about that a *beata*[2] of our Order, living more than seventy leagues from here, heard of me, and, happening to come this way, went some leagues out of her road to talk to me.[3] The Lord had inspired her, in the same year and month as He had inspired me, to found another convent of this Order; and, as He had given her this desire, she sold all she had and walked barefoot to Rome to obtain the necessary patent.

She is a woman greatly devoted to penance and prayer and the Lord granted her many favours. Our Lady had appeared to her and ordered her to undertake this task. She had done so much more than I in the service of the Lord that I was ashamed to be in her presence. She showed me the patents which she had brought from Rome and during the fortnight she was with me we made our plans as to how these convents were to be founded. Until I spoke to her, it had not come to my notice that our Rule, before its severity became miti-

---

[1] From January 1562 until the beginning of July of the same year.

[2] [A *beata* is a somewhat vague term denoting a woman who either lives in a religious community without being professed or keeping the full rule or lives under a rule in her own house, wearing a distinctive habit but belonging to no community.]

[3] Her name was María de Jesús. Born at Granada in 1522, she had been left a widow when very young and had entered the convent of the Calced Carmelites of her native city. But, believing that God had called her to found a reformed house of the Order, she left the convent before making her profession and journeyed with some friends to Rome, where she eventually obtained a Brief for this purpose. Her attempts to make a foundation in Granada failed and it was then that she came to see St. Teresa, as described in this chapter. Later Doña Leonor de Mascareñas gave her a house at Alcalá de Henares and the convent was founded in July 1563.

gated, had ordered us to possess nothing,[4] and I had had no idea of founding a convent without revenue, my intention being that we should have no anxiety about necessaries, and I did not think of all the anxieties which are entailed by the holding of possessions. Though unable to read, this blessed woman had been taught by the Lord, and so she knew quite well what I did not, despite my having so often perused the Constitutions. And when she told me this, I thought it a good idea, though I was afraid that no one would ever agree with me, but say I was being ridiculous and tell me not to do things which would cause suffering to others. If I alone were concerned, nothing whatever should hold me back: on the contrary, it would be a great joy to me to think I was keeping the counsels of Christ our Lord, for His Majesty had already given me great desires for poverty. For my own part, I had never doubted that poverty was the soundest basis for a foundation. I had been wishing for days that it were possible for a person in my state of life to go about begging for love of God and have no house or any other possession. But I was afraid that, if others were not given these desires by the Lord, they would live in a state of discontent, and also that the thing would cause some distraction. I had seen a number of poor monasteries in which there was no great degree of recollection, and it had not occurred to me that their distraction was not due to their poverty, but that their poverty was the result of their not being recollected. Distraction does not make people richer and God never fails those who serve Him. In short, my faith was weak, whereas the faith of this servant of God was not.

I sought the opinions of a great many people with regard to all this but found hardly anyone who shared my own—neither my confessor nor the learned men whom I consulted about it. They put before me so many contrary arguments that I did not know what to do; for, now that I had learned the nature of the Rule and realized that its way was that of greater perfection, I could not persuade myself to allow the house to have any revenue. True, they sometimes con-

---

[4] Chap. VI of the Rule says:—"Nullus fratrum sibi aliquid proprium esse dicat, sed sint vobis omnia communia." Gregory IX, by a Brief dated April 6, 1229, forbade the Carmelites to possess houses, lands or money.

vinced me; but, when I betook myself to prayer again and
looked at Christ hanging poor and naked upon the Cross, I
felt I could not bear to be rich. So I besought Him with tears
to bring it about that I might become as poor as He.

I found that the possession of revenue entailed so many
inconveniences, and was such a cause of unrest, and even of
distraction, that I kept on disputing about it with learned
men. I wrote to that effect to the Dominican friar who was
helping us,[5] and he answered me in a letter two sheets long,
full of refutations and theology; in this he told me that he
had made a close study of the subject, and tried to dissuade
me from my project. I replied that I had no wish to make use
of theology and should not thank him for his learning in this
matter if it was going to keep me from following my vocation,
from being true to the vow of poverty that I had made, and
from observing Christ's precepts with due perfection. If I
found anyone who would help me, I was delighted. The lady
with whom I was staying[6] was of great assistance to me here.
Some told me at the very beginning that they approved of
my plan, but afterwards, on looking into it farther, found so
many disadvantages in it that they once more urged me
strongly to give it up. I told them that, though they had
changed their opinions so quickly, I preferred to keep mine.
It was at this time that, through my entreaties, for the lady
had never seen him, the Lord was pleased that the saintly
Fray Peter of Alcántara should come to her house. As one
who was a great lover of poverty and had practised it for so
many years, he knew how much wealth there was in it, and
so he was a great help to me and told me that I must carry
out my plan without fail. Once I had his opinion and help,
which, as he had had the advantage of a long experience,
none was better able to give, I resolved to seek no further
opinions.

One day, when I was earnestly commending my plan to
God, the Lord told me that I must on no account fail to
found the convent in poverty, for that was His Father's will,
and His own will, and He would help me. I was in a deep
rapture at the time, the effects of which were so marked that
I could not possibly doubt that it had been of God. On an-

[5] P. Ibáñez, then at Trianos. (Cf. p. 313, n. 4.)
[6] Doña Guiomar de Ulloa.

other occasion He told me that money led only to confusion, and said other things in praise of poverty, and assured me that none would ever lack the necessaries of life if they served Him. For my own part, as I say, I was never afraid of being without these things. The Lord also changed the heart of the Presentado[7]—I mean, of the Dominican friar—who, as I have related, had written and told me not to make the foundation unless I had money. I was delighted at hearing this and at having the support of such opinions; I thought I had nothing less than all the riches in the world when I had resolved to live only on the love of God.

It was about then that my Provincial[8] revoked his order and released me from the obligation of obedience which he had laid upon me and which kept me in the place where I then was: he now left me free to do as I liked, so that I could go away for a time, if I wanted to do so, and, if I wanted to stay where I was, I could do that too. Just at that time there was to be an election in my convent, and I was warned that many of the nuns wanted to lay upon me the responsibility of being their superior. The very thought of this was such a torment to me that, though I was resolved and prepared to undergo any martyrdom for God's sake, I could not possibly persuade myself to accept this. For, apart from the great labour it would involve, on account of the large number of nuns there were, and for other reasons (such as the fact that I was never fond of such work, and had not wanted to hold any office—indeed, I had always declined to do so), I thought it would involve my conscience in grave peril, and so I praised God that I was not there. I wrote to my friends and asked them not to vote for me.

Just as I was feeling very glad that I should not be getting mixed up in that commotion, the Lord told me that I must on no account fail to go: if I wanted a cross, there was a good one all ready for me and I was not to reject it but go on bravely, for He would help me; so I was to go at once. I was terribly worried and did nothing but weep, for I thought that this cross meant that I was to become Superior, and, as

[7] This title, here given to P. Ibáñez, is an academic one, equivalent in the Order of St. Dominic to that of Licentiate [in English, to Bachelor of Arts, Divinity, etc.].

[8] P. Ángel de Salazar. He ordered St. Teresa to return from Toledo to Ávila to be present at the election of a Prioress.

I say, I could not persuade myself that that would do the least good to my soul or see any way in which it possibly could. I told my confessor[9] about it. He ordered me to see at once about going, saying that this was clearly the way of greatest perfection; but he added that, as the weather was very hot and it would suffice if I got there for the election, I could wait for a few days lest the journey should do me any harm. But the Lord had disposed it otherwise and I had to leave then and there, so great were my inward restlessness and my inability to pray and my fear that I was being false to the Lord's command, and that I would not go and offer myself for the work because I was comfortable and at my ease where I was. I felt that I was rendering God nothing but lip-service. Why, if I had the chance of living a life of greater perfection, should I not take it? If I had to die, let me die. Together with these thoughts came an oppression of soul and the Lord took all the joy out of my prayer. In fact, I found myself in such torment that I begged the lady to be good enough to let me leave, and, when my confessor saw the state I was in, he told me to do so: God had moved him just as He had moved me.

She was very sorry that I was leaving her, and this was a further trial, for it had cost her a great deal of trouble, and she had practised all kinds of importunities, to obtain permission from the Provincial for me to come. I thought it a very great thing that she should agree to my going, considering how she felt about it, but as she was a most God-fearing woman and I told her if I went I might be doing a great service to God, as well as giving her many other reasons, and held out the hope that I might possibly come and see her again, she acquiesced in it, though with the greatest regret.

For myself, I now no longer regretted going; for, as I realized that this would be conducive to greater perfection and to the service of God, and as pleasing Him always gives me pleasure, I bore my distress at leaving this lady, at seeing how sorry she was about it, and also at leaving others to whom I was greatly indebted—in particular, my confessor, a priest of the Society of Jesus, with whom I got on very well. The greater was the comfort which I sacrificed for the Lord's sake,

[9] P. Pedro Domenech, Rector of the Toledo house of the Society of Jesus.

the happier I was to forgo it. I could not understand how this was possible, for I realized clearly that I was being moved by two contrary feelings: that is to say, I was rejoicing and being glad and finding comfort in what was oppressing my soul, for I was calmed and comforted and had the opportunity of spending many hours in prayer. I saw that I was about to fling myself into a fire, for this the Lord had already told me, and that I was going to bear a heavy cross, though I never thought it would be as heavy as I afterwards found it to be. Yet, in spite of all this, I went off gladly, only chagrined that, since it was the Lord's will that I should enter the battle, I was not doing so immediately. Thus was His Majesty sending me strength and establishing it in my weakness.[10]

As I say, I could not understand how this was possible. But I thought of this comparison. If I possess a jewel, or something which gives me great pleasure, and if I happen to discover that some person wants it whom I love better than myself, and I am more anxious for her pleasure than for my own comfort, it will give me greater happiness to go without it than it has given me to have it, because I shall be affording that person pleasure. And as the pleasure of pleasing her transcends my pleasure in having the jewel myself, my regret at no longer having it, or anything else that I like, and at losing the pleasure it gave me, will disappear. In the same way, although I wanted to feel sorry when I found that I was leaving people who so much regretted losing me, especially as I am such a grateful person by temperament, I could not feel sorry any more, however hard I tried, though on any other occasion it would have been enough to cause me great distress.

It was so important for the affairs of this house that I should not delay for another day that I do not know how they would have been settled had I waited. Oh, the greatness of God! I am often astounded when I think about this and realize how specially anxious His Majesty was to help me carry out the business of this little corner of God's house (for such, I believe, it is) and this dwelling in which His Majesty takes His delight—once, when I was in prayer, He told me that this house was the paradise of His delight. So it seems that His Majesty had chosen the souls whom He has drawn to Him-

10 [An apparent reference to 2 Corinthians xii, 9.]

self and in whose company I am living, feeling very, very much ashamed of myself, for I could never have expected to have souls like these for this plan of living in a state of such strict enclosure and poverty and prayer. Such is the joy and happiness of their lives that each of them thinks herself unworthy to have merited coming to such a place. This is particularly true of some, whom the Lord has called from all the vanity and parade of the world, in which, according to its own standards, they might have been happy. But here the Lord has so multiplied their happiness that they clearly recognize that in place of the one thing they have forsaken He has given them an hundredfold, and they are never tired of giving His Majesty thanks. Others He has changed from good to better. To the young He gives fortitude and knowledge so that they may desire nothing else and may learn that, even from an earthly standpoint, to live far from everything that has to do with this life is to live with the maximum of repose. To those who are older and whose health is poor He gives strength, as He has done in the past, to endure the same austerity and penance as all the rest.

O my Lord, how abundantly dost Thou manifest Thy power! There is no need to seek reasons for what Thou willest, for Thou dost transcend all natural reason and make all things possible, thus showing clearly that we have only to love Thee truly, and truly to forsake everything for Thee, and Thou, my Lord, will make everything easy. It is well said, with regard to this, that "Thou feignest labour in Thy law",[11] for I do not see, Lord, and I do not know how the road that leads to Thee can be "narrow".[12] To me it seems a royal road, not a pathway; a road along which anyone who sets out upon it in earnest travels securely. Mountain passes and rocks that might fall upon him—I mean, occasions of sin—are far distant. What I call a path, and a cruel path, and a really narrow road, is that which has on one side a deep gorge into which one may fall, and on the other side a precipice: hardly has a man relaxed his care than he falls over it and is dashed to pieces.

He who truly loves Thee, my God, travels by a broad and a royal road and travels securely. It is far away from any prec-

[11] Psalm xciii, 20 [A.V., xciv, 20].
[12] St. Matthew vii, 14.

ipice, and hardly has such a man stumbled in the slightest
degree when Thou, Lord, givest him Thy hand. One fall—and
even many falls, if he loves Thee and not the things of the
world—will not be enough to lead him to perdition: he will
be travelling along the valley of humility. I cannot understand
why it is that people are afraid to set out upon the way of
perfection. May the Lord, for His name's sake, make us realize how unsafe we are amid such manifest perils as beset us
when we follow the crowd, and how our true safety lies in
striving to press ever forward on the way of God. Our eyes
must be fixed upon Him and we must not be afraid that this
Sun of Justice will set, or that He will allow us to travel by
night, and so be lost, unless we first forsake Him.

People are not afraid to walk among lions, each of which
seems to be trying to tear them to pieces—I mean among
honours, delights and pleasures (as the world calls them) of
that kind. The devil seems to be frightening us with scare-
crows here. A thousand times have I been amazed by this;
fain would I weep ten thousand times, till I could weep no
more, and fain would I cry aloud to tell everyone of my great
blindness and wickedness, in the hope that this might be of
some avail to open their eyes. May He open them Who alone
of His goodness can do so, and may He never allow mine to
become blind again. Amen.

CHAPTER XXXVI

Continues the subject already begun and describes the com-
pletion of the foundation of this convent of the glorious
Saint Joseph, and the great opposition and numerous
persecutions which the nuns had to endure after taking
the habit, and the great trials and temptations which she
suffered, and how the Lord delivered her from every-
thing victoriously, to His glory and praise.

After leaving that city I went on my way very happily, resolved to suffer with the greatest willingness whatever it
might please the Lord to send me. On the very night of my
arrival in these parts there arrived our patent for the convent

and the Brief from Rome.[1] I was astonished at this, and so were those who knew how the Lord had hastened my coming here, when they found how necessary it had proved to be and how the Lord had brought me here just in the nick of time. For here I found the Bishop and the saintly Fray Peter of Alcántara, and another gentleman,[2] a great servant of God, in whose house this saintly man was staying—he was one with whom God's servants could always find hospitality.

Between them, these two persuaded the Bishop to sanction the foundation of the convent. This was by no means easy,[3] as it was to be founded in poverty, but he was so much drawn to people whom he saw determined to serve the Lord that he at once inclined to the idea of helping it. The whole thing was due to the approval of this saintly old man and the way he urged first one person and then another to come to our aid. If, as I have already said, I had not arrived at this particular moment, I cannot see how it could have been done, for this saintly man was here only for a few days—not more than a week, I believe—and during that time he was very ill: not long afterwards the Lord took him to Himself. It seems as if His Majesty had prolonged his life until this business was settled, for he had for some time been in very poor health—I fancy for over two years.

Everything was done with great secrecy: had it been otherwise, nothing could have been done at all, for, as appeared later, the people were opposed to the plan. The Lord had ordained that a brother-in-law of mine[4] should fall ill, and,

[1] This Brief of Pius IV was dated February 7, 1562. It would have been the beginning of July when it reached Ávila.

[2] Probably not Don Francisco de Salcedo, as is generally supposed, but Don Juan Blázquez, father of the Count of Uceda, as it was he with whom St. Peter of Alcántara usually stayed when at Ávila.

[3] It certainly was not. When St. Peter of Alcántara reached Ávila, the Bishop was away. Fray Peter went to the village where he was staying to see him and found him completely opposed to the establishment of a convent without an endowment. He persuaded him, however, to come back to Ávila and visit St. Teresa at the Incarnation, and as a result of the interview he withdrew all his objections and became her staunch supporter.

[4] Don Juan de Ovalle. He had come to Toledo, while St. Teresa was there, to inform her of the progress being made with the house which was to become the Reformed foundation, and had intended

his wife not being with him, should be in such need of me that I was given leave to go and stay with him. This prevented anything from being discovered, and, though a few people must have been rather suspicious, they did not think there was anything in it. The remarkable thing was that his illness lasted only for just the time we needed for our negotiations, and, when it was necessary for him to be better so that I could be free again and he could go away and leave the house, the Lord at once restored him to health, and he was amazed at it.

What with one person and what with another, I had a great deal of trouble in getting the foundation sanctioned. Then there was my patient, and there were the workmen—for the house had to be got ready very quickly, so that it would be suitable for a convent, and there was a great deal which had to be done to it. My companion[5] was not here, for we thought it advisable that she should be away so that the secret might be the better kept. I saw that speed was of the first importance, and this for many reasons, one of them being that I was in hourly fear of being sent back to my own convent. So many were the trials I had to suffer that I began to wonder if this was my cross, though I thought it very much lighter than the heavy one which I had understood the Lord to say I should have to bear.

When everything had been arranged, the Lord was pleased that some of the sisters[6] should take the habit on Saint

---

to return thence to Alba. But he fell ill at Ávila on his way back: Doña Juana was, of course, at Alba. It was in these circumstances that St. Teresa was allowed to go and stay with him, which, as she suggests in the text, gave her the opportunity to complete the preparations for the new foundation in secrecy.

[5] Doña Guiomar was away at Toro.

[6] These were: Antonia de Henao (del Espíritu Santo), a penitent of St. Peter of Alcántara; María de la Paz (de la Cruz) who had been living with Doña Guiomar de Ulloa, in whose house she first met St. Teresa; Ursula de Revilla (de los Santos), recommended to the Saint by Gaspar Daza; María de Ávila (de San José), sister of Julián de Ávila. The names given in brackets are those taken by these nuns in religion. The Bishop deputed P. Daza to give them the habit. St. Teresa was present, with two of her cousins who were nuns at the Incarnation and later joined the Reform; and others who attended were Gonzalo de Aranda, Salcedo, Ovalle and his wife and Julián de

Bartholomew's Day and on that day too the Most Holy Sacrament was placed in the convent. So with the full weight of authority this convent of our most glorious father Saint Joseph was founded in the year 1562. I was there to give the habit, with two other nuns of our own house, who chanced to be absent from it. As the house in which the convent was established belonged to my brother-in-law, who, as I have said, had bought it in order to keep the matter secret, I was there by special permission, and I did nothing without asking the opinion of learned men, lest in any way whatever I should act against obedience. As they saw what benefits, in numerous ways, were being conferred upon the whole Order, they told me I might do what I did, although it was being done in secret and I was keeping it from my superiors' knowledge. Had they told me that there was the slightest imperfection in this, I think I would have given up a thousand convents, let alone a single one. Of that I am sure; for, though I desired to make the foundation so that I could withdraw more completely from everything and fulfil my profession and vocation with greater perfection in conditions of stricter enclosure, I desired it only with the proviso that if I found that the Lord would be better served by my abandoning it entirely, I should do so, as I had done on a former occasion, with complete tranquillity and peace.

Well, it was like being in Heaven to me to see the Most Holy Sacrament reserved, and to find ourselves supporting four poor orphans (for they were taken without dowries)[7] who were great servants of God. From the very beginning we tried to receive only persons whose examples might serve as a foundation on which we could effectively build up our plan of a community of great perfection, given to prayer, and carry out a work which I believed would lead to the Lord's service and would honour the habit of His glorious Mother. It was for this that I yearned. It was also a great comfort to me that I had done what the Lord had so often commanded me and that there was one more church here than there had pre-

Ávila. The Cathedral Chapter at Ávila still celebrates a solemn Mass, at St. Joseph's, yearly, on St. Bartholomew's Day, and a sermon is preached, in commemoration of the historic occasion.

[7] The Book of Professions belonging to St. Joseph's, nevertheless, shows that, on entering the convent, Antonia del Espíritu Santo and Ursula de los Santos brought small sums as alms.

viously been, dedicated to my glorious father Saint Joseph. Not that I thought I had done anything of all this myself; I never thought that nor do I now; I have always known that it was done by the Lord. The part of it which concerned me was so full of imperfections that I can see I ought to have been blamed rather than thanked for it. But it was a great comfort to me to see that in such a great work as this His Majesty had taken me, wicked as I am, to be His instrument. I was so happy, therefore, that I was quite carried away by the intensity of my prayer.

When everything was finished—it might have been about three or four hours afterwards—the devil plunged me into a spiritual battle again, as I shall now relate. He made me wonder if what I had done had not been a mistake and if I had not been acting against obedience in arranging it all without a mandate from the Provincial. It had certainly occurred to me that the Provincial would be rather displeased at my having placed the convent under the jurisdiction of the Ordinary, without having first told him about it, though, on the other hand, as he had not been prepared to sanction it and I had not altered my plans, I had also imagined that he might not trouble about it. The devil also asked me if people living under so strict a rule would be contented, if they would have enough to eat, and if the whole thing was not ridiculous—and what reason had I to mix myself up in it, seeing that I was already in a convent of my own? All that the Lord had commanded me, all the opinions I had been seeking and the prayers I had been saying almost continuously for over two years—all these things fled from my memory as if they had never existed. The only thing I remembered now was my own opinion; and faith, and all the virtues, were suspended in me, and I had not the power to turn any of them into practice or to defend myself against all these blows.

The devil would also put it to me how, when I was so often indisposed, I could want to endure so much penance, to leave such a large, pleasant house, where I had always been so happy, and to give up so many friends for people in this other convent who would perhaps not be to my liking. Then he suggested that I had undertaken a great deal and might possibly have to abandon it as hopeless. Indeed, he said, might it not be the devil himself who had induced me to do this, in order to deprive me of peace and quiet? And, once I was inwardly disturbed, I might be unable to pray, and then my soul would be lost. Things of this kind he suggested to me one after another, till I found it impossible to think of anything else, and at the same time he plunged my soul into such affliction and obscurity and darkness as I cannot possibly describe. When I found myself in this state, I went to visit the Most Holy Sacrament, though I felt unable to commend myself to God. I really think my anguish was like a death agony. And I dared not discuss it with anyone, for as yet I had not even been given a confessor.

Oh, God help me! What a miserable life is this! There is no happiness that is secure and nothing that does not change. Here I was, such a short time ago, thinking I would not exchange my happiness with anyone on earth and now the very cause of it was tormenting me so sorely that I did not know what to do with myself. Oh, if only we thought carefully about the things of life, we should each find by experience how little either of happiness or of unhappiness there is to be got from it! I certainly think this was one of the worst times that I have ever spent in my life; my spirit seemed to be divining all that it would have to suffer, though I never had to endure as much suffering as this would have caused me had it lasted. But the Lord did not allow His poor servant to suffer long: in all my tribulations He has never failed to succour me. So it was here. He gave me a little light, so that I should see that it was the work of the devil, understand the truth and know that this was simply an attempt to frighten me with falsehoods. Then I began to remember my firm resolutions to serve the Lord and my desires to suffer for Him. I realized that, if I was to carry them out, I must not go about looking for repose; that, if I was to have trials, this was the way to win merit; and if I was to be unhappy and used my unhappiness in order to serve God, it would serve me as a kind of purgatory.[8] What was I afraid of? I asked myself. I had been wanting trials, and here were some good ones, and the greater was the opposition I endured, the greater would be my gain. Why was I lacking in courage to serve Him to Whom my debt was so great? By means of these and other reflections, I made a great effort, and in the presence of the Most Holy Sacrament promised to do all I could to get per-

8 [A characteristic play upon words: cf. Translator's Preface, p. 21.]

mission to enter this new house, and, if I could do so with a good conscience, to make a vow of enclosure.

The instant I had done this, the devil fled, leaving me quiet and happy; and I remained so and have been so ever since. All the rules we observe in this house concerning enclosure, penance and other things of that sort I find extremely easy and there are not many of them. So great is my happiness that I sometimes wonder what earthly choice I could possibly have made which would have been more delightful. I do not know if this has anything to do with my being in much better health than ever before, or whether, because it is right and necessary that I should do as all the others do, the Lord is being pleased to comfort me by enabling me to keep the Rule, though it costs me something to do so. But my ability to keep it astonishes all who know my infirmities. Blessed be He Who gives everything and in Whose strength this can be done!

After this conflict I was sorely fatigued, but I laughed at the devil, for I saw clearly that it was his doing. As I have never known what it was to be discontented with being a nun—not for a single moment of the twenty-eight years and more that have gone by since I became one—I think the Lord permitted what had taken place so that I might understand what a great favour He had granted me in this, and from what torment He had delivered me, and also in order that, if I ever saw anyone in that state, I should not be alarmed, but should be sorry for her and know how to comfort her. When this was over, I wanted to get a little rest after dinner. (All the previous night I had had hardly any peace of mind; and on several of the preceding nights I had been continuously troubled and worried; so that during each day I had felt worn out. For now what we had done became known in my convent and in the city, and for the reasons I have given there was a great deal of commotion—not, it seemed, without some cause.) But the Superior[9] sent for me to come to her immediately. On receiving the order, I went at once, leaving my nuns terribly upset. I was well aware that there was ample trouble in store for me, but, as the thing was now done, I

[9] Gracián, in his notes, says that this was Doña Isabel de Ávila; but this Prioress was succeeded, on August 12, 1562, by Doña María Cimbrón, who seems therefore to be the person referred to.

cared very little about that. I prayed to the Lord and begged Him to help me and besought my father Saint Joseph to bring me back to his house. I offered up to God all I should have to suffer, very happy at having some suffering to offer Him and some service to render. I went in the belief that I should at once be put in prison. This, I think, would have been a great joy to me, as I should not have had to talk to anyone and should have been able to rest for a little and be alone—and I needed that very badly, for all this intercourse with people had worn me to pieces.

When I got there and gave the Superior my version of the affair, she relented a little, and they all sent for the Provincial[10] and laid the case before him. He came, and I went to hear his judgment with the utmost happiness, thinking that there would now be something for me to suffer for the Lord. I could not discover that I had committed any offence either against His Majesty or against the Order—indeed, I was striving with all my might to strengthen the Order and to do this I would willingly have died, for my whole desire was that its Rule should be observed with all perfection. But I remembered the trial of Christ and realized that this, by comparison, was nothing at all. I acknowledged my fault, as if I had acted very wrongly, and so in fact I must have appeared to have done to anyone who did not know all the reasons. The Provincial gave me a severe rebuke, though its severity was less than would have been justified by the report which many people had given him of my delinquency. I would not excuse myself, for I had already resolved not to do so, but begged him to forgive me, to punish me and not to be annoyed with me any longer.

In some ways I knew quite well that they were condemning me unjustly, for they told me that I had done this so as to win esteem for myself, to get well known, and so on. But in other ways it was clear to me that they were speaking the truth—in saying that I was more wicked than other nuns, and in asking how, if I had not kept all the numerous rules observed in that house, I could consider keeping stricter rules in another: I should be scandalizing the people, they said, and setting up new ideas. None of this caused me the least trouble or distress, though I gave the impression that it did,

10 P. Angel de Salazar.

lest I should appear to be making light of what they were saying. Finally, I was commanded to state my version of the matter in the presence of the nuns, so I had to do so.

As I was inwardly calm and the Lord helped me, my account of the affair gave neither the Provincial nor the others present any reason for condemning me. Afterwards, when I was alone with him, I spoke to him more plainly, and he was quite satisfied, and promised me, if my foundation succeeded, to give me permission to go there as soon as the city was quiet—for there had been a very great commotion in the city, as I shall now relate.[11]

Two or three days before, there had been a meeting between the Mayor and certain members of the City Council and of the Chapter, and they had all agreed that this new convent must on no account be sanctioned, that it would cause notable harm to the common weal, that the Most Holy Sacrament must be removed and that the matter must on no account be allowed to go any farther. They summoned a meeting of representatives of all the Orders—two learned men from each—to obtain their opinions. Some said nothing; others were condemnatory. Finally, they decided that the foundation must be dissolved at once. There was only one of them, a Presentado of the Order of Saint Dominic,[12] who was not opposed to the convent, though he objected to its poverty: he said that there was no reason for dissolving it, that the question should be gone into with care, that there was plenty of time for doing so, that it was the Bishop's affair, and other things of that kind. This did a great deal of good: to judge by their fury, it was fortunate for us that they had not proceeded to dissolve the foundation on the spot. The fact was that the convent had been destined to be founded, for its foundation was the Lord's will and against

11 [P. Silverio (I, 311, n. 1) gives a long independent account of the "commotion" mainly from Julián de Avila's biography of St. Teresa: I do not reproduce this, as St. Teresa's own narrative would seem sufficiently detailed. The Bishop's strong support of the new foundation is an outstanding feature of the events here related.]

12 P. Báñez, who wrote here, in the margin of the autograph: "This was at the end of August in the year 1562. I was there and gave this opinion. Fr. Domingo Bañes. And I sign this on May 2, 1575, when this Mother has founded nine convents in which the Rule is strictly observed."

that the whole body of them were powerless. They gave reasons for what they did and showed great zeal for what was good, and so, without offending God, made me, and all the people who were helping the project, suffer: there were a number of these and they all had to go through a great deal of persecution.

All this made such a commotion in the city that people talked about nothing else. Everybody was condemning me and going to see the Provincial and visiting my convent. I was no more distressed by all they were saying about me than I should have been if they had said nothing at all, but I was afraid that the foundation might be dissolved, and that distressed me a great deal, as it did to see that the people who were helping me were losing credit and suffering such great trials. I believe what they had been saying about me made me rather glad. If I had had a little faith, I should not have let it worry me at all, but a slight failing in a single virtue is sufficient to deaden all the rest. So I was greatly distressed during the two days in which these meetings I have mentioned were being held in the town. Once, when I was quite worn out, the Lord said to me: "Knowest thou not how powerful I am? What dost thou fear?" and He assured me that the foundation would not be dissolved. This brought me great comfort. They sent the information which they had obtained to the Royal Council and a reply came requiring a report to be made on how all this had arisen.

Here we were, then, at the beginning of legal proceedings. The city sent representatives to the capital, and it was clear that the convent would have to send some too, but there was no money for this and I had no idea what to do. However, the Lord provided, and my Father Provincial never ordered me to withdraw from the business, for he is a lover of everything that is good, and, though he did not help us, he would not take the other side. But until he saw what the outcome of all this was going to be, he did not give me permission to come and live here. So those servants of God were alone in the house and their prayers were more effective than all my negotiations, though I had to be extremely diligent about these. Sometimes it seemed that everything was going wrong: this was particularly so one day, before the arrival of the Provincial, when the Prioress ordered me to have no more to do with the matter and to give it up altogether. I went to God and said: "Lord, this house is not mine; it has been founded for Thee; and now there will be no one to carry on the negotiations, so Thy Majesty must do so." This calmed me and left me as free from worry as if I had had the whole world carrying on the negotiations for me; from that moment I felt quite sure they would prosper.

A priest, who was a great servant of God and a lover of all perfection, and who had always been a great help to me,[13] went to the capital to take the matter in hand and worked very hard at it. That saintly gentleman of whom I have made mention also did a very great deal in the matter and helped in every way he could. He suffered many trials and great persecution over this and I always found him a father in everything and find him so still. Those who helped me were inspired by the Lord with such fervour that each of them regarded the matter as if it were his own and as if his own life and reputation were at stake, when it had really nothing to do with them except in so far as they believed it to be for the Lord's service. It seemed clear, too, that His Majesty was helping the cleric I have referred to, who was another of my great helpers, and whom the Bishop sent to represent him at an important meeting which was held. Here he stood out alone against all the others and eventually pacified them by suggesting certain expedients which did a great deal to bring about an agreement. But nothing was sufficient to dissuade them from putting their whole weight, as we say, into smashing us. It was this servant of God of whom I am speaking who gave us the habit and reserved the Most Holy Sacrament for us,[14] and as a result found himself sorely persecuted. This commotion lasted for six months, and it would take a long time to give a detailed description of the severe trials which we had to suffer.

I was astonished at all the trouble that the devil was taking to hurt a few poor women, and how everybody thought that twelve women and a prioress (for I must remind those who opposed the plan that there were to be no more) could do such harm to the place, when they were living so strictly. If there had been any harm or error in their project it would have concerned themselves alone; harm to the city there

[13] Gonzalo de Aranda.
[14] Gaspar Daza (see p. 222, n. 5).

could not possibly be, and yet our opponents found so much that they fought us with a good conscience. Eventually they said they would allow the matter to go forward if the convent had an endowment. By this time I was so wearied, more by all the trouble my helpers were having than by my own, that I thought it would not be a bad idea to accept some money until the storm subsided, and then to give it up. At other times, like the wicked and imperfect woman I am, I would wonder if perhaps it was the Lord's will that we should have an endowment, as it seemed impossible for us to get anywhere without one. So in the end I agreed to this arrangement.

The discussion of it had already begun, when, on the very night before it was to be concluded, the Lord told me that I must not agree to such a thing, for, if once we had an endowment, we should never be allowed to give it up again. He said various other things as well. That same night there appeared to me the holy Fray Peter of Alcántara, who was now dead.[15] Before his death, knowing how much opposition and persecution we were meeting with, he had written to me[16] saying he was delighted the foundation was encountering all this opposition, for the efforts which the devil was making to prevent the establishment of the convent were a sign that the Lord would be very well served there; and he had added that I must on no account allow the place to have any revenue. He had insisted upon this in the letter two or three times, and said that, if I were firm about it, everything would turn out as I wished. Since his death I had seen him on two previous occasions and had had a vision of the great bliss that he was enjoying. So his appearance caused me no fear—indeed, it made me very happy, for he always appeared as a glorified body, full of great bliss, and it gave me the greatest joy to see him. I remember that, the first time I saw him, he told me among other things how great was his fruition, adding that the penances he had done had been a happy

---

[15] [This vision, then, occurred after October 18, 1562, the date of St. Peter's death.]

[16] Marchese, St. Peter of Alcántara's biographer, confirms this statement. Daza had been to Arenas to visit him a few days before his death and had brought him a letter from Salcedo telling of the opposition with which St. Teresa was meeting and of the reason for it. This news inspired him to write encouraging her to continue.

thing for him, since they had won him such a great reward.

As I think I have already said something about this, I will say no more here than that on this occasion he spoke to me with some severity. All he said was that I was on no account to accept any endowment and asked why I would not take his advice; he then immediately disappeared. I was astounded, and on the next day I told that gentleman what had happened, for I used to consult him about everything, as he was the person who helped us most. I told him on no account to allow the agreement about our endowment to be concluded, but to let the lawsuit continue. He was more definite about this than I and was delighted at what I said; he told me afterwards how much he had regretted having given the agreement his approval.

There then came forward another person, a zealous and devoted servant of God,[17] who suggested that, now this point was satisfactorily settled,[18] the matter should be put into the hands of learned men. This caused me a good deal of uneasiness, for some of my helpers agreed to that course and the unravelling of this tangle in which the devil now involved us was the most difficult task of all. Throughout everything the Lord helped me, but in this summary narrative it is impossible to give an adequate description of what happened in the two years between the beginning of the foundation and its completion. The first six months and the last were the most troublesome.

When the city was finally somewhat calmed, the Dominican Father-Presentado[19] who was helping us managed things for us very well. He had not previously been there, but the Lord brought him at a time which was very convenient for us,

[17] Mir (*Santa Teresa de Jesús*, Madrid, 1912, I, 559) suggests that this was P. Baltasar Alvarez, but gives insufficient evidence for the supposition, nor does any further evidence appear to exist.

[18] [This phrase, *ya que estaba en buenos términos*, presents some difficulty. Lewis translates, more or less literally, "the matter was in good train"; but, in actual fact, as the following lines make clear, it was not—only the acceptance of the endowment, it seemed, could have resolved the conflict. I take the author's meaning to be that, from her point of view, the position was clarified—there was a straight issue: she no longer had to contend with her own subconscious aversion from financial help.]

[19] P. Ibáñez.

and His Majesty seems to have done so for that end alone, for he told me afterwards that he had had no reason for coming and had only heard of the matter by accident. He stayed with us for as long as was necessary. When he left, he managed somehow—it seemed impossible that he could have done this in so short a time—to get our Father Provincial to give me leave to go and live in the new house and to take some other nuns with me so that we might say the Office and instruct the sisters who were there. It was the happiest of days for me when we went in.[20]

While at prayer in the church, before entering the convent, I all but went into a rapture, and saw Christ, Who seemed to be receiving me with great love, placing a crown on my head and thanking me for what I had done for His Mother. On another occasion, after Compline, when we were all praying in choir, I saw Our Lady in the greatest glory, clad in a white mantle, beneath which she seemed to be sheltering us all.[21] From this I learned what a high degree of glory the Lord would give to the nuns in this house.

When we had started to say the Office, the people began to be very much devoted to the convent. More nuns were received and the Lord started to move the people who had persecuted us most to help us and give us alms. So they now found themselves approving what previously they had so strongly condemned and gradually they abandoned the lawsuit and said they now realized the work was of God, since

---

[20] Despite his good will, the Provincial found certain obstacles in the way of his granting this permission, and, although apparently he did so verbally on July 3, 1563, it was not until August 22 that he was able to issue a patent giving leave to Doña Teresa de Ahumada, María Ordóñez, Ana Gómez and María de Cepeda to transfer to St. Joseph's. The Nuncio's confirmation of this patent, as far as it affected St. Teresa, was dated August 21, 1564. P. Jerónimo de San José infers from the Preface to the *Foundations* (Vol. III, p. xxi) that St. Teresa was living at St. Joseph's in December 1562 [though I do not myself think that, considering how near that convent was to the Incarnation, the words of the reference necessarily mean this]. Others think she went there in March 1563, the date given by María Pinel in her manuscript History of the Convent of the Incarnation. The earliest extant records at St. Joseph's give no help, as they date only from 1580.

[21] At one time every Discalced Carmelite convent had a picture representing this vision.

His Majesty had seen well to further it despite so much opposition. There is no one now who thinks it would have been right to give up the foundation, so they are very anxious to provide for us with their alms; and, without our making any appeals or asking anyone for money, the Lord inspires people to send it. We get on very well, then, and have no lack of necessaries; I hope in the Lord that this will be the case always. As the nuns are few in number I am sure His Majesty will never fail them if they do their duty, as at present He is giving them grace to do; nor will they ever have to be burdensome or importunate, for the Lord will take care of them as He has done until now. It is the greatest happiness to me to find myself among souls with detachment.

Their life consists in learning how to advance in the service of God. They find their greatest happiness in solitude and it troubles them to think of seeing anyone—even a near relative—unless doing so will help to enkindle them in the love of their Spouse. So none come to this house save with that aim; were they to do so it would give pleasure neither to themselves nor to the sisters. They speak only of God, and they understand no one who speaks of anything else, nor does such a person understand them. We observe the rule of Our Lady of Carmel, and we keep it without mitigation, in the form drawn up by Fray Hugo, Cardinal of Santa Sabina, and given in the year 1248, in the fifth year of the pontificate of Pope Innocent IV.

All the trials that we have suffered will, I believe, have been endured to good purpose. The rule is rather strict, for meat is never eaten except in cases of necessity, there is an eight-months' fast, and there are other ascetic practices, as may be seen in the primitive Rule. Yet many of these things seem to the sisters very light and they observe other rules which we have thought it necessary to make so that our own Rule may be kept the more perfectly. I hope in the Lord that what we have begun will prosper, as His Majesty told me it would.

The other house which the *beata* I spoke of[22] was en-

---

[22] María de Jesús. Cf. p. 331, n. 2. Having more fervour than discretion, this lady went to such lengths in the austerities which she imposed that life in her convent became impossible and in 1567 St. Teresa had to visit it in order to put things straight, which she did

deavouring to establish has also enjoyed the Lord's favour. It was founded in Alcalá and did not fail to meet with a great deal of opposition or escape severe trials. I know that all the observances of the religious life are practised in it, according to this our primitive Rule. May the Lord be pleased to direct it all to His glory and praise and to that of the glorious Virgin Mary, whose habit we wear. Amen.

I expect Your Reverence[23] will be getting impatient at the long account which I have given of this convent, though it is short enough when you remember how many trials the Lord has sent us and what marvellous things He has wrought. There are many witnesses who will be able to swear to these, so I beg Your Reverence, for the love of God, if you think it well to tear up everything else that is written here, to preserve what concerns this convent. Then, after my death, it should be given to the sisters here, for it will be a great encouragement in the service of God to those who come after us and will prevent this work that has been begun from falling to the ground and help it to prosper continually when it is seen what importance His Majesty must have attached to this house since He founded it through a creature as wicked and as base as I. And I believe myself that, as the Lord has been pleased to grant us such special help in its foundation, anyone will do great harm and be heavily punished by God who attempts to mitigate the perfection of the Rule which the Lord has initiated and encouraged here, and which works so smoothly. For it is quite evidently easy to endure and pleasant to carry out, and there is every facility for its being kept permanently by those who desire to rejoice in Christ their Spouse in solitude. This will always be the aim of our nuns— to be alone with Him only. There will not be more than thirteen of them,[24] for, after asking the opinions of many people, I have decided that that number is best, and I have seen by

---

by giving the nuns the same Constitution as that of St. Joseph's. This Alcalá convent, however, never came under the jurisdiction of the Order, which in 1599 founded a convent of its own there, known as Corpus Christi.

[23] P. García de Toledo.

[24] Later St. Teresa increased this number, as well as admitting lay sisters, of whom there were none at St. Joseph's when it was founded. To-day there are twenty-one nuns in each convent, eighteen of whom are choir-nuns.

experience that, if we are to preserve the spirituality which we now possess, and to live on alms, yet not to beg from anyone, it is impossible for us to admit more. May they always give the greatest credence to one who, with much labour and through the prayers of many, contrived to arrange things for the best. That this is the way which suits us will be evident from the great joy and gladness and the few trials which we have had during the years we have been in this house, as well as from our health, which has been far better than before. If anyone thinks the Rule a harsh one, let her blame her own lack of spirituality and not our observance; for it can be borne quite easily by people who are not in the least robust, but really delicate, if they have sufficient spirituality. Let those who have not go to some other convent, where they will find salvation and yet live according to the spirituality which they have.

CHAPTER XXXVII

Describes the effects produced upon her after the Lord had granted her any favour. Adds much sound teaching. Says how we must strive in order to attain one degree more of glory and esteem it highly and how for no trial must we renounce blessings which are everlasting.

It is painful to me to say more of the favours which the Lord has bestowed on me than I have said already; even these are so numerous that it is hard for anyone to believe they can have been granted to one as wicked as I. But in obedience to the Lord, Who has commanded me to do so, and to Your Reverences,[1] I shall speak of some of these things to His glory. May it please His Majesty that some soul shall be profited by seeing that the Lord has thus been pleased to help so wretched a creature—how much more will He help one who has served Him truly! Let us all strive to please His Majesty, since even in this life He gives such pledges as these.

First, it must be understood that, in these favours which God grants the soul, there are greater and lesser degrees of

[1] PP. Pedro Ibáñez and García de Toledo.

glory. For so far do the glory and pleasure and happiness of some visions exceed those of others that I am amazed at the diversity in fruition which is possible, even in this life. There can be so much difference between the consolations and favours given by God in a vision or in a rapture that it seems impossible there can be anything more in this life to be desired,[2] and so the soul does not desire, and would never ask for, any greater happiness. At the same time, now that the Lord has explained to me that there is a difference in Heaven between the fruition that can be experienced by one soul and by another, and shown me how great that difference is, I see clearly that here too, when the Lord is pleased so to give, there is no measure in His giving. I wish that the same were true of the service I render His Majesty, and that I employed my whole life and strength and health in this; I would have no fault of mine deprive me of the smallest degree of fruition. I can say, then, that if I were asked whether I should prefer to endure all the trials in the world until the world itself ends, and afterwards to gain a little more glory, or to have no trials and attain to one degree less of glory, I should answer that I would most gladly accept all the trials in exchange for a little more fruition in the understanding of the wonders of God, for I see that he who understands Him best loves and praises Him best.

I do not mean that I should not be pleased and think myself very happy to be in Heaven, even if I were in the lowest place there; for, as one who had merited such a place in hell, I should be receiving a great favour from the Lord if He were to grant me a place in Heaven at all: may it please His Majesty to bring me there and not to regard my grievous sins. What I mean is that, if the choice were mine, and the Lord gave me grace to endure great trials, even were it at the greatest cost to myself, I should not like to lose anything whatever through my own fault. Wretch that I am, who through my many faults had lost everything!

It should also be observed that, after every favour in the shape of a vision or a revelation which the Lord granted me,

[2] ["More to be desired than the highest of them, which are so incomparably greater than the lowest" is the meaning. As it stands, the sentence would seem to mean that the difference is between consolations and favours or between visions and raptures, but, as so often in St. Teresa, the true sense is indicated by the context.]

my soul was left with some great gain—after certain visions, with very many. After a vision of Christ there remained with me an impression of His exceeding great beauty, which I have preserved to this very day. And if one single vision sufficed to effect this, how much greater would be the power of all those which of His favour the Lord has granted me! One very great benefit which I received was this. I had a very serious fault, which led me into great trouble. It was that, if I began to realize that a person liked me, and I took to him myself, I would grow so fond of him that my memory would feel compelled to revert to him and I would always be thinking of him; without intentionally giving any offence to God, I would delight in seeing him and think about him and his good qualities. This was such a harmful thing that it was ruining my soul. But when once I had seen the great beauty of the Lord, I saw no one who by comparison with Him seemed acceptable to me or on whom my thoughts wished to dwell. For if I merely turn the eyes of my mind to the image of Him which I have within my soul, I find I have such freedom that from that time forward everything I see appears nauseating to me by comparison with the excellences and glories which I have seen in this Lord. Nor is there any knowledge or any kind of consolation to which I can attach the slightest esteem by comparison with that which it causes me to hear a single word coming from that Divine mouth—and more wonderful still is it when I hear many. And, unless for my sins the Lord allows this memory to fade, I consider it impossible for me to be so deeply absorbed in anything that I do not regain my freedom when I turn once more in thought, even for a moment, to this Lord.

This has happened to me with some of my confessors, for I always have a great affection for those who direct my soul, looking upon them as so truly in the place of God that I always like to follow their advice more than anything else. As I was feeling perfectly safe, therefore, I would show myself pleasant to them. But they, being God-fearing and God-serving men, were afraid that I might in some way become attached to them and drawn towards them—in a spiritual sense, of course—by the bonds of affection; so they would treat me quite unpleasantly. This happened after I became accustomed to obeying them; before that I had had no such affection for them. I used to laugh to myself when I saw how mistaken they were. I was not always telling them, in so many words, how little attachment I had to anybody, though secretly I knew this to be the case, but I would reassure them, and, when they got to know me better, they learned how much I owed to the Lord—for these suspicions which they had of me always came at the beginning. Once I had seen this Lord, I was so continually in converse with Him that my love for Him and trust in Him began to increase greatly. I saw that, although God, He was also Man, and is not dismayed at the weaknesses of men, for He understands our miserable nature, liable as it is to frequent falls, because of man's first sin for which He had come to make reparation. Although He is my Lord, I can talk to Him as to a friend, because He is not, I believe, like those whom we call lords on earth, all of whose power[3] rests upon an authority conferred on them by others. Such lords have fixed hours for audiences and persons whom they appoint for the purpose of speaking with them. If some poor man has business with them, he can only get it attended to by employing roundabout methods and currying favours and taking a great deal of trouble. If his business is with a king, and he is poor and not well-born, he cannot approach him directly, but has to find out who are his favourites. And you may be sure they will not be people who trample the world underfoot; for people who do that speak the truth, fear nothing and need fear nothing; they are not meant for palaces, for there they cannot do as they are wont, but must keep silence about anything they dislike and must not dare even to think about it or they will fall from favour.

O King of glory and Lord of all kings! Thy kingdom is not fenced in by trifles, but is infinite. No third party is required to obtain us an audience of Thee. We have only to look at Thy person to see at once that Thou alone deservest to be called Lord. Thou revealest Thy majesty; we need no sight of a retinue or guard to convince us that Thou art a King. An earthly king can scarcely be recognized as such in his own person; for, however much he may wish to be so recognized, no one will believe he is a king if there is nothing about him to distinguish him from others; his majesty must be seen to be

---

[3] ["Lords" is *señores*, and "power", *señorío*: there is thus a play upon words, almost as though we were to read: "lords of the earth, who *lord* it by authority."]

believed. So it is reasonable that kings should maintain this artificial authority, for, if they had none, nobody would respect them, as their appearance of power does not come from themselves and their authority must of necessity come from others. O my Lord! O my King! If one could but picture Thy majesty! It is impossible not to see that in Thyself Thou art a great Emperor, for to behold Thy majesty strikes terror. But my terror is greater, my Lord, when together with Thy majesty I behold Thy humility and the love that Thou bestowest on such a creature as I.

We can converse and speak with Thee about anything, just as we wish, when we have lost our initial fear and terror at seeing Thy majesty and acquired a deeper fear of offending Thee—but not a fear of punishment, my Lord, for that is of no account by comparison with loss of Thee! Here, then, are the benefits of this vision, setting aside other important ones which it leaves behind in the soul. If the vision is of God, its source will be recognizable by its effects, when the soul receives light—for, as I have often said, the Lord may be pleased for the soul to be in darkness and not to see this light, so it is not surprising if one who knows herself to be as wicked as I should be afraid.

Only quite recently it chanced that for a full week I was in such a condition that I seemed to have lost all sense of my debt to God and was unable to recapture it. I could not remember His favours; and my soul had become so stupid and so much occupied (I know not with what, or how: it was not that I had bad thoughts but that I was incapable of thinking any good ones) that I would laugh at myself and find it pleasant to realize how low a soul can sink when God is not forever working within it. In such a state, the soul sees clearly that it is not without God: this is not like the severe trials which I have said I sometimes experience. The soul collects wood and does all it can by itself, but finds no way of kindling the fire of the love of God. It is only by His great mercy that the smoke can be seen, which shows that the fire is not altogether dead. Then the Lord comes back and kindles it, for the soul is driving itself crazy with blowing on the fire and rearranging the wood, yet all its efforts only put out the fire more and more. I believe the best thing is for the soul to be completely resigned to the fact that of itself it can do nothing, and busy itself, as I have already suggested, in other meritorious activities, for the Lord may perhaps be depriving it of the power to pray, precisely so that it may engage in these other activities and learn by experience how little it can do of itself.

It is true that, while in converse with the Lord to-day, I have dared to complain of His Majesty. "How is it, my God," I have said to Him, "that it is not enough for Thee to keep me in this miserable life, which I endure for love of Thee, willing to live where on every hand there are obstacles to my having fruition of Thee? I have to eat, sleep, attend to my business and mix with people of every kind—and all this I endure for love of Thee. Well knowest Thou, my Lord, that this is the sorest torment to me. How few are the moments which remain to me for enjoying communion with Thee, and even during these moments Thou hidest Thyself! How does this agree with Thy mercy? How can Thy love for me endure it? Verily, Lord, I believe that, if it were possible for me to hide myself from Thee as Thou hidest Thyself from me, the love that Thou bearest me is such that Thou wouldst not endure it. But Thou art with me and seest me always. My Lord, this is not to be borne; consider, I beseech Thee, what a wrong is being done to one who so much loves Thee."

This and other things, as it chanced, I was saying, while realizing all the time how merciful was the place in hell assigned to me by comparison with the place I deserved. But sometimes love makes me foolish, so that I do not know what I am saying, and I use all the sense I have and make these complaints and the Lord bears with it all. Praised be so good a King! Should we be as bold as this in our approach to earthly kings? I am not surprised that we should not dare to speak to a king, for it is right that he and the lords who act as his representatives should be feared, but the world is now in such a condition that our lives will have to be longer than they are if we are to learn the new customs and details and methods of correct behaviour and yet spend any time in the service of God. When I see all that goes on, I can only cross myself in dismay. The fact is, when I came here[4] I did not know how I was going to live; for when we are careless and omit to treat people much better than they deserve it is not made light of, but considered as a real affront; if, as I said, we

---

[4] I.e., to St. Joseph's.

have been careless, we have to satisfy people that our intentions were good—and please God they may believe us!

Really, I repeat, I did not know how I was going to live: you could have seen that my poor soul was worn out. It hears itself being told always to occupy its thoughts with God and to be sure to keep them fixed on Him so that it may escape from all kinds of danger. On the other hand, it discovers that it must not fail to observe a single point of worldly etiquette, lest it should give offence to those who think this etiquette essential to their honour. I used to be simply worn out by all this: my attempts to satisfy people were never-ending, for, study to please them as I would, I was always making mistakes, and, as I say, these are never overlooked as being unimportant. And is it the case that in religious Orders excuses are made for all such things? It might be thought only reasonable that we should be excused from these observances. But no; they say that convents should be courts and schools of good breeding. Personally, I simply cannot understand this. It has occurred to me that some saint may have said that they ought to be courts to teach those who want to be courtiers of Heaven and that this saying may have been wrongly interpreted. But if we are careful, as it is right we should be, always to please God and to hate the world, I do not see how at the same time we can be so very careful to please those who are living in the world, in matters which are so often changing. If these things could be learned once and for all, it might be tolerable. But even for a matter like the addressing of letters we need a University professorship, and lectures would have to be given in that art, or whatever it is to be called. For in one case one part of the paper has to be left blank, and in another case, another part, and the title "Illustrious" has to be given to a man who formerly was not even described as "Magnificent".

I cannot think what we are coming to—for I am not yet fifty,[5] and even in my own short life I have seen so many changes that I have no idea how to live. What, then, will it be with those who are now being born and whose lives are still before them? I am really sorry for spiritual people who

[5] [Unless St. Teresa were mistaken about her own age—a by no means uncommon phenomenon in Spain: so modern a writer as Núñez de Arce (1832–1903) for long believed himself to be two years younger than he was—these lines must have been written before March 28, 1565.]

for certain pious reasons are obliged to live in the world: the cross they have to bear is a dreadful one. If they could all come to an agreement to remain ignorant of these sciences and be willing to be considered so, they would escape a great deal of trouble.

But what nonsense I have begun to write! I was discussing the wonders of God and I have descended so far that I am now talking about the pettinesses of the world. So, as the Lord has granted me the favour of allowing me to renounce the world, I will bring this to a close. Let those who toil over the adjustment of such trifles settle them to their own satisfaction. And pray God that in the life to come, where there are no changes, we may not have to pay dearly for them. Amen.

CHAPTER XXXVIII

Describes certain great favours which the Lord bestowed upon her, both in showing her certain heavenly secrets and in granting her other great visions and revelations which His Majesty was pleased that she should experience. Speaks of the effects which these produced upon her and of the great profit which they brought to her soul.

One night, when I was so unwell that I meant to excuse myself from mental prayer, I took a rosary, so as to occupy myself in vocal prayer, trying not to be recollected in mind, though, as I was in an oratory, I was recollected to all outward appearance. But, when the Lord wills it otherwise, such efforts are of little avail. I had been in that condition only a very short time when there came to me a spiritual impulse of such vehemence that resistance to it was impossible. I thought I was being carried up to Heaven: the first persons I saw there were my father and mother, and such great things happened in so short a time—no longer than it would take to repeat an *Ave Maria*—that I was completely lost to myself, and thought it far too great a favour. I was afraid lest it might be an illusion, but, as it did not seem to be so, I did not know what to do, for I was very much ashamed to go to my confessor about it—not, I think, because of any humility but for fear he might laugh at me and say: "What a Saint Paul she is, with her

heavenly visions! Quite a Saint Jerome!" Because these glorious saints had had visions of this kind, I was the more afraid,
and did nothing but shed copious tears, for I did not think it
possible that I had been sharing their experiences. In the end,
though feeling still worse about it, I went to see my confessor,
for, however much it troubled me to speak of such things, I
never dared to keep silence about them, so fearful was I of
being deceived. When he saw how worried I was about it,
he comforted me a great deal, and gave me a great many good
reasons for not being troubled.

With the progress of time, the Lord continued to show me
further great secrets: sometimes He does so still. The soul
may wish to see more than is pictured to it, but there is no
way in which it may do so, nor is it possible that it should;
and so I never on any occasion saw more than the Lord was
pleased to show me. What I saw was so great that the smallest
part of it was sufficient to leave my soul amazed and to do it
so much good that it esteemed and considered all the things
of this life as of little worth. I wish I could give a description
of at least the smallest part of what I learned, but, when I
try to discover a way of doing so, I find it impossible; for,
while the light we see here and that other light are both light,
there is no comparison between the two and the brightness of
the sun seems quite dull if compared with the other. In short,
however skilful the imagination may be, it will not succeed
in picturing or describing what that light is like, nor a single
one of those things which I learned from the Lord with a joy
so sovereign as to be indescribable. For all the senses rejoice
in a high degree, and with a sweetness impossible to describe,
for which reason it is better to say no more about it.

Once, when I had been for more than an hour in this state,
and the Lord had shown me wonderful things, and it seemed
as if He were not going to leave me, He said to me: "See,
daughter, what those who are against Me lose: do not fail to
tell them of it." Ah, my Lord, how little will my words profit
those who are blinded by their own actions unless Thy Majesty gives them light! Some persons to whom Thou hast given
it have profited by the knowledge of Thy wonders, but they
see them, my Lord, as revealed to a wicked and miserable
creature like myself, so that I think it will be a great thing if
there should be anyone who believes me. Blessed be Thy
name and Thy mercy, for I have found that my own soul at

least has notably improved. Afterwards I could have wished that my soul had remained in that state for ever and that I had not returned to this life, for I was left with a great contempt for everything earthly. It seemed to me like dung and I see how base are the occupations of those of us who are detained here below.

It happened on one occasion while I was staying with that lady whom I have mentioned,[1] and I was troubled with my heart (as I have said, I have suffered with this a great deal, though less so of late), that, being an extremely kind person, she had some very valuable golden trinkets and stones brought out for me, and in particular a set of diamonds, supposed to be of great price, thinking that they would cheer me. But I only laughed to myself, thinking what a pity it is that people esteem such things, remembering what the Lord has laid up for us and reflecting how impossible it would be for me to set any store by these things, even if I tried to make myself do so, unless the Lord were to allow me to forget those others.

The soul that feels like this has great dominion over itself— so great that I do not know if it can be understood by anyone who does not possess it, for it is a real, natural detachment, achieved without labour of our own. It is all effected by God, for, when His Majesty reveals these truths, they are so deeply impressed upon our souls as to show us clearly that we could not in so short a time acquire them ourselves. I was also left with very little fear of death, of which previously I had been very much afraid. Now it seems to me very easy for one who serves God, for in a moment the soul finds itself freed from this prison and at rest. This experience, in which God bears away the spirit in these transports and shows it such excellent things, seems to me very much like that in which a soul leaves the body; for it finds itself in possession of all these good things in a single instant. We may leave out of account the pains of the moment of its flight, to which no great importance need be attached: to those who love God in truth and have put aside the things of this world death must come very gently.

I think, too, that this experience has been of great help to me in teaching me where our true home is and in showing me that on earth we are but pilgrims; it is a great thing to see

[1] Doña Luisa de la Cerda.

what is awaiting us there and to know where we are going to live. For if a person has to go and settle in another country, it is a great help to him in bearing the trials of the journey if he has found out that it is a country where he will be able to live in complete comfort. It also makes it easy for us to die if we think upon heavenly things and try to have our conversation in Heaven. This is a great advantage for us: merely to look up towards the heavens makes the soul recollected, for, as the Lord has been pleased to reveal some part of what is there, the thought dwells upon it. It sometimes happens that those with whom I keep company, and whose presence comforts me, are those who I know live in Heaven: they, it seems to me, are the people who are really alive, while those who live on earth are so dead that it seems as if there is no one in the whole world who can be a companion to me, especially when those vehement impulses come upon me.

Everything I see is like a dream and what I see with my bodily eyes is a mockery. What my soul desires is what I have seen with the eyes of the soul; and, finding itself so far away from it all, it desires death. In short, this is a very great favour that the Lord grants to those on whom He bestows such visions, for by so doing He helps them greatly, yet at the same time gives them a heavy cross to carry, for all the things they have are powerless to satisfy them, but are simply impediments. If the Lord were not sometimes to allow these visions to be forgotten (though later they return to the remembrance), I do not know how one could live. Blessed be He and praised for ever and ever! May His Majesty grant, by the blood which His Son shed for me, that, seeing He has been pleased to give me some understanding of these great blessings, and I have in some degree begun to enjoy them, I may not share the fate of Lucifer, who by his own fault lost everything. For His own sake may He not allow this: sometimes I have no little fear that He will, although, as a general rule, the mercy of God gives me assurance, for, as He has delivered me from so many sins, He will not let me out of His hand and permit me to be lost. I beg Your Reverence to beg this of Him for me always.

The favours I have already mentioned are not, I think, as great as one which I shall now describe, for many reasons and because of the great blessings which it has bestowed on me, together with great fortitude of soul, although each of these favours, considered by itself, is so great that there is nothing with which it can be compared.[2]

One day—it was the vigil of Pentecost—I went, after Mass, to a very solitary spot,[3] where I used often to say my prayers, and began to read about this festival in the Carthusian's *Life of Christ*.[4] As I read about the signs by which beginners, proficients and perfect may know if the Holy Spirit is with them, it seemed to me, when I had read about these three states, that by the goodness of God, and so far as I could understand, He was certainly with me then. For this I praised God and remembered a previous occasion when I had read this passage and when I lacked much that I now have; this I saw very clearly, and, as I became aware how different I am now, I realized what a great favour the Lord had granted me. So I began to meditate on the place in hell which I deserved for my sins, and I gave great praises to God, for so changed was my life that I seemed not to recognize my own soul. While I was meditating in this way a strong impulse seized me without my realizing why. It seemed as if my soul were about to leave the body, because it could no longer contain itself and was incapable of waiting for so great a blessing. The impulse was so exceedingly strong that it made me quite helpless. It was different, I think, from those which I had experienced on other occasions, and I did not know what was the matter with my soul, or what it wanted, so changed was it. I had to seek some physical support, for so completely did my natural strength fail me that I could not even remain seated.

While in this condition, I saw a dove over my head, very

---

[2] [Cf. Translator's Preface, p. 21.]

[3] Anxious to make the life of the Reform as similar as possible to that of the primitive Carmelites, St. Teresa had a number of hermitages made at St. Joseph's, Avila and her other foundations. At the time of her Beatification there were four of these in the garden of St. Joseph's and one within the convent itself. To-day, also, there are four, but in the shape of divisions of a single building.

[4] The *Life of Christ*, written in Latin by Ludolph of Saxony, a Carthusian, was translated into Spanish by Ambrosio de Montesinos about 1502 under the title *Vita Christi cartuxano*. It is one of the books which St. Teresa recommends to her nuns in her Constitutions (Vol. III, p. 220). It is often referred to as "the Carthusian" and its two parts as "the first" and "the second Carthusian" respectively.

different from those we see on earth, for it had not feathers like theirs but its wings were made of little shells which emitted a great brilliance. It was larger than a dove; I seemed to hear the rustling of its wings. It must have been fluttering like this for the space of an *Ava Maria*. But my soul was in such a state that, as it became lost to itself, it also lost sight of the dove. My spirit was calmed by so gracious a guest, though I think it must have been disturbed and alarmed at experiencing this marvellous favour; as it began to rejoice in it, however, its fear left it, and with its joy came a return of its tranquillity, and it remained in rapture.

The glory of this rapture was surpassingly great; for most of the festal season I was so bewildered and stupid that I did not know what to do or how I could be capable of receiving so great a favour and grace. It was as if I could neither hear nor see, so great was my inward joy. From that time forward I became conscious of the greatest progress in the highest love of God and of a very great strengthening in virtue. May He be blessed and praised for ever. Amen.

On another occasion I saw the same dove over the head of a Father of the Order of Saint Dominic, though I thought the rays and the brightness of its wings extended much farther. I took this to mean that he was to draw souls to God.

On another occasion I saw Our Lady putting a pure white cope on a Presentado of this same Order of whom I have several times spoken.[5] She told me that she was giving him that vestment because of the service he had rendered her in helping in the foundation of this house, and as a sign that from that time forward his soul would remain pure and that he would not fall into mortal sin. I am sure that this came true, for a few years later he died, and both his death and the last years of his life were marked by such penitence, and his life and death were so holy, that, as far as one can understand, there is no possibility of doubt about it. A friar who had been present when he died informed me that, before passing away, he had told him that Saint Thomas was with him. He died with great joy and with a longing to depart from this exile.[6]

[5] According to Gracián's notes, both this and the preceding paragraph refer to P. Ibáñez.

[6] P. Báñez adds in a marginal note: "This Father died Prior of Trianos." The note confirms Gracián's statement just quoted. [It also helps to fix the date of the book, as P. Ibáñez died on February

Since then he has several times appeared to me in very great glory and told me a number of things. He was such a man of prayer that although, before he died, he was so weak that he would have liked to cease praying, he was so often in rapture that he could not do so. Shortly before his death, he wrote to me to ask what he ought to do; for no sooner had he finished saying Mass than he would go for a long time into rapture and was quite unable to prevent himself from doing so. In the end, God gave him the reward of the many services which he had rendered Him during his whole life.

With regard to the Rector of the Company of Jesus, whom I have already mentioned several times,[7] I have had a number of visions of the great favours which the Lord was bestowing upon him, but, lest I should write at too great length, I am not setting them down here. It once happened that he was in great trouble, having been sorely persecuted and finding himself in great distress. One day, when I was hearing Mass, at the elevation of the Host I saw Christ on the Cross. He spoke certain words to me, which He told me to repeat to the Rector for his comfort, and He added other things to warn him of what was to come and to remind him of what He had suffered for him and how he too must prepare to suffer. This brought him great comfort and gave him courage and everything has since happened as the Lord told me it would.

Concerning the members of the Order to which this Father belongs—namely, the Company of Jesus[8]—and of the entire Order itself, I have seen great things. On several occasions I

2, 1565. Taken in conjunction with the reference to St. Teresa's age (p. 359) it seems to give us almost the exact date of the composition of these final chapters.] But cf. p. 58.

[7] Gracián and María de San José assert that P. Álvarez is meant, but more probably the reference is to P. Gaspar de Salazar.

[8] Luis de León, in the *editio princeps*, altered this phrase to read: "Concerning those of a certain Order." A reason suggested for this is that in Chap. XL St. Teresa says that she does not name particular Orders, for fear of invidiousness, and that Fray Luis thought this to be an oversight. In another place, however, he leaves intact a reference to Dominicans and Franciscans and in the next line deletes one to St. Ignatius and his Society. The suppressions are more probably attributable to the strained relations existing between the Society and, on the one hand, certain religious Orders; on the other, the University of Salamanca. The correct reading in this present passage was restored by the Discalced Carmelites in their edition of 1627.

saw these Fathers in Heaven with white banners in their hands, and, as I say, I have seen other things concerning them which give cause for great wonder. Thus I hold this Order in great veneration, for I have had a great deal to do with its members and I see that their lives are in conformity with what the Lord has given me to understand about them.

One night, when I was at prayer, the Lord began to talk to me. He reminded me how wicked my life had been and made me feel very much confused and distressed; for, although He did not speak severely, His words caused me to be consumed with distress and sorrow. A single word of this kind makes a person more keenly aware of his advance in self-knowledge than do many days spent in meditating upon his own wretchedness, for it bears a stamp of truth the reality of which none can deny. He pictured to me the earlier movements of my will, showed me how vain they had been, and told me that I must prize the desire that I now had to fix upon Him a will which had spent itself as foolishly as mine had done, and that He would accept this desire. On other occasions He told me to remember how I used to think it honourable to oppose His honour. On others, again, to remember what I owed Him, for even when I was dealing Him the cruellest of blows, He was bestowing favours upon me. When I am committing any faults—and my faults are not few—His Majesty makes me so conscious of them that I feel entirely confused with shame, and so numerous are they that this happens often. Sometimes it has chanced that my confessor has rebuked me, and, when I have tried to find comfort in prayer, I have been soundly rebuked there as well.

Let me now return to what I was saying. As the Lord began to remind me of the wickedness of my past life, and in the midst of the tears which I shed at having till then, as I thought, achieved nothing, I wondered if He was about to show me some favour. For it is quite usual for the Lord to grant me some special favour after I have been beside myself with shame, so that I may the better realize how far I am from deserving it; I think this must be the Lord's doing. Soon after this, my spirit became so completely transported that it seemed to have departed almost wholly from the body: or, at least, there was no way of telling that it was in the body. I saw the most sacred Humanity in far greater glory than I had ever seen before. I saw a most clear and wonderful representation of it in the bosom of the Father. I cannot possibly explain how this happened, but, without seeing anything, I seemed to see myself in the presence of the Godhead. I was amazed, so much so that I believe several days must have gone by before I was completely myself again. I seemed all the time to have present with me that Majesty of the Son of God, although not in the same way as in the first vision. This I was quite well able to understand, but it remained so indelibly stamped upon my imagination that for some time, quickly as it passed, I could not rid myself of it: it is a wonderful comfort to me and it also does me a great deal of good.

I have beheld this same vision on three other occasions: I think it is the sublimest vision which the Lord has granted me grace to see, and it brings with it the greatest benefits. It appears to have a wonderfully purifying effect upon the soul and almost entirely destroys the power of our sensual nature. It is a great flame, which seems to burn up and annihilate all life's desires; for, although—glory be to God!—I had no desires for vain things, I was clearly shown here how everything was vanity, and how vain, how completely vain, are all worldly dignities. This is a wonderful way of teaching the soul to lift up its desires in purity of truth. It impresses on it a sense of reverence which I cannot possibly describe, but which is very different from anything that we can acquire on earth. The soul becomes astounded when it remembers that it has dared to offend His exceeding great Majesty and that there is anyone else who can dare to do the same.

I must have spoken several times of these effects produced by visions and other experiences of that kind, but, as I have already said, there are greater and lesser degrees of profit to be extracted from them, and it is this kind of vision that causes the greatest profit of all. Whenever I approached the altar to communicate, and remembered that exceeding great Majesty which I had seen, and considered that it was He Who was in the Most Holy Sacrament and that the Lord was often pleased that I should see Him in the Host, my hair would stand on end and I would feel completely annihilated. O my Lord! Didst Thou not cloak Thy greatness, who would dare to come so often to the union of such foulness and wretchedness with such great Majesty? Blessed be Thou, Lord. Let the angels and all creatures praise Thee, Who measurest things by our weakness, so that, while we are rejoicing in Thy sovereign favours, we may not be so much affrighted by Thy great power as not to dare, because we are weak and miserable creatures, to rejoice in those favours.

We might have the same experience as a certain peasant—and this is a thing which I know actually happened. He found some treasure, much more valuable than his dull mind was capable of grasping; and the mere possession of it gradually brought on a melancholy, so that eventually he died of pure distress and worry because he had no idea what to do with it. If he had not found it all at once, but had been given it by degrees, so that he could have lived upon it, he would have been happier than when he was poor and it would not have cost him his life.

O Wealth of the poor, how wonderfully canst Thou sustain souls, revealing Thy great riches to them gradually and not permitting them to see them all at once! Since the time of that vision I have never seen such great Majesty, hidden in a thing so small as the Host, without marvelling at Thy great wisdom. I cannot tell how the Lord gives me courage or strength to approach Him; I only know that it is bestowed on me by Him Who has granted me, and still grants me, such great favours. I could never possibly conceal this or refrain from proclaiming aloud such great marvels. What must be the feelings of a wretch like myself, weighed down with abominations, who has gone through life with so little fear of God, when she finds herself approaching this Lord of such Majesty, Whose will it is that my soul shall see Him? How can I open my mouth, which has uttered so many words against this same Lord, to receive that most glorious Body, full of purity and compassion? For the soul, knowing that it has not served Him, is much more grieved and afflicted by the love shining in that face of such great beauty, so kindly and so tender, than it is affrighted by the Majesty which it sees in Him.

What, then, must my feelings have been on two occasions when I saw the things that I shall now describe? Indeed, my Lord and my Glory, I am going to say that in some measure these great afflictions experienced by my soul have resembled acts performed in Thy service. Ah, I know not what I am saying, for I am writing this almost as though I were not myself speaking: I find I am troubled, and even somewhat distraught, as I recall these things to my memory. If these feelings really came from me, my Lord, I might well say that I had done something for Thee, but, as there can be no good thoughts unless Thou givest them, no thanks for them can be due to me. I, Lord, am the debtor, and it is Thou Who hast been offended.

Once, when I was about to communicate, I saw, with the eyes of the soul, more clearly than ever I could with those of the body, two devils of most hideous aspect. Their horns seemed to be around the poor priest's throat; and when I saw my Lord, with the Majesty which I have described, in the hands of such a man, in the Host which he was about to give me, I knew for a certainty that those hands had offended Him and realized that here was a soul in mortal sin. What must it be, my Lord, to see that beauty of Thine between two such hideous forms? In Thy presence they seemed so cowed and terrified that I think they would gladly have fled, hadst Thou allowed them to go. This upset me so much that I do not know how I was able to communicate, and I was sore afraid, for, I thought, had it been a vision from God, His Majesty would not have allowed me to see the evil that was in that soul. Then the Lord Himself told me to pray for him and said He had allowed me to see this so that I might realize what power there was in the words of consecration, and that, however wicked the priest who pronounces those words may be, God is always present without fail. He wanted me also to appreciate His great goodness in placing Himself in the hands of that enemy of His, and this solely for my good and for the good of all. This showed me clearly how much stricter is the obligation laid upon priests to be virtuous than upon other people, and what a terrible thing it is to take this Most Holy Sacrament unworthily, and how complete is the devil's dominion over the soul that is in mortal sin. It was of the very greatest help to me and gave me the fullest knowledge of what I owe to God. May He be blessed for ever and ever.

On another occasion something else of this kind happened to me which gave me a bad fright. I was in a place where a certain person had died after leading for many years, as I knew, a very bad life. But for two years he had been ill and in some respects seemed to have mended his ways. He died without making his confession, but in spite of all this I did not myself think he would be damned. While his body was being wrapped in its shroud, I saw a great many devils taking hold of it and apparently playing with it and treating it roughly. I was horrified at this: they were dragging it about in turn with large hooks. When I saw it being taken to burial with the same honour and ceremony that is paid to all dead persons, I kept thinking upon the goodness of God Who would not allow that soul to be dishonoured but permitted the fact of its having been His enemy to be concealed.

After what I had seen I was half crazy. During the whole of the funeral office I saw no more devils; but afterwards, when the body was laid in the grave, there was such a crowd of them waiting there to take possession of it that I was beside myself at the sight and had need of no little courage to hide the fact. If they were taking possession like this of the unfortunate body, I reflected, what would they do with the soul? Would to God that this frightful thing which I saw could be seen by everyone who is leading an evil life! I think it would be a great incentive to amendment. All this makes me realize better what I owe to God and what He has saved me from. Until I had talked to my confessor about it I was terribly frightened, wondering if it were an illusion produced by the devil to dishonour that person's soul, though he was not considered to be a very good Christian. In any case, illusion or no, the very remembrance of it always makes me afraid.

Now that I have begun to talk of visions about the dead, I will refer to some matters, in connection with certain souls, which the Lord has been pleased to reveal to me. For brevity's sake and because they are not necessary—for our profit, I mean—I will describe only a few of them. I was told of the death of a former Provincial of ours—at the time of his death he was Provincial of another province—whom I had had to do with and had reason to be grateful to for several kindnesses.[9] He had been a person of many virtues. When I heard of his death, I was greatly perturbed, for I was fearful about his salvation, as he had been a superior for twenty years—this always causes me misgivings, for it seems to me a very dangerous thing to have the charge of souls. So, greatly distressed, I went to an oratory. There I offered on his behalf all the good

[9] This could not be P. Salazar, who was still alive when the book was completed. It may be P. Gregorio Fernández (p. 306), whom we know to have been Prior of Ávila in 1541 and Provincial in 1551–3 and 1559–61.

I had done in my whole life, which must have been very little, and then I begged the Lord to make up the deficiency for that soul with His own merits so as to deliver it from purgatory.

While I was praying to the Lord for him to the best of my ability, he seemed to me to rise up, on my right hand, from the depths of the earth, and I saw him ascend to Heaven with the greatest joy. He had actually been very old, but, as I saw him then, he seemed to be about thirty, or even less, and his face was bright and shining. This vision passed very quickly, but I was so wonderfully comforted that I could never again grieve about his death, although I found people greatly distressed by it, for he was very much loved. So greatly was my soul comforted that nothing troubled me and I could not doubt that this was a genuine vision—I mean, that it was no illusion. He had not been dead more than a fortnight at the time; none the less, I did not cease trying to get people to commend him to God and to do so myself, except that I could not pray with the same fervour as if I had not seen this vision; for, once the Lord had revealed him to me in that way, I could not help feeling that to want to commend him to His Majesty was like giving alms to a rich man. I heard later about the kind of death which the Lord granted him—for he died a long way from here. It was one which caused me great edification; he was in such complete possession of his faculties when he died, and so repentant and humble, that everyone was astounded.

A nun who had been a great servant of God had died in our house,[10] and rather more than a day and a half later there occurred the following incident. The office for the departed was being said for her in choir; a nun was reading the lesson; and I was standing there to assist her with the versicle. Halfway through the lesson I saw the dead sister: her soul seemed to be rising on my right hand, as in the preceding vision, and to be going up to Heaven. This was not an imaginary vision, as the last had been, but was like the others to which I have referred already. There is no more reason for doubting it, however, than for doubting visions which are seen.

---

[10] This must refer to the Incarnation, for, when these lines were written, all the nuns of St. Joseph's were still living. There are independent testimonies to this occurrence.

Another nun who died in this same house of mine was about eighteen to twenty years old. She had always had poor health; and she served God well and was fond of choir and very virtuous. I certainly thought she would not have to go to purgatory, for not only had she suffered much from illness but she had superabundant merits. About four hours after her death, while the Hours were being said before she was buried, I perceived her in the same place, ascending to Heaven.

Once I was in a college of the Company of Jesus, suffering severely in soul and body, as I have said I sometimes used to, and still do, to such an extent that I was hardly capable of thinking a single good thought. On that night a brother of that house of the Company had died[11]; and, while I was commending him to God as well as I was able, and hearing a Mass which was being said for him by another Father of the Company, I became deeply recollected and saw him ascending to Heaven in great glory, and the Lord ascending with him. I understood that it was by a special favour that His Majesty bore him company.

Another friar of our Order—a very good friar—was extremely ill[12]; and while I was at Mass I became recollected and saw that he was dead and was ascending into Heaven without passing through purgatory. He had died, as I afterwards heard, at the very hour at which I saw him. I was amazed that he had not gone to purgatory. I learned that, as he had been a friar who had faithfully observed his Rule, the Bulls of the Order had been of avail to save him from going there. I do not know why I was allowed to learn this: I think it must have been to teach me that being a friar does not consist in a habit—I mean, in the wearing of the habit—and that this does not in itself imply the state of greatest perfection, which is that of a friar.

I will say no more of these matters, for, as I have said, it is unnecessary for me to do so, though the Lord has granted me the favour of seeing a great many such things. But from none of the visions that I have seen have I ever gathered that any

[11] This was Alonso de Henao, who had come from the Jesuit College at Alcalá and died on April 11, 1557.

[12] "Fray Matía," says Gracián's note. His full name was Diego (de San) Matías; for some time he was confessor at the Incarnation.

soul has escaped purgatory save the souls of this Father, of the saintly Fray Peter of Alcántara and of the Dominican Father whom I have mentioned.[13] The Lord has been pleased that I should see the degrees of glory to which some persons have been raised and has shown them to me in the places which have been assigned to them. There is a great difference between some of these places and others.

CHAPTER XXXIX

Continues the same subject and tells of the great favours which the Lord has shown her. Describes His promises to her on behalf of persons for whom she might pray to Him. Tells of some outstanding respects in which His Majesty has granted her this favour.

I was once earnestly importuning the Lord to give sight to a person to whom I was under a certain obligation and who was almost entirely blind; I was very sorry for him and feared that the Lord would not hear me because of my sins. He appeared to me as on former occasions, began by showing me the wound in His left hand, and then, with the other hand, drew out a large nail which was embedded in it, in such a way that in drawing out the nail He seemed to me to be tearing the flesh. It was clear how very painful this must be and I was sorely grieved at it. Then He said to me that surely, if He had borne that for me, He would even more readily do whatever I asked Him; that He promised me I should never ask Him anything which He would not grant; that He knew I should never ask anything that did not tend to His glory; and that therefore He would do what I was now asking of Him. I must remember, He added, that, even in the days when I did not serve Him, I had never asked Him for anything which He had not granted in a better way than I could have planned; how much more readily still would He not do it now that He knew I loved Him? Of that I must have no doubt. I do not think a full week had passed before the Lord restored that person's sight. My confessor heard of it at once. It may not,

13 P. Ibáñez.

of course, have been due to my prayer; but, as I had seen this vision, I felt certain that it was a favour granted to me and I gave His Majesty thanks for it.

On another occasion there was a person[1] very ill with a most painful malady, which, as I do not know its exact nature, I shall not now describe. His sufferings for two months had been intolerable and he was in such torture that he would lacerate his own body. My confessor, the Rector I have mentioned, who went to see him, was very sorry for him and told me that I must certainly pay him a visit—and it was possible for me to do this, as he was a relative of mine. I went and was moved to such pity for him that I began with great importunity to beg the Lord to cure him. This showed me clearly the way in which, as I firmly believe, He favours me, for, on the very next day, my relative was completely free from that pain.

I was once in the deepest affliction because I learned that a person to whom I was under great obligations wanted to do something which militated grievously against God and His honour and was firmly resolved that he would. I was so worried about this that I did not know what means I could employ to dissuade him: it seemed, in fact, that there were none. I besought God from the bottom of my heart to give me some such means, but until I found them I could get no relief from my distress. While things were in that position, I went to a very lonely hermitage, of which this convent has a number, and which contains a representation of Christ bound to the Column, and there I begged Him to grant me this favour. Then I heard a very soft voice, speaking to me, as it were, in a whisper. My whole body quivered with fear and I tried to catch what the voice was saying, but I could not, and very soon it was gone. My fear quickly left me, and, when it had passed, I experienced a calm, a joy and an inward delight, and it amazed me that the mere hearing of a voice with the bodily ears, unaccompanied by any understanding of what it said, should have such an effect upon the soul. I saw by this that what I was asking of God was to be granted me, and, although this had not then been done, my distress was as completely removed as if it had been. I told my con-

[1] "Her cousin, Pedro Mexía", according to Gracián.

fessors of it—for at that time I had two, very learned men and servants of God.[2]

There was someone who I knew had resolved to serve God in very truth; for some days he had been engaged in prayer, in the course of which His Majesty had granted him many favours. But certain occasions of sin then presented themselves and, instead of withdrawing himself from these occasions of sin, which were very perilous, he gave up his prayer. This caused me the greatest distress, for he was a person whom I dearly loved and to whom I was much indebted. I believe more than a month passed during which I did nothing but beg God to turn this soul to Himself. One day, when I was at prayer, I saw beside me a devil, in a great fury, tearing up some papers which he held in his hand. This brought me great comfort, for I thought it meant that what I had been praying for was granted me. And so it was, for I afterwards learned that this man had made a very contrite confession and had so truly turned to God that I hope in His Majesty that he will make continual progress. Blessed be He for everything! Amen.

In answer to my supplications Our Lord has frequently delivered souls from grave sins, and has led others to greater perfection. As to rescuing souls from purgatory and doing other such notable things, the favours which He has granted me here are so numerous that I should be fatiguing myself, and fatiguing the reader too, if I were to describe them. Many more of them have concerned the health of the soul than the health of the body. This fact has been generally recognized and there have been numerous witnesses to it. It used to cause me great scruples, for I could not help believing that the Lord was doing this because of my prayers —apart, of course, from the chief reason, which is His pure goodness. But now these favours have become so numerous and have been observed by so many people that it causes me no distress to believe this. I praise His Majesty and I grow ashamed, because I see I am more His debtor than ever, and I believe He increases my desires to serve Him and revives my love for Him. What astonishes me most has to do with favours which the Lord sees are not good for me: even if I try to do so, I am unable to beg Him to grant me these; when I

[2] PP. Báñez and García de Toledo.

attempt it, my prayers have very little power or spirituality or concentration; and, however much I try to force myself to do more, I cannot. Yet, when it comes to other things which His Majesty means to grant, I find that I can ask for these often and with great importunity, and though I may not be specially thinking of them they seem to come to my mind.

There is a great difference between these two ways of praying, which I do not know how to explain. When I pray for the first kind of favour, I may persist in forcing myself to beg the Lord for it, yet, even if it is a thing which touches me nearly, I do not feel that I have the same fervour as in praying for the other kind. I am like a person whose tongue is tied: desire to speak as he may, he cannot, or if he does so he cannot make himself understood. In the other case I am like a person speaking clearly and alertly to someone whom he sees to be eagerly listening to him. The first type of prayer, we might say, is like vocal prayer; the other is like contemplation so sublime that the Lord reveals Himself, and so we know His Majesty is hearing us and rejoicing at what we are asking of Him and delighting to bestow it upon us. May He be blessed for ever, Who gives so much when I give Him so little. For what can a man accomplish, my Lord, who does not wholly abase himself for Thy sake?[3] How far—oh, how far, how very far! I could say it a thousand times—am I from doing this! It is because I am not living as I should, in view of what I owe Thee, that I cannot desire to live at all, though there are other reasons for this also. How many imperfections do I find in myself! How feebly do I serve Thee! Sometimes I could really wish I were devoid of sense, for then I should not understand how much evil is in me. May He Who is able to do so grant me succour!

While I was in the house of that lady whom I have mentioned,[4] I had to be careful of my behaviour and constantly bear in mind the vanity inseparable from everything in this life, because of the high esteem and the great praise which were bestowed on me and the numerous things to which, had I looked only to myself, I might have become attached. But He Who sees things in their true light looked favourably upon me and suffered me not to escape out of His hand.

[3] [An untranslatable play upon words: the two verbs are "do" (*hace*) and "undo" (*deshace*).]
[4] Doña Luisa de la Cerda.

Speaking of seeing things in their true light, I call to mind the great trials which have to be borne in their dealings with others by persons to whom God has given a knowledge of what is meant by truth in earthly matters; for on earth, as the Lord once said to me, there is so much dissembling. Much that I am writing here does not come out of my own head; I have been told it by this Heavenly Master of mine; and so, in places where I distinctly say "I was told this" or "The Lord told me", I am extremely scrupulous about adding or subtracting so much as a single syllable. When I do not remember everything exactly, then, it must be understood that it comes from me and some of the things I say will come from me altogether. Anything that is good I do not attribute to myself, for I know there is nothing good in me save what the Lord has given me without my deserving it. When I say that a thing has "come from me", I mean that it was not told me in a revelation.

But, O my God, how is it that even in spiritual matters we often try to interpret things in our own way, as if they were worldly things, and distort their true meaning? We think we can measure our progress by the number of years during which we have been practising prayer. We even seem to be trying to set a measure to Him Who bestows on us measureless gifts, and Who can give more to one person in six months than to another in many years. This is something which I have so often observed, and in so many people, that I am amazed to find we can act so pettily.

I am quite sure that no one will be deceived in this way for long if he has a gift for the discernment of spirits and if the Lord has given him true humility: such a person will judge these spirits by their fruits and their resolutions and their love, and the Lord will give him light to recognize these. What He considers here is not the years which people have spent in prayer but the extent to which their souls have advanced and made progress; for one soul can attain as much in six months as another in twenty years, since, as I say, the Lord gives to whom He wills and also to him who is best prepared to receive. I find at present that among those coming to this convent are a number of girls, quite young in years.[5] God touches their hearts and gives them a little light

---

[5] St. Teresa may be thinking of Francisco de Cepeda's daughter, who professed on October 21, 1564, as Isabel de San Pablo, at the

and love—I mean, during some short period in which He has granted them consolation in prayer. They have not been expecting this and they put aside every other consideration, forgetting even their meals, and shut themselves up for good in a convent that has no money, like people who make no account of their lives for the sake of Him Who they know loves them. They give up everything; they have no wish to follow their own desires; and it never occurs to them that they may grow discontented in a place so circumscribed and so strictly enclosed. They offer themselves wholly, as a sacrifice, to God.

How glad I am to admit that they are better than I and how ashamed of myself I ought to be in God's presence! For what His Majesty has not consummated in me during the many years that have elapsed since I began to pray and He began to grant me favours, He consummates in them in three months—sometimes even in three days—though, while amply rewarding them, His Majesty gives them far fewer favours than He gives me. They have most certainly no cause to be dissatisfied with what they have done for Him.

For this reason I should like those of us who have been professed for many years, as well as others who have spent long years in the practice of prayer, to retrace that period in their memories. I have no desire, however, to distress those who in a short time have made more progress than ourselves by making them turn back and go at our own pace, or to make those who, thanks to the favours given them by God, are soaring like eagles move like hens with their feet tied. Let us rather fix our eyes on His Majesty, and, if we see that these souls are humble, give them the reins; the Lord, who is showing them so many favours, will not allow them to fling themselves down a precipice. They themselves put their trust in God and their trust makes the truth which they know through faith of avail to them. Shall not we, then, trust them too, instead of trying to measure them by our own standards, which are determined by the pettiness of our spirits? That we must never do: if we cannot produce fruits and resolutions equal to theirs, which cannot be properly understood except

___

age of seventeen. Three other young girls—María Bautista, María de San Jerónimo and Isabel de Santo Domingo—took the habit in 1563-4.

by experience, let us humble ourselves and not condemn them. For, by our apparent regard for their profit, we shall be impeding our own, as well as losing this opportunity, sent us by the Lord, of humbling ourselves and understanding our own faults; and we shall fail to realize how much more detached and how much nearer to God these souls must be than our own since His Majesty is drawing so near to them.

My only intention here—and I do not wish to suggest that I have any other—is to explain why I value prayer which has lasted for only a short time and yet is producing fruits so notable and so quickly apparent; for we cannot resolve to leave everything, in order to please God, without great potency of love. I prefer this to prayer which has continued for many years, but which, neither first nor last, produces any more resolutions to do things for God than a few of no weight or bulk, like grains of salt, which a bird might carry in its beak, and which we cannot consider as fruits of prayer or signs of great mortification. Sometimes we attribute importance to things we do for the Lord which, however numerous they may be, cannot fairly be so considered. I am like that myself—and I forget His favours at every moment. I do not say that His Majesty will not value the services I have rendered Him, since He is so gracious, but I have no wish to set store by them myself, or even to notice it when I do them, since they are nothing. Forgive me, then, my Lord, and blame me not if I try to take comfort from anything I do, since I am of no real service to Thee: if I served Thee in great matters, I should set no store by these nothingnesses. Blessed are they who serve Thee by doing great deeds. If I could accomplish anything by merely envying them and desiring to imitate them I should not be backward in pleasing Thee. But I am of no worth, my Lord. Do Thou put worth into what I do, since Thou hast such love for me.

One day, after I had obtained a Brief from Rome empowering me to found this convent without providing any revenue for it,[6] and the whole business, which I think really cost me some trouble, had been brought to a conclusion, I was feeling glad that it had been accomplished in this way and think-

---

[6] This Brief was dated July 17, 1565. [If it took as long as its predecessor (p. 339, n. 1) to reach Ávila, these lines cannot have been written before the very end of December 1565. But it may, of course, have come more quickly. Cf. p. 59.]

ing over the trials which it had cost me, and praising the Lord for having been pleased to make some use of me. Then I began to think of the things which I had gone through. And it is a fact that in every action of mine which I thought had been of some value I found any number of faults and imperfections. In some of them, too, I discovered signs of faint-heartedness, and in many of them a lack of faith. I can see now that all the Lord told me would happen with regard to this house has been accomplished, but previously I had never been able to bring myself resolutely to believe that it would be so, and yet I could not doubt that it would either. I cannot explain this. But the position is that while, on the one hand, it seemed to me impossible, on the other I could not doubt it—I mean, I could not believe that it would not turn out as the Lord had said. Eventually I found that He, on His side, had done all the good things, and I had done all the bad things, and so I stopped thinking about it; and I have no further desire to remember it lest I should recall to mind all my faults. Blessed be He Who, when such is His will, brings good out of them all! Amen.

As I say, then, it is dangerous to keep counting the years during which we have practised prayer, for, even though we may do so with humility, it is a habit which seems to leave us with a feeling that we have won some merit by serving God. I do not mean that our service is devoid of merit or that it will not be well rewarded; but any spiritual person who thinks that the mere number of years he has practised prayer has earned him these spiritual consolations will, I am certain, fail to reach the summit of spirituality. Is it not enough that God has thought him worthy to be taken by His hand and kept from the offences which he used to commit before he practised prayer? Must he sue God, as we say, for his money's worth? This does not seem to me very deep humility; I should rather call it presumption. My own humility is little enough, yet I do not think I have ever dared to do such a thing. It may be, however, that I have never asked because I have never served Him; if I had, perhaps I should have been more anxious than anyone else for the Lord to recompense me.

I do not mean that, if a soul has been humble in its prayer, it does not make progress, or that God will not grant us progress: what I mean is that we should forget the number of years we have served Him, for the sum total of all we can do is worthless by comparison with a single drop of the blood which the Lord shed for us. And if, the more we serve Him, the more deeply we fall into His debt, what is it we are asking, since, when we pay a farthing of our debt, He gives us back a thousand ducats? For the love of God, let us leave all this to Him to judge, for judgment is His. Comparisons of this kind are always bad, even in earthly matters: what, then, will they be in questions of which only God has knowledge? And this His Majesty clearly showed when He gave the same payment to the last workers as to the first.[7]

It has taken me such a long time to write all this (the last three sheets have taken as many days, for, as I have said, I have had, and still have, little opportunity for writing) that I had forgotten what I had begun to describe—namely, the following vision. While I was at prayer, I saw myself in a great field, all alone, and around me there was such a multitude of all kinds of people that I was completely surrounded by them. They all seemed to have weapons in their hands for the purpose of attacking me: some had lances; others, swords; others, daggers; and others, very long rapiers. Well, I could not get away in any direction without incurring mortal peril, and I was quite alone there, without anyone on my side. I was in great distress of spirit, and had no idea what I should do, when I raised my eyes to Heaven, and saw Christ, not in Heaven, but in the air high above me, holding out His hand to me and encouraging me in such a way that I no longer feared all the other people, who, try as they might, could do me no harm.

This vision will seem meaningless, but it has since brought me the greatest profit, for its meaning was explained to me, and soon afterwards I found myself attacked, in almost exactly that way, whereupon I realized that the vision was a picture of the world, the whole of which seems to take up arms in an offensive against the poor soul. Leaving out of account those who are not great servants of the Lord, and honours and possessions and pleasures and other things of that kind, it is clear that, when the soul is not on the look-out, it will find itself ensnared, or at least all these will strive their utmost to ensnare it—friends, relatives, and, what amazes me most,

[7] St. Matthew xx, 10.

very good people. By all these I found myself oppressed: they thought they were doing right and I did not know how to stand up for myself or what to do.

Oh, God help me! If I were to describe the different kinds of trial which I had to bear at this time, on top of the trials I have already mentioned, what a warning it would be to people that they should hate everything worldly altogether! Of all the persecutions I have suffered, this, I think, has been the worst. I mean that I found myself sorely oppressed on every side and could get relief only by raising my eyes to Heaven and calling upon God. I kept clearly in mind what I had seen in this vision. It was of great help to me in teaching me not to put much trust in anyone, for there is none who never changes save God. In these sore trials the Lord always sent me some person coming from Him who would lend me a hand, exactly as He had shown me that He would, and had revealed it to me in this vision, so that I had no need to cling to anything but pleasing the Lord. This has served to sustain the little virtue that I had in desiring to serve Thee. Blessed be Thou for ever!

Once, when I was very restless and upset, unable to recollect myself, battling and striving, turning all the time in thought to things that were not perfect, and imagining I was not as detached as I used to be, I was afraid, seeing how wicked I was, that the favours which the Lord had granted me might be illusions. In short, my soul was in great darkness. While I was distressed in this way, the Lord began to speak to me and told me not to be troubled: the state in which I found myself would show me how miserable I should be if He withdrew from me; while we lived in this flesh we were never safe. I was shown how well our time is spent in warring and struggling for such a prize and it seemed to me that the Lord was sorry for those of us who live in the world. But, He added, I was not to think myself forgotten, for He would never leave me, though I myself must do all that lay in my power. This the Lord said to me compassionately and tenderly, as well as other things in which He was very gracious to me and which there is no need to repeat.

Often His Majesty says to me, as a sign of His great love: "Now thou art Mine and I am thine." There are some words which I am in the habit of repeating to myself—and I believe I mean what I say. They are: "What do I care about myself,

Lord, or about anything but Thee?" When I remember what I am, these words and signs of love cause me the very greatest confusion; for, as I believe I have said on other occasions and as I sometimes say now to my confessor, I think more courage is needed for receiving these favours than for suffering the sorest trials. When they come, I almost forget the good I have done, my reason ceases to function and I can do nothing but picture to myself my own wickedness: this, too, I sometimes think, is supernatural.

At times there come to me yearnings for Communion so vehement that I doubt if I could put them into words. One morning it happened to be raining so heavily that I thought I could not leave the house. But, once I had started, I was so much carried away by my desire that, even if the raindrops had been spears levelled at my breast, I think I should have gone on through them—how much less did I trouble about drops of water! When I reached the church, I fell into a deep rapture. I thought I saw, not a door into the heavens, as I have seen on other occasions, but the heavens wide open. There was revealed to me the throne which, as I told Your Reverence, I have seen at other times, and above it another throne, on which (I did not see this, but learned it in a way I cannot explain) was the Godhead. The throne seemed to me to be held up by some beasts; I think I have heard something about these animals—I wondered if they were the Evangelists.[8] But I could not see what the throne was like, or Who was on it—only a great multitude of angels, whom I thought of incomparably greater beauty than those I have seen in Heaven. I wondered if they were seraphim or cherubim, for they were very different in their glory and they seemed to be all on fire. There is a great deal of difference between angels, as I have said, and the glory which I felt within me at that time cannot be expressed in writing, or even in speech, nor can it be imagined by anyone who has not experienced it. I felt that all the things that can be desired were there at one and the same time, yet I saw nothing. They told me—I do not know who—that all I could do was to understand that I was incapable of understanding anything, and to consider everything else as nothing at all by comparison with that. Afterwards my soul was dismayed to find that there was any

8 Apocalypse iv, 6–8.

created thing in which it could rest, still more that I
could come to have affection for any, for everything else
seemed to me a mere ant-hill.

I assisted at Mass and communicated. I do not know how
I did so. I thought I had been there only a very short time
and I was astounded when the clock struck and I found that
I had been in that state of rapture and bliss for two hours.
Afterwards I was amazed at having experienced this fire, which
seems to proceed from on high, and from the true love of
God, for, however much I desire and strive and am consumed
with the effort to attain it it is only when His Majesty so
pleases, as I have said on other occasions, that I am able to
obtain so much as a single spark. It seems to consume the
old man, with his faults, his lukewarmness and his misery; it
is like the phoenix, from the ashes of which, after it has been
burned (or so I have read), comes forth another. Even so is
the soul transformed into another, with its fresh desires and
its great fortitude. It seems not to be the same as before,
but begins to walk in the way of the Lord with a new purity.
When I besought His Majesty that this might be so with me
and that I might begin to serve Him anew, He said to me:
"The comparison thou hast made is a good one: see thou
forget it not, that thou mayest ever strive to amend."

Once when I was struggling with this same doubt that I
described just now, as to whether these visions were of God
or no, the Lord appeared to me and exclaimed sternly: "Oh,
children of men, how long will ye be hard of heart?" I was
to examine myself thoroughly, He added, on one matter: Had
I made a full surrender of myself to Him or no? If I had, and
was wholly His, I must have confidence that He would not
allow me to be lost. I felt greatly troubled at that exclamation
of His. So, very tenderly and consolingly, He told me again
not to be troubled, for He knew well that I would not know-
ingly fail to devote myself wholly to His service; and He
promised that all I desired should be performed. And in fact
what I was then beseeching of Him was granted me. He bade
me, too, consider the love for Him which was increasing daily
within me, and I should then see that this experience of mine
was not of the devil. He told me not to suppose that God
could allow the devil to have so much to do with His servants'
souls as to be able to give them the clearness of mind and the
quiet that I was experiencing. He gave me to understand that,
when so many persons, and such persons, had told me that

the visions came from God, I should be doing wrong not to believe them.

Once, when I was reciting the psalm *Quicunque vult*, I was shown so clearly how it was possible for there to be one God alone and Three Persons that it caused me both amazement and much comfort. It was of the greatest help to me in teaching me to know more of the greatness of God and of His marvels, and when I think of the Most Holy Trinity, or hear It spoken of, I seem to understand how there can be such a mystery and it is a great joy to me.

Once, on the Feast of the Assumption of Our Lady, Queen of the Angels, the Lord was pleased to grant me the following favour: in a rapture there was pictured to me her ascent into Heaven and the joy and solemnity with which she was received and the place where she now is. To explain how this happened would be impossible for me. Exceeding great was the glory which filled my spirit when it saw such glory. The fruits of the vision were wonderful and I was left with a great desire to serve Our Lady, because of her surpassing merits.

I was once in a college of the Company of Jesus[9] when the brethren of that house were communicating, and I saw a very rich canopy above their heads: this I saw twice. When other people were communicating I did not see it.

CHAPTER XL

Continues the same subject and tells of the great favours which the Lord has granted her. From some of these may be obtained most excellent teaching, and, next to obedience, her principal motive in writing has been, as she has said, to convey this instruction and to describe such favours as are for the profit of souls. With this chapter the narrative of her life which she has written comes to an end. May it be to the glory of the Lord. Amen.

Once, when I was in prayer, I felt within myself such great joy that, being unworthy of such a blessing, I began to think how much more I deserved to be in the place which I had

[9] The College of St. Giles, Ávila.

seen prepared for me in hell; for, as I have said, I never forget
the vision which I once had of myself there. As I meditated
in this way, my soul began to be more vehemently enkindled
and there came to me a spiritual transport of a kind which I
cannot describe. My spirit seemed to be plunged into that
Majesty of which I have been conscious on other occasions,
and to be filled with It. In this Majesty I was given to understand a truth which is the fulfilment of all truths, yet I cannot tell how, for I saw nothing. Someone said to me—I could
not see who, but I was quite clear that it was the Truth Itself: "This that I am doing for thee is no small thing, but one
of the things for which thou art greatly indebted to Me; for
all the harm which comes to the world is due to a failure to
know the truths of Scripture in the clarity of their truth, of
which not a tittle shall fail."[1] I thought that I had always
believed this and that all the faithful believed it. Then He
said to me: "Ah, daughter, how few are they who love Me in
truth! If people loved Me, I should not hide my secrets from
them. Knowest thou what it is to love Me in truth? It is to
realize that everything which is not pleasing to Me is a lie.
Thou dost not yet realize this, but thou shalt come to see it
clearly in the profit it will bring to thy soul."

And, praised be the Lord, I have indeed come to see it:
since that time I have looked upon all that I do not see being
directed to the service of God as vanity and lies. I could not
explain how it is that I realize this or say how much I pity
those whom I see living in darkness with respect to this truth.
From this, too, I have derived other advantages which I shall
here describe and many others which I cannot. On the occasion referred to, the Lord said one special thing which has
been of the greatest help to me. I do not know how this happened, for I saw nothing, but, in a way which I cannot explain, I acquired an extreme fortitude so that I became most
firmly resolved to carry out with all my might the very smallest thing contained in the Divine Scripture. I believe that
there is no obstacle that could present itself to me which I
could not overcome.

From this Divine Truth,[2] which was presented to me with-

[1] Cf. St. Matthew v, 18.

[2] [In this and the next paragraph I follow P. Silverio in the use of
capitals or lower-case letters for the word "truth".]

out my knowing what it was or how it came, there remained imprinted upon me one truth in particular. It gives me a fresh reverence for God, by granting me a knowledge of His Majesty and Power in a way which it is impossible to describe; but I can at least understand that it is a great thing. It gave me a very great desire to speak only of things which are very true and which go far beyond any that are treated of in the world, and thus living in the world began to cause me deep distress.[3] It left me filled with a great tenderness, consoled and humbled. I thought, without understanding how, that the Lord had now given me a great deal; I had not the least misgiving lest it should be an illusion. I saw nothing, but I understood what a great blessing it is to set no store by anything that will not bring us nearer to God. Thus I understood what it is for a soul to be walking in truth in the presence of Truth Itself. And what I understood comes to this: the Lord showed me that He is Truth Itself.

All that I have been saying I learned, sometimes by means of locutions, and sometimes without their instrumentality—and yet I grasped these latter things more clearly than others which were told me in words. About this Truth I learned the profoundest truths and more of them than if I had been taught them by many learned men. I do not think learned men could ever have impressed upon me so strongly or have shown me so clearly the vanity of this world. This truth which I am referring to and which was taught me is truth in itself, and is without beginning or end, and upon this truth all other truths depend, just as all other loves depend upon this love and all other greatnesses upon this greatness. This is an obscure way of putting the clear truth which the Lord was pleased should be revealed to me. And what the might of this Majesty must be when in so short a time it brings the soul such great gain and leaves such things as this imprinted upon it! Oh, my Majesty and Greatness! What art Thou doing, my Lord Almighty? Consider to whom Thou art granting such sovereign mercies. Dost Thou not remember that this soul has been an abyss of lies and an ocean of vanities and all through my own fault? Thou hadst given me a nature which abhorred lying, yet in many things I allowed myself to deal in

---

[3] [The numerous repetitions in this and the preceding sentences will be noted. Cf. Translator's Preface, p. 21.]

lies. How, my God, can it be thought fitting or tolerable for such great favours to be granted to one who has deserved so ill of Thee?

On one occasion, when I was reciting the Hours with the community, my soul suddenly became recollected and seemed to me to become bright all over like a mirror: no part of it—back, sides, top or bottom—but was completely bright, and in the centre of it was a picture of Christ Our Lord as I generally see Him. I seemed to see Him in every part of my soul as clearly as in a mirror, and this mirror—I cannot explain how—was wholly sculptured in the same Lord by a most loving communication which I shall never be able to describe. This, I know, was a vision which, whenever I recall it, and especially after Communion, is always of great profit to me. It was explained to me that, when a soul is in mortal sin, this mirror is covered with a thick mist and remains darkened so that the Lord cannot be pictured or seen in it, though He is always present with us and gives us our being; with heretics it is as if the mirror were broken, which is much worse than being dimmed. Seeing this is very different from describing it, for it cannot be properly explained. But it has helped me a great deal and has also caused me deep regrets at the many occasions when, through my faults, my soul has become darkened and so I have been unable to see the Lord.

This vision seems to me a very beneficial one for recollected persons, for it teaches them to think of the Lord as being in the very innermost part of their soul. This is a meditation which has a lasting effect, and, as I have said on other occasions, is much more fruitful than thinking of Him as outside us, as certain books do which treat of prayer, telling us where we are to seek God. This is particularly well put by the glorious Saint Augustine, who says that neither in market-places[4] nor in pleasures nor wheresoever else he sought Him did he find Him as he did within himself.[5] It is quite clear that this is the best way: we need not go to Heaven, nor any farther than to our own selves, for to do that is to trouble the spirit and distract the soul, without producing any great fruit.

[4] [Sp., *plazas*, squares, public places: i.e., in intercourse with men.]
[5] The quotation is taken from Chap. XXXI of the apocryphal *Soliloquies*, often published in Latin under the name of St. Augustine, and, in Spanish, at Valladolid, in 1515.

There is one thing which happens in a deep rapture and of which I want to give warning here: when the period has passed during which the soul is in union and its faculties are wholly absorbed—and this period, as I have said, is short—the soul will still be recollected, and be unable, even in outward things, to return to itself; two of the faculties—memory and understanding—will be quite bewildered, and almost in a state of frenzy. This, as I say, sometimes happens, especially at the beginning. It may, I imagine, be a result of the inability of our natural weakness to endure such spiritual vehemence, and of the weakening of the imagination. I know this happens to some people. I should think it a good idea for them to force themselves to give up prayer and to take it up again later, at some time when they have leisure, for if they try to pray while in that state they may come to great harm. And I have experience of this and of the wisdom of considering what our health can bear.

In all this we need experience and a director; for, when the soul has reached this stage, many things will occur which it will need to discuss with someone. Yet, if it seeks such a person unsuccessfully, the Lord will not fail it, for, even though I am what I am, He has not failed me. I believe there are few who have acquired experience of all these things, and without experience it is useless to attempt to bring a soul relief—one will bring it only disquiet and distress. This the Lord will also take into account, for which reason it is better, as I have said on other occasions, to discuss the matter with one's confessor. All that I am saying now I have said already, but I do not remember it very well, and I am sure the relations of penitent and confessor, and the type of confessor to be chosen, are very important matters, especially to women. The Lord gives these favours far more to women than to men: I have heard the saintly Fray Peter of Alcántara say that, and I have also observed it myself. He would say that women made much more progress on this road than men, and gave excellent reasons for this, which there is no point in my repeating here, all in favour of women.

Once, when I was in prayer, I saw, for a very brief time and without any distinctness of form, but with perfect clarity, how all things are seen in God and how within Himself He contains them all. Describe this I cannot, but the vision remained firmly imprinted upon my soul and is one of those great favours which the Lord has granted me and which, when I remember the sins I have committed, cause me the greatest confusion and shame. I believe, if it had been the Lord's will for me to have seen this vision earlier, and if it had been seen by those who offend Him, they would have neither the heart nor the presumption to do so. I cannot say with certainty that I saw nothing, for, as I am able to make this comparison, something must have been visible to me; but the vision comes in so subtle and delicate a way that the understanding cannot grasp it. Or it may be that I cannot understand these visions, which do not seem to be imaginary, though there must be an imaginary element in some of them; but, as they take place during raptures, the faculties are unable, after the rapture is over, to form the picture which the Lord has revealed to them and in which it is His will that they should rejoice.

Let us say that the Godhead is like a very clear diamond, much larger than the whole world, or a mirror, like that which symbolized the soul in my account of an earlier vision, except that it is of a far sublimer kind, to which I cannot do justice. Let us suppose, furthermore, that all we do is seen in this diamond, which is of such a kind that it contains everything within itself, because there is nothing capable of falling outside such greatness. It was a terrifying experience for me, in so short a space of time, to see so many things at once in the clear depths of that diamond, and whenever I think of it, it is a most piteous reflection, that so many foul things, like my sins, should have been pictured in that clearness and purity. So, whenever I remember this, I do not know how to bear it and at that time I felt so ashamed that I did not seem to know where to hide myself. Oh, that someone could reveal this to those who commit the most foul and dishonourable sins and could make them realize that their sins are not hidden; that, committed as they are in His Majesty's own presence, God justly grieves for them; and that we are behaving in His sight with the greatest irreverence! I saw how truly one single mortal sin merits hell; it is impossible to understand how grave an offence it is to commit such a sin in the sight of such great Majesty and how alienated such things are from His nature. And thus His mercy becomes ever the more clearly seen, for, though He knows that we are doing all this, He none the less bears with us.

This has also made me wonder, if one such experience as this leaves the soul so terrified, what the Judgment Day will be like, when His Majesty will reveal Himself to us clearly and we shall see the offences we have committed. Oh, God help me, how blind I have been! I have often been amazed at what I have written, but Your Reverence must not be amazed except at my being still alive when I see these things and consider what I am. May He Who has borne with me for so long be blessed for ever.

Once when I was in prayer, and deep in recollection, sweetness and quiet, I thought I was surrounded by angels and very near to God. I began to entreat His Majesty for the Church. I was shown what a great benefit would be conferred upon it in the latter days by one of the Orders and by the fortitude with which its members would uphold the Faith.[6]

Once when I was praying before the Most Holy Sacrament there appeared to me a holy man whose Order had been to some extent in a state of decline. In his hands he was holding a large book; he opened this and told me to read a few words which were in large and very legible print. "In the times to come," they said, "this Order will flourish; it will have many martyrs."[7]

On another occasion when I was at Matins in choir, I saw in front of me the figures of six or seven members of this same Order, with swords in their hands. I take this to mean that they are to defend the Faith. For at another time, when I was in prayer, my spirit was carried away and I thought I was in a great field where many people were fighting and the members of this Order were doing battle with great fervour. They had lovely faces, quite lit up with zeal; many were vanquished and laid low by them; others were killed. This, I thought, was a battle against the heretics.

[6] Ribera (Bk. IV, Chap. V) thinks that the Society of Jesus is meant; but Gracián, in his notes, has "the Order of St. Dominic".

[7] This, too, according to Gracián's annotation, refers to the Order of St. Dominic. Ribera agrees here. Yepes (Bk. III, Chap. XVII) says: "For certain honourable motives the holy Mother refrained from naming this Order; but I know that she is speaking of the new Reform which she founded." A number of Carmelite writers take this view, but P. Silverio inclines to agree with Gracián and Ribera. [So do I: the language of the following paragraphs suggests the Order of Preachers—certainly not the Discalced Carmelites.]

I have seen this glorious Saint several times and he has told me various things and thanked me for praying for his Order and promised to commend me to the Lord. I do not name these Orders. If the Lord wishes it to be known which they are, He will make it clear, and in that case the rest will not be offended. Each Order, and every individual member of an Order, should strive that the Lord may use it and him to bless it so that it may serve Him in the Church's present great necessity. Blessed are the lives which are spent in doing this.

I was once asked by someone to beg God to tell him if he would be serving Him by accepting a bishopric.[8] And after Communion the Lord said to me: "When he has quite clearly and truly realized that true dominion consists in possessing nothing, then he may take it." By this He meant that anyone who is to hold a position of authority should be very far from desiring or wishing for one, or at least from trying to obtain one.

These and many other favours the Lord has granted this sinner and still grants her continually. But there is no need, I think, for me to describe any more of them, for from what I have said can be gathered what progress my soul is making and how much spirituality the Lord has given me. Blessed be He for ever, Who has had so much care for me!

Once He told me, by way of consolation, not to worry—and He said this very lovingly—for in this life we could not always be in the same condition. Sometimes I should be fervent and at other times not; sometimes I should be restless and at other times, in spite of temptations, I should be tranquil. But I was to hope in Him and not to be afraid.

One day I was wondering if I was too much attached to the world because I was happy when I was with the people to whom I speak about my soul and had an affection for them, and because, when I see that anyone is a great servant of God, I always find comfort in his company. And the Lord told me that if a sick man had been at death's door, and attributed his recovery to a physician, it would be no virtue in him to fail to thank him and not to love him. What would have become of me, He continued, but for these people?

---

[8] This, says Gracián, was the Inquisitor Soto, who later became Bishop of Salamanca.

The conversation of good people never did any harm, and provided my conversation was always carefully considered and virtuous I should not cease mixing with them, and I should find that they would do me good rather than harm. This comforted me a great deal, for I used sometimes to think myself over-attached to them and would want to have nothing to do with them at all. The Lord would always give me counsel about everything, even to the point of telling me how I must deal with people who were weak and with certain others. He never fails to look after me; sometimes I am distressed when I see of how little use I am in His service and how I am obliged to spend so much more time than I should like in a body as weak and miserable as mine is.

Once, when the time came for me to go to bed, I was in prayer, and I was suffering very great pain and beginning to experience my usual sickness. Seeing how tied I was to my body, yet how, on the other hand, my spirit craved time for itself, I became so depressed that I started to shed floods of tears and to be in great distress. This happened not only once but, as I say, often: it seemed to make me exasperated with myself, and whenever that happens I regard myself with abhorrence. But as a general rule I do not think I regard myself so, nor do I fail to do anything I see to be necessary for me. Please God I do not often do more than is essential, though sometimes I am bound to. On this occasion, as I say, when I was so distressed, the Lord appeared to me and comforted me a great deal and said I was to do these things for love of Him and to put up with everything, for my life was necessary now. I think I have never found myself distressed since I resolved to serve this Lord and Comforter of mine with all my might; for, though He would let me suffer a little, He would comfort me in such a way that it is nothing to me to desire trials. So there seems to me now to be no other reason for living than this, and it is for this that I pray to God most earnestly. I sometimes say to Him with my whole will: "To die, Lord, or to suffer! I ask nothing else of Thee for myself but this." It comforts me to hear a clock strike, for when I find that another hour of life has passed away, I seem to be getting a little nearer to the vision of God.

At other times I am in a state in which I do not feel I am

alive and yet I do not seem to want to die⁹: as I have said is frequently the case, I experience a kind of lukewarmness and everything is dark as a result of the great trials I am suffering. When the Lord was pleased that these favours which His Majesty is granting me should become publicly known (which He told me some years ago would happen), I was greatly troubled, and, as Your Reverence knows, it has caused me no little suffering down to this very day, for everyone interprets them as he likes. It has been a comfort to me that they have become known through no fault of mine, for I have been very careful, and at great pains, never to talk about them except to my confessors and to people to whom I have known that my confessors have spoken about them: this I have done, not from humility, but because it has distressed me to speak of them even to my confessors. Now, however, though, out of a zeal for righteousness, people may speak very ill of me, and others are afraid to have anything to do with me or to hear my confessions, while still others say all kinds of things to my face, I care about it—glory be to God!— very little; for I believe the Lord has chosen this means of helping many souls, and I know quite well how much the Lord Himself would suffer for the sake of just one soul: I often call that to mind. I do not know if it is for that reason that His Majesty has put me in this little corner,¹⁰ where I live in such strict enclosure, and where I am so much like a dead thing that I once thought nobody would ever remember me again. But this has not been so to the extent that I should like, as there are certain people to whom I am obliged to speak. Still, I am not in a place where I can be seen, so the Lord seems to have been pleased at last to bring me to a haven, which I hope in His Majesty will be a safe one.

As I am now out of the world, and my companions are few and saintly, I look down upon the world as from above and care very little what people say or what is known about me. I care more about the smallest degree of progress achieved by one single soul than for all the things that people may say about me; for, since I have been here, it has been the Lord's will that this should become the aim of all my

⁹ [Or "in which I am not sorry I am alive, nor do I seem to want to die." But the context, I think, favours the rendering given in the text.]

¹⁰ St. Joseph's, Ávila.

desires. He has given me a life which is a kind of sleep: when I see things, I nearly always seem to be dreaming them. In myself I find no great propensity either to joy or to sorrow. If anything produces either of these conditions in me, it passes so quickly that I marvel, and the feeling it leaves is like the feeling left by a dream. And it is really true that, if later I should want to be glad about that occasion of joy or to feel sad about that cause for sorrow, I am no more capable of doing so than is a sensible person of either grieving or glorying over anything he may have dreamed. My soul has been awakened by the Lord from a condition in which I used to feel as I did because I was neither mortified nor dead to the things of the world; and His Majesty will not let me become blind again.

It is thus, dear Sir and Father,[11] that I live now. Your Reverence must beseech God either to take me to be with Him or to give me the means of serving Him. May it please His Majesty that what is written here may be of some profit to Your Reverence, for the little opportunity I have of writing has made it a laborious task for me. But the task will be a happy one if I have managed to say anything for which one single act of praise will be made to the Lord. This alone would make me feel rewarded, even were Your Reverence then to burn what I have written immediately.

I should prefer it not to be burned, however, before it has been seen by the three persons, known to Your Reverence, who are or have been my confessors;[12] for, if it is bad, it would be well that they should lose the good opinion they have of me, and, if it is good, they are virtuous and learned men and I know they will recognize whence it comes and praise Him Who said it through me. May His Majesty ever keep Your Reverence in His hand and make you so great a saint that your spirituality and light may enlighten this miserable creature, so lacking in humility and so presumptuous as to have dared to resolve to write upon subjects so sublime. May it please the Lord that I may not have erred in this, for my intention and desire have been to be accurate and obedient and I have hoped that through me some praise might be

---

[11] P. García de Toledo. [On the form "Sir", see p. 213, n. 6.]

[12] Two of these would be PP. Báñez and García de Toledo. The identity of the third cannot be given for certain.

given to the Lord, a thing for which I have prayed for many years. And as no works which I have performed can accomplish this, I have ventured to put together this story of my unruly life, though I have wasted no more time or trouble on it than has been necessary for the writing of it, but have merely set down what has happened to me with all the simplicity and truth at my command.

May it please the Lord, since He is powerful and can do what He will, that I may succeed in doing His will in all things, and may He not allow this soul to be lost which so often, by so many methods and devices, His Majesty has rescued from hell and drawn to Himself. Amen.

LETTER WRITTEN BY THE SAINT TO FATHER GARCÍA DE TOLEDO WHEN SENDING HIM HER "LIFE"[13]

I. H. S.

May the Holy Spirit be ever with Your Reverence. Amen. It would not be a bad idea if I were to exaggerate the importance of this task of mine to Your Reverence so as to impose upon you the obligation to commend me earnestly to Our Lord, as well I might after what I have suffered through finding that I have written about so many of my miserable deeds and have thus called attention to them; though I can truly say I have felt more keenly having to write of the favours which the Lord has bestowed upon me than of the offences which I have committed against His Majesty. I have done what Your Reverence commanded me, and written at length, on the condition that Your Reverence will do as you promised me and tear up anything that seems to you wrong. I had not finished reading through what I had written when Your Reverence sent for it. Some things in it may be badly explained and others set down twice, for I have had so little time that I have been unable to re-read all that I have written. I beseech Your Reverence to amend it, and, if it is to be sent to Father-Master Ávila, to have it copied, for otherwise someone might recognize the handwriting.

I am most anxious that the order shall be given for him to

[13] This letter is found in the autograph, at the end of the last chapter. It was probably written to P. García de Toledo. [But see p. 59. The heading is not, of course, in the original.]

see it, as it was with this intention that I began to write it; and, if he thinks I am on the right road, this will be a great comfort to me, for I can only do what lies in my power. Your Reverence must act in everything as you think best and realize your obligations to one who thus entrusts you with her soul.

I shall commend Your Reverence's soul to Our Lord all my life long. Be assiduous, therefore, in serving His Majesty, so as to help me, for Your Reverence will see from what I have written here how well we use our time if we do as Your Reverence has begun to do and give ourselves wholly to Him Who gives Himself to us without measure.

May He be blessed for ever, and I trust in His mercy that Your Reverence and I shall see each other in a place where we shall realize more clearly what great things He has done for us and praise Him for ever and ever. Amen.

This book was ended in June of the year MDLXII.[14]

[14] P. Báñez appends the following note: "This date is to be understood as referring to the first draft of the *Life*, before it was rewritten and divided into chapters. To this version Mother Teresa of Jesus added many things which happened after this date, such as the foundation of the convent of St. Joseph, Ávila. . . ."

OTHER IMAGE BOOKS

A 79 – 1

46A